The Battle Hymn of the Republic

THE
BATTLE HYMN
OF THE
REPUBLIC

A Biography of the
Song That Marches On

John Stauffer

AND

Benjamin Soskis

OXFORD
UNIVERSITY PRESS

OXFORD
UNIVERSITY PRESS

Oxford University Press is a department of the University of Oxford.
It furthers the University's objective of excellence in research,
scholarship, and education by publishing worldwide.

Oxford   New York
Auckland   Cape Town   Dar es Salaam   Hong Kong   Karachi
Kuala Lumpur   Madrid   Melbourne   Mexico City   Nairobi
New Delhi   Shanghai   Taipei   Toronto

With offices in
Argentina   Austria   Brazil   Chile   Czech Republic   France   Greece
Guatemala   Hungary   Italy   Japan   Poland   Portugal   Singapore
South Korea   Switzerland   Thailand   Turkey   Ukraine   Vietnam

Oxford is a registered trade mark of Oxford University Press
in the UK and certain other countries.

Published in the United States of America by
Oxford University Press
198 Madison Avenue, New York, NY 10016

© John Stauffer and Benjamin Soskis, 2013

Textual design elements courtesy of Washington National Cathedral

Library of Congress Cataloging-in-Publication Data
Stauffer, John, 1965–
The battle hymn of the republic : a biography of the song that marches on /
John Stauffer and Benjamin Soskis.
pages cm
Includes bibliographical references and index.
ISBN 978-0-19-983743-4
1. Battle hymn of the republic (Song).
2. Protest songs—United States—History and criticism.
3. Music—Political aspects—United States—History.
4. Social movements—United States—History.
I. Soskis, Benjamin. II. Title.
ML3561.B25S73   2013
782.42′15990973—dc23   2012043908

1 3 5 7 9 8 6 4 2
Printed in the United States of America
on acid-free paper

★

For Erik and Nicholas
and
For Mira and Daphna

CONTENTS

Contents

viii

ACKNOWLEDGMENTS

ONE OF THE PLEASURES of writing a book that covers quite a bit of territory is incurring quite a number of debts. Many people helped to bring this book to fruition, in ways big and small, and we are immensely grateful to all of them.

Margaret Shannon was incredibly generous with her time and assistance in helping us understand the place of the "Battle Hymn" in the 9/11 memorial ceremony at Washington National Cathedral. Richard H. Hulan offered his unparalleled expertise on early American hymnody, as well as several images from rare hymnbooks in his collection. Steven Brown at the University Archives at the University of Georgia helped us unravel the mysteries of the origins of "Glory, Glory to Old Georgia." John Bell and Helen Hannon provided heroic research assistance. Danny Smith shared important insights on Julia Ward Howe's family history.

We offer special thanks to Robert D. Shuster, archivist of the Billy Graham Center Archives at Wheaton College, who went out of his way to help us find sources and whose knowledge and generosity were invaluable; to Dell Moore, executive administrative assistant to Cliff Barrows, who helped us set up an interview with Barrows and sent us the recording of the interview; to Cliff Barrows, for kindly agreeing to an interview; to Morgan Miller, for his extraordinary collection of IWW material and knowledge of the organization; to the archivists at the Washington State Historical Society, at the West Virginia Memory Project, at the Library of Congress, and at the Labadie Collection, Special Collections, University of Michigan; and to Peter Accardo, archivist at Houghton Library, Harvard University.

Eric Foner, Franny Nudelman, Blake Gilpin, Michael Sean Winters, Valarie Ziegler, and David Walls answered other important research queries. A number of scholars and friends gave us valuable feedback after reading parts of the manuscript, including David Brion Davis, Jon Butler, Michael Kimmage, Casey King, Jessica Covitz, and Colin Bossen.

We would like to thank as well our agent, Wendy Strothman, who helped shepherd this project through in its earliest phases. And we owe a gigantic debt of gratitude to our editor at Oxford University Press, Timothy Bent, and his assistant, Keely Latcham. Tim and Keely's editorial judgments were exquisite. They cracked the whip firmly but gently and were probably more patient than we deserved. This book is immensely better for their attentions.

Finally, we thank our families, whose love and support sustained us through this project. Carole and Davis Soskis offered words of encouragement and, when called upon, astute editorial judgments. Our children, Mira and Daphna, Erik and Nicholas, offered us the best sorts of distractions. And we thank our wives, Deborah Cunningham (an accomplished musician who played for us several early American hymns and in doing so helped us to untangle the roots of "Say Brothers") and Rebecca Deutsch, both of whom in many ways bore the brunt of this book and did so (on most days) with graciousness and good humor. We are grateful to you all.

The Battle Hymn of the Republic

★ ★ ★

INTRODUCTION

Sounding Forth the Trumpets

TUESDAY, SEPTEMBER 11, 2001, was for White House staffers—as it was for most Americans—a day of shock, confusion, sadness, and rage. When the second plane hit the Twin Towers in New York, confirming the awful scale of the terrorist plot unfolding, Secret Service personnel hastily evacuated the office of the president. Press aides and policy analysts scattered and pooled in the streets around the White House, as colleagues comforted each other and whispered what they knew. A select few congregated in the Situation Room with Vice President Dick Cheney, while President George W. Bush, who had been visiting a second-grade classroom in Florida when he first learned of the attack, made his way back to the capital on *Air Force One*.

On Wednesday morning, with the air around the Pentagon still heavy with acrid smoke, White House staffers regrouped. A number of high-level officials assembled in a room at the Eisenhower Executive Office Building to coordinate President Bush's response. As Karl Rove, Bush's top political advisor, recalled, the senior staffers assembled strained to maintain a sense of calm, "compensating for the previous day's trauma by pressing a bit too hard for normalcy." In the days ahead, these officials understood, the president would face a daunting challenge: he would need not only to comfort a stricken nation but also to lead it out of its grief, to help it translate its sadness and rage into resolve. Bush had taken a first step in doing so by charging

3

the first lady and one of his leading advisors, Karen Hughes, with planning a memorial service to be held that Friday, which he declared a national day of prayer and remembrance. At the Wednesday meeting, officials began discussing the service and tasked Timothy Goeglein, the president's liaison to the conservative Christian community, with devising a preliminary draft of its program.

Officials had initially assumed the service would be a small, intimate one, possibly held at Saint John's Church in Lafayette Square, across the street from the White House. But Goeglein pushed for the service to be larger, grander, and more inclusive and suggested Washington National Cathedral, the imposing Gothic edifice perched atop Mount Saint Albans in northwest Washington, as the appropriate venue. Goeglein, as well as many other White House officials, felt strongly that the service should be interdenominational and ecumenical, and he began reaching out to leaders of different faiths who might participate. He also started to piece together the liturgy, working closely with cathedral officials, who sent over a record of all the services that had ever been held there in times of national tragedy.

Goeglein made his initial suggestions and then passed them on to Hughes for review. The first lady had emphasized the "soothing" capacities of music, and so Hughes focused on the hymns, making sure to include several that would be familiar to those in the pews or watching the service on television. She added a few of her personal favorites, as well, including "O God, Our Help in Ages Past." When it came time to select the concluding hymn for the service, she found herself in perfect agreement with Goeglein; they both favored a nineteenth-century song, the "Battle Hymn of the Republic."[1]

That Friday morning, four former presidents, all nine Supreme Court justices, hundreds of senators and congressmen, a lineup of four-star generals, and scores of other dignitaries crowded the pews in Washington National Cathedral. The service culminated in an address from President Bush, in which he held the note of righteous anger struck earlier by Billy Graham, the octogenarian evangelical preacher who had served as the White House's unofficial spiritual advisor for more than four decades (and who had orchestrated the personal conversion of the president as a younger man). In failing health, Graham had recently turned down requests to speak in public. But he mustered the strength to deliver a stirring sermon. "We are facing a new kind of enemy," he said, "and we need the help of the spirit of God." When Bush spoke, he too sought God's blessing for coming battles, which the nation would wage in order to fulfill its "responsibility to history" and to "rid the world of evil." And so, from the pulpit of Washington National Cathedral, the president declared war.

A hush fell over the pews when Bush finished his address and returned to his seat; his father, the former president, reached across the first lady and gave his hand a reassuring squeeze, though he did not look in his son's direction. The silence was broken as sixteen members of the Navy's Sea Chanters, dressed in formal whites, filed onto the steps leading to the pulpit and were greeted with a clash of snare drums and a trumpet fanfare. The audience rose, a bit tentatively. And then, accompanied by the cathedral's 10,600-pipe Great Organ, the singers launched into the first verse of the "Battle Hymn of the Republic."[2]

"Mine eyes have seen the glory of the coming of the Lord," they began. Almost immediately the audience took up the song. By the time the Sea Chanters had reached the end of the first stanza, which spoke of God's loosing the fateful lightning of His terrible swift sword, tears had begun to stream down the face of House Majority Whip Tom "the Hammer" DeLay, a politician not known for easy displays of sentimentality. Michael Gerson, the president's chief speechwriter, recalled that when he heard that verse, he suddenly understood that the United States was at war. Others experienced a similar awakening. National Security Adviser Condoleezza Rice pointed to the singing of the hymn's final verse, which called on Americans to "die to make men free" as the moment "when it [all] turned": "We were done with the mourning," the song announced. "It was time to protect the country." Indeed, as those assembled rose to sing the hymn, she later recalled, "you could feel the entire congregation . . . stiffen, and this deep sadness was being replaced by resolve."[3]

The song, originally the leading anthem of the Union cause during the Civil War, had over the past century and a half frequently been called upon by Americans in moments of crisis and peril. When she had made her selections Karen Hughes stressed that the "Battle Hymn" would allow the service to end on "a note of defiance." Goeglein hoped that the song might provide a sense of "continuity and stability." As he later remarked, "If there was ever an appropriate time outside of the nineteenth century for the hymn, it was that occasion."

Yet White House officials had raised concerns about the "Battle Hymn." For one, it was long, stretching out across five stanzas, each constructed around a "Glory, glory, Hallelujah!" chorus. And its words and images were unabashedly militant. Hughes felt the need to run the selection by the president. She let him know that some churches considered the song excessively bellicose and had removed it from their hymnals. Yet she needn't have worried; the hymn received enthusiastic support from both the first lady and the president. "Defiance is good," Bush reassured her.[4]

Defiance was good. "Battle Hymn of the Republic" quickly became the unofficial anthem of the nation's response to the September 11 attacks. An interfaith service at Yankee Stadium hosted by Oprah Winfrey opened with the "Battle Hymn," which played as a procession of representatives from the Protestant, Catholic, Jewish, Muslim, Sikh, and Hindu faiths marched onto a podium set up in center field. The song even marked the finale of a service of remembrance for victims of the 9/11 attacks held at London's St. Paul's Cathedral. Queen Elizabeth, visibly moved, bit her lip and fought back tears. Outside, thousands filled the streets surrounding the cathedral and took up the song, the "Glory, glory, Hallelujah" chorus cascading through the crowd.[5]

Appropriately solemn, the hymn affirms the need to mourn and to memorialize. Yet it is hardly a dirge; from its opening lines, the "Battle Hymn" urges listeners to honor the dead with a belief in the decency of the American character and in the nation's inevitable triumph over her enemies. Indeed ever since its composition in 1861 by Julia Ward Howe, a distinguished Boston reformer, the hymn has proven itself an exceptionally potent amalgam: a saber-rattling tearjerker. Just as it had for Northern audiences in the early days of the Civil War, the "Battle Hymn" consoles and fortifies in equal measure.

In the case of 9/11, listeners heard in the song the stirrings of the moral and spiritual renewal they believed the terrorist attacks had awakened. The image of Democrats and Republicans belting out the hymn at Washington National Cathedral suggested a nation coming together in steely determination under the vaulting expanse of its own righteous resolve. Many commentators were also heartened by the song's insistence on regarding the nation's fate in terms of God's providential designs. Perhaps most important, the song expressed the conviction of most Americans that the 9/11 attacks had sparked a war whose ultimate conclusion was never in doubt. As the foreign policy scholar Walter Russell Mead wrote in the *Washington Post*, "The terrorists who attacked the United States . . . made the gravest blunder any human being possibly could commit": they had "loosed the fateful lightning of a terrible, swift sword."

However, not everyone cheered the prominence of the "Battle Hymn" in the wake of 9/11. For those who resisted a providentially grounded belief in American exceptionalism, the song seemed an affirmation of views both theologically heterodox and geostrategically imprudent. The song's inclusion in the 9/11 memorial service, claimed Richard Hughes, a professor of religious history at Messiah College, promoted the "facile confusion of the purposes of the Christian faith with the purposes of the American state." In doing so, these critics argued, it also portended the development of an irresponsible, absolutist foreign policy. The progressive evangelical Jim Wallis pointed to the hymn's culmination of the 9/11 memorial service as an illustration of "bad theology" practiced by President Bush and his supporters, an unreflective worldview in which evil resides only in "them" and not in "us."

In the weeks following the attacks many Americans took inspiration from the final lines of the "Battle Hymn," linking Christ's crucifixion to the sacrifices made by Union soldiers in the name of freedom: "As He died to make men holy / Let us die to make men free." Some religious leaders, however, found the call to military sacrifice more troubling than inspiring—and not for the first time in the hymn's history. Indeed in the past century several denominations had altered the verse in their hymnals so that it read "let us *live* to make men free." The White House, after considerable deliberation, had insisted on using the original version. The move, applauded by many, served as a sort of lyrical girding on of armor. It was a "portent," claimed the columnist George Will, that—as had been the case when the song was composed during the Civil War—"there is some dying to be done." And, of course, Will might have added, some killing as well. Yet for spiritual leaders who maintained that religious faith should counsel peace, especially when there was no peace, the popularity of the "Battle Hymn" was not a sign of a righteously defiant nation, but of a wounded and morally compromised one.[6]

In fact when the White House finalized the service's program, some cathedral officials were ambivalent about the selection of the "Battle Hymn." Washington National Cathedral is an Episcopalian institution, and like many within the denomination, the cathedral's clergy and staff tended to hold generally progressive views on foreign policy and were not entirely comfortable with aggressive celebrations of American militarism; a decade earlier, the cathedral's presiding bishop had been in the forefront of demonstrations against the first Gulf War. In fact, as Douglas Major, the cathedral's long-time organist, told the *Washington Post* shortly after the memorial service, the "Battle Hymn" had rarely been performed there over the past several decades, except for occasional appearances at services honoring the armed forces. For some, he later explained, the hymn carried a hint of the reactionary that seemed out of place within the cathedral's walls.

And yet the "Battle Hymn of the Republic" has had a much stronger presence within the cathedral than that uneasiness would suggest. For carved into the Lincoln Bay, at its west end, are seven bosses (ornamental keystones) depicting the hymn's most vivid images. Emerging from the vaulting cathedral walls are representations of the "trumpet that shall never call retreat," of "the watch-fires of a hundred circling camps," of the trampling of the "grapes of wrath" and the loosing of the "fateful lightning" of the "terrible swift sword," of "burnished rows of steel," of a military encampment and of a cluster of Easter lilies, in whose beauty "Christ was born across the sea." And in the central boss, five Union soldiers stand with their faces lifted in song above a pennant that declares "Hallelujah!" These icons, as the cathedral's provost explained at a dedication ceremony when they were unveiled in February 1978, were "carved symbols of love and sacrifice for the United States" that might inspire "that higher patriotism which has preserved us, one nation under . . . divine law."[7]

As with the cathedral, so too with the nation itself. A century and a half of military conflicts, of political campaigns and reform movements, of public moments full of tragedy and exaltation have etched the "Battle Hymn of the Republic" deep into our own cultural memory. The song has long helped Americans to express what they mean when they talk about sacrifice, about the importance of fighting—in battles both real and allegorical—for the values they believe the United States represents. It conjures up and confirms some of our most profound conceptions of national identity and purpose. And yet ever since it was first published in the February 1862 edition of the *Atlantic Monthly*, the song has also exposed the fragility of those ideals. For if it has celebrated the sense of mission and national exceptionalism that have bound Americans together in times of trial, it has also highlighted, and even deepened, the fractures running through those ideas.

THIS BOOK TELLS THE STORY of that paradox. The dynamic between the forces of unity and dissolution pulsing throughout the song was perhaps most evident at the moment of its composition. For the "Battle Hymn," which celebrates the divinely guaranteed power of the Union, was born out of the nation's supreme moment of disunity; the hymn portrayed fellow Americans, those fighting for the Confederacy, as diabolical serpents to be crushed underfoot.

Yet the story of the hymn stretches back decades before, as do those tensions. Its origins can be traced to the revivalist camp meetings of the early nineteenth century. One of the songs popular at such revivals, "Say Brothers Will You Meet Us," was adapted by Union troops during the Civil War and transformed into one of the army's most popular marching anthems, "John Brown's Body." The reference to John Brown was inspired—though only partly, as we shall see—by the fiery abolitionist of that name who, in 1859, led a raid on the federal arsenal in Harpers Ferry in the hopes of instigating a general slave uprising. He failed, though not before he and his men killed four local citizens—including the mayor—and one marine, and he was hanged for treason and murder. The song represented his installation as one of the presiding geniuses of the Union cause. And yet while some Northerners celebrated Brown as a martyred visionary who was willing to die to make men free, many others were uncomfortable with his embrace of righteous, divinely sanctioned violence in service of his cause.

Julia Ward Howe was one. She composed the "Battle Hymn of the Republic" in an effort to provide more elevated lyrics for the "John Brown's Body" tune. Yet her poem inherited many of the tensions within the marching song that had proved so popular with Union troops—between unity and discord, between the glories and the perils of righteous enthusiasm. In fact, the "Battle Hymn" intensified those tensions and helped to inscribe them in the American literary canon.

Howe's poem is full of strange, redolent images: grapes of wrath, serpents being crushed under heel, sounding trumpets. Yet when it first appeared, many Americans would have found these images intimately familiar and perhaps even comforting, for these were the stuff of the apocalyptic sections of the Old and New Testaments. Americans of the mid-nineteenth century possessed a deep biblical literacy, and such texts were essential elements of a common cultural patrimony. The books of Isaiah, Daniel, Matthew, and especially Revelation sketched out the final scenes of human history in terrifying, vivid detail. These works were simultaneously prophetic and symbolic, foretelling the end times while providing a series of archetypal crises that the events of the intervening years would prefigure: A divinely dispatched Redeemer would return to Earth, his advent foretold by a series of cataclysmic events, in which the faithful people of God would experience immense tribulations and undergo a great, ultimate, judgment. The redeemer's return would either precede or follow a thousand-year period of perfect peace—a foretaste of the heavenly kingdom that has become known as the millennium. Its conclusion would be marked by a final battle between the forces of good and the forces of evil—in Revelation, identified as occurring at a place called Armageddon—and with the victory of God's army, human history would terminate and the divine kingdom descend upon the Earth.

Millennial and apocalyptic thought held a particular attraction in the United States. From the first pilgrims who set foot on its shores, many of its inhabitants have been convinced that divine providence favored this new land and that it would be the seat of the world's redemption. (Those brought over in the hulls of slave ships did not share this view.) Waves of religious revivals in the eighteenth and nineteenth centuries intensified these beliefs, as did the Revolutionary and Civil Wars, each of which could be imagined as introducing fiery trials that tested and confirmed the nation's elect status and that inaugurated a new—and perhaps final—epoch in human history. The final verse of the "Battle Hymn" articulates more profoundly than perhaps any other line in American letters the nature of the responsibilities attending that election, which blended the spiritual and the secular: the United States would redeem the world by making it free. Such thinking laid the foundation for an American civil religion, one that merged patriotism and piety in order to honor the nation's divinely favored status.[8]

The certainty that the United States served as a millennial instrument did not specify the exact way that redemption would play out in history; the millennial tradition itself fostered a variety of eschatological timeframes and mechanisms. Was Christ's return imminent? Would it follow or precede the millennium? Would the breaks between secular and sacred time be marked by earthquakes and fire from heaven? Or would the transition to the establishment of the Kingdom of God on Earth be gradual and imperceptible? Would redemption come at the hand of a transcendent God or through His historical agents and human institutions?

The millennial and apocalyptic images that fill the "Battle Hymn of the Republic" allowed for all these variations. The song called forth all the enthusiasms of eschatology while leaving the details of the final days open to interpretation. It has thus been supremely adaptable to the particularities of the current crisis and to the doctrinal partialities of particular audiences. The expansiveness of those images has also allowed the song to be adapted for non-American contexts. A 1917 article in the *Atlantic Monthly*, for instance, invoked the hymn in a discussion of the Russian Revolution. It quoted a recent Russian émigré, remarking that on hearing the news of the upheaval she "thought first of all of that line in your hymn, 'Mine eyes have seen the glory of the coming of the Lord.'" During World War I, many Britons sang the "Battle Hymn" during their church services, even, one observer noted, the "fervant [*sic*] un-English refrain of 'Glory, glory, Hallelujah!'" By the time the hymn was sung in 1965 at the funeral of Prime Minister Winston Churchill, who requested its inclusion as a tribute to his American mother, the congregants at St. Paul's Cathedral who rose to sing it could find broader meanings in the words to reflect their own national ideals.[9]

The hymn's universality underscores a tension at the heart of America's civil religion. Belief in the nation's providential identity must strive for inclusivity—even of a circumscribed, Judeo-Christian sort—to do justice to the population's religious diversity, while at the same time tapping powerful strains of religious thought fueled by particular doctrines. Unmoored from concrete dogma, a civil religion can dissipate into ethereal exhortations, but rooted in too concrete a theology, it can alienate those it should energize.

That tension is another that has long coursed through the "Battle Hymn." The imagery in much of the hymn, definitively biblical without being explicitly dogmatic, has allowed it to assume a degree of ecumenism. Yet its last verse, the very lines that many consider the repository of its inspirational power, makes a valedictory break toward a specifically Christian theology by gesturing to Christ's atoning sacrifice. Some have claimed that narrowing of vision prevents the song from speaking to all Americans. Others have sought to secularize the hymn. The radical labor movement, for instance, attempted to harvest the song's millennial enthusiasm while dropping the sectarian chaff, appropriating the tune for the union anthem "Solidarity Forever."

The song has also been repudiated for being overly sectional as well as excessively sectarian. Ever since Appomattox, many Southerners have regarded the song warily, as a relic of Northern hostility. (Such suspicions doomed the candidacy of the hymn when Congress deliberated on the selection of a national anthem in the first decades of the twentieth century. In 1931 it eventually selected the less combustible—for all its bombs bursting in air—"Star Spangled Banner.") In 1937 the United Daughters of the Confederacy announced a contest, with a $25 prize, to rewrite the text of the "Battle Hymn" so as to represent a more national perspective. They denounced the original version for "giv[ing] the approval of the Lord for one side and promis[ing] reward with his Grace in proportion to the success they have in crushing the opposing soldiers who are designated as serpents and enemies of God."

Yet the submissions ultimately disappointed. As one of the judges commented on the eventual winner, it lacked the "fire, fervor, zim and zest" that great national songs possessed, forged out of "some great emotional crisis." His assessment suggests a paradox of American historical memory that parallels the dilemmas of our civil religion. No emotional crisis has touched the United States more profoundly than the Civil War, and yet the fire and fervor that it sparked among citizens also produced political and moral fissures that split the nation for generations. In the decades after the Civil War, promoters of sectional reconciliation sought to rechannel the millennial energies of the song into imperial projects and America's global responsibilities. And yet the history of the "Battle Hymn of the Republic" begs the question: Do the historical events possessing the necessary "fire, fervor, zim and zest" to support a unifying national identity also threaten to stoke sectarian and sectional divides?[10]

The postbellum efforts to disentangle the "Battle Hymn" from the antagonisms of the Civil War and to employ the song in the service of fresh battles underscore another element of the hymn's adaptability: its wide-ranging political uses. In the early decades of the nineteenth century, millennial thought found its firmest purchase among the Federalist clergy and those citizens committed to upholding the social order. Indeed throughout American history, conservatives have been attracted to those strains within millennialism that recognize the United States as a providential instrument and therefore highlight the need to preserve its dominant institutions and traditions.

But millennialism has also strengthened a prophetic current in American thought, exposing the nation's sins in the light of its ideals and emphasizing the need to repent and reform in order to be true to its divine election—and to avoid divine wrath. Such admonitions have always been destabilizing. As a New York minister explained to his congregation in 1860, "agitation is the inevitable consequence" of the conviction that the United States was a Christian nation that had "deliberately made God's revealed will its standard of morality." This strain of millennial thought, by calling the nation's attention to its moral failings, suggested that the greatest threat to its survival lay in its betrayal of its divine covenant. Such a chastisement could be directed inward, provoking efforts at self-purification or national reconciliation. It could also be directed at suspect others, identifying subversive elements within the population responsible for calling forth God's fury and stoking internecine conflict. The apocalyptic elements intertwined with millennial thought encourage such suspicions. For they posit a grand conspiracy at the heart of the cosmic drama unfolding in history and envision a series of cataclysmic clashes necessary to overturn that ultimate evil.[11]

As a chief expression of such apocalyptic visions, the "Battle Hymn of the Republic" has encouraged this nation's citizens to imagine conflicts of transcendent significance erupting all around them; and its inspirational rhetoric has primed them for battle. Not surprisingly, the hymn has experienced resurgence during nearly every major American military engagement. Rooted in the emancipatory imperatives of the Civil War, the hymn has allowed subsequent generations of Americans to perceive their own engagements—in Cuba, in the Philippines, in the fields of France, and in the jungles of Vietnam—as the most recent fulfillment of their millennial mission to make men free.

And yet critics of American foreign policy have long lamented the valorization of the nation's military as the preeminent millennial instrument. If the United States would hope to usher in the Kingdom of God, they insisted, it should do so as a peacemaker. In this reading of American exceptionalism, the popularity of the "Battle Hymn" becomes a mark of the steady deterioration of the nation's once vibrant tradition of Christian pacifism. When he was compiling his anthology, *Songs of Three Centuries*, the great Quaker poet and devout pacifist John Greenleaf Whittier initially sought to exclude all warlike poems. In searching for a contribution from Julia Ward Howe, he initially disqualified her most famous composition. But, as he later explained, he ultimately "got over [his] Quaker scruples, or rather stifled them," and included the hymn, though not without a certain degree of ruefulness.

Such was the stature of Howe's hymn. Yet the scruples continued to nag. Those uncomfortable with the hymn's celebration of an uncompromising holy war struggled to reconcile the universality of its millennial themes with its promotion of particular national interests. If the song could grant providential sanction to the "terrible, swift sword" wielded by the American military, could other nations claim the prerogatives of righteous combat as easily as they took up the tune? In a 1920s tract, the California pacifist Fanny Bixby Spencer warned that the "Battle Hymn" actually vitiated the nation's claims to exceptionalism. For, she insisted, it was difficult to differentiate the "war intoxication" the song encouraged from the bloodlust of the "Turks when they go out to kill the Armenians. They, too, have read a fiery gospel writ in burnished rows of steel," foretold in their own holy book. The popularity of the "Battle Hymn" has undercut America's status as a moral exemplar by celebrating the brutality we claimed to disdain in our enemies, Spencer lamented. Ultimately the song would only confirm the suspicion of Muslims that Christianity was "a religion of blood."[12]

Through such apprehensions, the ghost of John Brown has continued to haunt the "Battle Hymn of the Republic." And in that sense, by charting the course of "John Brown's Body" and the "Battle Hymn," this book tells something of a ghost story. Both songs remained popular in the decades following the Civil War. Yet by the turn of the century, the "Battle Hymn" had eclipsed the song from which it sprang. Even so, Brown's ambiguous legacy would continue to shadow the hymn in the years to come, for the figure of the nation's most celebrated—and most vilified—holy warrior lurked within its millennial themes. Brown's ghostly presence forced Americans to confront their own history of apocalyptic violence. For, while Brown has been claimed by radicals of nearly every persuasion as an inspiration, he has never been comfortably assimilated into the pantheon of celebrated American personages. His place in our history remains unresolved. Can we celebrate him for his uncompromising opposition to the evils of slavery without encouraging others to take up his "terrible, swift sword?"

In this day of polarized politics and "clashing civilizations," and in the midst of our current war on terror, the task of grappling with the memory of John Brown has become even more pressing. As the historian David Blight asked in 2002, "Can John Brown remain an authentic American hero in an age of Timothy McVeigh, [O]sama Bin Laden, and the bombers of abortion clinics?" Freighted both with the menace of apocalyptic violence and with the fervor of ardent abolitionism, the haunting echoes of "John Brown's Body" have become more insistent, even as the song itself has retreated into the cultural shadows. In fact when the "Battle Hymn" was played at the 9/11 memorial service, those familiar with the hymn's lineage noted that it mingled uneasily with the rhetoric of righteous retribution emanating from the pulpit. As one writer explained, "Buried inside the melody of the song . . . was the rotting corpse of an American terrorist."

Some commentators chastised the organizers of the memorial for their assumed ignorance of the hymn's origins in antislavery zealotry. But the "Battle Hymn's" inclusion did not represent an episode of historical amnesia. It was instead a moment of historical revelation, bringing to light discomforting continuities. The song's millennial and apocalyptic themes bridge the gulf between the Charles Town scaffold where John Brown met his end—but not before calling down God's wrath on a sinful nation—and the Washington cathedral where the nation's political and spiritual leaders asked for divine assistance in their own battles with their diabolical adversaries. And the bridge extends farther still, joining early nineteenth-century camp meetings on the southern frontier to southern city streets in the next century, where African Americans marched to secure their rights and providing common ground for imperialists, anticommunists, progressive reformers, and conservative firebrands.[13]

As the scope of those enthusiasms makes clear, reducing the "Battle Hymn" to a celebration of militarism does it a grave disservice and slights the rich complexities of its historical development. For the hymn has provided a call to arms of a different sort: it has heralded the commencement of allegorical battles in which military combat merely provided a symbolic representation of the personal service necessary to usher in the Kingdom of God. Such an understanding of the hymn reflects the development over the past century and a half of a progressive Christianity that insists on the need to redeem society itself and not merely the souls of individual sinners.

And so the "Battle Hymn" has been embraced as an anthem for nearly every single reform movement in American history, from temperance to civil rights and to the pro-life movement. The song has even been invoked by antiwar activists, its vision of a millennial age of perfect peace overshadowing its apocalyptic images of violent conflict. It has fostered generations of "culture warriors," who have regarded conflicts over their particular reforms as transcendent contests between irreconcilable antagonists. While such an outlook has introduced an additional dose of immoderation into our political life, it has also pierced the pall of resignation that is often as great a threat as immoderation.

Of course, if the Lord is *coming*, He has not yet arrived. The heightened state of expectancy stoked by the "Battle Hymn" is difficult to sustain; millennialism has long encouraged moments of urgent, even ecstatic hopefulness, followed by periods of disillusionment, exhaustion, and withdrawal. The frequency with which the "Battle Hymn" has been adapted as a protest anthem reflects this dialectic, and perhaps no other song has contributed more to the storehouse of American parody. On the one hand, the hymn's tune has frequently been appropriated for use in doggerel and ditties for the same reason that Union troops used the Methodist hymn to sing of Old John Brown: its familiarity and its infectious, driving cadence. It was likely these attributes that led paratroopers during World War II to borrow the tune for their song, "Blood on the Risers," with its macabre chorus of "Gory, gory, what a hell of a way to die!" And similar reasons led generations of grade school students to belt out a version of the song that opens with a rousing "Glory, glory Hallelujah, teacher hit me with a ruler!" and ends with some adolescent vision of vengeance (though the profundity of a second-grader's conception of injustice should not be underestimated, and in this sense, the song has inherited some of Brown's legacy). But, at their most powerful, parodies do not merely subvert; they monumentalize an ideal against which their mischief is measured. It is the widespread recognition of the solemnity and significance invested in the "Battle Hymn," and not just its catchy tune, that makes the song ripe for parody.[14]

The tension between millennial expectancy and disappointment that these parodies have often enacted has been a central theme in the song's development over a century and a half. It was that tension that drew John Updike to the hymn and led to one of its more striking contemporary appropriations: the use of one of its final phrases for the title of his 1996 epic, *In the Beauty of the Lilies*. As Updike explains, the phrase comes from the first line, so "odd and uplifting," of the hymn's concluding stanza: "In the beauty of the lilies Christ was born across the sea." For Updike, that arresting image captured the America that he would hymn: a nation possessed of an intense spiritual yearning both sustained and frustrated by its separation from the realm of the holy; its citizens were "severed from Christ by the breadth of the sea." It is significant that Updike finds in this verse a representation of the nation's spiritual alienation, for those same lines have also been a source of great spiritual consolation and inspiration for generations of Americans. The paradox is not of Updike's invention. The hymn's popularity has long been fueled by these internal contradictions: between unity and divisiveness, between national triumphalism and chastisement, between visions of perfect peace and of cataclysmic violence, between America's millennial promise and the recognition of how far we have fallen short of its glory. The story of this great American song is the story of those contradictions too.[15]

I

★ ★ ★

ORIGINS

The Hymn and the Man

FOR FIVE DAYS AT the end of May 1807, some four thousand men and women congregated in a backwoods community called Boiling Spring, about thirty miles east of Richmond, Virginia, to sing the praises of God and allow Christ into their hearts. They didn't just sing, they "shouted from the top of the mountains," as the biblical prophet Isaiah had instructed. Some even spoke in tongues, barking like dogs. Others collapsed and lay prostrate on the ground or convulsed and screamed. Such emotional displays were viewed as signs of conversion, of the spiritual turmoil associated with repenting one's sins and accepting Jesus as one's personal Savior. At Boiling Spring, seventy souls professed conversion, according to Stith Mead, the organizer and one of nine ministers presiding over this "camp meeting revival," as it was called.[1]

On one level, the Boiling Spring camp meeting could be regarded as a failure. After all, only seventy of the four thousand who had gathered there professed conversion. But Stith Mead did not measure success in these terms. "We see 'the race is not to the swift, nor the battle to the strong,' but to God, who is merciful," he wrote in response to the number of converts.[2]

For almost twenty years Mead had been living through Christ and repudiating the "gay and frolicksome" things of the world. The son of a wealthy Georgia planter, he had been born again as a twenty-two-year-old in 1789.

His conversion had alienated him from his family, whom he thought would "dance in hell" unless they repented their sins and repudiated their worldly pleasures. Now forty, he worked as an itinerant Methodist minister, in charge of the Williamsburg, Virginia, circuit. The hardships of riding circuit had left him looking like a pauper, with ill-fitting clothes and a haggard appearance.[3]

But Mead's spirit was more alive than ever. The Boiling Spring camp meeting inspired him to publish a collection of "new and admired hymns" that he had heard there and at other camp meetings. One month after Boiling Spring, he published his new hymnbook in Richmond. In his preface he emphasizes the importance of hymns: they were the most effective way to bring sinners to Christ, "especially when the compositions are adapted to suit the times." Singing hymns could "melt and move the most obdurate heart." They could "cheer and comfort the most dejected mind." Indeed hymns possessed "superior charms to any other part of divine worship." Why? Because they originated in the soul, and souls sang even after death: "Preaching and prayer will cease at death—but singing is the employment of the glorified, and will continue forever."[4]

Among the songs in Mead's 1807 hymnal likely sung at Boiling Spring and other southern camp meetings was Hymn 50, "Grace Reviving in the Soul." It is better known as the "Say Brothers" or "O Brothers" hymn:

O brothers will you meet me, O brother[s] will you meet me,
O brothers will you meet me, on Canaan's happy shore?
By the grace of God I'll meet you, by the grace of God I'll meet you,
By the grace of God I'll meet you, on Canaan's happy shore.
[*Chorus*]
There we'll shout and give him glory, We'll shout and give him glory,
We'll shout and give him glory, for glory is his own.

The music of "Say Brothers" stuck, even if the lyrics did not. Union soldiers stationed at Boston Harbor in 1861 would base "John Brown's Body" on the "Say Brothers" hymn. Julia Ward Howe would write the lyrics of the "Battle Hymn of the Republic" to the song. And in the twentieth century, Ralph Chaplin set the workers' anthem "Solidarity Forever" to the "Say Brothers" tune. If "Say Brothers" originated in the soul, as Mead claimed, then, in a larger sense, these "battle hymns" expressed a *national* soul that united a southern camp meeting hymn with northern lyrics.[5]

★

"SAY BROTHERS" IS A folk hymn, meaning that it adapted religious texts to a secular tune. Folk hymns were quite common in early America, especially in the South, where "Say Brothers" achieved its greatest popularity. They circulated and evolved chiefly through oral tradition rather than through print. As a result, when folk hymns were finally published in hymnbooks, they had already been "orally current," as the folklorist George Pullen Jackson noted in his 1943 classic. Mead's 1807 hymnbook consists of 151 folk hymns, or, as he said, hymns in which "the compositions are adapted to suit the times." He probably heard "Say Brothers" at Boiling Spring or an earlier camp meeting, admired it, and included it among his selections.[6]

"Say Brothers" is a particular kind of folk hymn known as the "revival spiritual," as Jackson called it. Revival spirituals were characterized by short, repetitive lines that were easy to memorize and sing without a hymnbook. They often emerged extemporaneously in camp, sometimes growing out of a chorus or refrain that had been written by ministers, based on intricately worded British hymns that were long and difficult to memorize.[7]

The emergence of "Say Brothers" and other revival spirituals coincided with the rise of evangelical camp meetings and reflected a shift in American religious expression. Camp meetings emerged around 1800, mainly in and around Kentucky, as part of a massive wave of revivals sweeping the South and West. They were a major social and religious institution in the South. In effect they constituted "the beginnings of the Bible Belt," as the religious historian Christine Heyrman has emphasized. Lasting several days, camp meetings brought together thousands of frontier folk who lived in sparsely settled communities without the resources to build their own churches. Participants slept in tents surrounding the camp, huts made out of pine branches, or in the open. They spent most of their days and part of their nights praying, listening to sermons, and, most of all, singing. Revivals attracted young and old, rich and poor. They also brought together men and women and blacks and whites, though the meetings were physically segregated along racial and gender lines, reflecting the highly structured culture of southern country folk. During formal worship, white men and white women were separated by a center aisle, and blacks congregated at the back.[8]

Although camp meetings have often been identified as Methodist, they originated with the Presbyterians and were in practice ecumenical.

They united Methodists, Baptists, and Presbyterians, the three dominant denominations in the South. No single denomination authorized or regulated camp meetings. But church leaders endorsed them even if they also sometimes criticized their religious "enthusiasm."[9]

Camp meetings were highly charged events. One scholar has characterized them as "extended emotional orgies." The "jerking"—sometimes violent movement and free-form dancing—was so rampant that the Methodist minister Peter Cartwright once reported seeing five hundred people simultaneously writhing in one camp. Preachers often encouraged such behavior. A standard routine during a sermon was for the preacher to be lifted off the ground and then drop a handkerchief and cry out, "Thus, O sinner, will you drop into hell unless you forsake your sins and turn to God."[10] The frenzy in camps at times provoked panic over losing self-control. In 1801 the twenty-year-old James Finley traveled from western North Carolina to the bluegrass region of Kentucky to attend his first camp meeting, the great Cane Ridge revival that attracted some twenty thousand people. The experience overwhelmed him: "Some of the people were singing, others praying, some crying for mercy in the most piteous accents, while others were shouting most vociferously. While witnessing these scenes, a peculiarly strange sensation, such as I had never felt before, came over me. My heart beat tumultuously, my knees trembled, my lip quivered, and I felt as though I must fall to the ground. A strange supernatural power seemed to pervade the entire mass of mind there collected." Finley fled to the woods. "I strove to rally and man up my courage. . . . My pride was wounded, for I had supposed that my mental and physical strength and vigor could most successfully resist these influences."[11]

Returning to the camp, Finley again became terrified by the sight of hundreds of people collapsing to the ground, "as if a battery of a thousand guns had been opened upon them." Again he fled to the woods, where he suddenly realized "the awful truth": "if I died in my sins I was a lost man forever." He finally gave in, dropping to his knees and crying "aloud for mercy and salvation." The experience was a turning point; Finley became a prominent Methodist minister.[12]

To frontier folk, camp meetings seemed like strange new worlds. Accustomed to living in communities of ten or twenty, they suddenly found themselves in camps of four thousand or twenty thousand, with everyone singing and praying. "The noise was like the roar of Niagara," according to Finley. Moreover these frontier folk were used to quiet evenings and early bedtimes. Camp meetings at night must have seemed phantasmagoric.

Fires blazed in a circle surrounding the camp, illuminating preachers whose "prophesies of doom" grew "more lurid and alarming," according to another observer. He remembered that "the volume of song burst all bonds of guidance and control." The hordes of people, the noise, and the surreal nights brought both terror and delight, inspiring faith in God's sublimity.[13]

The emotional intensity of camp meetings was stoked by the high stakes: eternal damnation or salvation. Antebellum Southerners recognized that they could escape the fires of hell and be free from the bondage of sin only if they acknowledged their wickedness and experienced conversion, which gave them the grace to believe in Jesus as their personal Savior. As the historian Christine Heyrman has put it, "all Southerners spoke the language of Canaan," the biblical promised land and metaphor for place of heavenly rest and spiritual redemption.[14]

They sang the language of Canaan as well, and "Say Brothers" offered those at camp meetings an especially powerful means of doing so. Repeating the lines "Say Brothers, [or Sisters] will you meet us / on Canaan's happy shore" inspired people to repent and seek the land of heavenly peace.[15]

The structure of "Say Brothers" also contributed to its popularity. Its simple repetitions were ideally suited for camp meetings and encouraged mass participation. By contrast, the older folk hymns usually contained six or more stanzas, with little repetition from line to line, which made them difficult to memorize. And the nighttime sermons and frenzy around the fires, coupled with the illiteracy of many participants, made hymnbooks useless. The words of "Say Brothers" encouraged mass singing. The hymn's form, as Pullen Jackson wrote, "is not a hindrance to general participation but an irresistible temptation to join in."[16]

Stith Mead's 1807 hymnbook was among the first to include revival spirituals. He describes his book as containing "hymns and spiritual songs," or folk hymns and revival spirituals. But most of the entries are long, highly poetic and allusive hymns drawn from such British hymnodists as Isaac Watts and Charles and John Wesley, the founders of Methodism.[17] We know that "Say Brothers" predates the Boiling Spring camp meeting of 1807 because its first known publication is in an 1806 North Carolina hymnbook edited by David Mintz. Given the infrequent circulation of southern hymnbooks during this period, the publication of "Say Brothers" in these two hymnbooks, Mead's and Mintz's, suggests that it was already orally current in both states. The version in the 1806 hymnbook is very different from Mead's: it appears as the last stanza of an older, more elaborate folk hymn, "Almighty Love Inspire," followed by the chorus, "Oh give him glory":

> Oh! Brothers will you meet me,
> Oh! Sisters will you meet me,
> Oh! mourners will you meet me,
> On Canaan's happy shore?
> By the grace of God, I'll meet you, [x3]
> Where parting is no more.
>   Oh give him glory, [x3]
>   For glory is his own.
>   And I will give him glory, [x3]
>   For glory is his own.[18]

The coupling of "Say Brothers" to "Almighty Love Inspire" appears to be an anomaly. Mintz's hymnbook is the only known instance in which the two songs are yoked together. Moreover their melodies are different, based on a hymnbook published two years earlier, in 1804, that includes the lyrics and music of "Almighty Love Inspire" (obviously without the "Say Brothers" stanza).[19]

The two songs do not seem to share a common origin. "Almighty Love Inspire" has been attributed to Caleb Jarvis Taylor, a Kentucky Methodist minister whose hymns and sermons were popular in early America. "Say Brothers" has never been attributed to any particular individual. It emerged out of the collective spiritual yearnings of the camp meeting, likely originating more from the congregants than from a minister. It is possible that Mintz heard it sung at a camp meeting directly after hearing "Almighty Love Inspire," liked the combination, and added it to the end of "Almighty Love" as an additional chorus or refrain. Thematically this coupling makes sense: both are songs of Christians rejoicing, and they share the same chorus ("I will give him glory, / for glory is his own").[20]

Significantly Mead's 1807 hymnbook features "Say Brothers" (Hymn 50) immediately after "Almighty Love Inspire" (Hymn 49), as though he also appreciated the thematic parallels of the two hymns (or as though the hymns followed one another at meetings he attended). In his hymnal, "Say Brothers" also includes the chorus of "Almighty Love," "O Give him Glory!" Mead added an introductory and two concluding stanzas to "Say Brothers," reflecting the oral circulation and adaptability of revival spirituals. His version is worth quoting in its entirety because it offers another clue to the song's origins:

I feel the work reviving, I feel the work reviving,
I feel the work reviving, reviving in my soul.
I'm on my way to Zion, I'm on my way to Zion,
I'm on my way to Zion, the new Jerusalem.
            [*Chorus*]
We'll shout and give him glory, we'll shout and give him glory,
We'll shout and give him glory, for glory is his own:

O Christians will you meet me, O Christians will you meet me,
O Christians will you meet me, on Canaan's happy shore.
    There we'll shout and give him glory, & c.

Question. O brothers will you meet me, O brother will you meet me,
O brothers will you meet me, on Canaan's happy shore?
Ans. By the grace of God I'll meet you, by the grace of God I'll meet you,
By the grace of God I'll meet you, on Canaan's happy shore.
    There we'll shout and give him glory, & c.

Question. O sisters will you meet me, & c.
Ans. By the grace of God I'll meet you, & c.
    There we'll shout and give him glory, & c.

Quest. O Sinners will you meet me, & c.
O will you try to meet me on Canaan's happy shore.
I am sorry for to leave you, & c.
I am sorry for to leave you, to leave you in your sins.

Fare you well my dearest Brethren & c.
Fare you well my dearest Brethren, until we meet again,
I am sorry for to leave you, & c.
I am sorry for to leave you, to leave you all behind.
    But we'll shout and give him glory, & c.[21]

What is especially significant about Mead's version of "Say Brothers" are the call-and-response directions between minister and congregants, which typified the basic form and structure of African American spirituals. George Pullen Jackson first noted the fluidity between what he called "white spirituals" and "negro spirituals." He acknowledged that "Say Brothers" was immensely popular among both blacks and whites. Indeed "Say Brothers" has frequently been published in black hymnbooks—probably more frequently than in white. Jackson and other scholars have also noted that the "Glory, glory Hallelujah" chorus that would eventually replace "We'll shout and give him glory" is especially popular in African American spirituals.[22]

Jackson argued for a "white-to-black direction of influence." But in the past several decades, scholars have acknowledged the African influence of the call-and-response technique, and musicologists have emphasized the mutual sharing of black and white sacred music. We know that Mead preached to slaves. At one point his brother-in-law complained that Mead's preaching would "spoil his negroes." Did Mead hear "Say Brothers" from blacks? Based on the call-and-response structure of the hymn, coupled with the interracial makeup of camp meetings and the fact that Mead preached to blacks, it seems possible that the origins of "Say Brothers" were as much African as white American.[23]

Anecdotes of slaves singing "Say Brothers" support this biracial origins thesis. At Hilton Head, South Carolina, on Christmas night 1861, plantation slaves built a pine fire and sang "Say Brothers" in their Gullah dialect. The hymn was the finale of their Christmas celebration. Their "shouting exercise," as they called the song, resembled a ring shout, an African religious ritual in which people gathered in a circle, sang (or shouted), danced, and used a call-and-response form "with much repetition." In a call-and-response format, these Hilton Head slaves invited sisters, soldiers, preachers, and other groups to meet them "on Canaan's happy shore." Their performance was a syncretism of African and American religious expressions, a "serenade to Jesus," as they called the song.[24]

Nearly a thousand miles away, in Arkansas, plantation slaves sang "Say Brothers" in a strikingly similar fashion. Here again the performance capped a religious celebration in the middle of the night, and the field hands performed it as a ring shout. They formed a circle, stomped their feet, clapped their hands, and shouted in call-and-response, "O brothers!" or "O sisters! ain't you goin' to meet me on Canaan's happy shore." In both settings, the song grew "wilder and louder." And each group shouted to Jesus in a style that was as much African (and non-Christian) as camp meeting, another version of "Say Brothers" specially "adapted to suit the times."[25]

There are also examples of slaves singing spirituals in a ring shout at camp meetings. Evangelical ministers prohibited dancing, and while many accepted the ring shout as a form of devotion, not everyone endorsed this practice. The Methodist minister John Watson published a book on the "errors" of those "who indulge in extravagant emotions," including slaves who sang and danced in a ring shout at camp meetings. In the black section of camps, "the coloured people get together, and sing for hours . . . scraps of pledges or prayers, lengthened out with long repetitious *choruses*." Their manner of singing looked like slaves' dancing at a "husking-frolic" and "also very greatly like the Indian dances." This "evil," he lamented, "has already visibly affected the religious manners of some whites."[26]

Many scholars now agree with Watson that the slaves' ring shout—and other forms of ecstatic behavior—shaped the way whites behaved at camp meetings. Slaves merged "African patterns of response" with evangelical Christian expressions of conversion. The *manner* (or pattern) in which the spiritual was sung greatly influenced the religious *message* of rapturous surrender to the awesome and redeeming power of God. As one southern black preacher noted, "At camp-meeting[s] there must be a ring here, a ring there, a ring over yonder, or sinners will not get converted."[27]

Slave owners also embraced "Say Brothers," and it remained popular among white Southerners at camp meetings through the Civil War. The Confederacy sponsored hymnals that included it. And after the war, Confederate veterans sometimes sang the "old familiar hymn, 'Brother, Will You Meet Me'" at their reunions.[28]

"Say Brothers" thus spoke powerfully to blacks and whites, slaves and slaveholders. Neither group substantially altered the words, but each group interpreted the song differently. In the antebellum era, many if not most southern whites envisioned "Canaan's happy shore" as a slave society, a heavenly version of their own moral universe. They referred to the southwest, the region of growth for the slave South, as "new Canaan." And they called the North, where slavery had been outlawed, "Egypt." Near the end of the war, with Union victory a certainty, the Confederate nurse Kate Cumming wrote in her diary, "More woe and sorrow in store for us! The Egyptian will not let us go!" In much the same way, southern whites sang "Say Brothers" as a *Southern* hymn, wherein Canaan was "a metaphor of the South" that offered deliverance from sin without threatening the institution of slavery.[29]

For slaves, however, "Canaan's happy shore" meant deliverance from bondage. Their Canaan was a heavenly place, but it also pointed to a place in this world. When Frederick Douglass first schemed to run away from slavery, he and his conspirators sang hymns and made "joyous exclamations, almost as triumphant in their tone as if we had reached a land of freedom and safety." They repeatedly sang "O Canaan, sweet Canaan, / I am bound for the land of Canaan." As Douglass noted, Canaan meant "something more than a hope of reaching heaven": "We meant to reach the *north*—and the north was our Canaan."[30]

A famous fictional slave similarly imagined Canaan as a place that blurred distinctions between heaven and earth. Harriet Beecher Stowe largely derived Uncle Tom and the other characters in *Uncle Tom's Cabin* from the writings of ex-slaves. Like many other slaves, Tom "got religion at a camp meeting." He and Eva—the little white girl he rescues from drowning—read the Bible together, particularly Revelation, and Tom sings of flying away "to Canaan's shore," a place both otherworldly and just north of the terrestrial world they then inhabited:

> O, had I the wings of the morning,
>   I'd fly away to Canaan's shore;
> Bright angels should convey me home,
>   To the new Jerusalem.[31]

While "Say Brothers" likely first gained wide circulation in southern camp meetings, it soon migrated to the North. It did so during an era in which the Northeast was the "principal generating center" of folk hymns, according to the historian Charles Johnson. Two years after the publication of Mintz's hymnal, "Say Brothers" appeared in the 1808 *Boston Collection*, a hymnal designed for "Baptist churches in Boston and its vicinity," as the preface states.[32] The *Boston Collection* version seems a weaker variant of the southern version, omitting the crucial millennial symbol of Canaan. Instead of urging brothers and sisters to "meet us on Canaan's happy shore," it asks them merely to love Christ:

> O Brethren, don't you view him? [*Repeat*]
> Most precious to your souls?
> Then rise and give him glory [x3]
> For glory is his due.

Only in the hymn's final stanza does it evoke a promised land:

> We're on our way to glory, [*Repeat*]
> To th' New Jerusalem.

Whereas Canaan was "a metaphor of the South," according to Christine Heyrman, New Jerusalem was comparatively more common among Puritans and their descendants.[33]

The publication of "Say Brothers" in the 1808 *Boston Collection* apparently had little impact on the hymn's circulation in the North; the hymn did not become truly popular in the North until the 1840s and 1850s. What did effect northern circulation was the dramatic decline of camp meetings in the South in the 1840s. There were many reasons for this. As improved transportation systems brought people together, frontier areas became settled communities, and people built churches, reducing the demand for the open-air camp meeting. Then, too, Methodists and Baptists evolved from supposedly subversive sects to "denominational institutions within the existing southern social order," as one scholar puts it. As camp meetings declined, publication of hymnals featuring the spirituals that had been sung there increased, especially in the North. The books preserved, and indeed replaced, the experience of singing spirituals at camp meetings.[34]

Most Northerners were thus introduced to "Say Brothers" in a hymnal rather than at a camp meeting. Northern revivals and millennialist aspirations flourished in the 1840s and 1850s, also contributing to the hymn's popularity. "Say Brothers" was most often associated with Methodists, partly owing to the sect's explosive growth; by 1850 more Americans identified themselves as Methodists than any other denomination. When Lydia Maria Child, a shrewd observer of religious and cultural trends, first heard "John Brown's Body" in 1861, she connected the melody to the Methodists. "The tune is an exciting, spirit-stirring thing, hitherto unknown outside Methodist Conventicles," she wrote. But by then groups as disparate as Baptists, Mormons, Millerites, the American Sunday School Union, and the Sons of Temperance all claimed "Say Brothers" as their own.[35]

Divorced from its camp meeting setting and stripped of its lyrics, the "Say Brothers" melody was so adaptable that it was called not only a spiritual but a fighting song and work song. The musicologist William Lichtenwanger aptly summarized the tune's protean nature: it "is so simple and repetitive that it is hardly possible to speak of 'writing it.'" Rather it was a question of mixing it with "the appropriate words and metric pattern." The metric pattern of "Say Brothers" (and eventually of the "Battle Hymn") of A-A-A-B, which refers to rhyme and meter, was "quite popular" in the 1840s and 1850s, according to Lichtenwanger. The tune was simply "in the air."[36]

Indeed the melody was so pervasive that it was sometimes attached to lyrics that were anything but religious. In 1855 the Boston minstrel team of R. Bishop and G. Swain Buckley published sheet music for "She Had Such Wheedling Ways." The chorus tune is essentially that of the "Say

Brothers" chorus, and the rest of the melody loosely resembles that of the "Battle Hymn":

> Oh! she was a perfect screamer,
> Oh! how much I did esteem her,
> Oh! I wish I'd never seen her
> She had such wheedling ways.

Southern evangelicals would have been horrified by such desecration of their sacred hymn. The song had certainly left the confines of the camp meeting.[37]

★

IN THE DECADES TO COME, it was a Northerner who would become most closely associated with the "Say Brothers" hymn and with the adaptations it spawned: John Brown. His memory would help spread the tune that had sounded out at Southern camp meetings even farther throughout the nation, in the form of the song "John Brown's Body." In one sense, this incarnation of the tune would have repulsed many camp meeting revivalists nearly as much as "Wheedling Ways," since Brown was a leading abolitionist who despised slaveholders. In another sense, though, the song honored its camp meeting origins, for John Brown loved hymns. His favorite was "Blow Ye the Trumpet, Blow," a millennialist tune by Charles Wesley:

> Blow ye the trumpet blow,
> The gladly solemn sound,
> Let all the nations know,
> To earth's remotest bounds
> The year of Jubilee is come,
> Return ye ransomed sinners home.

Brown sometimes sang it with Frederick Douglass, Gerrit Smith, and other abolitionist friends. Although he never attended a camp meeting, he made his own camps—those of a warrior fighting against slavery. And he purportedly also sang, in a Kansas camp, the "Say Brothers" hymn, though he would not live to see the tune take on his name.[38]

Who was this man whose eponymous song would encourage countless other soldiers to sacrifice their lives? In October 1859 John Brown invaded the South as part of his grandiose scheme to incite a massive slave insurrection that would free the slaves. With a band of five black men and sixteen whites he captured the federal arsenal at Harpers Ferry, about sixty miles northwest of Washington, D.C. But they were soon overpowered by federal troops, and after being tried and sentenced, on December 2, 1859, Brown was hanged for murder, treason, and conspiring to incite a slave insurrection.

The raid on Harpers Ferry immediately made Brown the most contentious figure in America, a national symbol embodying contradictions: a Christ-like hero and satanic demon, a martyr and madman. For some he was the nation's archetypical freedom fighter; for many others, a dangerous fanatic.

Both Northerners and Southerners understood his raid on Harpers Ferry to be the central catalyst leading to secession and war. On the eve of Harpers Ferry, the vast majority of Southerners considered secession "a madman's dream," as the *Richmond Whig* put it. But the raid revolutionized the South, presenting undeniable evidence that the North was in the grip of a conspiracy of radical abolitionists who would stop at nothing to destroy the pillars of Southern society; six weeks after Brown's capture, secessionist voices had become dominant. The *Richmond Enquirer* described this transformation: "The Harpers Ferry invasion has advanced the cause of disunion more than any other event that has happened since the formation of [our] government."[39]

The abolitionists and their sympathizers also appreciated the import of Harpers Ferry. "John Brown swinging upon the gallows will toll the death-knell of slavery," declared the antislavery New York *Independent* a week before Brown's hanging. After the Civil War, Douglass concluded that Brown began "the war that ended slavery." The great nineteenth-century German scholar Hermann von Holst likened the slavery question to a boat flowing downstream toward an apocalyptic waterfall. As politicians tried steering the boat to an island, Brown gave it "a mighty shove away from the shore." He was the first to be destroyed in the depths below; "but was there now any chance that the leaky skiff should not follow him over the Falls?"[40]

It seems appropriate that the man widely viewed after his death as "a meteor of war" lived a life marked by failure. From a young age, Brown neither trusted nor cared much for the material world around him. His autobiographical sketch, a letter to Henry Stearns written in 1857—and the primary source of knowledge of his first twenty years—emphasizes above all else his trials and tribulations. Born in Torrington, Connecticut, on May 9, 1800, he was the son of Owen Brown, a local farmer and tanner, and Ruth Mills. His father was a stern mentor, deeply pious, and a zealous opponent of slavery. By his own reckoning, Brown learned at an early age to rely on his spiritual enthusiasms and to have faith in the treasures of heaven.[41]

Eventually, though, Brown sought to make his home and country a heaven on earth. This calling came through a series of tragedies. His mother died when he was eight, and he described his feelings of emptiness as "complete and permanent." The War of 1812 introduced to him firsthand the horrors of slavery. During the war he worked for his father, rounding up cattle and driving them to army outposts. After one cattle drive, he stayed with a landlord and saw him savagely beat a slave, a boy about Brown's age, with an iron shovel for no apparent reason. He concluded that masters acted like malicious demigods. Slavery was the embodiment of all evil, which stood in the way of his vision of America as the site and source of Christ's Second Coming.[42]

In 1816 Brown decided to pursue a career in the ministry. He studied at schools in Plainfield, Massachusetts, and Litchfield, Connecticut, where he memorized long Bible passages, a talent for which he became known throughout his life. But a year later he returned to Ohio, where his family had moved, flat broke and suffering from inflammation of the eyes. Instead of working for his father he set up his own tannery in New Richmond, Pennsylvania. He wanted independence from employers and society. To do that, he believed, he needed to be a leader and a patriarch. In 1820 he married Diane Lusk; they would have seven children. She died in 1832; the following year he married Mary Day, and with her he had thirteen more children.[43]

Brown's serious troubles began in the 1830s, a transformative decade in America marked by the rise of demands for immediate abolition, anti-abolition mob violence, and the emergence of aggressive proslavery leaders who tried to silence debates over slavery. In 1835, with his tannery faltering, he moved Mary and the children to the village of Franklin Mills, Ohio, and began speculating in land. A new canal had been completed that ran from Akron to Franklin Mills, and Brown thought that it would transform his town into a great manufacturing center. He purchased large blocks of land with borrowed money, plotted out imaginary towns and subdivided lots, and envisioned the day when he would serve as town patriarch, leading his community in the ways of righteousness. But money got tight, banks refused to pay specie, and creditors began foreclosing. The Panic of 1837 and subsequent depression was under way. Former friends and associates "sued him for loans he could not repay, land payments he could not make, contracts he could not fulfill." He lost his farm, despite keeping a creditor at bay with a shotgun, and was accused of being dishonest and incompetent. He staved off bankruptcy until 1842 only by borrowing money in other states to pay off old debts. His material world seemed to bring him almost nothing but failure.[44]

It would be almost impossible to comprehend Brown's crusade against slavery outside the context of these failures. He never would have become the militant abolitionist he did had he not gone bankrupt. With the Panic and bankruptcy he became a "passionate outsider," rejecting the values of his material world and revising his understanding of God and the permanence of sin. He wrote to his family in January 1839 that they should not become discouraged by any of the recent misfortunes that had befallen them but should simply trust in God and seek to "serve Him with a perfect heart." The last phrase is crucial, suggesting Brown's belief that it was possible for men and women to rid themselves of all sin. This uncompromising perfectionism lay at the root of his millennial vision. As his world crumbled around him, his belief in the need to bring about God's dominion only strengthened. In the wake of the Panic, he began defining himself as a prophet who would not merely foretell but would help to usher in a new perfect age.[45]

The effect of the Panic on Brown's abolitionism became apparent in November 1837. Elijah Lovejoy, an abolitionist publisher from Alton, Illinois, tried to protect his fourth press at gunpoint, after his first three presses were destroyed by proslavery mobs. He was murdered in a shootout. Brown attended a memorial service for Lovejoy, and at the close of the service stood up near the back of the room, lifted his right hand, and announced to the assembly, "Here, before God, in the presence of these witnesses, from this time, I consecrate my life to the destruction of slavery." Lovejoy's death came to signify for Brown all that was wrong in the country, in much the same way that the Slave Power later symbolized for Northerners the source of all their fears and anxieties.[46]

In June 1846 Brown left his family in Ohio and moved to Springfield, Massachusetts, to embark on the final business venture of his life. The company he established, Perkins and Brown, consisted of an empty warehouse that he planned to fill with wool from western growers and then sort, grade, and sell to manufacturers. His partner, Simon Perkins, a wealthy businessman from Akron, financed the venture while Brown managed it and brokered the wool. Once again, Brown had visions of great success.[47]

Four months later his optimism turned to despair. His one-year-old daughter was scalded to death when an older daughter accidentally dropped a pot of boiling water. Brown blamed himself and concluded that he had failed as a father and husband. "If I had a right sense of my habitual neglect of my family's Eternal interests; I should probably go crazy," he wrote to his wife. In Springfield things were no better. The recently passed Walker Tariff, which drastically reduced import duties (and appeased Southern planters), coupled with the declaration of war with Mexico by a proslavery president, caused wool prices to plummet. Brown refused to adjust his prices for manufacturers and soon had a warehouse filled with wool he could not sell and a ledger filled with debt he could not erase.[48]

John Brown had entered a world of desperation best understood by African Americans. More than ever before, he sought out blacks for comradeship and community. In late 1847 he met Frederick Douglass, the nation's preeminent black leader, who had recently begun editing the *North Star*. In his paper Douglass wrote that Brown, "though a white gentleman, is in sympathy a black man, and as deeply interested in our cause, as though his own soul had been pierced with the iron of slavery." A few months later Brown urged blacks to be proud and self-determined and to resist the racism blanketing the country. He wrote an essay for *Ram's Horn*, a militant black abolitionist paper edited by Willis Hodges, a friend of Douglass. In the essay, Brown affects the voice and tone of an urban black Northerner and criticizes himself and other black Americans for "tamely submitting" to whites instead of "nobly resisting their brutal aggressions" and affirming their black manhood. Hodges, already a friend of Brown, knew him to be white but preserved his assumed black identity by publishing the essay anonymously.[49]

By 1848 Brown wanted to escape the toils of business and white society. He was intrigued with the new black community in the New York Adirondacks that settlers called North Elba or "Timbucto," after the fabled city in West Africa. It had been created by Gerrit Smith, a wealthy white abolitionist who in 1846 gave away 120,000 acres of land in Franklin and Essex Counties to three thousand poor blacks. Amounting to forty acres a person, it was, in theory, enough land for settlers to become independent farmers and voters. (New York State required blacks to own $250 in property before they could vote.)[50]

Brown decided to settle his family at Timbucto. Though he had never met Smith, he had heard of Smith's gift and made a pilgrimage to his home in Peterboro, New York, and proposed an offer: "I will take one of your farms myself, clear it up and plant it, and show my colored neighbors how such work should be done." Smith was impressed by Brown and gave him 244 acres. In the fall of 1848 Brown went to Timbucto, met with the twenty or thirty families who had settled there, and liked what he saw. "I can think of no place where I think I would sooner go; all things considered than to live with those poor despised Africans, to try and encourage them; and to show them a little so far as I am capable how to manage." He moved some of his family members there in the spring of 1849.[51]

Brown effectively created an interracial utopia at Timbucto. He brought several barrels of pork and flour, a wagon, a team of oxen, and a small herd of Devon cattle, all for communal use. In 1849 the well-known Boston author Richard Henry Dana, while hiking in the Adirondacks, chanced upon Timbucto. Though himself an abolitionist, Dana was amazed to find Brown treating blacks as full social equals: he and his family not only ate and lived with the settlers but addressed them "by their surnames, with the prefixes of Mr. and Mrs."[52]

It was Timbucto that inspired Brown's war on slavery. He had read histories of guerrilla warfare, notably of the Haitian Revolution and its leader Toussaint Louverture, which he treated as a sort of personal guidebook. From his reading he concluded that mountains were the route to freedom. He wanted Timbucto to serve as the base of operations for what he called a "Subterranean Pass Way," a militant alternative to the Underground Railroad and the seed of his scheme to invade the South and liberate the slaves. The scheme entailed an elaborate network of armed men in the Allegheny Mountains that extended into the Adirondacks and Timbucto for the purpose of raiding slaveholders' property and running fugitives north to Canada. His immediate objective was to "destroy the money value of slave property," he told Douglass: "If we could drive slavery out of one county, it would be a great gain [and would] weaken the system throughout [Virginia]." Douglass, though skeptical, thought Brown's plan had "much to commend it." Moreover they both knew that the South was a "slumbering volcano," as Douglass phrased it, for slavery deprived slaveholders "the feeling of security." A Subterranean Pass Way would only heighten Southern anxieties.[53]

The Kansas-Nebraska Act of 1854 further radicalized Brown. The act opened Northern territories to slavery by applying the doctrine of popular sovereignty, calling on settlers to vote slavery up or down. Its immediate effect was to turn Kansas into a battleground between proslavery and antislavery emigrants. Brown, Douglass, and Smith became founding members of the Radical Abolition Party, which emerged in the wake of the conflict in Kansas. The party was aptly named: members embraced immediate and universal abolition, full suffrage for all Americans, the redistribution of land to prevent stark inequalities of wealth, and violent intervention against slavery. They called slavery a state of war and argued that it was the "highest obligation" of the people of the free states to make war on slavery in order to preserve the peace. And they relied on Pentecostal visitations (messages from God) to help them pave the way to their new world.[54]

Brown attended the inaugural convention in Syracuse, New York, in late June 1855. He was on his way to Kansas. Three of his sons were already there, and at the convention Smith read two letters from them, one of which described "thousands of the meanest and most desperate [proslavery] men, armed to the teeth with Revolvers, Bowie Knives, Rifles & Cannon." Brown then spoke and quoted Hebrews 22, reminding his listeners that "without the shedding of blood there is no remission of sin." He appealed for money and guns to bring with him to Kansas. His speech electrified his audience. Most members agreed that armed resistance was the only course left to the friends of freedom in Kansas, prompting Douglass to ask for contributions, which yielded Brown about $60 and a few guns.[55]

In Kansas things were worse than Brown's sons had described in their letters. The territory was in a state of civil war between proslavery "Border Ruffians" and antislavery emigrants, many from New England. President Franklin Pierce supported the proslavery legislature and proclaimed its opponents treasonable, thus sanctioning proslavery violence. One antislavery leader was hacked to death with hatchets and knives. On May 21, 1856, 750 Border Ruffians attacked the town of Lawrence, an antislavery stronghold. They destroyed the newspaper offices, burned and looted homes, and blew up the Free State Hotel. The invaders wore red flannel shirts, and some carried flags or banners proclaiming "THE SUPREMACY OF THE WHITE RACE" and "ALABAMA FOR KANSAS." The next day Charles Sumner, the abolitionist senator from Massachusetts, was brutally assaulted and almost killed on the Senate floor by a congressman from South Carolina, Preston Brooks, for his "Crime against Kansas" speech.[56]

Brown decided to make a retaliatory strike against proslavery settlers. On the night of May 24 he and seven men, including four of his sons and a son-in-law, entered the proslavery settlement along Pottawatomie Creek. They approached three cabins along the creek, woke up the settlers, dragged five men out into the dark night, and hacked them to death one by one with broadswords. One victim was decapitated and another's windpipe "entirely cut out," according to the *New York Tribune*.[57]

Rhetorically, at least, Radical Abolitionists endorsed this kind of retaliatory action. Four days after Brown's massacre, at the second annual Radical Abolition convention, Douglass responded to the news of civil war in Kansas and Congress by declaring, "Liberty must either cut the throat of Slavery, or have its own cut by Slavery." Brown's responsibility for the Pottawatomie massacre was largely obscured in the press until Harpers Ferry, and for the rest of his life he denied or evaded culpability for it. But Radical Abolitionists knew that he employed savage means to preserve freedom in Kansas, and some of them, along with other friends and supporters, no doubt knew that he was responsible for the massacres. They continued to support him because they viewed his violence within the context of civil war.[58]

At some point in the late 1850s Brown's plan to invade the South evolved from a subterranean route into a raid on Harpers Ferry. He put together a small army, consisting mostly of white comrades with whom he had fought in Kansas and black neighbors from Timbucto. He received support from Gerrit Smith and five influential Boston area abolitionists: Thomas Wentworth Higginson, Franklin Sanborn, George Luther Stearns, Theodore Parker, and Samuel Gridley Howe. The "Secret Six," as they became known, had been radicalized by the nationalization of slavery in the 1850s. They resisted the Fugitive Slave Act of 1850, which suspended habeas corpus and turned Northern soil into hunting grounds for slave catchers. And the Bostonians helped form the Massachusetts Kansas Committee, which gave guns and supplies to free-state Kansas settlers and to Brown for his raid on the South.[59]

Brown also gained the respect of Boston's preeminent intellectuals. Between 1857 and 1859 he visited Boston seven times and went twice to Concord, where he thrilled his audiences with descriptions of the war in Kansas, including accounts of how one son was murdered and another "crazed" by the violence.[60] Emerson and Thoreau heard him speak on both occasions and were much impressed. They invited him to their homes, supported his violent agenda, and gave money to his cause. After Brown's 1857 talk, Emerson wrote in his journal:

> Captain John Brown of Kansas gave a good account of himself in the Town Hall, last night. . . . One of his good points was, the folly of the peace party in Kansas. . . . He believes on his own experience that one good, believing, strong-minded man is worth a hundred, nay twenty thousand men without character. . . . The first man who went into Kansas from Missouri to interfere in the elections, he thought, "had a perfect right to be shot."[61]

During one Boston visit Brown called on Charles Sumner and asked about the assault by Preston Brooks. Sumner, still recovering from the head wounds sustained in the attack, told Brown, "The coat I had on at the time is hanging in that closet. Its collar is stiff with blood. You can see it, if you please, Captain." Brown took down the coat "and looked at it for a few minutes with the reverence with which a Roman Catholic regards the relics of a saint," according to the Unitarian minister James Freeman Clarke, who was at the meeting. As a senator, Sumner felt compelled to "deplore" Brown's extralegal violence. But he considered Brown "a most remarkable character," admiring "many things in the man."[62]

Brown's greatest supporters, however, were blacks—from nationally renowned leaders to his neighbors at Timbucto. Harriet Tubman, a friend whom Brown called "General Tubman," helped him plan the raid. So did Lewis Hayden, a neighbor of Sumner's, with whom Brown stayed while in Boston. In early October 1859 Hayden sent Brown crucial last-minute support in the form of $600, guns, and another comrade (Francis Meriam), which "removed the last delay," according to one historian. Martin Delany arranged a convention in Chatham, Canada, in 1858, where about fifty men, mostly blacks, approved Brown's plan to invade Harpers Ferry and a "Provisional Constitution," which was designed to govern those areas Brown hoped to liberate from slavery. It called slavery a state of war, sought to fulfill "those eternal and self-evident truths" in the Declaration of Independence, and repudiated laws that "degraded" blacks and women and denied them their equal rights as citizens.[63]

Brown had raided the South to liberate slaves even before Harpers Ferry. In December 1858 a Missouri slave who had just escaped asked for help, saying that he and other slaves "were about to be sold." Brown was back in Kansas, and he and eighteen men traveled into Missouri, raided three farmhouses, and liberated eleven slaves at gunpoint. One owner resisted and was killed. The news created a sensation and made national headlines. President James Buchanan and the Missouri governor offered rewards for Brown's capture. Over the next three months, Brown and his comrades eluded proslavery posses and took the fugitives safely into Canada. He defended his actions in the *New York Tribune*: "Eleven persons are forcibly restored to their 'natural and inalienable rights,' with but one man killed, and all 'Hell is stirred from beneath.'" During the 1,100-mile trek to freedom, one female fugitive gave birth and christened the child John Brown.[64]

One final indication of Brown's willingness to sacrifice his life for blacks: in 1857 he went to Canton, Connecticut, in order to take back to Timbucto the tombstone of his grandfather and namesake. Captain John Brown had been a Revolutionary War soldier and had died defending his country. The face of the tombstone bore the inscription "In Memory of Captn John Brown, who died at New York, Sept. ye 3, 1776, in the 48 year of his Age." On the reverse side Brown inscribed an epitaph for his son Frederick, who had died in Kansas. He placed the tombstone about twenty yards from the front door of his house at Timbucto, near a large granite boulder. For the next three years, whenever family members left the house, they were reminded of the significance of their name: Browns were willing to die for the cause of freedom. In December 1859 three more names would be added to the tombstone.[65]

★

THE RAID ON HARPERS FERRY began at 8 P.M. on October 16, when Brown gave the command "Men, get on your arms; we will proceed to the Ferry." They were renting a farmhouse a few miles from Harpers Ferry, known as the Kennedy Farm. Three men stayed behind to guard the weapons; the remaining eighteen raiders followed Brown down the road toward the federal arsenal. It would be a physically grueling and exhausting ordeal, and Brown was twice the age of his fellow warriors, old enough to be their father. But his faith made up for any loss of energy that came with age. He felt quite certain that he was an instrument in God's hands, acting out His designs for the nation. That design was to take over the arsenal and then distribute arms to blacks, launching a slave insurrection that would bring about an end to slavery.[66]

By midnight Brown's plan was succeeding well. He and his men had gained control of the federal armory, which held about 100,000 guns, and taken as prisoners the armory's guards. So far there had been no casualties, though he recognized that might change. "I want to free all the negroes in this state," he told one prisoner. "I have possession now of the United States armory, and if the citizens interfere with me, I must only burn the town and have blood."[67]

But in the wake of this early success, Brown delayed unnecessarily. Part of the problem was that he had never thought through precisely *how* he would distribute the 100,000 armory guns, plus additional arms and one thousand pikes financed by his Northern accomplices, to the state's 500,000 blacks, mostly slaves. He hoped that the town's two hundred blacks, 10 percent of the population, knew of his scheme and would quickly join it and that the insurrection would then spread like wildfire.[68] Martin Delany and Harriet Tubman had been confident that local blacks would come to his aid.

The black raider Osborne Anderson also believed the region's blacks could be relied upon, estimating that at least 150 slaves had been informed of the raid by word of mouth. But Brown had no idea how many blacks knew of his plan. He clearly hoped that thousands would join his insurrection.[69]

And so in the early hours of October 17, Brown waited and hoped for black reinforcements. Meanwhile he acquired more prisoners. His men raided the homes of local elites and brought masters and their slaves to the armory. By dawn he had about forty prisoners, twice the size of his own army. His white hostages could be used as ransom, allowing him to escape to the mountains unmolested, he calculated. And he hoped that his black captives would join the revolution.[70]

But between the blacks Brown had captured and the thousands of male slaves in the six-county region surrounding the Ferry, only a handful of people came to his aid. One newspaper noted that local blacks "had at least cognizance of" Brown's plans. But blacks were also aware of the suicidal nature of almost all slave insurrections, and they preferred to remain alive. In their prudence they echoed Douglass, whom Brown had tried hard to recruit a month before the raid. Douglass had refused, telling Brown that "he was going into a perfect steel-trap, and that once in he would never get out alive."[71]

The most distinguished prisoner was Lewis Washington, the great-grandnephew of George Washington. "I wanted you particularly for the moral effect it would give our cause, having one of your name as a prisoner," Brown told him. Other "moral effects" had also been confiscated: a dress sword purportedly given to General Washington by Frederick the Great and a pistol that had been a present from Lafayette.[72] Brown loved the symbolic value of these items. He had planned his raid for July 4, in order to highlight the contradictions between revolutionary ideals and existing realities.[73]

The first victim of Brown's war on slavery was a black man. While Brown was in the armory collecting prisoners, his men cut the telegraph lines and captured guards on the covered railroad bridge through which trains entered the town. They captured one guard, but an Irish watchman named Patrick Higgins resisted. Higgins punched his captor in the face, sprinted to the end of the bridge, and dove through the window of a hotel to safety. At 1:25 A.M. the eastbound train to Baltimore arrived at the bridge. Higgins and the hotel clerk, fearing sabotage, stopped it. The train conductor and some other trainmen, including Heyward Shepherd, a free black baggage handler, went into the covered bridge with a lantern to investigate. Brown's men ordered them to halt. Ignoring the order, Shepherd turned to flee. He received a bullet in the back that just missed his heart. It was a fatal wound and a bad omen for Brown and his men.[74]

The shooting created panic among the train's passengers and effectively sounded the alarm. But rather than keep the passengers hostage, Brown let the train continue on to Baltimore. He also imprudently divulged his scheme to the conductor, who stopped en route to send a wire to his manager in Baltimore: "Express train bound east, under my charge, was stopped this morning at Harpers Ferry by armed abolitionists. They have possession of the bridge and the arms and armory of the United States. . . . They say they have come to free the slaves and intend to do it at all hazards. . . . You had better notify the Secretary of War at once."[75]

Militia companies began arriving at Harpers Ferry on Monday morning, October 17. Brown and his men took refuge in the armory's engine house, and within a few hours they were surrounded. Two of his sons were with Brown and would soon die at his side. Secretary of War John Floyd, a former governor of Virginia, ordered a company of U.S. Marines, led by Colonel Robert E. Lee and J. E. B. Stuart, to Harpers Ferry. On Tuesday morning, as two thousand spectators looked on, Lee's company battered down the doors of the engine house and captured seven survivors. Brown and Aaron Stevens were severely wounded. The five other raiders received only minor injuries or were unhurt.[76]

Less than forty-eight hours after it began, John Brown's raid ended as a military campaign. Casualties were light: ten raiders were killed in action, plus two slaves who had joined them. Five raiders escaped to free soil. On the Southern side, four citizens and one soldier were killed, nine wounded. Brown and six other captured raiders were convicted of murder, treason, and conspiracy to incite a slave insurrection. Five raiders were hanged in December, the other two in March 1860.[77]

Compared to other slave insurrections, Harpers Ferry was comparatively peaceful. Brown and his men displayed considerable restraint. They neither burned the town, as Brown had threatened, nor killed any white prisoners. Indeed had Brown shown less respect for human life and executed a few prisoners he might have been able to escape to the mountains surrounding the town. But in his last order to his men before marching on Harpers Ferry he had proscribed unwarranted violence. "You all know how dear life is to you, and how dear your life is to your friends," he told them. "Do not, therefore, take the life of any one if you can possibly avoid it; but if necessary to take life in order to save your own, then make sure work of it."[78]

★

BROWN WAS A MAN of action who had long scorned the equivocations of politicians. A few months before the raid he had complained in Boston, "Talk! talk! talk! . . . will never set the slave free."[79] But it was his words that transformed his military failure into an extraordinary success. At his trial and in his letters and interviews from prison, which were soon published and widely distributed throughout the North, he stoically defended his actions. He was a primitive Christian heeding the law of God. When a reporter visiting his cell asked him whether he considered himself "an instrument in the hands of Providence," he responded simply, "I do." On November 2, before being sentenced to hang, he championed revolutionary violence in a speech to the court that its listeners never forgot:

> [The Bible] teaches me . . . to "remember them that are in bonds as bound with them." I endeavored to act up to that instruction. I say, I am yet too young to understand that God is any respecter of persons. I believe that to have interfered as I have done, as I have always freely admitted I have done, in behalf of His despised poor, was not wrong, but right. Now, if it is deemed necessary that I should forfeit my life for the furtherance of the ends of justice, and mingle my blood further with the blood of my children, and with the blood of millions in this slave country whose rights are disregarded by wicked, cruel, and unjust enactments—I submit: so let it be done.[80]

Brown believed his sacrifices would expiate the sins of the nation. He likened himself to Samson, the biblical martyr who brought down the Philistines' temple upon himself and his foes. "God has honored but comparatively a very small part of mankind with any possible chance for such mighty and soul satisfying rewards," he had written in 1858. "I expect to effect a mighty conquest even though it be like the last victory of Samson." He now rejoiced in the face of death, for he believed that he had earned his death by confronting the nation's greatest sin: slavery.[81]

The happiest moments of Brown's life occurred while he was in prison waiting to die. Despite saber cuts on his head that affected his hearing and vision and bayonet wounds in his kidney, he felt "quite cheerful in the assurance that God reigns and will overrule all for his glory and the best possible good," as he wrote his wife and family. His calamities would last but a moment compared to the "exceeding and eternal weight of glory" that was dawning. In another letter to his family he said he felt confident that his violent actions would bring the peace of God. He looked forward "to a time when 'peace on Earth and goodwill toward men' shall everywhere prevail," as he wrote in a prison letter. He compared himself to the apostle Paul and felt as happy as Paul had when "*he* lay in prison." Paul thought his own martyred death would advance the cause of Christ, and Brown felt the same way.[82]

To his final moments, John Brown never wavered in his belief that he had acted out God's will in expiating the country's sin through bloodshed. On December 2 he began his procession to the gallows. As he left his cell, he handed a note to a guard that read, "I John Brown am now quite *certain* that the crimes of this *guilty land: will* never be purged *away*; but with Blood. I had *as I now think: vainly* flattered myself that without *verry much* blood-shed; it might be done." He then climbed onto the open wagon and sat on his oak coffin. As the wagon started toward the field where the gallows had been built, he looked around and exclaimed, "This is beautiful country. I never had the pleasure of seeing it before." Upon reaching the gallows, which had been erected in nearby Charles Town, he noticed the town's mayor and the prosecutor who had tried him. "Gentlemen, good-bye," he told them. He stepped firmly onto the gallows, received the hood and noose willingly, and during his ten-minute wait in the dark asked only that he not be detained any longer than was absolutely necessary. His gravestone was ready for him at North Elba. His God awaited him in heaven.

John Brown's words and actions circulated through the press and the national consciousness like a long fuse that eventually exploded, ripping the nation apart. And his name awaited a song that could match his righteous resolve.[83]

II

★ ★ ★

"HIS SOUL IS MARCHING ON!"
"John Brown's Body" and the Civil War

SEVEN WEEKS AFTER SUPERVISING the capture of John Brown, Colonel Robert E. Lee once again found himself in Harpers Ferry, this time leading four companies of U.S. artillerymen. Governor Henry Wise of Virginia, convinced that the abolitionist's allies would stage a last-gasp rescue attempt before Brown's December 2 execution, had asked Lee to return. As Lee informed his wife, Mary, in a letter composed shortly after his arrival, he had quickly placed his men at key access points to the town, in order "to insure timely notice of the approach of the enemy." The good soldier had done his duty—but he had taken little pleasure in it. In fact he found his involvement in the entire John Brown affair rather distasteful; it was not, he believed, dignified work for regular troops. When Wise had called him back to western Virginia, Lee told his friends that he had been recruited for the *"Harper's Ferry war."* But he would leave it quickly, he informed them, and get back to his real vocation as a soldier: fighting the Comanches out west.

"The night has passed off quietly," Lee assured Mary after he had positioned his men. "Tomorrow will probably be the last of Captain Brown." His comment doubtless reflected the expectation that the execution would proceed on schedule. But it also betrayed a deeper hope, one shared by many nervous Southerners, that Brown's hanging would end not merely his life but his allure. Indeed Lee regarded Brown's raid as the act of a "madman" and assumed that other responsible citizens shared his view. It was these sober and judicious Americans, he hoped, who would determine the fate of the Union. Initially many in the North seemed to agree. Even a staunchly antislavery paper such as Horace Greeley's *New York Tribune* echoed Lee in denouncing the "deplorable affair" as "the work of a madman."[1]

In the aftermath of the raid, however, this belief was soon overwhelmed by the conviction that Brown's assault represented the spearhead of a vast Northern conspiracy, with radical abolitionists and their Republican abettors at its center. Governor Wise stoked these fears, conjuring up visions of Brown's conspirators girding themselves for another assault. Wise had even heard rumors that he himself was the subject of a kidnapping plot by Brown's Boston allies, who would seek to exchange the governor for the imprisoned raider.

This time, Wise vowed, Virginians would not be taken by surprise. Along with Colonel Lee, he enlisted some three thousand soldiers and state militia members to guard Charles Town on the day of the execution and to seal it off from Northern interlopers. The careful staging of the execution, the display of Southern military power, the restrictions placed on the authorized witnesses were all efforts to shape Brown's posthumous legacy. Wise sought to guarantee that December 2, 1859, would indeed be the last of Captain Brown, the last Southerners saw of him—and heard of him too. He even suggested handing over the body to a Southern medical school for dissection, a fate usually reserved for the most marginal, maligned citizens. Wise might have been responding to the advice of one correspondent, who had encouraged disposing of the corpse in such an ignominious fashion as the best means of avoiding a "triumphal procession through all the Eastern states" that might secure to Brown the status of a "hero martyr."[2]

Ultimately Southerners were right to fear the hold that Brown would have over the public mind after his death, though their reaction to his raid did nothing to weaken it. His execution amplified the waves of sympathy that had been building since his imprisonment, which crested on December 2 at prayer meetings and memorial services throughout the North. Northern pews were crowded on the day of the execution, and thousands kindled to the tributes offered to Brown by leading intellectuals like Henry David Thoreau and Ralph Waldo Emerson. Bells tolled his death in Worcester, Massachusetts, and in Portland, Maine; from pulpits throughout the region came comparisons of Brown's death to Christ's crucifixion. "The gallows from which he ascends into Heaven, *will be in our politics*, what the cross is in our religion," declared one New Hampshire minister. John Brown had become, as Governor Wise's advisor had feared, a "hero martyr."

"His Soul Is Marching On!"

The advisor was also right to worry about the galvanic power of Brown's body. Yet he need not have focused on the lifeless corpse. Brown's wife had taken it to New York, where it was treated and dressed for a brief public viewing and then sent on to Brown's homestead in Timbucto, where a small circle of family and friends saw it lowered into the earth, next to the spot where his grandfather lay. It was "John Brown's Body," the popular song, that wielded more power. Even those Northerners who had not marked his death with a special commemoration would soon help ensure his immortality by intoning its opening lines: "John Brown's body lies mouldering in the grave / His soul's marching on!"[3]

The "apotheosis of old John Brown is fast taking place," declared one Illinois journal in August 1862. "All over the country the old John Brown song may be heard at all times of the night or day in the streets of Chicago and all other cities; it is the pet song among the soldiers in all our armies." In fact Oliver Wendell Holmes Sr., the eminent Bostonian physician and man of letters, argued that given the wartime popularity of the song, Brown's raid should no longer be considered his failed attempt to take over the federal armory at Harpers Ferry, but should be heralded as his more successful posthumous campaign, when "his soul marched at the head of half a million men, shaking the continent and the world with the chorus of Glory Hallelujah."[4]

Holmes's redefinition raises several important questions: What precisely was the relationship between these two raids, the first on a federal armory, the second on the nation's penny songsters? To what extent did Brown's soul, fired by his commitments to racial justice, inspire the Union men who belted out his song? And to what degree did those who fought the Civil War assimilate Brown's millennial fervor? The history of "John Brown's Body" reveals a complex relationship between these two John Browns, the man and his legacy, the one mouldering in the grave and the other marching on.

★

IN THE DECADES AFTER the Civil War, the song's history was defined more than anything else by its obscurity. Attempting to track the song's genealogy back through thickets of surmise, spurious claims, and popular lore, the *Nation* magazine commented in 1887, "A more confused and muddled account of anything has seldom fallen under our notice." Yet to the song's admirers, this muddle served as a testament to its authenticity. Commentators praised "John Brown's Body" as "a self-made song, which sang itself into being of its own accord." It was a "fatherless" and "unwritten" air, elemental and wild, that had emerged organically from the soul of the Union over the course of the war, the primal expression of fighting men who did not deign to sign their name.[5]

These descriptions often appeared in the context of retrospective accounts of the songs of the Civil War. Nearly all of them noted, with varying degrees of satisfaction, that most of the tunes crafted by professional songsmiths to honor the Union's cause had been quickly forgotten. These postbellum commentators frequently mentioned a campaign to create a national hymn that was initiated shortly after the surrender of Fort Sumter by a group of prominent New Yorkers. An anonymous gentleman offered a prize of $500 to the writer who submitted the best coupling of lyrics and melody, to be judged by a committee of distinguished citizens. The Committee for a New National Hymn received more than 1,200 submissions, but, after wading through mounds of patriotic platitudes, they decided that none of them merited selection and refused to award the prize. The decision prompted the knowing chuckles of those who had always doubted the possibility of crafting an expression of nationalist sentiment "to order." Those who derided the committee's campaign held up "John Brown's Body"— spontaneously and not commercially generated—as an illustrative counterexample. As the abolitionist journal the *Liberator* declared in 1862, "John Brown's Body" could be the "National Hymn that the thirteen wise men of Gotham went a-fishing for last May, baiting their hooks with golden eagles, and getting many nibbles, but no bites." It was to the song's credit that it had no authors to claim a prize.[6]

Yet "John Brown's Body" was too fortunate an offspring to remain orphaned for long. A series of queries regarding the composer of the song's melody that appeared in Boston and New York papers in the mid-1870s sparked an effort to resolve the question of its origins and opened the door to a host of pretenders claiming paternity. The most prominent among them was Thomas Brigham Bishop, a successful songwriter from Maine who also listed (dubiously) the popular "Shoo Fly! Don't Bother Me" and the music to "When Johnnie Comes Marching Home" among his compositions. According to Bishop, he composed the song in 1858, after a visit from a religious brother-in-law who objected to Bishop's devotion to worldly music. He himself could never listen to the devil's music, the pious in-law announced, since he was "a soldier in the army of the Lord—glory, glory, hallelujah!" Those phrases instantly assumed musical form in Bishop's mind, and he quickly put them to paper. The brother-in-law then imported the song to a revival meeting, from which it spread throughout the country. A trip to Harpers Ferry the following year inspired Bishop to add the famous verse about John Brown's body. Yet, Bishop explained decades later, the song was really just "a joke upon [his] sanctimonious brother-in-law."[7]

Among all the claimants, the most successful was perhaps the most obscure: William Steffe, a native South Carolinian who settled in Philadelphia and worked as a bookkeeper and insurance agent. According to posthumous reports, Steffe had a fine musical ear but lacked a record of published composition. He claimed that in the mid-1850s he had been asked to compose a tune in honor of a visit from a Baltimore fire company to Philadelphia and came up with "Say, Bummers, Will You Meet Us?," the progenitor, at least in his telling, of the Methodist camp song. Steffe could produce no evidence to support his story, nor could he locate corroborating witnesses. As he told an inquiring journalist in 1885, he had been unable to locate the original score he had written decades ago, while all those who could have verified his story were "gathered to their fathers." A year later he claimed that he had sent a copy of the music to the journalist but that it had been lost in the mail. Given the lack of confirming evidence, the facts that no early version of "Say Brothers" cited Steffe as the tune's composer and that the "Say Brothers" line itself predates Steffe's composition by several decades, it seems most likely that he put down on paper and added new words to a tune that had been circulating for years. And yet, to this day, Steffe is widely credited as the composer of the music for "John Brown's Body" and the "Battle Hymn of the Republic."[8]

But though such dubious claims to paternity did little to dispel the murkiness clouding the song's origins, the controversies surrounding those claims in the 1870s and 1880s did prompt the published reminiscences of individuals who could shed light on the song's true birthplace and legitimate parents. This attention revealed one of the great ironies of the history of "John Brown' Body": that the Brown referred to in the song was not, initially at any rate, the Brown of Southern fear and Northern veneration.

IN THE HEADY DAYS after the fall of Fort Sumter in April 1861, Boston men rushed to join the handful of existing military units, and one of the more popular was the Second Battalion, Light Infantry. "The Tigers," as the unit was popularly known, could trace its lineage back to a company established in 1784 and had been maintained since then largely for social and ceremonial purposes. Recruits from the city's upper tier—students, clerks, merchants, and professional men—quickly flooded its ranks, giving it an early reputation for attracting "kid-gloved soldiers." On April 29, 1861, Governor John Andrew ordered the battalion, under the command of Major Ralph W. Newton, to garrison Fort Warren in Boston Harbor. Construction of the fort had begun in the 1830s but had been left uncompleted. When the men entered, they found it strewn with garbage and great mounds of dirt. They spent their first weeks of wartime service alternating between intensive drilling and cleaning the fort grounds. And to pass the time when engaged in either activity, the men sang. "We lustily sang all the popular songs of the day," one veteran recalled, "whether wielding the shovel, swinging the pick, trundling the wheelbarrow, or rolling heavy stones away. During our long evening in quarters, too, we sang almost continuously."[9]

One of the young Bostonians to join the Tigers was a short, broad-shouldered, and genial Scotsman named John Brown, who before the war had served as a clerk in his brother's tobacco firm. His comrades frequently needled him about bearing such an illustrious name, and one of their favored pastimes was making sport of the incongruities between the severe John Brown who had raided Harpers Ferry and the jovial John Brown hauling rocks around the fort. If Brown was a bit late falling into company line, some wag would quip, "Come, old fellow, you ought to be at it if you are going to help us free the slaves." And when a soldier returned from leave and asked for the latest news, the reply would often come, "John Brown's still dead—but he's a pretty lively corpse to go marching around." The Scottish Brown's good-natured protests only increased the ribbing. "This cannot be John Brown," his comrades would insist. "John Brown is dead." And then solemnly, with downcast eyes to maximize the comic effect, someone would intone: "His body lies mouldering in the grave."[10]

As it happened, Brown possessed a fine tenor voice and, with several other members of the battalion, formed a choral group (often referred to as a "quartet" but with an amorphous membership) that performed for the men and officers. One member recited Juliet's final soliloquy from Shakespeare's play, which he capped off by stabbing himself with a penholder and falling dead on a mattress. Brown regaled the battalion with Scottish folk ballads. The group also sang the popular songs—religious and secular—of the day. Among their favorites was "Say Brothers Will You Meet Us?"

Years later, when members of the singing group recalled the origins of "John Brown's Body," they offered various explanations for how the Methodist hymn came to their attention. Some claimed it appeared in a popular hymnal, the *Melodeon*, numerous copies of which were either peddled by the book's publisher or donated by a local Young Men's Christian Association. Other veterans of the Second Battalion claimed that members of the singing group, including Brown himself, had heard the hymn years before at camp meetings. One contemporary Bostonian dismissed these accounts; anyone who lived in the city during the war, he wrote, would have heard the hymn at least once a day. It was, he recalled, a favorite of students, who "were much given to street signing, especially at night."[11]

Eventually the good-natured taunting of Brown made its way into the choral group's program. On one particularly frolicsome night, when soldiers began marching around the parade grounds after dinner, James E. Greenleaf, an occasional member of the choral group as well as the organist in a nearby church, grafted one of the more popular lines that had emerged from the ribbing of the Scotsman—"John Brown's body lies mouldering in the grave / His soul's marching on"—onto the "Say Brothers" tune. The line stuck, in part because it reiterated the joke's basic premise: the incongruity between the two Browns, the dead abolitionist and the living soldier. It also likely borrowed its vivid image of corporeal decay and spiritual rebirth from other popular songs of the period, including from a variant of "Say Brothers" that emerged in the decade before the Civil War. "Rest in Heaven" (or "Rest in Home") used a similar tune as "Say Brothers" and incorporated a stanza asking "Brothers," "Sisters," and "Sinners" whether they would meet the singer among the "blest in heaven." It featured a new chorus, though, emphasizing the immortality of the soul:

> When this poor body lies mouldering in the tomb
> When soft winds gently sigh o'er its quiet home,
> When strange, sweet flower in beauty o'er it bloom;
> I shall rest at home.

It is possible that this variant originated in slave camp meetings. After the war several Southerners recalled having heard slaves in the field singing a similar air, whose opening lines declared, "My poor body lies a-mouldering in the clay / While my soul goes marching on!" The Fort Warren singers also likely found inspiration in local political culture; in the 1860 Massachusetts gubernatorial race, for instance, Democrats had taunted the Republican abolitionist John Andrews with songs emphasizing the emphatic deadness of John Brown, to which Andrew's supporters had responded with various songs declaring Brown's immortality.[12]

The day after Greenleaf's adaptation, the choral group took up the song. Soon the entire battalion was singing it. With that first verse as its foundation, and with the pace of the hymn quickened to support the marching of the men, over the next few weeks the song expanded with improvisations. After each stanza, which ended with some variation of "His soul's marching on," the singers added the "Glory, hally, hallelujah" chorus taken from "Say Brothers." In one verse they continued to work the theme of the merging of the two John Browns: "He's gone to be a soldier in the army of the Lord." In another they continued their teasing of the living Brown, based on a humorous incident from their first weeks at the fort. On the day knapsacks were issued and the men were given their first lessons in packing them, Brown, squat and determined, appeared before his fellow soldiers with his pack looming over him. Someone called out, "Say, knapsack, where are you going with that man?" Another cautioned Brown that he wouldn't make it far south with such a load. Brown, somewhat exasperated, shouted back, "John Brown's knapsack is strapped upon his back, and his soul will march on as far as any of you!" That retort was incorporated into the song as the line, "John Brown's knapsack is strapped upon his back."

In yet another of the more popular verses to attach themselves to the song, the soldiers allowed their pent-up aggression, and some of their youthful scatological exuberance, to vent upon the Southern leader who would soon serve as the Confederacy's first president. "We'll feed him sour apples till he has the di-ar-rhee," the men would gleefully chant. By the time the song had made its way outside the walls of the fort, however, this threat was considered a bit too vulgar, and another was substituted for it that had cropped up in several other Boston popular songs: "We'll hang Jeff Davis to a sour apple tree."[13]

"There was just a flavor of coarseness, possibly of irreverence, about [the song] slightly objectionable to the more fastidious 'Tigers,'" recalled one member of the battalion. Among those offended was the battalion's commander, Major Newton, who was not keen on his unit's gaining a reputation for rabid abolitionism or on needlessly inflaming the enemy by invoking the memory of Harpers Ferry. He suggested that if his men wanted to "howl that John Brown tune," they substitute some other worthy personage in Brown's place. As a suitable surrogate, he proposed Colonel Elmer E. Ellsworth, the leader of the New York Fire Zouaves and a lawyer who had worked on Lincoln's election campaign, who was shot and killed in May 1861 while pulling down the Confederate flag in Alexandria, Virginia, and mourned as the war's first prominent casualty. The men dutifully incorporated Ellsworth into their improvisations, adding verses like "When Ellsworth died, he died as a brave" and "His pet lambs [a reference to his fellow Zouaves] will meet him on the way." The changes held some appeal, especially for those who did not care to have Old John Brown marching at the front of the Union ranks. In the coming months, several song sheets appeared featuring the Fort Warren verses, substituting Ellsworth's name for Brown's. Other publishers printed both names in brackets, leaving it up to the singer to determine his or her presiding martyr—and, in a sense, determining the Union's animating cause: the defense of the national government or the abolition of slavery.[14]

In the vast majority of the published versions of the song, however, John Brown refused to yield pride of place. The men of the Second Battalion, for their part, made clear whom they preferred. According to one member of the battalion, the men resisted dislodging Brown because their "anti-slavery sentiment was intense and irrepressible." Many also no doubt relished tweaking their commander, and respectable opinion more generally, and in doing so channeled some of Brown's unruly anti-authoritarianism. In maintaining Brown's name, the men of the Second Battalion also preserved within the song's stanzas their appreciation of Brown's double identity, which bequeathed to future versions of the song a predisposition to parody. This was especially the case with adaptations of "John Brown's Body" that addressed the polarities of military life. The coupling of the severe and daunting abolitionist and the diminutive, good-natured Scotsman through their shared name expressed itself in the juxtaposition of high ideals and low humor of the song's lyrics, and in turn embodied the paradoxically double experience of war itself: by turns tedious and terrible, senseless and glorious.[15]

The men of the Second Battalion quickly embraced "John Brown's Body" as their distinctive anthem. The song also caught the ears of members of two professional bands that regularly played at the fort for the soldiers' entertainment: Gilmore's Band and the Brockton (Brigade) Band. James Greenleaf whistled the tune to a member of the Brockton Band, which gave the first public performance of the song at a flag-raising ceremony on May 12. After hearing the men singing the song, the leader of Gilmore's Band, Patrick Sarsfield Gilmore, who would go on to become the nation's preeminent bandmaster, asked the choral group quartet to teach it to him so he could incorporate it into his band's repertoire. One night the members of the singing group retired with Gilmore to a corner of the fort and performed the song, while Gilmore tooted along on a cornet and scribbled notes until he had enough to write out a proper score. He then began playing "John Brown's Body" at Boston events.[16]

On May 25, because the Second Battalion did not have the requisite number of companies to form a regiment, it was relieved of garrison duty and replaced at Fort Warren by the newly recruited members of the Twelfth Massachusetts Volunteer Infantry. The Twelfth was led by Fletcher Webster, the eldest son of the eminent Massachusetts senator Daniel Webster. The association endeared the regiment to Boston's upper crust; the *Chicago Tribune* dubbed the unit "the pet corps of Boston conservatism." Many men of the Second Battalion, including the core members of the choral group, joined the regiment. They brought "John Brown's Body" along with them and passed it on to the other regiments, the Eleventh and the Fourteenth, that soon joined them in the fort.[17]

The song quickly overran Fort Warren's walls. In July an advertisement from a Boston music-publishing firm for a printing of "*Glory! Hallelujah*" announced, "At this time one can hardly walk on the streets for five minutes without hearing it whistled or hummed." In the first months of the war, a lack of major military operations meant that most units set up for considerable stretches of time near major cities and towns, integrating the civilian and military populations and allowing popular songs to make their way back and forth between parlor rooms and military camps. Greenleaf had earlier facilitated this exchange. He requested that C. S. Hall, a Boston associate with strong abolitionist views, assist him in printing a version of the song. Hall sifted through the dozens of verses that had been improvised and selected five, adding one of his own composition: "Now, three rousing cheers for the Union! / As we are marching on!" Sometime in late May or early June, Hall published the "John Brown Song" as a penny ballad on thin paper with a filigreed black border and the six verses, interspersed with the "Glory, Hally, Hallelujah" chorus. (In future versions of the song, the middle "Hally" transformed into another "Glory.") The sheet quickly sold out. In mid-July Hall published a sturdier, full-sheet version of the song, complete with words and music (arranged by C. B. Marsh, a well-known local musician), which announced "Fort Warren" as the song's origin.[18]

Music publishers in the city smelled a hit. Just over a week after Hall copyrighted the music on July 16, the same Boston court clerk issued three other publishers' copyrights on the same song. Within a year numerous other Boston music publishers had issued their own versions of the song, as did publishers in New York, Philadelphia, Cincinnati, Chicago, Rochester, Cleveland, and San Francisco. Boyd Stutler, a collector who has conducted the most exhaustive research into the song's origins, counted sixty-five separate pieces of sheet music based on the "John Brown's Body" tune published during the war, as well as innumerable penny song sheets.[19]

If the "John Brown Song" struck a powerful chord, it did so among a public primed to be struck. The Civil War amplified what had been a robust public culture of singing that had developed by the mid-nineteenth century, one in which friends and strangers, men and women of different classes and social background, felt comfortable making music in each other's company. This was especially the case when the songs being sung at public meetings or rallies were patriotic offerings that celebrated the Union and the "boys in blue" who were defending it. In this context, war music emerged as an especially profitable business. The 1850s had witnessed a dramatic increase in piano production, which lessened the price of the instrument to the point that many middle-class families could afford to bring one into their homes. Songwriters and music entrepreneurs had responded to the ensuing demand for parlor music, one that the start of the war only intensified. Sheet music and songbooks shot forth from printing presses. One leading historian of Civil War music has estimated that between nine thousand and ten thousand different songs were published as sheet music during the war, with popular songs regularly selling tens of thousands of copies, a few even reaching the hundreds of thousands. "By the 1860s," he notes, "sheet music publishing in America had become the most profitable printed medium."[20]

The esteem in which much of Boston held the Twelfth Regiment coupled with the city's demand for patriotic music created a climate ripe for the John Brown song. On July 18 the regiment left Fort Warren to be reviewed by the governor on Boston Common and to be honored with an address by the noted orator Edward Everett. Major Newton, the Second Battalion, and the Gilmore Band met the regiment at the wharf, and the band played the song as the regiment marched up State Street, singing along "in a spirited manner." Five days later the 1,040 men of the regiment, equipped with Enfield rifles, neatly folded overcoats, and bulging knapsacks, left the fort for good and headed to the railway station, where twenty-one passengers cars and twenty baggage wagons waited to take them southward. Along the way the regimental band struck up "John Brown's Body" to the wild cheers of those crowding the streets to see them off, "creating a great popular furore."

The regiment arrived in New York on July 24, just as news was reaching the city of the first significant Union defeat at Bull Run. Thousands of spectators crowded the sidewalks and watched from alleyways, windows, and door fronts as the Twelfth Massachusetts marched up Broadway to the City Hall Park barracks. When the regiment began playing the John Brown song, the onlookers "seemed to be crazy with enthusiasm and delight" and joined along in the chorus. Perhaps the Webster Regiment, generally credited with being one of the best drilled in the army, restored something of the city's faith in the North's military prowess. The enthusiastic reception given the song was enough to get the attention of several reporters in the crowd; one from the *New York Tribune* managed to commandeer a copy of a song sheet, and a few days later his paper published the lyrics. In accounts of the procession, newspapers dubbed the Twelfth the "psalm-singing regiment from Boston" and the "Hallelujah Regiment." The latter sobriquet stuck, permanently linking the Webster Regiment in the public mind to "John Brown's Body."[21]

★

THROUGH SHARED ENCAMPMENTS AND joint engagements, "John Brown's Body" soon spread from the Massachusetts regiment to the entire Army of the Potomac, becoming its most beloved song. (As early as the end of July 1861 a version of "John Brown's Body" issued by a major Boston music publisher referred to it as "The Popular Refrain of Glory, Hallelujah as sung by the Federal Volunteers Throughout the Union.") Often soldiers left intact the Fort Warren lyrics, especially the verses about Brown's mouldering body and the arboreal retribution to be exacted upon Jeff Davis. But they also dropped some of the more obscure references to private battalion jokes and replaced them with lyrics that suited regimental particularities or that burnished regimental pride. The Fourth Battalion of the Massachusetts Thirteenth Regiment, for instance, added the verse "Nimble feet in Dixie when they hear the rifles crack / Of the Old Bay State's Thirteenth." A sergeant in an Ohio infantry regiment snuck in a verse poking fun at an unlucky major who had lost his company in a regimental reorganization.[22]

It is not a coincidence that a favorite song at military camps borrowed a tune that had been a favorite at camp meetings. Both settings cultivated conviviality and intimacy among strangers; both pulsated with the energy generated by the anticipation of future conflicts, military or spiritual in nature. One Illinois soldier wrote to his fiancée, explaining what camp life was like, "Imagine yourself to be at a campmeeting where the ladies are minus." The utility of "John Brown's Body" during both the rushes and lulls of protracted military campaigns suited it even more firmly for army life.

"The effect of this song, when heard in camp or on the march was simply indescribable," recalled one New Hampshire lieutenant, "and often, when tired and lank, both weariness and hunger disappeared, for the time being, when some bold spirit struck up the refrain." Late in the war, as his regiment marched through the swamps of South Carolina, a young Wisconsin private described to his mother in similar terms the song's power. Even though they frequently found themselves "in water to [their] knees for miles at a time . . . the boys don't grumble." He conjured up the scene of his mates belting out "John Brown's Body," "all feeling good and jolly," their singing and cheering mingling with the occasional curse when a soldier tumbled into the water.[23]

But the song did not just cheer men, of course; it also inspired them. One of the main justifications for the installment of a military band within each regiment was to rally troops in the heat of battle, and perhaps more than any other song, "John Brown's Body" proved effective at doing so. "The leaders of the Union army acknowledge its superhuman power for inspiring the ranks," wrote one journalist during the war. "One of the most eminent of Department commanders has said that the song 'made heroes of all his men.'" In fact one Union officer required that his troops sing the song every day, as a daily tonic he believed would imbue them with "Cromwellian earnestness," referring to the pious leader of the Parliamentarians in the seventeenth-century English Civil War, who was convinced he too was a soldier in the army of the Lord. The song, with its steady, determined cadence, steeled men for battle. "My old Brigade sang it softly," John Habberton, the *New York Herald*'s longtime literary critic, noted after the war, "but with a swing that was terrible in its earnestness, as they lay behind their stacks of arms just before going into action." "John Brown's Body" provided a particularly powerful boost to troop morale during the siege of Yorktown, in April 1862, where exhausted Union troops faced imposing Confederate entrenchments. One of the regimental bands began playing "John Brown's Body," and the song quickly spread. With the singing, "the wearied forms grew erect," one veteran recalled, "and beneath the bursting shells and to the accompaniment of the deep double bass of cannon, the ranks cadencing their steps to the inspiring melody, debouched upon the plain, deployed, and were arrayed to face the foe." The veteran suggested that its effect upon the men that day secured the song's status as "the marching song of the [entire] Army."[24]

It is a sad irony that just as "John Brown's Body" reached the peak of its popularity among the troops, the men of the Hallelujah Regiment lost their zeal for singing it. On June 6, 1862, outside Fort Royal, Virginia, John Brown and some other soldiers crossed the Shenandoah River to serve on picket duty. When the bridge that the men had used washed away, they boarded a hastily constructed raft to return to camp and avoid capture. But the flimsy craft disintegrated, and Brown drowned. Two months later, Fletcher Webster, the regiment's commander, was killed at the Second Battle of Bull Run. To honor both men's memories, the regiment stopped singing the song they had made famous. In July 1864, when the Twelfth Regiment returned to Boston and marched through the city—now with just eighty-five men, and Brown's Company A holding but three—a colonel made an effort to get the troops singing the old song again. The crowd cheered them on, but the men refused.[25]

That silence symbolically confirmed the abolitionist John Brown as the song's presiding spirit. Not until the origins of "John Brown's Body" became the topic of a nationwide discussion more than a decade after the war's conclusion was the memory of the Scottish John Brown revived. The association between the song and the abolitionist was further strengthened as Union forces marched through Charles Town, the site of Brown's execution, and Harpers Ferry. The latter changed hands twelve times during the war and suffered considerable damage; the jail in which Brown spent his final weeks lay in ruins. The soldiers who passed through the town took a special pleasure in noting its desolation. (They also took the opportunity to pocket souvenirs from landmarks of the raid: bricks from the firehouse where Brown was captured, splinters of wood from the gallows on which he died.) "Whenever our army or any part of it had occasion to pass through this town," recalled one surgeon in a New York regiment, "the bands always struck up this air, as if to taunt the inhabitants with the memory of their victim, and played it from one limit of the town to the other. So John Brown was revenged!" The Webster Regiment passed through Charles Town in late July 1861 and, circling around the still-standing gallows, belted out an especially stirring rendition of the song. A member of the Pennsylvania 132nd remarked that his regiment sang "John Brown's Body" with "peculiar zest" when passing through Harpers Ferry because of the "poetic justice" of Union troops reclaiming the ground that Brown had once briefly held.[26]

But what exactly did it mean for Union soldiers to sing "John Brown's Body" with peculiar zest? When soldiers declared that John Brown's soul was marching on, did they thereby channel his commitment to the emancipation of enslaved Africans? Few of the most popular songs of the war's first year engaged the military conflict as a struggle over slavery; they were mostly sentimental tributes to soldiers' mothers and patriotic tributes to the Union. To the extent that the mention of John Brown inevitably conjured up abolitionist furies, the song that bore his name proved somewhat exceptional, and even inconvenient, at a time when Union leaders were attempting to reassure border states that the war was being waged not to free the slaves but to preserve the Union. Such was the assessment of an editorialist at the *Chicago Tribune* who noted the curious fact that "the favorite song of the new volunteers is a negro doggerel in which John Brown is glorified as living in spirit in this campaign." If even Fletcher Webster's Boston's troops, the darlings of New England conservatism, were singing such a song, the "Virginians will think John Brown is worshipped as the Northern hero, in spite of all denials," he concluded. "So on all hands Providence seems to be involving slavery with the war, notwithstanding the most sincere efforts of patriotism and statesmanship to keep the constitutional lines distinct."[27]

There were some in the North, of course, who celebrated and promoted this interpretation of the song—and of the war itself. The Hutchinson Family, a popular Northern singing group with strong abolitionist sympathies, quickly incorporated "John Brown's Body" into their repertoire, and it became a staple at antislavery rallies. Missionaries and abolitionists who traveled south to minister to freed slaves taught it to their new pupils. As one historian has noted, "A typical school for freedmen might well begin with prayer, followed by the reading of a Bible passage and the singing of 'John Brown's Body.'" For those early enlistees in the Union army who were impelled by abolitionist fervor—a small but vocal minority—"John Brown's Body" served as a rallying cry. "I want to sing 'John Brown' in the streets of Charleston," announced one Massachusetts infantry captain to his mother, "and ram red-hot abolition down their unwilling throats at the point of the bayonet."[28]

For those who joined the fight out of abolitionist principles, "John Brown's Body" struck a note of defiance not merely against Southern antagonists but against Union military or political leaders who sought to tamp down those principles. The song was particularly popular among Kansas regiments, made up of men who had sharpened their blades clashing with proslavery "ruffians" in the border skirmishes of the 1850s; many had fought alongside Brown himself. In many ways the Kansas regiments merely continued those unrestrained guerrilla battles into the war years, adopting the tactics that Brown had employed—and that General Sherman would soon as well—plundering towns, requisitioning supplies, freeing slaves along the way. The Jayhawker units quickly gained a reputation for antislavery zeal and unruly, almost anarchic bravado. From all over the North, men flocked to join Kansas regiments because, as one enlistee explained, "no fugitive slaves [would] be returned by them." William Cody, who would later win renown as Buffalo Bill, joined the Seventh Cavalry Regiment. So too did John Brown Jr., the abolitionist's son. He recruited a company of sixty-six "sharpshooters"—"hunters, lumbermen . . . all first-rate shots"—from across the North. Passing through Chicago, his men sang "John Brown's Body" through the city's streets. Once they arrived in Kansas, they introduced the song to their comrades, and it quickly became the regiment's favorite. At dusk the men would huddle together near the captain's tent and listen to speakers who, in low, impassioned tones, would stoke the men's abolitionist fervor. They would always end by vowing to avenge the death of John Brown and by singing "John Brown's Body."

The Union military hierarchy regarded the Kansas regiments warily. They were particularly incensed by the penchant of Jayhawker officers to contravene official policy regarding the return of escaped slaves. When a colonel from the Seventh Cavalry issued an order declaring that any soldier who returned a fugitive slave to his master would "be summarily and severely punished," one general, John A. Logan, into whose territory the men had passed, ordered the regiment to move outside his lines. When the Kansas regiment was slow in complying, Logan sent an aide to issue the command again, this time more insistently: "General Logan orders this d—abolition regiment outside his lines or he will order out a battery and drive it out." This only stiffened the Kansans' resolve. They mounted their horses but did not move, daring Logan to make good on his threat and to see "how quick this d—abolition regiment will take it." Eventually a compromise was struck, and the Seventh moved to a nearby camp. As the men marched past the general's headquarters, the regimental band played "John Brown's Body," a fitting valediction from the damned abolition regiment.[29]

But no group appreciated the emancipationist associations of the song more than did African Americans, both enslaved and free. Northern visitors frequently expressed surprise when they encountered Southern blacks' familiarity with the song. A doctor in charge of a Florida school for freed slaves was moved to tears when, at a pause at the conclusion of the daily exercises, a young girl suddenly began singing "John Brown's body lies a-mouldering in the grave." Then, as if "by magic, the whole singing-class, sixty in number, chimed in," reported the teacher. "Where they had learned it he could not conjecture." The townspeople who congregated around the school's open window to listen to the singing seemed equally perplexed. If Northerners regarded the popularity of "John Brown's Body" among slaves with wonder—often depicting the song as the untutored and primal expression of slaves' yearning for freedom—it was because they disregarded the elaborate systems of communication slave communities had developed to pass on valuable bits of information. The same channels that had relayed to slaves news of Brown's raid also transmitted the song that bore his name. The popularity of "Say Brothers" within black churches and among Southern slaves likely primed African Americans for their reception of "John Brown's Body." The hymn's evocative image of crossing over into the promised land of Canaan had expressed the slaves' yearning for freedom, with the call for spiritual redemption cloaking the more illicit desire for political and economic liberation. But in singing "John Brown's Body" they demonstrated that the time of codes was passing. To invoke the figure of John Brown in the South, and not to do so with scorn, was to speak plainly and defiantly.

Such boldness was on display in a Charleston, South Carolina, guardhouse, in the final weeks of the war, when Union forces occupied the city. A Northern visitor came upon a group of freedmen and asked them to sing some old plantation songs. After they had performed some of their "strange, hum-drum, droning airs," someone asked if they knew the "John Brown song." They immediately began singing the first verse. When asked if they knew any more of the song, they replied that they knew the second verse as well. "We'll hang Jeff Davis to a sour apple tree / *On Canaan's happy shore!*" they sang. The apposition deeply moved one onlooker. "So simple and ludicrous, is the admixture of ideas in the minds of these untutored Africans!" he concluded. "In their guiltless ignorance, they see no reason why 'Canaan's happy shore' may not be an excellent place for an execution." Yet he admitted there might be "some true philosophy" in this conflation of Methodist hymn and soldier's war song, the spiritual and the corporeal. John Brown himself provided the bridge between the two, linking millennial hopes with retributive violence.[30]

Even before Union victory became certain, the song clearly held subversive attraction for bondsmen and -women who intuited that freedom was no longer a distant vision but an imminent actuality. A Boston paper relayed a story from its New Orleans correspondent of a master who was entertaining a number of Northern visitors at a nearby plantation and, in order to show his guests his slaves' contentment, ordered one of them to sing. "Whereupon the fellow struck up the 'Old John Brown' song, more to the amusement of the guests than of the host." A visitor to Virginia during the war expressed similar surprise in hearing the slaves singing "John Brown's Body" while laboring in the fields. When he asked their master why he allowed them to do so, the master replied that he was powerless to stop them.[31]

"John Brown's Body" occupied a central place in both spontaneous and planned celebrations of emancipation. At an interracial celebration of the Emancipation Proclamation held at Camp Saxton, near Port Royal, South Carolina, on New Year's Day 1863, an audience that included white missionaries, black soldiers, and thousands of now free men and women concluded the lengthy service with the John Brown song, which, a participant recorded in her diary, "all the colored people know." That same day the First Regiment of Kansas Colored Volunteers capped off their own celebration of the Emancipation Proclamation with a barbecue, some "strong drink," and a spirited rendition of "John Brown's Body." In February 1865, to celebrate emancipation in Missouri, a border state whose slaves were not officially freed until two years after those in the Confederate-controlled South, African American citizens in Kansas City organized a massive procession though the city's streets. According to one observer, "With music and banners and transparencies and mottoes [they] paraded the street, singing that great American hymn of freedom—the John Brown Song."[32]

"John Brown's Body" held a particularly strong attraction for African American troops, who had not only taken up Brown's cause of racial justice but had adopted his means of holy violence as well. According to Thomas Wentworth Higginson, a former ally and friend of Brown who commanded a volunteer slave regiment in South Carolina, the song was "a great favorite" among his men. As Higginson rested at night, he frequently heard the troops, seated around the campfire, "singing [the song] at the top of their voices," in a ritual that recalled the tune's camp meeting roots.[33]

From its very inception, the Fifty-fourth Massachusetts, the first black regiment to be created, embraced "John Brown's Body" as a potent expression of their aspirations. In April 1863, at Mother Bethel Church in Philadelphia, Frederick Douglass delivered a speech urging African Americans to "get an eagle on your button" and enlist in the regiment. He informed the crowd that he had just come from New York, where he had recruited nearly a full company of the states' citizens, who would soon march down Broadway "timing [their] footsteps to the time honored music of old John Brown." He called for the African American men in the pews to yell out their names if they would join the regiment. One did. There was a moment of hesitating silence, so Douglass began singing, "John Brown's Body lies mouldering in the grave," and before he arrived at the second line, the whole audience had joined in. When they finished the song, three more men added their names to the list, and by the end of the event nearly enough for an entire company had been recruited.

On May 28 the full ten companies of the Fifty-fourth (including two of Douglass's own sons) were reviewed on Boston Common and then marched to Battery Wharf, where a transport ship waited to take them to the Sea Islands of South Carolina. On the way the men took a moment to pause before the spot where, a century before, in the Boston Massacre, Crispus Attucks had shed the first blood of the American Revolution. At that moment, while one of the largest crowds in the city's history looked on, the regimental band struck up "John Brown's Body." The Fifty-fourth sang the song again, when they were among the first troops to enter Charleston in February 1865, marching behind a black Union soldier riding a mule and carrying a banner declaring "Liberty," and then yet again, three and a half decades later, when sixty-five veterans of the Fifty-fourth marched past Augustus Saint-Gaudens's newly unveiled monument to the regiment's slain colonel, Robert Gould Shaw, on Boston Common.[34]

Another black regiment, the First Arkansas Volunteer Infantry (African Descent), forged an especially strong attachment to the song by crafting a variant expertly molded to fit their own needs and aspirations. This regiment of former slaves, established in May 1863, had suffered horrible atrocities in late June at Goodrich's Landing, Mississippi, where they were stationed to protect plantations confiscated by the Union army that supplied food to troops. A large force of Confederates attacked Goodrich's Landing and the surrounding Union plantations in the hopes of destroying this supply line. They captured two companies of the First Arkansas and treated the black prisoners as slave insurrectionaries, killing or reenslaving nearly all of the men.

The Rebels also set fire to the plantations and burned down "every negro quarter," according to the commanding Union officer. Hundreds of black civilians, mostly women and children, burned to death in the conflagration. A few months after it witnessed those apocalyptic scenes, the First Arkansas was revitalized under the command of Captain Lindley Miller. A wealthy lawyer from New Jersey, Miller had also experienced a recent tragedy. He had grown up in an antislavery family, and when the war came he joined the New York Seventh, known as the "Silk Stocking" regiment for its fashionable members. In 1862, while still in uniform, he married Anne Tracy, a Manhattan socialite. Anne soon got pregnant, and in early July 1863 she was at home in Manhattan and at term when the draft riots erupted. For four days mobs of working-class Democrats, protesting that they were being drafted "to fight for the Niggers" who would come north and steal their jobs, went on a rampage throughout the city. They destroyed the homes and businesses of notable Republicans and killed or maimed nearly every African American they could get their hands on. Anne's father took her to the Catskills for safety, but she died in childbirth; the infant died a week later. Lindley was devastated and sought solace among African Americans, requesting a commission to serve as an officer of a black regiment. He was assigned to the First Arkansas.[35]

Miller got along with his troops well enough to write "a song for them to the tune of 'John Brown,'" as he wrote his mother in January 1864. Entitled "The Marching Song of the First Arkansas (Negro) Regiment," it was one of the most revolutionary songs of the Civil War. Appropriately Miller wrote it at Goodrich's Landing, which the First Arkansas had retaken from the rebels. Comprising eight stanzas and written in slave dialect, the song combines militant bravado with millennial expectancy, using both to stake the soldiers' claims to social and legal equality:

> Dey will hab to pay us wages, the wages of their sin,
> Dey will hab to bow their foreheads to their colored kith and kin,
> Dey will hab to gib us house-room, or de roof shall tumble in,
> As we go marching on.

In this remarkable stanza, the former slaves combined the idiom of the free labor ideology, the very antithesis of slavery, with the threat of rough retributive justice; the slaveholders owed blacks a debt of biblical proportions ("the wages of sin is death"), which justified the black soldiers' repaying them with violence of their own. Then, in the following verse, by insisting that the Rebels would have to show respect, and even deference, to "their colored kith and kin," the soldiers both gestured toward their common humanity and hinted at the shameful history of the sexual exploitation of slave women. The reparations the First Arkansas would win through the force of their arms would not stop at equality; they would require that Southerners reckoned with their own iniquities.[36]

When folk music enthusiasts and Civil War scholars rediscovered the song a century later, it was often celebrated as the unmediated expression of African American racial pride. But its lyrics in fact point to a collaboration between Lindley and the black soldiers. The song's characterization of the unit as "the sable army of 'African descent'" seems a literary flourish more likely to have come from the pen of the regiment's white officer, while some of the song's more combative images suggest that Lindley transcribed and edited words that his troops themselves sang. Of course, in its use of rather crude blackface dialect, the "Marching Song" also bears some resemblance to the demeaning minstrel songs popular among Northern audiences. But whereas minstrelsy featured unthreatening, buffoonish performers who could assuage white fears of African Americans, the "Marching Song" brandishes an unrestrained militancy. Lindley himself appreciated that it would make many listeners uneasy. "You will not like it I fear," he warned his mother. To another associate he wrote, "While it is not very conservative, it will do to fight with." His troops certainly seemed to agree. They sang it on dress parade "with an effect which can hardly be described," Miller noted.[37]

Miller's brother-in-law sent the "Marching Song" to the *National Anti-Slavery Standard*, a New York City abolitionist newspaper, where it was published in February 1864. A recruiting agent discovered it and published a broadside to help recruit black troops. The song helped Miller inspire his men. In fact he so impressed his superior officers that they promoted him to the rank of major and asked him to take command of a new black regiment in Missouri. Soon after arriving there, however, he came down with a high fever. He went home to try to recover but died soon after.[38]

The song reached a wider audience with help from Sojourner Truth. Among the best-known black leaders of her day, Truth lived in Battle Creek, Michigan, during the war and likely discovered the "Marching Song" in late 1863 or early 1864. She liked it so much that she sought to broaden its appeal. She changed the title and first verse to "The Valiant Soldiers" in order to generalize it, and she deleted two stanzas so that it would be easier to memorize. Truth circulated "The Valiant Soldiers" as part of her effort to recruit black regiments. Hers became the standard version, and until quite recently, when Miller's authorship was discovered, she was generally credited as the song's original author, adding a dash of feminist brio to the song's militancy.

"The Marching Song," coupled with its variant, "The Valiant Soldiers," spread to numerous black regiments during the war. The song resonated with the hopes of black soldiers in the imminence of a revolutionary moment, when their dreams of freedom and equality hung in the balance. Both songs did so by representing the war as a millennial conflict, with racial justice as its underlying issue; as one verse declared, "When de Massas hear us yellin' dey'll tink it's Gabriel's horn," comparing their battle cries to the call of judgment day. If they had altered the body of the John Brown song, they had stayed true to its soul.[39]

★

HOWEVER, WITHIN THE UNION ARMY more generally, as well as on the home front, many who sang along with "John Brown's Body" did not share Brown's views on slavery. Initially few Northerners enlisted out of abolitionist imperatives, and only a minority considered the destruction of slavery to be one of the war's primary aims. This is not to suggest that most Northerners harbored proslavery sympathies. Many claimed to detest slavery, but, like President Lincoln himself, they were willing to sheath that hatred when it seemed to interfere with their primary commitment: the preservation of the Union. Indeed in the first year, a considerable number of Union soldiers regarded these two objectives—the emancipation of the slaves and the preservation of the Union—to be at odds. A prominent New York minister made this point when cheering the Twelfth Massachusetts, the Hallelujah Regiment that would spread "John Brown's Body" through the army, as it passed through the city to the Southern theater. This struggle was "an uprising of the people . . . in defense of the constitutional government," the minister declared to the soldiers and the assembled dignitaries who had come to see them off. "This is not a war against slavery." A variation on the John Brown song, published by a New York firm in 1862, expressed a similar vision of the war's ends, with the rousing yet hardly radical exhortation, "Come fight for the Union as it was my boys! While we go marching on." The song depicted the war not as a crucible out of which the nation would emerge chastened and transformed, but as an essentially conservative struggle.[40]

Yet war, by its very nature, destabilizes what was, and in fighting to preserve the Union Northern troops necessarily transformed it. In fact there is considerable evidence that by the fall of 1861, just as "John Brown's Body" was spreading through the Union ranks, the experience of the war was changing soldiers' attitudes toward slavery. The twinned convictions of slavery as the root cause of the war and emancipation as the best means of ending it impressed themselves upon Northern troops. This acknowledgment led some to embrace "practical abolitionism," a strategic and tactical calculation as opposed to a humanitarian impulse. Practical abolitionists appreciated that each contraband slave represented a diminution of the Confederacy's labor resources and that every slave that donned the Union uniform represented a body that could absorb a Confederate bullet in place of a white soldier. They advanced toward emancipation haltingly, making sure to signal along the way that they had not undergone any dramatic change in their racial attitudes. "I am no Nigger worshipper," a Pennsylvania artilleryman assured his father in January

1863, but "nothing will end this war sooner" than the emancipation of the slaves.[41]

The experience of war could also promote a more radical ideological transformation; like a camp meeting, combat could induce mass conversions. Sheltering runaway slaves from masters determined to bring them back; encountering cruelty to African Americans at close range; watching former slaves perform nobly in combat; witnessing the slaves' jubilant response to the president's Emancipation Proclamation; and channeling the contempt that was building for the antiwar Copperheads on the home front—all led many soldiers to develop attitudes toward slavery, and even toward race itself, that would have been deemed radical before the war began.[42]

As emancipation became entwined with the military struggle, and as Unionist aims became associated with the soul of Old John Brown, his song increasingly served as the anthem of the spiritualization of the war effort. In November 1861 a Boston Unitarian minister, James Freeman Clarke, traveled to Washington, D.C. in the company of Julia Ward Howe, and during visits to Union encampments in Virginia, they heard soldiers singing "John Brown's Body." Clarke encouraged Howe to write new lyrics for the song, and early the next morning she would do exactly that. Though Clarke recognized its deficiencies, he was still moved by "John Brown's Body." As he recorded in his diary, the tune "seemed true in the deepest sense. John Brown's soul is marching on! For what is the soul of John Brown but his unconquerable hatred of slavery, and his fervent desire of seeing it abolished? And is not that desire and feeling marching on? Is not slavery recognized more and more as the cause of the war . . . and something which must be destroyed, if the life of the nation is to be saved?"[43]

And yet the fact that Northern crowds cheered along with a song that celebrated John Brown and seemed willing to install him as the Union's presiding spirit does not mean that they universally embraced his attitude toward slavery. Brown's soul, after all, could be revived in many different ways. The "great American hymn of freedom," at least in its classic Fort Warren version, does not actually mention freedom, or any of its cognate principles. For those abolitionists who embraced the song, the figure of Brown said enough. But others in the antislavery camp sought to provide new words that would deliver an unambiguously abolitionist message. None of these, however, matched the popularity of the original version, whose greatest asset might have been its ideological indeterminacy; the John

Brown of the song could stand for many principles. Soldiers who did not claim abolitionist sympathies could belt it out without fear of radical taint.

The image of Brown's soul "marching on" encouraged an open-ended interpretation of the song. The persistence of his spirit after his death, the insistence that the South would not be able to exterminate the principles for which he martyred himself, proved the most prominent trope in the posthumous celebrations of Brown. In a speech Thoreau delivered in Concord, for instance, he insisted that Brown had not really died. For, transformed into a force of pure spirit, he was "more alive than ever he was." Laudatory poems written in honor of his death invoked the empty tomb and the unsettled grave to suggest that Brown would continue to stalk the South.

Such claims were, in a sense, self-fulfilling. To speak of Brown's endurance was to guarantee it, without referencing any particular principle that would live on with him. It was to focus attention on his postexecution resurrection, as opposed to the gospel that had led him to the gallows. The attraction of a hero who lived on after his death at the hand of Southern scoundrels no doubt held a special attraction for large swaths of the Northern public, as well as for many Union soldiers, grappling with the enormity of death around them. The scale, then as now, defied belief: some 620,000 Northerners and Southerners were killed in the war, about 2 percent of the nation's total population. (A similar proportion would yield six million deaths today.) If John Brown's soul could go marching on, so too could that of a friend or a father, killed in battle or by disease. And so too might their own souls. The song instructed soldiers in the necessity and glory of sacrifice, a sacrifice that could be abstracted from any particular political, economic, or racial reformist program.[44]

But the song was not only about survival. It was also about revenge. When Northern troops sang "John Brown's Body," they tended to give special emphasis to the description of the indignities that would be visited upon Jefferson Davis. They were attracted not merely to claims of the persistence of the spirit when the body suffers but to the prospect of exacting suffering on some other body; they celebrated the enduring incorporality of war's aims *and* the vivid corporality of war's effects. Those lines about hanging Davis to a tree (or giving him "the di-a-rhee") held a strong appeal to some civilians as well, especially, according to one contemporary writer, "the small boys, the hard men, and the rough people generally" in a crowd. The moment when an audience arrived at that verse, the writer Mary Abigail Dodge noted, often proved a somewhat awkward one, in which the aesthetic, temperamental, political, and moral divisions bridged by Unionist fervor were momentarily exposed. At the conjuring of the image of the Confederate president dangling from a tree, "the civilized people look a little startled . . . [and] lean upon each other for support, smile compromisingly, and conclude to keep on. But all the wild beasts are mad with delight; they find their blood lust legalized; their tumultuousness is orthodox."[45]

For these particular admirers of "John Brown's Body," the violence that the song celebrated had little connection to Brown's holy purpose; it held an attraction all its own. To the extent that Brown's soul marched on besides these troops or inspired those bellowing the song in some concert hall, it was not Brown's antislavery principles so much as his unembarrassed embrace of violence as a means of achieving them that inspired. To many of Brown's partisans his success stemmed largely from his willingness to beat the proslavery toughs at their own game; as one contemporary journalist announced, Brown "brought southern tactics to the northern side." For decades, Southern proslavery apologists had become habituated to and more than a little contemptuous of the nonviolent principles of the leaders of the abolitionist movement. John Brown had upset that complacency. Before Brown's raid, the abolitionist stalwart Wendell Phillips remarked, the men "who believed in bowie knives" were largely Southerners attacking abolitionists. But since Harpers Ferry, "the tables have been turned . . . and the men who believe in violence . . . are ranged on the side of liberty."[46]

Southern condemnation of Brown's brutality and his disregard for human life also served as a means of exonerating the brutality of proslavery defenders—and, in a sense, of the violence at the heart of the institution of slavery itself. For Southerners and their allies, the fact that Union troops marched to battle singing a tribute to John Brown offered definitive confirmation of Northern depravity. In an 1863 speech Congressman Samuel Cox from Ohio, a Democrat closely allied with the leading Copperhead Clement Vallandigham, invoked the song to demonstrate the extent to which the entire North had been infected with "the Constitution-breaking, law-defying, negro-loving Phariseeism of New England." As proof of the North's fanaticism he pointed to the fact that its "Marseillaise is a hymn of apotheosis to a horse-thief and a murderer."

In fact the song seemed to possess the power to drive some Southerners into a fury. For Susan Bradford, a Tallahassee belle ensconced in her family's Pine Hill plantation, a rendition of "John Brown's Body" unleashed the pent-up bitterness generated by wartime deprivations and humiliations. The normally demure nineteen-year-old recorded in her journal, "For the first time in all my life I have laid hands in violence upon a *negro*." Actually she used a whip. In the waning days of the war, the presence of Union troops, including a contingent of African American soldiers stationed just two miles from the plantation, emboldened the family's slaves. As night came on, the family would sit by the window, listening nervously to the sounds outside, convinced that slaves were spying on their conversations to bring news to the nearby Union camp. One night Susan heard footsteps and saw "some twenty or more half-grown negro boys and girls." When they reached the house, they began to sing, "We'll hang Jeff Davis on a sour apple tree / As we go marching on," clearly relishing the effect the song would likely have on those huddled inside. "The negroes were evidently expecting to make us angry but they had not counted on the reception they received," Susan recorded. She grabbed a carriage whip and ran out to the yard: "I rushed in their midst and, laying the whip about me with all the strength I could muster, I soon had the whole crowd flying toward the [slave] Quarter, screaming as they went."[47]

Northerners, like the slaves lurking outside Susan Bradford's window, appreciated that the specter of John Brown continued to unnerve Southerners. And so "John Brown's Body" could serve as an especially potent anti-Confederate weapon. Such a motive was not necessarily divorced from a desire to trumpet the North's antislavery ideals. But the song could also be sung as a sort of musical thumbing of the nose, without specifying any ideological foundation for the gesture. The thought of Brown as a fearsome figurehead leading the Union army to victory was enough to rally the troops. It was not surprising that "Brave McClellan Is Our Leader Now," a song written to welcome the installation of George McClellan as commander of the Army of the Potomac after a string of military disappointments, used the "John Brown's Body" tune. Although the figure of Brown appeared nowhere in the song, when the men sang "We've had our last retreat, my boys," his soul surely marched along.[48]

Some of the more popular songs among Union troops touched on sentimental themes that could bridge the sectional divide. When camped near each other, Union and Confederate troops frequently engaged in musical duels, with the bands of each regiment playing their favored sectional songs. Sometimes they would end in a gesture of transsectional solidarity, communicating the shared vicissitudes of war, as with alternating tunes about loved ones left back at home. At the battle of Fredericksburg, after the bands traded "The Star Spangled Banner" and "Dixie," when Union musicians started playing "Home, Sweet Home," the men on both sides cheered.

"John Brown's Body" offered no such common ground; its sentiments, intertwined with specific or cryptic referents birthed at Fort Warren, staked it to the heart of the North. Within these exchanges, the song exhibited a particular power to infuriate. On one occasion, after the men of a Massachusetts regiment serenaded the Confederates camped nearby with it, "twenty [Confederate] canons thundered an answer to the insolent song."[49]

A leading contemporary literary critic once praised the words of "John Brown's Body" as the "verbal equivalents of rifle-bullets and cannon-balls." In the song's power to fuel and sustain defiance, it did seem to boast a certain degree of firepower. When a number of the men from the Sixteenth Connecticut Regiment were captured by a detail of North Carolinians, "they howled into the ears" of their Confederate captors "John Brown's Body." The defiant gesture allowed for a momentary power reversal, though one that was short-lived; the men would soon be dispatched to the infamous Andersonville Prison, where more than a quarter of all prisoners died from malnutrition, disease, or exposure to the elements. "[Hearing the fierce singing,] one would have supposed that we were the captors and they the prisoners," a veteran recalled.[50]

Not surprisingly Union troops often chose to mark their triumphant conquest of Confederate cities by singing "John Brown's Body." The song became a sort of anthem for General William Tecumseh Sherman's March to the Sea, the scorched-earth campaign he led from Atlanta to Savannah. (Southerners too associated the song, and Brown's willingness to inflict violence upon civilians, with Sherman's embrace of "total war.") After Sherman's troops burned down much of Atlanta and prepared to leave the city, the regimental band of the Thirty-third Massachusetts began playing the song. As one soldier recalled, "the men took up the words wedded to the music, and, high above the roaring flames, above the crash of falling walls, above the fierce crackling of thousands of small arms cartridges" could be heard the "triumphant refrain" of "Glory, glory Hallelujah." Upon leaving the smoldering city, Sherman himself commented, "Never before or since have I heard the chorus of 'Glory Glory Hallelujah' done with more spirit or in better harmony of time and place." When Charleston, South Carolina, fell to Union troops in February 1865, thousands of soldiers and former slaves marched through this marrow of the Confederacy singing "John Brown's Body." A parade of ten thousand, including two thousand black children, sang the song during the entire two-and-a-half-hour procession, many marching beneath a large banner that read, "The spirit of John Brown still lives." A Massachusetts abolitionist had volunteered to teach the city's black children the John Brown song for the parade, but had been persuaded by the school superintendent to leave out the verse about hanging Jefferson Davis, supposedly because of the superintendent's opposition to capital punishment. But many of the children knew the song already, and after singing the bowdlerized version a few times, began singing *only* the banned verse, to the consternation of the march's organizers and of the city's sullen white inhabitants who might have been watching.[51]

By 1864 "John Brown's Body" had become closely associated not merely with Northern military campaigns but with electoral ones as well. On the night of Lincoln's reelection, his jubilant supporters sang the song. But partisans of Lincoln's Democratic opponent, General George McClellan, who had run on a peace platform that would have allowed the South to maintain its independence, also sang their own version. Each camp could assume the pose of defying a powerful opponent—the Lincoln's National Union Party defied the Confederacy, while the Democrats stood up to the blood-soaked Black Republicans. Both camps shared a certainty in the justice and urgency of their cause, which linked them to the spirit of John Brown, if not necessarily to his millennial vision of racial egalitarianism. The young Confederate sympathizers in San Francisco who needled their neighbors by marching through the streets singing, "We'll hang Abe Lincoln to a Southern apple tree," were perversely appropriating Brown's legacy of principled defiance, though for a cause he would have scorned.[52]

These various appropriations of "John Brown's Body" took full advantage of its open-ended improvisational form and suggested an overarching theme of anarchic, democratic vitality, even if its contending usages—by abolitionists and Southern sympathizers, by those who cherished Brown's memory and those who scorned it—undermined any ideologically grounded meaning. For some, these incongruities were the song's most appealing feature. "There is high, religious fervor; a sense of poetic justice and righteous retribution; a scorn of grammar and rhetoric and rhyme and reason; an incoherence, a brutality, a diabolism, a patriotism, and a heroism" in the song, announced one journalist. "It appeals to all the emotions."

Yet others found the combination of high and low impulses incomprehensible. For Oliver Wendell Holmes Sr., the elevated, "almost sublime" ideals of the early verses, declaring the persistence of Brown's spirit and his service in the army of the Lord, were drawn down into the muck by the vulgarity of the verses vowing violent retribution toward Jefferson Davis.

If "John Brown's Body" had ended at its first stanza, claimed Holmes, "it would have stood, vivid and majestic, the Marseillaise of the civil war just past." Instead it "committed a felo de-se [suicide] in the fourth stanza," expiring ignobly as doggerel. In an 1866 compilation of Civil War literature, Richard Grant White, the prominent literary critic who had honed his connoisseurship of worthy songs as a leader of the Committee for a New National Hymn, dismissed "John Brown's Body" as a "senseless farrago." But, straining to explain its popularity, he also cited the song's relentless "presentation of a single idea."[53]

How could a song exhibit both senselessness and single-mindedness? A similar conundrum confronted Americans who struggled to extract some measure of meaning from the death and destruction brought on by the war. Doing so was made more difficult by the multitude of reasons soldiers fought: for home, for friends and comrades-in-arms, for their personal and familial honor, for their God, for their nation and its values.[54] Yet by the war's final months, a single idea *did* seem to propel the conflict to its conclusion, endowing the conflict with a sacred purpose. The war had secured, in Lincoln's words, "a new birth of freedom," both for a regenerated Union and for emancipated slaves, more than 100,000 of who had taken up arms to fight for their own liberty. For those who had emerged from such battles, "John Brown's Body" proved a means of celebrating this new birth. When the men of the 111th Pennsylvania Regiment received news of Lee's surrender, "caps were flung in the air, laughter rang out, jokes were cracked, and 'John Brown's Body'... rolled back and forth through the inspired ranks in endless melody."

Just as it had during the course of the war, the song also allowed Northern soldiers to taunt their Southern antagonists in the moment of victory. When the Fourth Michigan Cavalry, the regiment that captured Jefferson Davis, marched to Macon, Georgia, with their prize prisoner, the regimental band played "John Brown's Body," with all the soldiers joining in at the verse about the sour apple tree. Davis, riding in an ambulance, promptly pulled down the curtains. His wife complained bitterly that while her husband languished in prison, Union soldiers tutored his young son Billy in the rudiments of Northern morals, lessons that included the "John Brown's Body" verse in which his father figured prominently. Eventually the child confronted his mother and declared himself a Yankee.[55]

"John Brown's Body" was always more popular with troops on the march than with those on the home front. But in the war's waning days, the song's rhetorical swagger and its unyielding martial cadence also allowed civilians far from the scene of battle to participate vicariously. Upon hearing reports of Richmond's falling to Union forces in April 1865, American residents of Honolulu paraded through the streets singing "John Brown's Body." When the same news reached the Massachusetts Senate, its members immediately adjourned the body and rushed into the house chambers to announce the news. The house adjourned as well, and as friends and family members began streaming into the gallery, the legislators decided to hold an impromptu celebratory meeting. They first sang "America," then offered cheers for General Grant and President Lincoln. Then they erupted into the John Brown song, with those on the floor uniting with those in the galleries at the chorus. At the song's conclusion, they gave another three cheers for John Brown himself. And when Governor John Andrew entered the chamber, they had an excuse to launch into "John Brown's Body" yet again.[56]

Perhaps no occasion harnessed the emancipationist meanings of the song more powerfully than did the festivities in Charleston, South Carolina, at the close of the war. On April 14 General Robert Anderson returned to Fort Sumter to raise the flag that four years earlier he had lowered in surrender. Thousands of freedmen and a host of Northern politicians, missionaries, journalists, and abolitionists packed the fortress to witness the ceremony. Afterward a large procession of African Americans marched triumphantly through the city's streets; among them were black soldiers from a Pennsylvania regiment whose band erupted into "John Brown's Body." If Brown's raid on Harpers Ferry could in many respects be perceived as the opening salvo in the Civil War, the joyous rendition of the song that bore his name represented a bookend to the conflict. William Lloyd Garrison, for decades the nation's leading abolitionist, certainly appreciated the moment. As he listened to "John Brown's Body," he gripped the arm of a friend and burst into tears. "Only listen to that in Charleston streets," he exclaimed.[57]

The cessation of hostilities didn't dampen the public's enthusiasm for "John Brown's Body." The song was a favorite among veterans' groups and a staple at regimental reunions in the first years after the war. As Alfred S. Roe, a Massachusetts editor and politician, declared in 1883, "Put into one sum the times the name of Lincoln, the Martyred President, and Grant, the Peerless General, have been uttered and it would not make a hundredth part the number of times that represent the utterance of John Brown's name in this song."[58]

But in the decade after the war, as the Northern project of radical Recon-struction faltered and as a commitment to white supremacy became further entrenched in the South, Brown's reputation declined and the nation's memory of the war as an emancipationist struggle melted away. "John Brown's Body" was ultimately pushed aside by one of its musical offspring, another song that could summon its millennial energies and, freed from a direct association with the martyred abolitionist, offered an even greater range of interpretations for a nation newly committed to sectional reconcil-iation and imperial ambition.

III

★ ★ ★

JULIA WARD HOWE AND THE MAKING
OF THE "BATTLE HYMN OF THE REPUBLIC"

ONE DAY IN OCTOBER 1861, Rev. William W. Patton, pastor of Chicago's Washington Street Congregational Church, traveled by train to Cairo, Illinois, to inspect Union troops for a local sanitary agency. The government's reluctance to make emancipation an explicit war aim weighed heavily on Patton, and as he stared out the window and ruminated on how he might advance the antislavery cause, the tune of "John Brown's Body" drifted through his head. He had always found the melody "uncommonly taking" but dismissed the words as largely "meaningless." The idea of John Brown's soul marching on held strong appeal for Patton—it was, he thought, "too good to be lost"—yet he was repulsed by the image of Jefferson Davis dangling from a tree. "Why not have some better stanzas, with a proper rhythmical swing and a good anti-slavery moral, yet based on John Brown's history?" he thought to himself. So he started scribbling on the back of an envelope, and by the time he had arrived at his destination he had written an alternate version of the song. This he soon sent to the *Chicago Tribune* with the title "The New John Brown Song." Patton had retained the first verse of "John Brown's Body" and its "Glory, Hallelujah" chorus but had installed lyrics of an explicitly abolitionist bent. The song quickly spread, and in some pockets of the antislavery North rivaled its precursor in popularity. The most frequently cited stanza declared:

John Brown was John the Baptist of the Christ we are to see
Christ who of the bondsman shall the Liberator be
And soon throughout the sunny South the slaves shall all be free,
For his soul is marching on![1]

Patton's version was one of many adaptations of "John Brown's Body" that sought to sift from the song its improvisational dross. Henry Howard Brownell, famous for his Civil War battle poems, seemed especially offended by the song's lack of literary merit. "If people WILL sing about Old John Brown," he sniffed, "there is no reason why they shouldn't have words with a little meaning and rhythm in them." These he proceeded to supply, in five metrically neat stanzas of his own device.[2]

Paradoxically all these staid revisions took their license from the original's improvisational volatility. Patton, Brownell, and the others hoped to harness the millennial energies generated by the figure of John Brown and to direct them to respectable, reformist ends, without unleashing the vulgarity or the unrestrained apocalyptic violence that those energies could also spark.

The most successful of these efforts was Julia Ward Howe's "Battle Hymn of the Republic." Howe too believed that the sacred sentiments contained within "John Brown's Body" deserved a more dignified vessel. In fact her revision, more than any other, eclipsed the original song. But Howe's composition was not a simple act of lyrical supersession. For though she banished the figure of Brown from her "Battle Hymn," her cultivation of millennial and apocalyptic themes provided room for Brown's soul to continue its onward march. And though she managed to impose some discipline over the unruly forces swirling around the "Glory, glory, Hallelujah" chorus, her own song employed images and ideas that were ultimately not so easily restrained.

It is fitting that Julia Ward Howe had some success in corralling the anarchic energies of "John Brown's Body" within the bounds of high-culture respectability, for she had long sought to reconcile conventional social strictures with her own ambitions and impulses. She was born into a prominent New York family. Her father, Samuel Ward, had become a partner of a large New York banking house at the age of twenty-two. Her mother, Julia Cutler, was a woman of literary inclinations and intense evangelical piety who died at twenty-seven after giving birth to her seventh child. Her death devastated Samuel—for days he refused to even look at the new baby—and he turned to religion for consolation. He soon sought to impose his strict evangelical Calvinism on his children. His attentions fell especially hard on his oldest daughter, Julia, who was forced to serve as surrogate mother to her younger siblings.[3]

Leaving behind a house suffused with grief, Samuel Ward moved his family uptown, to what was then the northern periphery of the city. He built a spacious brownstone, and by convincing his brothers and father to buy up the surrounding lots, he created a cloistered urban enclave, where, as Howe recalled, he could shield his children from "the dissipations of fashionable society, and even [from] the risks of general intercourse with the unsancti-fied many." Ward boarded up his extensive wine cellar; he forbade his chil-dren to attend the theater. His eldest son, Sam, who would go on to have a checkered career as a speculator, author, and lobbyist, had already devel-oped a carapace of independence that insulated him from his father's over-bearing religiosity. Julia, on the other hand, absorbed it without such mitigations and soon developed a precocious piety. At nine, she devoured *Pilgrim's Progress* and slept with the Bible under her pillow to protect herself from the devil.[4]

Julia's father provided her with some of the city's finest tutors; she stud-ied German, French, Latin, Italian, mathematics, and declamation. A famous Italian singing master, whose father had written the libretto for Mozart's *Don Giovanni* and *Marriage of Figaro*, trained her voice. Fiercely committed to her studies—she would instruct her siblings to tie her to her chair and not to release her until she had completed her lessons—Julia possessed enor-mous intellectual ambition. "Through all these years," she later wrote, "there went with me the vision of some great work or works which I myself should give to the world. I should write the novel or play of the age." Her father, however, proved less interested in stoking her literary aspirations than in securing her intellectual and moral deference to his authority, a dis-position that would also be exhibited by her husband, and the mixture of reverence and resentment that she felt toward the former would ultimately be transferred to the latter.[5]

When her father died in November 1839 and an older brother succumbed to typhoid fever soon after, Julia sought to manage her grief by throwing herself into the religious revival that had swept through New York City. Her inability to experience a personal conversion brought her more anguish—though for the rest of her life, even as she settled comfortably within the provinces of liberal Protestantism, she never cut her ties to evangelical Christianity, and a deeply personal relationship with Christ would bring her much comfort in the midst of the loss and heartache she would endure in the years to come. In the days after her father's death, however, it was her intellectual and literary commitments that served as balm. Though emotionally devastating, her father's death freed Julia from his domineering presence. Her social horizon expanded dramatically when her older brother, Sam, married a granddaughter of John Jacob Astor, then the richest man in the United States. Sam introduced her to New York society, and she was smitten.

Samuel Ward's isolating and austere domestic regime had bottled up his eldest daughter's effervescent social instincts; when they finally had the opportunity for release, they revealed Julia to be an exceptionally gifted debutante—admired for her witty and learned conversation and her well-trained voice—and even something of a heartbreaker. As a childhood friend of Julia's recalled to her daughter Louisa, when the city's most eligible bachelors "saw [her] mother they just *flopped*." Vivacious, sophisticated, with red hair, a pale complexion, and mischievous gray eyes, "Diva Julia," as her admirers called her, reeled in a string of suitors, singing duets with one, reading German poetry with another, studying Anglo-Saxon with a third. Sam frequently escorted her to Boston and made introductions to some of that city's leading young writers and intellectuals, such as Henry Wadsworth Longfellow and Charles Sumner.[6]

On one of her trips to Boston, Julia visited the Perkins Institution and Massachusetts Asylum for the Blind, whose director, Samuel Gridley Howe, was one of the nation's most prominent philanthropists. As a young doctor, Howe had first made a name for himself by lending his services to the Greeks in their revolutionary struggle against the Turks; in appreciation, the Greek government had granted him the title of chevalier of the Greek Legion of Honor, which led his close friends to nickname him "Chev." He returned to the United States with Lord Byron's helmet, an imperious and vaguely military bearing, and a reputation as a leading humanitarian. Julia had visited the Perkins Institution with her friends Sumner and Longfellow, hoping to meet Laura Bridgman, the deaf and blind girl who was Howe's most famous pupil. She also clearly hoped to gain an introduction to the dashing, bewhiskered Chev.

In *Reminiscences*, her memoir, Julia recalled the moment she saw through a classroom window the approach of "a noble rider on a noble steed." Soon after, a friendship blossomed between the two, separated by eighteen years, and within a year, and after a somewhat tempestuous courtship, they were married.

★

IT WAS TO BE one of the great unhappy couplings in the annals of American matrimony. Though progressive in many arenas of reform, Howe held decidedly conservative views regarding a woman's role in marriage. He loved Julia deeply, but he demanded absolute, adoring submission to his authority. He assumed that her primary, indeed her only responsibility was to himself and to their children and that she would gladly put aside her literary aspirations, like so many childhood toys, to focus on her duties as wife and mother.[7]

Doubts about her marriage began to percolate even during their courtship. Julia was reluctant to give up her independence and knew her limits as a homemaker. By the time of their European honeymoon, during which Chev often left his new bride unattended at social events while he basked in the attention of his admirers, those doubts had grown even more severe. She began composing poems that registered her sense of loss and confinement. "Hope died as I was led / Unto my marriage bed," lamented one. In another, written two days after the wedding, she compared marriage to a crown of thorns. Indeed she seemed to transfer the Calvinist notions of man's fallen state that she had imbibed as a youth onto marriage. The sacrifices brought on by a woman's responsibilities as wife and mother, which she believed would sap her own creative faculties, she eventually accepted, but stoically, and even remorsefully. "Marriage, like death," she confided to her younger sister, "is a debt we owe to nature." To another sister she extended the analogy even further: "God knows one's wedding day may be worse than the day of one's death, . . . [since] one's husband may prove anything but a comfort and support."[8]

Such resignation did not spell absolute surrender to her husband's will. Her decision to preserve her maiden name—she would henceforth be known as Mrs. Julia Ward Howe and not as Mrs. Samuel Gridley Howe— hints at a resolve to maintain a degree of matrimonial independence. For his part, in the early days of the marriage, Chev seemed blissfully unaware of his wife's discontent. After the birth of their first daughter, in Rome, he praised Julia's "entire self-forgetfulness and the total absorption of her nature in this new object of love." He wrote their mutual friend Charles Sumner rapturously of the transformation his wife had undergone in just a year, from an artificial "New York belle" to "a wife who lives only for her husband, & a mother who would melt her very heart, were it needed, to give a drop of nourishment to her child."

He would soon give Julia plenty of opportunity to make good on that penchant for maternal sacrifice. On returning to Boston, he installed the family in the drab and drafty confines of the doctors' wing of the Perkins Institution, located two miles from the center of Boston. Without a carriage, Julia could travel into the city only on an omnibus that arrived every two hours. Once again she found herself isolated, without intellectual companionship, and at the whims of an overbearing patriarch. The isolation only fueled the growing estrangement between Julia and Chev, as her intellectual, spiritual, and emotional needs, untended by her husband, grew wildly within her private sanctuary of imagination and introspection.[9]

The couple sparred over Julia's supposed failures as a homemaker and often over money, as Chev insisted on assuming control of the financial trust that Julia had received from her father. He would eventually wrest it from her and squander the funds on unsound Boston real estate investments; for the rest of her life, Julia would be strained for money, and financial insecurity added fuel to her literary ambitions. A trip to Rome, much of it spent without Chev, functioned as a sort of trial separation—after his early departure home, she danced around her apartment exclaiming, "Liberty!"—and deepened the chasm that had grown between them.

The tension between husband and wife flared even more violently in late 1853, after Julia published the poems she had begun to write while on her honeymoon. Although *Passion-Flowers* came out anonymously, her authorship became common knowledge in her social circle, and the poems' intimate disclosures of her emotional tumult, including a handful of gauzily veiled verses that detailed the attempts of an overbearing husband to control his spirited wife, scandalized Chev. This would not be the last time that Julia's restive literary imagination defied Chev's idealized notions of domesticity. In the next decade she would work on a novel that featured a hermaphroditic and sexually voracious protagonist and would complete a play, largely shunned by scandalized New York audiences, revolving around a betrayed heroine who revenges herself upon an unfaithful husband.

But it was this first transgression of Chev's notion of the decorous, deferential wife that wounded him most deeply. The brewing acrimony between them pushed both to the brink of mental and physical collapse. Deeply shamed, Chev called for a separation; Julia, meanwhile, began to fear that he had taken a mistress, a suspicion that Chev confirmed in the final year of his life. She salvaged the marriage only by agreeing to another child, her fifth. Yet the thought of another pregnancy—haunted by the memory of her own mother's death during childbirth, she regarded the prospect with dread—and of another child to "pick her bones," led her deeper into despair. "It is a blessed thing to be a mother, but there are bounds to all things, and no woman is under any obligation to sacrifice the whole of her existence to the mere act of bringing children into the world," she wrote to her sister Louisa, advising her to put off maternity. Worse, she confronted the fact that she would be forced to bear those sacrifices in a home lacking emotional warmth or intellectual camaraderie. "Where shall I go to beg some scraps and remnants of affection to feed my hungry heart?" she implored her sister.[10]

Chev's unrelenting hostility and the weight of the domestic burdens did not diminish Julia's intellectual ambitions. Throughout the 1850s and 1860s she took refuge in works of theology and philosophy, and from the various thinkers she encountered—Transcendentalists, the Swedish spiritualist Emanuel Swedenborg, Immanuel Kant—she developed a rationale for her regimen of reading and writing that rested on the primacy of individual conscience and the necessity of free expression. It was every man's and every woman's duty, and not just their right, to give vent to their God-given "inner voice"; "internal necessity," she insisted, must be allowed "to conquer the external." Chev dismissed such statements as Julia's excuses for her self-aggrandizing literary pretensions and domestic derelictions. But she maintained that neither self-conceit nor a desire for praise motivated her to write; her pen was simply stirred by the hand of God. "I never made a poem," she insisted in one. "Not a word I breathe is mine. . . . My master calls at noon or night." This was an empowering apologetic, one that minimized her authorial ambitions even as it justified her verse as divinely inspired.[11]

Julia's literary identity, with its strong sense of divine calling and its willingness to contravene social conventions, shared significant affinities with contemporaneous abolitionist thought, especially the elevation of a "higher law" beyond the Constitution. Championed by Senator William Seward of New York, this theory defended the defiance of the terrestrial laws that protected slavery in the United States. Julia's insistence that the ability to "obey a transcendent command of conscience" was "the divine right of the human soul" linked her as well to John Brown. But her connection with Brown ran deeper still, for Chev had been an ardent supporter of Brown's, serving as one of the "Secret Six" who had supplied the funds for his Harpers Ferry raid.[12]

Chev had been initially cool to the abolition movement, but a series of provocations, including the recapture of a number of fugitive slaves in Boston and the savage beating of Charles Sumner on the Senate floor, catalyzed him into antislavery militancy. He took the lead in establishing vigilance committees to protect escaped slaves from slave catchers in Boston and helped to arm the Free Soilers who were heading to Kansas to wrest the territory from proslavery settlers. In 1857 he brought Julia along with him to Kansas, where he transferred to Brown funds he had raised back east. Julia did not meet Brown there, though Chev did speak much about him.

He described to her a remarkable man, whom she would be sure to hear about sooner than later, who "seemed to intend to devote his life to the redemption of the colored race from slavery, even as Christ had willingly offered his life for the salvation of mankind." With such praise, Chev perhaps planted the seed that would later flower in the final verse of the "Battle Hymn," with its convergence of spiritual and political salvation in the figures of Christ and the Union soldier. It was around a year later before Julia would actually get an opportunity to meet Brown. Chev had offered their Boston home as a meeting place for the Secret Six. One day Chev told her to expect another visitor to those meetings, who would arrive when Chev was out: John Brown.[13]

Sure enough, Brown appeared later that afternoon. He seemed to Julia "a Puritan of the Puritans, forceful, concentrated, and self-contained," and they spoke briefly. She saw him only once more, when he visited Chev's office, and after that heard nothing more of him till the whole nation buzzed with news of his raid. When Chev's involvement in the raid's funding came to light shortly after Brown's capture, he fled to Canada. More than a little disingenuously, Chev insisted that he had possessed no advance knowledge of the raid itself and that he had trouble reconciling it with Brown's "characteristic prudence, and his reluctance to shed blood." Julia, seven months pregnant, remained in Boston and was able to visit and console Brown's wife when she passed through the city after her husband's execution. But Julia also made sure to temper her admiration for Brown with circumspection, echoing Chev in insisting, falsely, that no one in Boston had known anything of the raid's planning. She wrote to her sister, "The attempt I must judge insane but the spirit *heroic*."[14]

Julia had a similarly ambivalent relationship with the abolitionist movement more broadly. Her maternal grandmother hailed from South Carolina, and through her mother's family Julia had imbibed notions of slavery as a beneficial system. Early in 1859—while John Brown was finishing preparations for his raid—Julia accompanied her husband to Cuba and, while there, wrote a number of travel pieces for the *Atlantic*. She painted a deeply unflattering portrait of the island's black inhabitants, depicting them as indolent, ugly, and stupid. These qualities, she suggested, represented the undiluted racial characteristics of the "negro among negroes," who had not benefited from the moral and intellectual tutelage of whites, as African Americans had. These considerations prompted her to reflect on the South and its "peculiar institution." Given the degraded condition of black Cubans, she wondered whether "compulsory labor be not better than none," and went on to declare her affection for "the pleasant Southern land . . . [and] those who dwell in it." William Lloyd Garrison singled out those comments for rebuke in the *Liberator*, the nation's leading journal of abolition. At the time Julia had made clear her own distaste for what she considered the incendiary and vulgar nature of much abolitionist rhetoric, attacking radical antislavery proponents in her *Atlantic* articles for their "self-congratulation and vituperation of their brother man" and for their "habitual sneer."[15]

Within a little more than a year, she had perfected a sneer of her own. Like much of the North, she was galvanized by John Brown's raid, which, because of her husband's complicity, had an even greater immediacy for her. By the beginning of the war itself, any doubts regarding the absolute evil of slavery or warmth toward her Southern countrymen seemed to have melted away. Indeed in May 1861, when she returned from New York to Boston by boat and found herself sitting near a woman she believed "had a southerly aspect," she could not help glaring at her "like a tigress." When the fighting began, both Julia and Chev were desperate to assist with the war effort. Governor John Andrews gave Chev an opportunity when he requested that he travel to Washington to inspect the sanitary conditions of Massachusetts troops. These duties ultimately led him to a position with the U.S. Sanitary Commission, a private organization charged with coordinating Northern relief efforts. In November Julia joined her husband on a trip to the capital, accompanied by her pastor, James Freeman Clarke, Governor Andrews, and his wife. As they drew closer to their destination, Julia could look out the train window and see vivid evidence of the war; she was particularly struck by the sight of the campfires, shimmering in the dark, from the pickets set up around the city to guard the railroad line. As they neared Washington, her sense of powerlessness grew stronger. "I thought of the women of my acquaintance whose sons or husbands were fighting our great battle; the women themselves serving in the hospitals," she later wrote. But her husband was too old to fight, and her sons were not yet of military age. "I could not leave my nursery to follow the march of our armies," she said, "neither had I the practical deftness which the preparing and packing of sanitary stores demanded. Something seemed to say to me, 'You would be glad to serve, but you cannot help anyone; you have nothing to give and there is nothing for you to do.'" To her, there was no stronger self-rebuke.[16]

Arriving in the city, the group installed themselves at Willard's Hotel, Washington's most distinguished accommodation, passing the clusters of congressmen and foreign dignitaries who conducted much of the city's unofficial business at the establishment's bar. The hotel buzzed even more than usual. A large mass of Confederate troops had stationed themselves just a few miles away, and the Army of the Potomac had formed a protective ring around the city, which assumed the air of a gigantic military camp. "Mounted officers and orderlies galloped to and fro," Julia recalled, and the rutted streets were clogged with army ambulances depositing their human cargo. From her hotel window she could see "the ghastly advertisement of an agency for embalming and forwarding the bodies of those who had fallen in the fight or who had perished by fever."

The next few days would prove to be some of the most consequential of Julia's life. Through Governor Andrews, she gained a brief audience with President Lincoln. The conversation, largely between Lincoln and the governor, "was rather formal and perfunctory," and she was most taken not with the dialogue but with "the sad expression of [the president's] deep blue eyes." She also spoke in public for the first time. While visiting the camp of the First Massachusetts Heavy Artillery, the regiment's leader, an old family friend, asked Julia to say a few words to his men. She demurred and hid in a hospital tent. But the colonel tracked her down and practically dragged her to his headquarters, where she told the assembled soldiers how much she appreciated their service and sacrifice. Despite her reservations, her daughter Florence Howe Hall noted in her 1916 history of the "Battle Hymn," the colonel "must have read in her face something of the emotion which poured itself out" in the poem. In accounts of the hymn's composition, this halting inaugural public address established Julia Ward Howe as a reluctant orator, setting up the idea that some force larger than her own authorial ambition bestowed the poem upon her.[17]

★

ON NOVEMBER 18 SHE joined Governor Andrews, his wife, and Reverend Clarke in a carriage and, along with a crowd of other sightseers, drove to witness a review of troops taking place across the Potomac River, in Bailey's Crossroads, Virginia. But a Confederate raiding party broke up the affair when it threatened to cut off a small group of Union soldiers stationed nearby. The men who were to be reviewed were ordered back to their quarters, joining the sightseers who were attempting to return to Washington in jamming the roads. To pass the time as they inched toward the city, the group joined with the soldiers in singing the popular songs of the day. Julia's strong mezzo-soprano voice rose above the din. The troops seemed especially taken with her singing of "John Brown's Body," shouting "Good for you!" Reverend Clarke turned to Julia and suggested that she "write some good words for that stirring tune." She replied that she had often thought of doing so, but the words had not yet come to her.[18]

They soon did. She went to bed that night and, as usual, slept soundly. She later recalled, "I awoke in the gray of the morning twilight; and as I lay waiting for the dawn, the long lines of the desired poem began to twine themselves in my mind. Having thought out all the stanzas, I said to myself, 'I must get up and write these verses down, lest I fall asleep again and forget them.'" She jumped out of bed, found an old stump of a pen nearby, and scrawled the verses on the back of a piece of Sanitary Commission stationery, "almost without looking at the paper."

In the mythology that developed around the creation of the "Battle Hymn," the suddenness of the inspiration suggested a supernatural visitation. But such episodes of nocturnal creativity were not at all unusual for Julia Ward Howe and had as much to do with the exigencies of her domestic routines as with divine guidance. Throughout her life she frequently experienced what she termed "vivid thought and mind pictures," which she was able to mold into verse and which she attributed to her "red-haired temperament." She experienced them frequently while in bed, perhaps the only place where she could snatch a moment of quiet reflection in a house full of children and chores. She had in fact grown used to scribbling notes in barely sufficient light, so as not to wake the baby invariably sleeping beside her. And she knew that she had to review the composition once she rose to be able to interpret the scrawl; many poems were no doubt wrecked on the shoals of indecipherability.[19]

What happened that night at Willard's had happened on countless other nights in her Boston bedroom—with the important difference that what she scribbled that night endured. She went back to sleep in the breaking of the early November dawn with what she later recalled was a drowsy sense of satisfaction. "I like this better than most things that I have written," she thought to herself. When she awoke in the morning, she could not remember what she had written, but she turned to the sheet of paper next to the bed and found six stanzas. With only minimal changes—most notably, the jettisoning of the final stanza—the poem appeared much as it would in its published form, two and a half months later.[20]

The story of that night at Willard's Hotel, the climax of the poem's "origin myth," became so intertwined with the hymn's renown that it served almost as an extra stanza itself. Much as with accounts of earlier incarnations of the tune—"Say Brothers" sung by revivalists and the "fatherless" "John Brown's Body" shouted out by Union troops—the hymn's beginnings transcended individual claims to authorship. With Julia Ward Howe acting as medium, channeling the North's righteous resolve, the hymn became "the song that wrote itself," a first-person vision that solidified its author's celebrity, yet at the same time was classified as an essentially "impersonal" composition. As Florence Howe Hall declared, "the soul of the vast army of the American people struggling for utterance in the greatest crisis of its existence" found expression in the hymn. It was "the work not of an individual, but of a nation."[21]

But if the song seemed to write itself, this was not necessarily a testament to its impersonality. In his influential 1887 article on Civil War songs, Brander Matthews noted that the greatest war hymns were almost always written in a single burst of inspiration, the product of a sudden venting of "fiery feeling long confined," requiring "immediate relief." Julia seemed to intuit that composing the hymn represented the release of such pressures and for this reason often prefaced her accounts of the hymn's composition at Willard's with the scene of her struggling with the gnawing sense of uselessness on the train to Washington. The poem—and the poem's origins—gave her a use, one compatible with contemporary gender conventions as well as her own self-conception.[22]

On the one hand, the poem allowed Julia to circumvent the most frequent criticism of women's wartime charitable contributions: that they were excessively sentimental and inefficiently distributed. The leaders of the Sanitary Commission, the organization on whose stationery the poem was composed, had sought to discipline those contributions. According to the Commission's president, its aim was to encourage "impersonal" wartime giving, directed to the nation, and not to any particular individual or regimental unit. With the poet's perspective, not as wife or as mother, but as a loftily perched millennial witness, Julia could claim to be offering precisely such a gift. That perspective also assuaged her feelings of powerlessness, since on the providential heights from which she glimpsed the coming of the Lord human agency had no sway.[23]

Moreover by cultivating the identity of prophetess, both inspired and inspiring, she gained an opportunity for public recognition without challenging the Victorian propriety that largely restricted women's service to the domestic realm. Women were encouraged to contribute their energies and talents to the war effort so long as they deferred to male authority. Julia's inspiration in her room at Willard's Hotel, a safely domestic setting, could exemplify this reconciliation of the active and the passive, the self-promotional and the deferential. Speaking before an audience of Bryn Mawr students, for instance, Senator George Hoar of Massachusetts pointed to the composition of the "Battle Hymn" as instructing women that their "greatest power would be as a stimulant to some man's heroism." Chev could not have put it better himself.[24]

All this fit nicely with Julia's own constructed identity, enabling her to enhance her public standing even as she declined literary authorship. She fed her ambition while merely claiming to serve as a vessel for higher powers. Indeed Julia Ward Howe's literary identity as the author of the "Battle Hymn" shared a profound symmetry with the national identity that the hymn expressed and encouraged: the conception of America as an exceptional nation, serving divinely mandated, millennial purposes through its own expansion and aggrandizement. In narratives explaining the prominence of Howe and the United States, both were *called* to greatness.

The origin story also served the interests of the North. In Julia's early accounts of her night at Willard's Hotel, she did not specify the source of the inspiration. Others, however, were quick to find within it evidence of divine intervention, confirming for Northerners God's favor for their cause. In this sense Julia echoed the earlier comments of Harriet Beecher Stowe, who attributed the initial inspiration for *Uncle Tom's Cabin* to a sudden "tangible vision," while sitting in church, of the death of Uncle Tom that left her shaking and sobbing. To an admirer who congratulated her for writing the novel, she made clear the source of the inspiration. "I did not write it," she insisted. "God wrote it." Of course, such a demurral was not an expression of self-effacement as much as a validation of the abolitionist and Unionist cause itself.[25]

Americans had long supposed their nation to be specially favored by God, a New Israel providentially founded and directed. The religious revivals that swept across the land in the early nineteenth century had nurtured these ideas, until, on the eve of the war, they were particularly ripe.

Accordingly, across the North and South, ministers heartened new enlistees on the way to battle with the good news that they left with God's favor. "It is a holy and righteous cause in which you enlist," Rhode Island's Episcopal bishop informed the state militia in a farewell service before the men left for the front. "God is with us. . . . The Lord of Hosts is on our side." But a hint of doubt lurked beneath these confident pronouncements. In the run-up to the war, some religious leaders had wondered whether the sectional crisis suggested that the nation had in fact lost God's blessing. Furthermore while Southerners could rally around the defense of hearth and home, Northerners were confronted with the challenge of fueling war enthusiasm for the defense of a national government that rarely touched the lives of most Americans. Few doubted the depth of the patriotic surge that swept across the North when Sumter fell. However, some worried whether the North had sufficient cultural and intellectual resources to sustain this patriotism through the difficult months that lay ahead.[26]

It was this concern that precipitated the campaign in May 1861 for the creation of a new national hymn. Although the submissions it prompted led even its initial promoters to portray it as something of a farce, the anxieties regarding American national identity it sought to assuage were real. Lincoln himself had borrowed a history of the campaign from the Library of Congress (though, since the authors of the book filled it with some of the campaign's worst submissions, perhaps he sought in it some comic relief in the dark days of the war). And Julia Ward Howe had saw fit to contribute to the contest a poem of her own, the forgettable "Our Country." In many regards, however, the poem that she composed the following year at Willard's Hotel would fulfill the campaign's mandate.[27]

HOWE HAD BORROWED MANY of the most vital images in her poem from the key apocalyptic texts of the Old and New Testaments, specifically from Revelation and, to a lesser extent, from Isaiah, Ezekiel, Joel, and Daniel. Indeed one explanation for the apparent effortlessness with which the poem was written is Howe's intimate familiarity with the Bible. Starting as a child, she had read a passage from it daily and thus had ready access to its vast storehouse of idioms and images. Moved by the sight of the military buildup surrounding Washington that she had glimpsed on the train, she invested the images of bivouacking troops—the "watch-fires of a hundred circling camps"—with a millennial import.

By the mid-nineteenth century most American Protestants were post-millennialists. The coming of the Lord called to mind not the imminent Second Advent of Christ but the arrival of the thousand years of earthly bliss *after* which He would arrive. God's "marching on," invoked in the song's chorus, suggests a progressive unfolding consistent with postmillennial thought. American Protestants had also begun to see in great crises a prefiguring of the ultimate Apocalypse, perhaps in the distant future, that would bring about a messianic kingdom. Yet the vividness of the poem's apocalyptic images strained against the bounds of metaphor and gave a note of urgency to its prophetic call. Where precisely the poet—and thus the nation—stood on the border between temporality and eternity remained powerfully ambiguous.[28]

In the poem's opening lines, with their archaic King James phrasing (echoing, for instance, Isaiah 6:5), Howe establishes herself at the juncture between secular and sacred time; she presents the scenes of the capital's militarization not merely as epochal moments in the history of the nation but as millennial portents. The image of God's winepress, which Howe borrowed from Revelation (14:19–20), communicates temporal ripeness; the iniquity of those who have sinned against God during the long reign of the Beast has run its course and will now be reaped through the "terrible swift sword" (the analogue of the "sharp sword" with which God "shall smite the nations [Revelation 19:15]), which Howe equates with the forces of the Union.[29]

In the following stanzas, Howe further establishes the war within an apocalyptical timeframe and identifies the Army of the Potomac with the divine armies that would crush the forces of evil and inaugurate the millennium. In the third stanza, she makes use of a frequent trope in artistic depictions of the conflict: the representative of the Union and the agent of the Lord (in this case, Christ, "the Hero, born of woman," prophesied in Revelations 12) crushing a serpent underfoot.[30] In the following verse, she merges secular and sacred time by conscripting biblical allusions into double duty: the imagery describes the Northern military efforts and prophesies the actual coming of the Lord. Thus "the trumpet that shall never call retreat" is both the bugle of advancing Union troops and the blast that will announce God's final judgment. In these depictions the Union army, and the North more generally, appears not merely as a subject of that final judgment but as its instrument. And the killing of Confederates represents not merely the bitter fruit of military defeat but the actual verdict of God's "righteous sentence," the "sifting out the hearts of men before His judgment-seat."[31]

Most Americans at the time would have recognized these images. Millennial modes of thought had a wide currency, extending well beyond those religious groups that incorporated strong apocalyptic themes into their theology. To some extent, Howe was a surprising spokesperson for this apocalyptical and millennialist dispensation. The community of Boston Unitarians and theological liberals who were her social and intellectual peers clung to notions of progress and human perfectibility that would seem to leave little room for ultimate battles between the forces of good and evil. Yet the confidence in an intelligible pattern within the mysterious workings of the world provided a significant point of convergence between visions that seemed more at home in theologically orthodox denominations and a religious liberalism informed by Enlightenment rationality. Indeed the Boston reform community, and especially abolitionists, had long made use of apocalyptic themes in order to stress the divine judgment that would fall on the nation for the sin of slavery. In Harriet Beecher Stowe's 1856 novel *Dred*, for instance, a prophetic slave employs the winepress image to explain a cholera outbreak in the South as God's just retribution. Howe, with her Calvinist childhood, her later drift toward Unitarianism, and her loose affiliations with the abolitionist community, embodied millennialism's broad appeal.[32]

As the likelihood of war approached, a millennial framework offered several different means of interpreting the conflict. The belief that the United States served as a millennial instrument led some Northern religious leaders to insist on preserving national unity even at the cost of placating the South and endorsing the perpetuation of slavery. Others were willing to let the South secede and to accept disunion as God's will, insisting that only a righteous, purified nation could be true to its millennial purpose. It was not until the flag was lowered at Fort Sumter that calls for forbearance yielded to full-throated endorsements of war. Even many devout pacifists like William Lloyd Garrison rallied to the conflict once they understood its violence to be providentially delivered. For Northern Christians of both liberal and orthodox denominations, that militancy was understood as furthering an eschatological struggle, a holy war in which good and evil contended, with the fate of the entire world hanging in the balance. As New School Presbyterians declared at their 1862 general assembly in Cincinnati, "We . . . Americans . . . are here by the ordering of Providence in charge of the final theater and final problems of history."[33]

The patriotic surge that overwhelmed the North in the early months of the war swept aside almost all reckonings with the North's own moral failings. The North was instead portrayed as the unblemished defender of freedom and democracy for all humanity and for all of history, a providential instrument that demanded absolute and unconditional loyalty on the battlefield and in the ballot box. Those who refused to give such loyalty, or actively opposed the Union cause, increasingly took on diabolic form. Thus in her "Battle Hymn" Howe could claim to read "a fiery gospel writ in burnished rows of steel": that God would extend His grace to those who dealt with His "contemners" with the necessary severity.[34]

Confederates too regarded the conflict in Manichaean terms, as a clash between the forces of light and the forces of darkness. Much as Northerners often depicted the South as the seat of a satanic conspiracy, Southerners wielded apocalyptic imagery to portray Northern corruption, materialism, and irreligion. They increasingly described the North as a fallen Babylon, the city in Revelation used to symbolize the seat of God's enemies at the end of world. One Tennessee preacher described the Union forces as "antichrist, the Beast that [is to] ascend from the bottomless pit." Even as Northern and Southern armies butchered each other, this convergent vision produced a common bond between them; the notion of the holy war allowed, for instance, John Brown to serve as a model citizen for both sections. In calling for Southern troops, Henry Wise, the Virginia governor who had presided over Brown's hanging and had denounced Brown as a bloodthirsty fanatic, invoked the memory of the abolitionist to express the war as an apocalyptical opportunity: "I rejoice in this war. It is a war of purification. You want war, fire, blood, to purify you and the Lord of hosts has demanded that you shall walk through fire and blood—You are called to the fiery baptism and I call you to come up to the altar. . . . Take a lesson from John Brown."[35]

This understanding of the war deepened as the casualties mounted on both sides. Two months after the "Battle Hymn" was published, Union forces engaged Confederates at Shiloh, the bloodiest battle in the Western Hemisphere to date; more Americans died during those two days of fighting than in the Revolutionary War, the War of 1812, and the Mexican War combined. Given the sacrifice borne by the North, Northerners could assume, wrote one missionary, that the "great Captain is about to push the warfare to a final victory." The North's millennial expectancy was heightened as well by President Lincoln's issuance of the Preliminary Emancipation Proclamation in September 1862. Many Protestant clergy saw God's hand in the transformation of the war from one fought to preserve the Union into one to free the slaves. Northern religious leaders portrayed slavery as the ultimate enemy at the seat of the apocalyptical conspiracy. As such, it could be understood as something fundamentally alien to the American character and destiny—as defended by Union troops and defined by Union leaders—whose removal would usher in a perfect age.[36]

Such a conception clearly blinded Northerners to their own complicity in the maintenance of the slave system. Yet as the fighting continued and the heady expectations of the war's early days confronted the reality of a protracted, bloody campaign, apocalyptic idioms also promoted a more self-critical understanding of the conflict. Such self-reflection fostered an understanding of the war as God's chastisement of his chosen people for a variety of sins, including the *national* and not merely the sectional sin of slavery. Union military setbacks inevitably brought forth from Northern pulpits a tide of jeremiads, urging listeners to repent and assuring them that if they did so and honored their covenantal relationship, they would once again receive God's favor. Such exhortations did not challenge the claim that the United States, and particularly the North, assumed a unique role in God's plan to establish his Kingdom on Earth and that the Union would therefore ultimately emerge victorious from the conflict. But it did make sense of both Northern and Southern suffering, as well as of Northern and Southern sinfulness. The North was undergoing a time of testing, burning off its own imperfections in the cataclysmic furnace of battle, from which it would emerge spiritually regenerated and recommitted to its holy purpose. So when, in the autumn of 1864, a Methodist hymn invoked the winepress image, it emphasized that the blood that flowed was both Southern *and* Northern and that the continued suffering represented not merely an apocalyptic judgment upon God's enemies but also a divine rebuke of the North for its own sins.[37]

This emphasis on the shedding of soldiers' blood represented a momentous shift in American millennial thinking. In the decades before the war, many Americans had assumed they could usher in the Kingdom of God through moral suasion, evangelization, and voluntary reform—decidedly nonviolent means. But the Civil War installed the military as the most powerful of millennial instruments, with killing as its sacred mission; America's strength of arms would justify its election as a New Israel. In this holy war, it became increasingly common to regard the conflict as a means of national as well as human redemption. Soldiers became (and perceived themselves as) martyrs, dying not just for their country but for the promotion of God's Kingdom; their military camps, as in Howe's poem, were transformed into "altars," the sites of ritual sacrifice. Indeed the day before Howe's fateful trip to watch the military review, Octavius Frothingham, a prominent Boston minister, preached a sermon in which he likened the "regenerating" force of the sacrifices offered by the martyred Union soldier to that offered by Christ on the Cross.

The analogy, echoed in pulpits across the nation, helps make sense of the final stanza of the "Battle Hymn," with its almost jarring introduction of the lily-enwrapped Christ, presiding over the ending of a poem that, until that point, had been dominated by a wrathful battlefield God. Here the poem becomes not merely a vision but a call to action. Howe achieves a final reconciliation of the secular and sacred perspectives in which she regards the conflict. The "glory in [Christ's] bosom that transfigures" each believing man and woman echoes the glory of the coming of the Lord.

Battlefield death would have meaning for the Union soldiers both as impersonal agents of divine retribution, killing in God's name, and as individual Christians and Americans, dying to make men free and thereby embodying Christ's sacrificial love. These were not novel theological or political claims that Howe forwarded. The religious and secular press were full of similar offerings. Yet more than any of the war's other cultural productions, the "Battle Hymn" managed to distill Northerners' understanding of their national identity into a poetic essence whose potency would sustain American exceptionalism for generations to come.[38]

WHEN HOWE RETURNED TO Boston after her Washington sojourn, she sent the poem to James T. Fields, the editor of the *Atlantic Monthly*, one of the nation's premier literary journals, with a circulation of thirty thousand, based largely in New England. Fields's Boston publishing house had brought out *Passion-Flowers*, and, after taking the helm of the *Atlantic*, Fields had accepted several of Howe's other poems and travel pieces. She meanwhile had buffeted him with correspondence, insisting on higher fees for her submissions, griping about the copy-editing, and questioning his editorial judgment; by 1863 the tensions between the two had mounted to such an extent that Howe refused to publish any more in the journal. Yet in December 1862 she still regarded Fields as a literary ally. In the letter accompanying her latest offering, she let slip the mask of reluctant prophetess to speak instead in the voice of the confident, self-promotional—if also a bit self-mocking—woman of the world: "Fields! Do you want this, and do you like it, and have you any room for it in January number? . . . I am sad and spleeny, and begin to have fears that I may not be after all, the greatest woman alive."

Fields did have room in the February issue and paid her $5 for the submission. It was he who provided the poem's title, "Battle Hymn of the Republic." He placed Howe's submission on the cover, but without her name. The decision did not necessarily constitute a slight or a deliberate editorial statement; Fields had done the same with nearly all the poems and articles featured on the journal's cover. But the poem's anonymity nonetheless encouraged the idea that it expressed the collective voice of the righteous North, paradoxically bolstering Howe's celebrity as that voice's instrument.[39]

In *Reminiscences* Howe notes that though the poem received some praise after its publication, "the vicissitudes of the war so engrossed public attention that small heed was taken of literary matters." She neglected to mention that just a few weeks after the appearance of the hymn in the *Atlantic*, Oliver Ditson, one of Boston's most prominent music publishers, put out a broadsheet of the "Battle Hymn." Howe herself read the poem at an Emancipation Day celebration on January 1, 1863, at the home of a leading Boston abolitionist. Adopting the passive voice, she wrote that the poem "found its way" to the military camps, where it encountered an enthusiastic reception among the soldiers.[40]

She preferred to displace the promotion of the song onto another figure— a man of God, no less—heightening the suggestion that her celebrity was the product of providence, not of ambition. It was, she suggested, Charles McCabe, a newly ordained Methodist pastor from Ohio and Civil War chaplain, who did most to sow the hymn's early popularity. McCabe had read Howe's poem in the *Atlantic* and was so taken with it that he committed it to memory before getting up from his chair. Yet it was not until he heard the "Battle Hymn" sung at a massive war rally in Zanesville, Ohio, that he realized the poem had been written to accompany the tune to "John Brown's Body" (which suggests that the song had already achieved considerable popularity before it reached McCabe). In October 1862 McCabe joined the 122nd Ohio Volunteer Infantry as chaplain. After the Union withdrawal from the Battle of Winchester on June 16, 1863, he stayed behind to tend to wounded soldiers and was captured by Confederate troops. Instead of returning him to his unit, as was common practice with chaplains who fell into enemy hands, General Jubal Early declared that Northern ministers had been responsible for fomenting the war and dispatched McCabe to Libby Prison in Richmond. A converted tobacco warehouse, Libby Prison was used mainly to hold officers, and though the building was large, it became so overcrowded with men that the prisoners had to sleep in the "spooning" position, turning in unison at a prearranged signal. Chaplain McCabe immediately set to work ministering to the prisoners, tending to both their spiritual and material needs; through a personal connection with the prison's commissary, he was able to procure rare luxuries like bathtubs and books for his fellow inmates.[41]

McCabe also made use of his rich baritone singing voice. When the prisoners' spirits sagged, one would inevitably turn to McCabe and request, "Chaplain, sing us a song." When the inmates heard reports that a great battle had recently taken place at Gettysburg, that it had been a decisive Confederate victory, and that tens of thousands of Union soldiers had been taken prisoner, an especially heavy gloom settled over them. Men sank on the floor and cried like babies. But early the next morning, an old slave who had been allowed to sell newspapers to the prisoners arrived with the latest editions. He looked around at the dejected men and then announced, "Great news in de papers!" The men huddled around the slave and by the light of a candle read that Gettysburg had in fact been the scene of a decisive Union victory. The prisoners' dejection suddenly turned to elation. McCabe later likened the scene to a mass resurrection. He seized the moment, jumping onto a box to lead the men in the "Battle Hymn." As he recalled, "the very walls of Libby quivered in the melody as five hundred" prisoners joined to sing the "Glory, Hallelujah" chorus.[42]

After suffering a nearly fatal bout of typhoid fever, McCabe was released from Libby Prison in October 1863. Soon after, a Philadelphia Sunday school class asked him to speak about his experience. McCabe didn't want to confront the children with the "horrors of prison life," so he composed a lighter speech, "The Bright Side of Life in Libby Prison." Full of tales of Northern pluck and perseverance, the talk climaxed with the stirring retelling of the Gettysburg revelation, with McCabe reprising his singing of the "Battle Hymn." As an agent for the Christian Commission, an agency dedicated to promoting the spiritual and physical health of Union troops, he gave the speech countless times throughout the nation, at military camps and political meetings, in hospitals, schools, and churches. In doing so, he popularized the "Battle Hymn," introducing it to those who were unlikely to have encountered the poem in the pages of the *Atlantic*. As his biographer claimed and as Howe herself agreed, "He with his glorious voice introduced it to the country and made it popular with the people."[43]

On February 2, 1864, the Christian Commission held a meeting inside the hall of the House of Representatives, with Vice President Hannibal Hamlin presiding and President Lincoln making an appearance midway through. The organizers asked McCabe to give a version of his "Bright Side" speech. His performance of the "Battle Hymn" electrified the audience, and when he reached the chorus, they stood up as one to sing along. At the final verse—"As He died to make men holy, let us die to make men free"—the men and women in the House chamber seemed to go wild. Some dropped the pretense of a tune entirely and simply shouted the words out. "It was as though all the patriotic fire of the Nation had centered on these lines and at this place," recalled one witness. Lincoln was especially moved by that equation of Christ's sacrifice on the Cross and the Union troops' sacrifice on the battlefield. With tears welling in his eyes, in the silence following the thundering of the final chorus he shouted out, "Sing it again!" A few weeks later, when Lincoln met McCabe at a White House reception, he told the chaplain, "Take it all in all, the song and the singing, that was the best I ever heard."[44]

The Christian Commission meeting in the House chamber, with its recently completed magnificent dome, seemed perfectly suited to amplify the elevated themes of the "Battle Hymn of the Republic." Yet there is some question as to whether the song held its attraction in less majestic surroundings. In her history of the song, Florence Howe Hall insisted that the "Battle Hymn" was a favorite among Northern troops. She recounted a scene during a long march through eastern Tennessee in the middle of a freezing rainstorm, when one of the Union soldiers began singing, "Mine eyes have seen . . ." The men in front and behind him immediately picked up the song, and it traveled up and down the line, from the front to the rear, with hundreds of men joining along. "Thereafter," she wrote, "the wet aching marchers thought less that night of their wretched selves, thought more of their cause, their families, their country."[45]

Yet even Hall conceded that the song's primary usage was ceremonial, turned to in times of national crisis or thanksgiving. And the historical record does suggest that Union soldiers preferred other songs—"John Brown's Body" among them—to express their hopes, calm their fears, and relieve the tedium of war. In fact one of the leading scholars of Civil War music has recently reported that he has found only a handful of references to soldiers actually singing the "Battle Hymn."

For some, these two songs' divergent centers of popularity—the campfire and the town square—came to represent a cultural divide between soldiers and civilians. In the decades after the war, when the "Battle Hymn" was being considered as a potential national anthem, Northern veterans were some of the most skeptical of its stature, dismissing the song as highfalutin, cumbersome, and lacking concrete meaning. One declared in a letter to the *New York Times*, "I can imagine nothing that would provoke the jeers of a regiment of United States soldiers so surely as the attempt of some man in the ranks to sing the words: 'In the beauty of the lilies Christ was born across the sea.'" And yet, he claimed, if that same man had started up with the words "Hang Jeff Davis to a sour apple tree" a thousand voices would have joined with him.[46]

In fact in the years following the Civil War the "Battle Hymn" and "John Brown's Body" coexisted somewhat uneasily. Sung at different venues, the two were not necessarily in active competition; perhaps, at times, the popularity of one bolstered that of the other. A recent scholar of music history, however, in exploring the relationship between the two, has echoed the veteran quoted above and stressed their antagonism. The "Battle Hymn" and the origin myth that accompanied it, Anne J. Randall has argued, represented a deliberate attempt to expunge the radicalism of "John Brown's Body" by denying the song's associations with terrorism and fundamentalism. She links the absence of Howe's name on the *Atlantic* cover with the absence of the "Glory, Hallelujah" chorus and links both to the removal of John Brown from the song's lyrics. While the author's name might have called to mind Samuel Gridley Howe, the militant abolitionist who had funded Brown's Harpers Ferry raid, the chorus might have conjured up the camp meeting origins of the tune, with all its anarchic spiritual energy.[47]

Exchanging the beauty of the lilies for the vindictive pungency of sour apples certainly does suggest a taming of the more unruly elements of "John Brown's Body." And as subsequent chapters of this book document, removing the person of John Brown from the song did leave it open for appropriation by those who did not share his radicalism or racial progressivism. Yet, in many ways, with their explicit apocalyptic and millennial overtones, the lyrics of the "Battle Hymn of the Republic" suited John Brown's spirit more closely than did those of "John Brown's Body," whose words had as much to do with soldiers' comic extemporizing than with their radical enthusiasms. In the years after the composition of the "Battle Hymn," it was by no means clear that by banishing Brown from the lyrics, Howe had exorcised his soul from the song. Admirers often described the hymn's spirit as "Cromwellian" or "Puritan," precisely the terms that had been used to characterize Brown's uncompromising and providentially mandated militancy. Most abolitionists who sought to infuse the Union army with the spirit of Brown's devotion to emancipation certainly did not interpret the "Battle Hymn" as a repudiation of his legacy. At the John Brown Party, held on Emancipation Day, January 1, 1863, at the Massachusetts estate of the wealthy abolitionist and Brown supporter George L. Stearns, the host unveiled a marble bust of the abolitionist martyr and Howe recited her "Battle Hymn" to an audience that included many of the nation's leading antislavery activists. No one complained that the hymn did not fit the grandeur of the moment.[48]

John Brown's soul stirred most violently in the song's final lines. One of the central tropes in the Northern exaltation of Brown after his capture and execution was the explicit comparison between his martyrdom and Christ's redemptive self-sacrifice. Howe expanded that analogy by bringing Union troops within its fold. If Brown, in the words of Ralph Waldo Emerson, made "the gallows glorious like the cross," Northern soldiers could lend the battlefield a similar sanctity with their blood. The Brown-Christ analogy served as the hymn's most powerful motif. It would also prove one of the more vexing, providing a point of common opposition for the theologically orthodox and pacifist critics of the song, both of whom rejected the conflation of Christ's atoning sacrifice and military service. Even in the early years of the "Battle Hymn," as that final verse stirred Lincoln and countless others to greater devotion to the Union cause, it rankled other Americans. The Hutchinson Family, the North's most prominent abolitionist singing group, for instance, insisted on changing the lyrics when they performed the song, singing "As He died to make men holy, let us *live* to make men free." The group's leader, John Hutchinson, traveled in the same reformist circles as Howe and often argued with her about the moral legitimacy of the hymn's final militant exhortation. After one heated exchange, an exasperated Howe turned to Hutchinson's granddaughter and implored her, "Sing it as I wrote it." The young girl graciously complied, but her grandfather continued to sing his preferred version, a tradition that many future generations of peace-minded performers have maintained.[49]

In the final year of the war, the association between military sacrifice and spiritual (and national) redemption intensified, as the capture of Richmond and Lee's surrender at Appomattox inspired parallels to Babylon's fall. The series of epochal events that marked the spring of 1865, falling in such rapid succession, suggested the nation had entered a time pregnant with eschatological significance. Rebecca Harding Davis, a Philadelphia writer, concluded, "God was dealing with us as with his chosen people of old—by such great visible judgments that we almost heard his voice and saw his arm." As the North's favored expression of millennial expectation, the "Battle Hymn" secured its status as a leading war hymn during these months. The song's prominence only increased with the assassination of Abraham Lincoln on Good Friday. The president's death represented the final blood sacrifice necessary for the expiation of the nation's sins and the inauguration of a millennial age over which a perfected, *United* States would preside. Lincoln had fulfilled the concluding analogy of the "Battle Hymn"; he had become the Christ figure who died to make men free, joining John Brown as the nation's preeminent abolitionist martyr. "Lincoln died for we, Christ died for we, and me believe him de same mans," declared one South Carolina freedman shortly after the president's death.

Given those resonances, as well as Lincoln's own stated appreciation of the song, it is not surprising that the organizers of a memorial service for the president in Chicago asked Chaplain McCabe to sing the "Battle Hymn." As he began to sing, he was nagged by doubts as to the hymn's appropriateness; he had so long associated it with the North's military triumphs that it seemed strange to offer it up in the hour of the nation's greatest loss. But as he built up to those final stanzas, he came to appreciate that in its exaltation of sacrifice, the song fit the moment superbly. It became "the natural expression of our gloomy joy."[50]

Lincoln clearly held the "Battle Hymn" in high regard, and the song seemed to help Northerners make sense of the extraordinary events that marked the end of the war. But in one important regard, McCabe was right to express some resistance to singing the song as a tribute to the fallen president. Not long before his death, Lincoln had himself offered a meditation on the meaning of those events and on the identity of the United States as a providentially chosen nation: his Second Inaugural Address. These two statements, Howe's "Battle Hymn" and Lincoln's Second Inaugural, represent the most enduring, perhaps the only enduring theological reflections on the meaning of the Civil War. As Mark Noll, the preeminent historian of nineteenth-century American religious life, has commented, though the most respected theologians of the day produced countless sermons considering the war's ultimate meaning, no one outside of a few academic specialists pays attention to them today. Yet Americans still stir to Lincoln's Address, as they still do to Howe's hymn. If the "Battle Hymn" has endured, it is because it so powerfully encapsulates and amplifies the themes rehearsed in those forgettable war sermons. Lincoln's Second Inaugural, on the other hand, offers a striking alternative to the certainties they offer regarding the intelligibility of God's will and the nation's relation to it.[51]

★

A STEADY RAIN FELL upon Washington on the morning of March 4, 1865. The city's streets became so clogged with mud that engineers considered putting down pontoons on Pennsylvania Avenue to accommodate the crowds. Due to the downpour, formal proceedings began inside the Senate chamber, where Vice President Elect Andrew Johnson delivered a rambling, drunken speech. When the rain stopped, the somewhat stunned crowd was relieved to move outside for the president's remarks, to the east front of the Capitol. Just as Lincoln began to speak, the sun broke through the clouds. It seemed an especially auspicious sign for the expectant crowd. And yet Lincoln's speech, which grappled with the gap between man's aims and God's will, was marked by its willingness to defy the expectations of its listeners. He began by denying the need to review the recent Union military victories, despite the fact that those in the crowd almost certainly were primed to have their sectional allegiances stoked; the loudest applause during the speech came when Lincoln spelled out the basic divisions between North and South. Yet he would offer no victorious paeans to Northern military might, no bold predictions about continued Union success.

Instead he recalled his first inauguration, when he spoke to the still-united nation and tried to preserve its integrity and prevent war by reassuring the South that he had no intention of abolishing slavery where it already existed. Southerners too at that time had hoped to avoid war but regarded the dissolution of the Union as the only means of doing so. And yet, Lincoln recognized, despite the efforts of North and South, "the war came." The conflict was of a greater magnitude and intensity than either section expected, and confronted with its awesome costs, both turned to the same God for succor. "The prayers of both could not be answered; that of neither has been answered fully," Lincoln remarked. "The Almighty has His own purposes." In attempting to explain what those purposes might be, Lincoln imagined the war as a providentially delivered chastisement for the *national* sin of slavery, of which both North and South were guilty. Both sections had been judged; both were afflicted.[52]

Like the "Battle Hymn of the Republic," the Second Inaugural was steeped in biblical, and decidedly apocalyptical, references and idioms. Lincoln's declaration that slavery was one of those "offenses" that "in the providence of God, must needs come," but that it would be removed "at his appointed time," bore the distinctive understanding of evil, of history, and of God's mysterious purposes that permeates Revelation. But Lincoln and Howe advanced two very different perspectives on the relationship between the war and God's providential plan. Lincoln assumed a posture of humility, based on the fundamental inscrutability of God's purposes. In contrast, from the first line of her hymn, Howe establishes the transparency of providence. When she writes, "Mine eyes have seen the glory of the *coming* of the Lord," she describes a process literally unfolding before her. Her act of witness is confidant, triumphant. Lincoln employs the same verb to describe the same conflict, but in a decidedly different manner. When he states, "And the war *came*," he relegates his own position to that of a passive observer, denoting the ways the war confounded the expectations of human agents. He recognized that he was offering not a transparent vision like the "Battle Hymn" but one obscured by human fallibility and partiality.[53]

There was considerable boldness in this humility. Especially after the Union's military setbacks of 1862–63, other political and religious leaders had described the war as a divine chastisement of both North and South, for both sections' complicity in the sin of slavery. But most remained confident that if its citizens repented, God's favor would surely fall on the Union. What distinguished Lincoln's remarks from other theological reflections of the time was his refusal to assume that he—and by extension, the North more generally—had privileged access to God's purposes. Though Lincoln believed the speech the best he had ever written, he also appreciated that it was not "immediately popular." And he understood why. "Men are not flattered by being shown that there has been a difference of purpose between the Almighty and them," he explained to one correspondent.

Yet he did not mean this lack of certitude to diminish the Union's resolve to bring the war to its conclusion. Theological modesty would not induce military timidity, but, as he made clear in the speech's final paragraph, it would recommend a certain way of treating the North's antagonists after victory had been secured: "With malice toward none; with charity for all; with firmness in the right, as God gives us to see the right, let us strive on to finish the work we are in; to bind up the nation's wounds; to care for him who shall have borne the battle, and for his widow, and his orphan—to do all which may achieve and cherish a just, and a lasting peace, among ourselves, and with all nations." Lincoln implicitly established a relationship between an appreciation for the mysteriousness of providence and the just treatment of fellow Americans; in doing so, he also suggested that absolute confidence in the intelligibility of God's will might make it more difficult to sustain a charitable regard for one's former enemies. Those who believed that they had clearly seen the Lord's coming in Union advances were most likely to call on Him to crush their opponents under His heel.

The "Battle Hymn" offered its own corrective to Lincoln's Second Inaugural and of the theological modesty that informed it. A reckoning with the mysteriousness of providence could ultimately encourage a paralyzing fatalism, an intellectual and spiritual malady with which Lincoln himself struggled. And as the foundation of governance, charity could have its limits, for, as the history of Reconstruction would demonstrate, a charitable treatment of some (white Southerners) could lead to an uncharitable fate for others (the freed African Americans who lived among them). With its abolitionist associations, the "Battle Hymn" could give some sustenance to those who appreciated that "finish[ing] the work" of the war might require, if not a measure of malice, then a willingness to let some of the nation's wounds remain unbound until the freed slaves had been accorded justice as well as charity. And yet, ultimately, as the next chapter will show, the "Battle Hymn" was able to assimilate much of the reconciliationist spirit of the Second Inaugural, while maintaining the uncompromising militancy of Howe's vision, by focusing that militancy onto an international arena.[54]

In the decades after the war, it was Howe's growing celebrity more than Lincoln's memory that installed the "Battle Hymn" in the pantheon of American civil religion. Ironically, despite the fame that would follow her for more than four decades after the hymn's composition, the poem represented the high-water mark of Howe's literary production. Indeed postbellum commentators often classified her as a "mono-poet," or what we would now term a one-hit wonder. She chafed at being defined by a single night's work. In May 1864, after visiting a hospital with some friends, she complained in her diary about being "tormented" by constant introductions as "Mrs. Howe, author of the Hymn." Four decades later she was still laboring to loose herself from its fetters, declaring that though she was glad "it was given to [her] to write it," the hymn was "a thing of the past" and her soul was "in the future." Her frustration with her literary progeny is understandable. During nearly all the thousands of social events she attended in the years between those complaints, she was buffeted by requests to recite the hymn or to copy out a few stanzas and sign them. In light of these demands, one friend compared the poem to "Frankenstein's monster." But she rarely turned down a request.[55]

Some critics regarded Howe's desire to uncouple herself from an exclusive identification with her "Battle Hymn" as an act of ingratitude or impudence. "Julia Ward Howe recently confessed to being bored to death by the constant allusions to her 'Battle Hymn of the Republic,'" one Kansas paper sniffed. "Let the good lady have patience. The hymn is her only title of immortality on earth." Yet such sniping failed to appreciate the nature of Howe's celebrity or its relationship to the "Battle Hymn." The hymn funded her literary renown, but once established, she did not merely subsist off the poem's reserves. Through an intense engagement with reform causes and social clubs, she cultivated a public persona that itself augmented the hymn's stature.[56]

Indeed, somewhat paradoxically, in straining against her identity as a poet she secured the status of her most famous poem. Although she continued to compose verse, she increasingly found herself less enthused with the medium—and with its disappointing public reception and financial recompense. None of her subsequent works of poetry matched the popular acclaim that met *Passion-Flowers*; many were ignored, and much to Howe's dismay, some were gently disparaged. Even *Latter Lyrics*, the book of war poems that she published in 1866, which contained the "Battle Hymn," sold poorly and was largely ignored by critics. As her status as a published poet dimmed, she took some solace in the enthusiastic applause that invariably greeted her poems or essays when she read them at social events. Her *Atlantic* editor James T. Fields had once explained his rather low opinion of some of Howe's verse that had been praised by her friends by noting that her manner of reading made the poems sound better than they actually were. Howe took offense, yet she ultimately followed Fields's perhaps unintended advice. Soon after the war's conclusion, she began to craft a new public identity fueled less by the printed page than by the spoken word. She recalled in *Reminiscences* of the years after the war, "It was borne in upon me . . . that I had much to say to my day and generation which could not and should not be communicated in rhyme, or even in rhythm." She began to mine the lode of her own dynamic intellect and personality.[57]

Tragedy also helped push her beyond the borders of her established literary identity. Devastated by the death of her three-year-old son, Sammy, during the war, Howe threw herself into the study of religion and philosophy. She began to compose her own systematic theological and philosophical reflections. By September 1863, four months after her son's death, she could claim in her journal, "[I have] built up a greater coherence between things natural and things divine than I have seen or heard made out by anyone else." She held small gatherings in her home, where she addressed intimate crowds on religious and philosophical themes. These domestic lectures soon led to more public appearances. Chev proved even less supportive of his wife's new vocation than of her career as a writer. He managed to turn their children, and many of their mutual friends who had supported her literary aspirations, against her ambitions as a public speaker. After one confrontation, Howe confided to her journal, "I never knew him to be so cruel and unjust as today." Considering Chev's record of malice, this was an impressive benchmark. But the opposition of her family and friends did not deter her in pursuing her new calling in "a profession of ethical exposition." That first term neatly encapsulated her desire for a recognized public identity that accorded with the promptings of her inner voice. "If I am sent for and have the word to say, I should say it," she insisted.[58]

Chev's death in January 1876 inaugurated what Howe termed her "new life." Although she was deeply wounded by the revelations of his infidelity, his deathbed disclosure that he had not been faithful assuaged some of her guilt at her own marital shortcomings. Despite the keenness of her mourning for her companion of more than three decades, she experienced the removal of the pall cast by Chev's unyielding criticisms and demands for constant attention as a sort of liberation. His death did mean, however, that her economic well-being, somewhat precarious after Chev squandered much of her inheritance and left her little in his will, rested now entirely on her own shoulders. Building her public persona—through reform commitments, associational ties, and her writing—also provided a means of establishing a degree of financial security. She threw herself into various causes: the women's suffrage movement, world peace, antiprostitution, Russian freedom, Armenian relief. Well into her eighties, she insisted on keeping a hectic schedule of speaking engagements across the country that would have exhausted many women half her age. She seemed to possess preternatural stores of energy for social engagements. Indeed when Oliver Wendell Holmes remarked that Howe was "eminently *clubable*," he was not threatening violence but offering one of the most profound compliments available in his wood-paneled milieu. Howe boasted an impressive talent for sowing new groups wherever she traveled and for helping to sustain them with her charm and organizational zeal. Chev had once dismissed his wife's inexhaustible appetite for reform meetings, especially those associated with women's suffrage, as an excuse to enjoy elegant teas and fine food in the company of like-minded peers—and outside the bounds of his supervision. But Howe regarded these social engagements as the best means of using her God-given talents for the greater good. As she replied after an especially congenial club meeting, "Why, we may be living in the Millennium without knowing it!"[59]

In the final decades of her life, Julia Ward Howe ripened into a nationally revered celebrity, a walking monument to American idealism. As she outlived many of her compatriots in the reform campaigns of the nineteenth century—she was making public appearances just two weeks before her death at age ninety-one—she came to embody for a postbellum generation anxious about its own excessive materialism the heroic spirit of an earlier, more selfless age. As the *New York Times* declared in 1909, "She fills the national imagination as no other woman has, by her identification with a great chapter in human liberty and by her constancy in support of human uplift." In the national pride invested in her person, in fact, she came closer than any of her countrymen to assuming the status of American royalty. Indeed ever since Howe had visited England during her honeymoon, she had been told that she bore a striking resemblance to the young Queen Victoria, three days her senior. In her later years those comparisons were invoked again, this time to suggest not merely her physiognomic similarities but her regal embodiment of Victorian respectability and decency as well.[60]

For all of her domestic turmoil, as Howe's renown grew, so too did her dedication to the principle of social order. During the war, in an 1863 lecture titled "Moral Triangulation," she first developed the social theory that would bolster this commitment. There was, she declared, "a third party" in "all twofold relations": "the compact which originally bound them together." This compact had a life independent of those bonded and demanded deference in its own right. Respect for these bonds was the real adhesive that held society together, providing a measure of order when law failed or love disappointed. Fidelity to these bonds could justify to her both the discontents she endured while remaining married to Chev and the rebuke of the Confederate states for violating the sanctity of the Union.[61]

The depth of those commitments fueled a zeal for a benevolent moderation and allowed Howe, as one Boston acquaintance noted, to provide "a bridge between the world of society and the world of reform." Just as in the decade before the Civil War Howe had embraced an antislavery identity that positioned itself in opposition to the belligerence and absolutism of the Garrisonian abolitionists, in the postbellum years she distanced herself from the more uncompromising proponents of women's suffrage, such as Elizabeth Cady Stanton, and sided with those who were willing to yield to the priority of black enfranchisement, like Lucy Stone. Although in her private writing she continued to lambaste patriarchal folly, in her public lectures she rarely troubled conventional gender norms. She sought to deepen, but not necessarily to challenge, women's fundamental identities as wives and as mothers by insisting they should no longer be considered ancillary to those assumed by men. In fact, with her children and Chev no longer making demands on her time, she no longer portrayed her domestic responsibilities as in tension with her moral, spiritual, or intellectual development. Reinventing herself as the exemplary Victorian wife and mother, she could champion a harmony between internal and external necessity. And so in her 1899 autobiography, the woman who always seemed to resent the encroachments of domestic life into the private realm of reflection and imagination praised the benefits of homemaking. "Surely no love of intellectual pursuits should lead any of us to disparage and neglect the household gifts and graces," she instructed her readers. The few readers old enough to recall the young Mrs. Howe may have allowed themselves a brief chuckle at that remark.[62]

Because it was so closely intertwined with Howe's public identity, the "Battle Hymn" tracked her own development—and domestication. At nearly every event at which she graced the podium, her "Battle Hymn" made an appearance as well. And so, besides its powerful antislavery resonances, the song developed associations with the various strains of postbellum reform Howe championed—and several that she did not. Feminists and women's suffrage proponents sang it at their rallies; peace activists and temperance reformers concluded their proceedings with the hymn; and the members of the Dallas Freethinkers Association, a group of secularists committed to exposing the inanities of religious thought, took inspiration in Howe's vision of the coming of the Lord.[63]

The song had become a catch-all expression of the reformist impulse, though in the process it had lost something of its wartime radical edge. For many, the "Battle Hymn" heralded a parlor millennialism, one that middle-class citizens could comfortably champion. In the bold yet measured confidence the hymn inspired, it reflected a broader shift among mainstream Protestants toward the eventual secularization of postmillennialism in the decades after the war. In these visions of the coming of the Lord, Christ's return to Earth would follow—not precede—the thousand-year period of perfect peace, which would unfold gradually, without radical discontinuities or ruptures, through the steady work of human hands and earthly institutions.[64]

During the war, the radical and conservative strains of millennialism coincided. *Preserving* the United States as a millennial instrument ultimately led to *transforming* the nation. If the North at first fought on behalf of constitutional order and the integrity of the Union, the fighting led to the emancipation of four million men and women, a "new birth of freedom" that opened the possibility for dramatic social upheaval. A performance of the "Battle Hymn of the Republic" during the war could honor both efforts simultaneously. In the years that followed, however, many of those who had embraced the transformative potential of the conflict sought instead social order and pursued more modest reforms. As the two strains of millennialism began to diverge, the public meanings of the "Battle Hymn" did as well. In the decades to come, Howe's hymn would offer contending interpretations of America's millennial identity, both celebrating and rebuking the nation. It would serve as the anthem of the jingo and of the Jeremiah and, in the intermingling of those voices, of the many who stood somewhere in between.[65]

IV

★ ★ ★

THE RECONSTRUCTION
OF THE "BATTLE HYMN"

IN FEBRUARY 1866 A local teacher named James Whann and his wife set up a
school for black children in Brenham, Texas, a rough railhead situated halfway
between Houston and Austin. New attendees streamed in weekly and soon
overflowed the small room that Whann had rented. So, with the assistance of
the regional commissioner of the Freedmen's Bureau, the governmental
agency charged with protecting the rights of the newly freed slaves, Whann
organized a Fourth of July picnic to raise money for a new schoolhouse. As a
fundraiser, the event was far from a success; in fact after settling the bills,
Whann was $11 poorer. But the freedmen and women left in good spirits and
announced their intention to continue the festivities in a march through town.
Both Whann and the local Freedmen's Bureau commissioner, a former Union
cavalry officer named Samuel Craig, hesitated to grant permission. Brenham
had long been wracked by racial tension; white residents had recently beaten
a group of African Americans for celebrating too rowdily when a circus came
to town. But the freedmen offered assurances that they would avoid any disorderly conduct. So, dressed in their red, white, and blue finest, they paraded
through Brenham's streets, singing songs to fit the holiday spirit. Among
them was "John Brown's Body." And they sang the verse about hanging Jeff
Davis to a sour apple tree with more holiday spirit than any other.

The sight of newly freed slaves marching through the streets besmirch-
ing the honor of the former Confederate president proved too much for

many of the town's white residents to bear. Like many Texans, they bitterly resented the persistence of military control over the state even after President Andrew Johnson had declared the rebellion there to be over. They also resented the Freedmen's Bureau as the unwelcome, meddling institution of an occupying power, upending a racial hierarchy that they saw no reason to upset, despite the end of slavery. The editor of the local paper, a fiercely unreconstructed former Confederate officer, denounced the parade as a monstrous provocation and used the occasion to lodge an attack on Whann's school and on the Freedmen's Bureau. The Whanns soon received threatening letters suggesting that they take the next train out of town.

Commissioner Craig was happy to let them go, but his Freedmen's Bureau supervisors ordered him to protect the Whanns, reminding him that African Americans had a right to sing whatever Union songs they wished. They also instructed Craig to inform the editor that any further disparagement of the Whanns or the Bureau would "subject [him] to official action." When the editor refused to back down, Craig fined him $200, and when he did not pay the full amount, arrested him and threw him into jail. The editor's imprisonment became a cause célèbre within the South, and Craig soon began receiving threats on his own life. Not long after, Freedmen's Bureau officials moved him to another post more than one hundred miles away. But before they did, the smoldering resentments in the town finally erupted. In September a group of Northern soldiers brawled with some locals and a number of the U.S. troops were shot. Later than night the soldiers burned the city's entire business section to the ground, including the office of the Brenham *Banner*. The unreconstructed editor never published another edition.[1]

Even in the North, the "Glory, Hallelujah" chorus roused passions that exposed the fractures within communities. In May 1863 the principal of a high school in New York's Ninth Ward expelled a sixteen-year-old Catholic girl named Catherine McGean for refusing to sing the "Battle Hymn of the Republic" in class. McGean deemed "irreverent" the chorus's claim that Union military triumphs constituted evidence of God's "marching on." A committee assigned by the Board of Education reviewed the incident and determined that McGean was justified in refusing to sing the chorus. The members "expressed their surprise that a song of this character should have been tolerated for one moment in any of the Public Schools of this city." However, the school's ward trustees, who held ultimate authority over all disciplinary matters, refused the Board's request to reinstate McGean. The Board then threatened to withhold salaries from teachers and staff in the ward until the local trustees relented. For a brief period, all payments for school purposes stopped, though the trustees did order that the hymn no longer be sung in the ward's schools. The controversy continued to fester for months, until the state supreme court denied a request to review the case.[2]

Although ward trustees and the central Board often sparred because of the uneasy division of authority between them, the contest over whether a student who refused to sing a Unionist hymn was guilty of "insubordination," as the trustees claimed, implicated broader issues than those that normally preoccupied the educational bureaucracy. This was especially the case given the broader tensions roiling New York at the time; while the Board was deliberating, draft riots erupted in the city. A large segment of New York's laborers, many of them Irish Catholic Democrats, had resented the incorporation of abolitionism into the war effort. Why, they demanded, should their own blood be spilled on Southern battlefields so that freed slaves could move north and steal their jobs? When Congress, against strenuous Democratic objections, instituted a draft in March 1863 that included provisions allowing citizens to name a substitute or buy out their obligation, resentments simmered until they boiled over in a July rampage. Mobs roamed through the city, killing scores of African American men and women and attacking symbols of abolitionism, the city's industrial elite, and the Republican establishment. Converging on the office of the *New York Tribune*, the city's leading organ of Republican thought, the mob announced its plans for the paper's editor by parodying "John Brown's Body": "We'll hang old [Horace] Greeley to a sour apple tree!" City authorities restored order only by calling in federal troops, some fresh from the recent fighting at Gettysburg.

The same tensions that set the city ablaze informed the press's coverage of the McGean controversy, in which the "Battle Hymn," referred to as an "abolitionist" or "Protestant" song, was granted a clearly defined sectarian and partisan identity. While McGean's father was a prominent Catholic merchant and Democratic booster, the Ninth Ward trustees were dominated by leaders of the Protestant and Republican establishment, men prominent in organizations like the Union League and the American Bible Union.[3] The city's public schools had long been key arenas in which partisan and sectarian battles were waged; less than a decade before, nativists had conspired to take control of key board committees to ensure that only native-born Protestants were appointed principals. The Board's Democratic chairman, William E. Curtis, was acutely sensitive to partisan and sectarian infiltration of the school system. The imperious actions of the ward trustees no doubt roused his suspicions. As one contrite trustee wrote to the Board, apologizing for the fact that the other trustees refused to reinstate McGean, "If the scholars of our schools can be dismissed so summarily on so slight a pretense as this, we may next hear that our own daughters, having refused to scrub the floors of our School-houses, have been dismissed for insubordination." Indeed the resentments over the controversy lingered within the New York Irish community long after the Board moved on to other issues. Seven years later a New York paper reported that continued sectarian clashes in the public schools ensured that the "case of Miss McGean" was "still fresh in the minds of many."[4]

During the Civil War and in its immediate aftermath, the "Battle Hymn of the Republic" stoked the sectional, sectarian, and partisan divisions at the heart of the conflict. In the decades that followed, the song would also help to quell many of those antagonisms. As the North and South cast aside the animosities of the war and, in the words of old Horace Greeley himself, clasped hands across the bloody chasm, the song became an anthem of national cohesion. In the process the meaning invested in the "Battle Hymn" underwent a significant transformation, one that reflected the shifts in attitudes toward the reconstruction of the South and toward the Civil War itself. Just as in the 1870s, the North's commitment to promoting the civil and political rights of freedmen and women began to wane, and just as an interpretation of the war's significance that centered on the emancipation of the slaves gave way to one that emphasized the depoliticized valor of soldiers from both North and South, the abolitionist associations that had animated the "Battle Hymn" began to fade as well. Instead the song was endowed with meanings appropriate to the providentially sanctified nation-state that emerged out of the crucible of the war. The hymn became a call to arms for other campaigns, a rallying cry for economic development and for military expansion, crusades in which North and South could join together with equal zeal. Ironically "John Brown's Body," the song that had absorbed so many improvisations during the war, found its meaning to be less malleable. It could not as easily shed its associations with a defiant sectionalism or a devout abolitionism.

And so the paths of the "Battle Hymn of the Republic" and "John Brown's Body" began to diverge. While the former marched triumphantly into the new century, securely installed in the liturgy of American civic religion, the latter took up a more humble place in street songs and popular protest culture. This split accelerated during the Spanish-American War of 1898, when religious and political leaders embraced the "Battle Hymn" as the anthem of the nation's burgeoning imperial ambitions. "Just now the poem by Mrs. Julia Ward Howe . . . is on the mind and frequently on the lips of patriotic people the world over," an Omaha paper declared in July 1898, a week after the city of Santiago had surrendered to American forces. "John Brown's Body," on the other hand, rarely found itself on the program of celebratory church services or public rallies. This did not mean that Americans consigned the song to cultural oblivion; it had burrowed too deep in the popular mind to be so easily dislodged. In one of the great naval engagements of the short war, in which the Americans destroyed much of the Spanish fleet as it tried to escape from Santiago, the men in the engine room of the battleship *Brooklyn* sang of old John Brown while they fervently shoveled coal.[5]

★

YET IN THE PERIOD immediately after the war, "John Brown's Body" could rival the "Battle Hymn" in its prominence. During the heady days of Radical Reconstruction, when the defeated South seemed to lay prostrate before the victorious North and open to the possibility of dramatic social upheaval, John Brown's spirit really did seem to be marching on as triumphantly as ever. And his song could speak to both the punitive policies directed toward Confederate leaders and the ambitious calls for the expansion of rights for freedmen and women, the two pillars of the postwar program favored by the ascendant Radical Republicans. In March 1868, at the North Carolina Constitutional Convention, the white loyalists and black Republicans who made up the vast majority of the delegates (many Democratic opponents of Reconstruction had abstained from voting, and the few Democratic delegates walked out of the proceedings) called upon Brown's spirit to mark the occasion. The constitution they framed abolished slavery, provided for universal male suffrage, and instituted a "uniform system of Public Schools" throughout the state. It represented the fruits of the first statewide election in which blacks were allowed to vote. At the convention's adjournment, the delegates joined hands, formed a circle, and performed what one observer called "a sort of cornfield dance" while singing "John Brown's Body." They continued dancing even as a "young rebel" in the gallery shouted out, "Three cheers for Jeff Davis!" to a smattering of applause.

Indeed, for some, the John Brown song served as a sort of surrogate loyalty oath. Southerners frequently complained, for instance, about Northern teachers who were installed in classrooms when the Union army occupied Southern territory and who instructed their students to sing the song. In testimony to Congress, one native New Yorker, who had moved to New Orleans more than a decade before the war began, seemed to confirm those protests. The teacher had been dismissed from her school because of her Unionist sympathies in 1860 but had been reinstated by the occupying Union forces two years later. The local superintendent had forbidden her to teach "patriotic" songs to her students, but she had continued anyway. The senators seemed especially interested in the sorts of songs she had taught. Was "John Brown's Body" included, one asked? The teacher replied in the affirmative. "It was pretty hard to get some of the girls to sing it," she admitted, but she insisted that they do so.[6]

In September 1866 the song helped to neutralize one of the most famous cases of apostasy from the Radical Reconstruction cause. Before the war few had more enthusiastically rallied Northerners to take up arms against the Confederate rebels than Henry Ward Beecher, pastor of Plymouth Congregational Church and the nation's most prominent preacher. After the war, however, Beecher became a leading evangel of national reconciliation. Christianity, he insisted, demanded forgiving one's enemies, even as they continued to trespass. "You must not be disappointed or startled because you see in the newspapers accounts of shocking barbarities committed upon" the freed slaves, he warned the readers of the New York *Independent*, a leading journal of Northern progressive thought. Some racial violence was to be expected, Beecher counseled; the North must have patience with their white Southern brethren while they adapted to new moral, political, and social realities. In September 1866 Beecher wrote a letter to the planners of a Cleveland convention promoting sectional reunion which seemed to offer support for President Andrew Johnson's call for a speedy reintegration of Confederate leaders into the federal government, as well as the president's desire to roll back federal protection of the freedmen in the South. His congregation rose up in revolt. One of its most prominent members, Theodore Tilton, editor of the *Independent*, turned the plaster bust of Beecher that had graced his mantle to face the wall. (Tilton would soon have an even greater reason to bear a grudge; a few years later his wife would confess to having had an affair with Beecher, sparking the Gilded Age's greatest social scandal.)

To reaffirm Plymouth Church's commitment to Radical Reconstruction, Beecher's congregants invited a contingent of Southern "loyalists" who were touring the North to speak at the church. While a Southern loyalist gave a speech upholding the right of Northerners to avenge themselves upon Southern traitors, the audience hooted and hissed at every mention of

Andrew Johnson and cheered "every inferential disapproval of the course of the pastor of the Church." After he finished, and the crowd awaited the arrival of another speaker, a church organist filled the silence with some music. The audience received his selections indifferently until he hit on "John Brown's Body." According to one reporter, those assembled immediately took up the song "with the wildest glee." When the congregation "sang in perfect unison and with grand effect—'We'll hang Jeff Davis to a sour apple-tree,'" their radical bona fides had been fully restored.[7]

Indeed the song's popularity after the war had as much to do with vindictiveness toward Davis as with admiration of Brown. In those early postbellum years, it was just as frequently referred to as "Hang Jeff Davis" as "John Brown's Body"; the fear that the unreconstructed Confederate leader would ultimately triumph over his captors through their abandonment of Reconstruction was just as strong as the conviction that Brown had triumphed over his own, through the emancipation of the slaves. So in August 1867, when Davis, after his release from prison, received an invitation from a sympathetic resident of Stanstead, Vermont, to discuss investment opportunities nearby, other citizens of the town serenaded him with the song. (One women threw rocks as well.) Some even cited the popularity of "John Brown's Body" in support of executing Davis, claiming that such a punishment would respect the "voice of the people."[8]

The postwar Republican Party also laid claim to the song. It was, in this sense, the musical accompaniment to the waving of the bloody shirt, the strategy employed by Republicans to remind voters of the devastation caused by Confederates and their Northern Democratic allies and of the need to remain loyal to the Republican cause in order to ensure that the war's sacrifices were not endured in vain. In the 1868 presidential race, when the celebrated Civil War general Ulysses Grant faced the Democratic candidate Horatio Seymour, a viciously racist former governor of New York who advocated the immediate termination of Reconstruction and the institution of Southern home rule, Grant's partisans insisted that Seymour's campaign represented a Southern "rebellion at the polls" that must be quashed as decidedly as was the South's military uprising. In Bellows Falls, Vermont, Grant supporters marched to the polls in unison, and after voting tramped through the town's streets singing the John Brown song. And when Andrew Johnson vacated the White House to make way for the victorious Grant, an immense crowd gathered to see him off, including a number of Northerners who entertained the crowd by singing "We'll hang Andy Johnson on a sour apple tree."[9]

Four years later Grant faced a surprising opponent for the presidency in Horace Greeley, who had bolted from the Republican ranks to head up the Liberal Republican Party, whose platform centered on a speedy sectional reconciliation. Not surprisingly, Greeley also received the Democratic nomination. He began touring the country, urging his countrymen to put the war behind them, embracing a general amnesty for all Confederates and urging an end to federal protection of the freedmen. He offered generous rhetorical olive branches to the South, even questioning whether his past opposition to slavery "might have been a mistake." Greeley's supporters portrayed these conciliatory gestures as the essence of Christian charity. Senator Charles Sumner, who, like Greeley, had once been a stalwart of the radical camp (and whose body had never recovered from the beating he had received on the Senate floor for that dedication), insisted that God had inspired Greeley's challenge to Grant as a means of redirecting Americans to a proper respect for the virtues preached in Christ's Sermon on the Mount.

Republicans, on the other hand, insisted that an electoral victory for Greeley would hand the South ultimate victory in the Civil War. After Grant had been officially nominated at the Philadelphia Republican convention, the large crowd "cried out for the music of John Brown, until the band began to play it, the whole convention rising and signing it with great enthusiasm." Two months later, at a massive Republican campaign rally in Cleveland, with as many as fifteen thousand in attendance, speakers affirmed their party's commitment to protecting the rights of the freedmen and likened the foes that Grant had vanquished on the battlefield to those he faced now at the polls. "There is no difference," one speaker declared, "between [Greeley] and Jeff Davis." The rally ended with the crowd singing a version of "John Brown's Body" with "great gusto." Once again Horace Greeley found himself swinging from a sour apple tree, but this time the crowd who rhetorically deposited him there were loyal Republicans, and he was now joined, in successive verses, by Jefferson Davis and a host of other prominent Democratic politicians.[10]

Of course, there was more to "John Brown's Body" than the sour apple tree. The spirit of Brown himself still animated the song, and so it expressed the desire not merely to punish the South but to transform it. It memorialized an understanding of the Civil War as a struggle over slavery and of the postbellum years as a struggle for racial justice. Throughout the nation the John Brown song assumed a prominent place at commemorations of the Emancipation Proclamation. It also had a prominent place in the celebration of the first Decoration Day—the precursor to Memorial Day—which freed slaves helped organize on May 1, 1865, at the site of a former Confederate prison in Charleston, South Carolina. The prison had been built on a horseracing track, with the Union soldiers crowded in the track's interior. Without adequate food or shelter, many succumbed to disease and were buried in unmarked graves behind the judge's stand. In April 1865, after the city fell into Union hands, freed slaves insisted on giving these soldiers a proper burial and built an enclosure where they could be reinterred. On May 1 some ten thousand men and women, many of them former slaves, assembled to decorate the graves. Three thousand black schoolchildren, carrying roses, marched around the racetrack singing "John Brown's Body" and garlanded the ground around the soldiers' tombstones. A few years later the leading Union veterans' organization, the Grand Army of the Republic (GAR), called on all veterans to mark that same day by honoring their fallen comrades in a similar fashion.[11]

Soon after the period was brought to a close with the removal of federal troops from the South in 1877, the attacks of Reconstruction's reactionary critics, for whom it reeked of corruption and hubristic folly, converged with those of its radical challengers, bitterly disappointed by the period's reformist timidity, to lend Reconstruction a general air of disrepute that has not entirely dissipated to this day. But the attacks the period endured should not obscure the dramatic, and salutary, changes that those years imposed upon the South. A series of civil rights bills passed by Congress, and then the Fourteenth (1868) and Fifteenth (1870) Amendments ratified by the states, extended to African Americans national and state citizenship and secured for them universal manhood suffrage. During Reconstruction some two thousand African Americans held federal, state, and local public offices in the South. The changes were most profound in the years after 1867, when radical Republicans in Congress, after nearly impeaching Andrew Johnson, gained control of Reconstruction policy and set an aggressive course. But by the 1870s the North's commitment to Reconstruction had begun to ebb, as President Grant refused to slow the torrent of Confederate pardons that Johnson had initiated and as Northern Republicans authorized the dismantling of the Freedmen's Bureau.

In part the North's retreat was in response to a massive Southern countermobilization to Northern occupation. Southerners sought to preserve the labor discipline that had reigned during slavery through a campaign of vigilante violence against African American political and social leaders and their white allies. They torched schools, lynched black elected officials, and chased out Northern teachers who had come south to instruct the freed slaves. The retreat from Reconstruction also reflected a general exhaustion among Northerners with the intractable "Negro problem." Confronted with the daily dislocations of a rapidly urbanizing and industrializing society—mounting labor unrest, a major economic panic in 1873, a blight of political corruption at all levels of governance, and a growing immigrant population—the Northern public seemed to crave stability and peace. Northern businessmen were also reluctant to let sectional animosity stand in the way of the profits that could be made from a developing Southern economy. If the price of peace and profits was to leave the freedmen to their former masters, who were more than happy to work them as hard as sharecroppers and contract laborers as they had as bondsmen, it was one most Northerners were willing to pay.[12]

Thus for many in the North, white transsectional fraternity came to trump interracial solidarity. The retreat from Reconstruction required another conception of the Union's bonds, strengthened not merely in constitutional provisions but in the sentimental ties among its white citizens. It also required a reinterpretation of the nation's millennial promise, emphasizing the imperatives of reunion more insistently than those of racial justice. The foundations of such an understanding were laid in the early days after the Confederate surrender at Appomattox by one of the North's leading theologians, Horace Bushnell, at Yale's 1865 commencement ceremony. "The unity now to be developed, after this war-deluge is over," he informed the students and faculty, "will be no more thought of as a mere human compact . . . always to be debated by the letter, but it will be that bond of common life which God has touched with blood; a sacredly heroic, Providentially tragic unity, where God's cherubim stand guard over grudges and hates and remembered jealousies, and the sense of nationality becomes even a kind of religion."[13]

Paradoxically the transcendent nationality that emerged from the crucible of the war was channeled into a national government with relatively modest reformist ambitions. The postbellum decades witnessed a general dimming of the humanitarian fervor that had burned so brightly among antebellum Northern reformers. For some Northern clergy, the recognition that Reconstruction would not bring about the radical upheaval in Southern institutions and values foretold in their millennial visions produced a profound sense of disappointment and even led to calls for "a second interposition of divine grace to save the nation." But for many others, the ordeal of Reconstruction merely left them exhausted, craving stability and "peace," and harboring a newfound respect for authority and discipline.

The Reconstruction of the "Battle Hymn"

Perhaps there is no better representative of this receding reformism than Thomas Wentworth Higginson, who had been one of John Brown's most zealous partisans and who had led a regiment of African American troops during the Civil War. After the war ended, he supported the strict punishment of Confederate leaders, the enfranchisement of the freedmen, and the redistribution of rebel land to them. Establishing a strong federal presence in the South was necessary, he insisted, to check Southern intransigence. Yet as the region continued to smolder and occasionally to erupt in bursts of racial violence, his disillusionment with federal intervention in the South grew. He came to view the massive federal power that Reconstruction demanded as a greater danger to the nation's health than the occasional assaults on freedmen's rights. Ultimately he determined that, armed with the ballot, freedmen and women could fend for themselves, selecting leaders who would secure their interests. And so what the freedmen needed was not John Brown's apocalyptic militancy but patience. A trip to the South taken in 1877, the year that marked the official end of Reconstruction, convinced him that their status had already improved significantly. African Americans were "still a subordinate race, doubtless, but what a difference in the degree of subordination!" he wrote in a report to *Woman's Journal* (edited, at the time, by Julia Ward Howe).

Two years later Higginson returned south for his honeymoon—to Harpers Ferry. Visiting the ruins of the famous landmarks—the jail where Brown spent his final days and the site of the gallows where he was executed—Higginson and his new wife encountered a Southern lady who claimed to be a cousin of Robert E. Lee. She reassured Higginson with her warm "interest in the condition of the Negroes, whom she heartily and warmly praises and thinks are making great progress." On the ground haunted by the ghosts of sectional antagonism, there could be no more comforting apparition for those committed to reunion.[14]

INDEED BY THE 1870s both Northerners and Southerners had come to agree that peace depended on letting the unwholesome ghosts of war slumber, on cultivating a measure of salutary forgetfulness. In 1869 Robert E. Lee had set the tone by refusing an invitation to travel to Gettysburg to help with the erection of a monument to mark the famous battle that had been fought there. He thought it "wiser," he said, "not to keep open the sores of war." Throughout the North the veterans' organizations struggled to retain members; by 1875 only 2 percent of those eligible to join the Grand Army of the Republic had done so. By the late 1870s many communities in the North had even stopped funding Decoration and Memorial Day activities. "Progress in forgetfulness is wonderfully rapid," remarked a local paper in Westboro, Massachusetts, noting the cancellation of a Memorial Day program there. This embrace of oblivion fit into a broader cultural desire for regeneration. Forgetting held out the promise of a national spiritual rebirth. The termination of Reconstruction was understood as a second emancipation that would free the nation from the chains of sectional bitterness and inaugurate an age in which a regenerated *United* States could fulfill its muscular, millennial destiny. "The past is dead," announced one Trenton newspaper in 1882. "Let us live in the present and act the part of men."[15]

The 1880s did witness a revival of Civil War reminiscence and a reassertion of the prerogatives of memory, but only if those memories were depoliticized and sentimentalized. Memorialization of the war turned away from a focus on the emancipation of the slaves as the war's ultimate triumph and toward an emphasis on the sacrifices borne by soldiers of both sections. Such an understanding of the war, premised on a recognition of the valor and sacrifice of erstwhile enemies, fostered sectional reconciliation and provided the raw material for an ascendant civil religion. Both sections could embrace a renewed memorialization of the conflict, so long as attention was paid to the soldiers' common bravery and not the cause for which they fought.[16]

The "Battle Hymn of the Republic" was more comfortably incorporated into this culture of reunion than "John Brown's Body." Its status as the chief Union anthem had been solidified in the decade after the war, when it became a standard at Memorial Day celebrations and veterans' meetings, such as those sponsored by the GAR. The hymn also maintained something of its partisan associations, serving as a campaign song at countless Republican Party rallies. It had certainly not shed its sectional identity entirely, and yet it fit the reconciliationist ethos so superbly because of the balance it could strike between memorializing and forgetting. At Memorial Day observances and at veterans' reunions, the song clearly conjured up memories of the Civil War. It was also, by definition, forward-looking, boldly anticipating the coming of the Lord and thus unburdened by the past it evoked. Its final lines, invoking the sacredness of battlefield death, honored a unified "republic of suffering" in which both North and South had earned a place.[17]

And so the "Battle Hymn" was welcomed into various ceremonies of reconciliation. On these occasions the song was often paired with "Dixie," the jaunty minstrel tune (in fact written by a Northern composer) that became the favored battle hymn of the Confederacy. This coupling was often on show in a ritualized exchange of musical appreciation, in which a Northern performer would play (or a Northern audience would request) "Dixie" and a Southern performer would reciprocate with the "Battle Hymn." During the mobilization for the Spanish-American War, for instance, the First Connecticut Voluntary Infantry was brigaded in Virginia with the state's First Volunteer Corps. The Northern troops worried about the reception they would receive from their Southern hosts, but these concerns were quickly put to rest when the Virginia regimental band escorted the Northerners to their camp to the tune of the "Battle Hymn." The Connecticut band quickly responded by playing "Dixie."[18]

It was therefore not surprising that on Memorial Day 1895, one Massachusetts newspaper invoked the "Battle Hymn" to suggest that the "coming of the Lord," an image that in Howe's poem had represented the cataclysmic defeat of the Confederacy, could now be detected in the strengthening ties between the North and South. The author cited the lack of bitterness directed toward the South by Northern veterans and toward the North by Southern veterans. He touted as well the remarks of a South Carolina politician who had rejected the fear of "negro domination" as "demagogic." After all, the politician had explained, Southern blacks were now quite willing to defer to "those better fitted for government than themselves." All these signs, suggested the Massachusetts author, could be read as a "partial fulfillment of [the hymn's] prophecy," an indication that "the cause for which our heroes gave their lives is still 'Marching on.'"

He did not mention, of course, the race riot in New Orleans that had occurred just a few months before and that had resulted in the deaths of six African Americans, or the scores of lynchings of black Americans throughout the South; that year would witness more than one hundred. To do so would not merely have suggested that the demagoguery of "negro domination" had by no means lost its persuasiveness but would have also threatened the foundations of section reconciliation, clearly struck on Southern terms. Indeed, through such evasions, by the last decade of the century the "Battle Hymn" had become inoffensive enough to Southern sensibilities that the University of Georgia could use its melody for its football fight song, "Glory, Glory to Old Georgia." And by 1905 the students of Jackson, Mississippi, could celebrate the birthday of Robert E. Lee with a program that included both the "Battle Hymn" and "Dixie."[19]

In the final decades of her life, Julia Ward Howe lent her full support to the culture of reunion. She composed a poem for the January 1907 centennial of Robert E. Lee's birth (read at the celebration in Richmond by the leading Lost Cause scribe, Thomas Page Nelson). "A gallant foeman in the fight / A brother when the fight was o'er," Howe's poem began, and went on to celebrate the love that had healed the nation's wounds and united it after the war. Howe also endorsed the rededication of her "Battle Hymn" to the service of sectional reconciliation. In 1884 she traveled to New Orleans to head up the Women's Department of the World's Fair. She was deeply moved when, during a reception at the home of one of the sponsors of the exhibit, guests asked her to recite the "Battle Hymn." "I count it the greatest boon that God has given me," she later declared, "that I have heard my reunited country sing, North and South together, that cry of my heart when brother hand turned against brother, and blood flowed like rivers through the land." Such a claim represented an almost comic act of historical revision. Howe had not written the "Battle Hymn" in a spirit of anguished fraternity. Her poem had not mourned the flowing of blood, but granted it a providential, glorious meaning.[20]

In her history of the "Battle Hymn," Florence Howe Hall reinforced this reinterpretation. The poem's impersonality gave it an ideological slipperiness that allowed it to wriggle out of its sectional moorings. Though composed during the Civil War, she wrote, "there is no word of North or South, no appeal to local pride or patriotism, no word of sectional strife or bitterness." Such a reading required more than a bit of exegetical legerdemain. Hadn't her mother urged the "Hero" to "crush the serpent with his heel"? Yes, Hall explained, but she was not referring to the South per se. The serpent of the song was slavery itself: the sin and not the sinner. Even this interpretation found itself vulnerable to the culture of reunion, which pushed slavery aside from a discussion of the causes of the war. It was the fact that Northern and Southern soldiers fought for a cause—not the cause itself— that made them "adorable" to the subsequent generation of Americans.[21]

In fact certain facets of the poem made it especially amenable to appropriation by the cult of reunion. In the midst of an apocalyptic war, the hymn might have reflected the glare of sectional antagonism, but in the light of sectional cohesion, it gave off a gentler glow. The biblical images studding the poem could be detached from one particular referent—the struggle against the Confederacy and slavery, for instance—and easily applied to another; the hymn's battle could become whichever one Americans happened to be fighting at the time.[22]

Some of the references in the song that might have troubled national reunion with intimations of the conflict over slavery could be reinterpreted in ways that would not offend Southern honor. During the Civil War, urging soldiers to die to make men free might have suggested a crusade to rid the nation of slavery. But freedom is one of the most versatile values in the American panoply; Southerners, after all, also claimed to be fighting for freedom. Unionist and Confederate partisans called forth two very different sets of values with that one word; for Northerners, freedom meant the right of individuals to enjoy the fruits of their own labor, while for Southerners, it meant local self-government and security of property, including property in other human beings.[23]

Yet when the war ended, one particular definition of freedom provided common ground on which Northerners and Southerners could meet—at least white Northerners and white Southerners. This conception of freedom pushed aside the more transformative, radical one that freedmen and women had anticipated in their songs about crossing into Canaan and entering a promised land. Instead many Northerners assumed that once the Thirteenth Amendment had abolished slavery, and freedmen were given the opportunity to enter into labor contracts, they had secured their measure of freedom. Emancipation was understood as an apocalyptical event, instantaneously revolutionary and radically discontinuous from that which had come before it—an attitude that, ironically, guaranteed that what came after was not especially radical. It did not demand a protracted, vigilant campaign to ensure that the fruits of freedom were enjoyed by those who had been enslaved. Instead the realization of freedom became analogous to the sinner's sudden conversion into grace or the world's inauguration into a millennial age. The system of free labor would work its magic, transforming the South and elevating the freedmen in an inexorable tide. In this context the hymn's final lines about dying to make men free could take on a conservative cast. Union soldiers *had* died to make slaves free; now it was up to the freedmen and women themselves, and their Southern countrymen, to make the most of that freedom.[24]

It is not surprising that "John Brown's Body" assumed an awkward and sometimes unwelcome place within the culture of reunion. The song still retained its hold; as late as 1903 the *New York Times* could announce that, if called upon to do so, "every one of a chance multitude of ten thousand could sing" the song, "though nine thousand out of ten were born since the days when it was current and meant something as sung by the troops marching through cities on their way to the battle fields of the civil war." But by the turn of the century, the song held quite different resonances than it did when it "meant something" to Union troops. Then it had been the expression of triumph, sung as Northerners marched into defeated Confederate cities. In the final decades of the century, however, "John Brown's Body" was more often sung as an expression of protest by those who found themselves on the wrong side of history.[25]

"John Brown's Body" was regularly employed as a Republican campaign song in the 1870s and 1880s, often with inventive improvisations involving the Democratic bogeyman of the moment. For those who resisted the appeal of reunion, the song remained a compelling anthem. During a torchlight procession through the town of Bethany, Missouri, in 1876, local Republicans used as a makeshift banner an actual bloody shirt, pocked with bullet holes and splattered red, with the phrases "Republican Blood" and "Democratic Bullets" inscribed on the top and bottom. The crowd made its way to the town courthouse for a campaign rally, where it heard a rousing speech from Benjamin Prentiss, the Union general who had been one of the heroes of the Battle of Shiloh. At the end of the night all those assembled joined together to sing "John Brown's Body."

Four years later, at a Republican rally at New York's Academy of Music's four-thousand-seat auditorium, the crowd championed the presidential campaign of James Garfield, another former Union general. The high point of the event came when, after a pause in the proceedings, a group in the corner of the auditorium took up the John Brown song. Then the entire audience "at once caught up the refrain and there swelled up a great chorus that actually seemed to make the walls vibrate." When they reached the line about hanging Jeff Davis, such "a wave of enthusiasm swept over the vast multitude . . . that, at the conclusion of the stanza, the thousands who had been singing broke out into great applause, as if by an irresistible impulse."

Davis's reemergence in the 1880s as an unrepentant symbol of the Confederate Lost Cause provoked some Northerners into defiant incantations of the song. In April 1886, for instance, Davis delivered a speech in Montgomery, Alabama, at the laying of the cornerstone for a monument to honor the state's Confederate dead. Thousands descended on the city from across the South to pay tribute to their old leader and to hear him declare that the Confederacy's fight was "a holy war" and that "the spirit of Southern liberty is not dead." Spectators insisted that his reception eclipsed that given him during his inauguration in that same city a quarter century before. In response, a group of citizens in Albany protested "the resurrection of Davis from the oblivion to which a loyal and patriotic people had consigned him." The gathering served as a rally in defense of memory. "It is too soon to forget the sufferings and sacrifices of a loyal people; it is too soon to forget treason and traitors," the organizers declared. They concluded the meeting with a rousing version of the anthem of that smoldering memory, "John Brown's Body," or, as they called it, "We'll hang Jeff Davis on a sour apple tree."[26]

The John Brown song held out the possibility of fanning the cooling embers of sectional antagonism. At an 1883 concert in Philadelphia, a reporter noted that the audience showed little enthusiasm for the old war songs that had once been performance staples. "Only one line of one song awakened an answering throb of the war spirit," that which pledged to hang Jeff Davis to a sour apple tree. Yet many in the North preferred to let "John Brown's Body" moulder in the ground of Radical Reconstruction, a period whose politics they had no wish to disinter. Democratic journals began to gloat that among Northern audiences, the "John Brown sour apple tree lament does not enthuse as it" once did. "We suspect that it isn't a good year to flaunt the ensanguined garment or to attempt to make a campaign on the issue of hanging Jeff Davis to a sour apple tree," advised a Boston journal in 1878. "Sensible people are tired of it, and know that it is folly to talk about it. A sound currency and the preservation of the national honor is *the* issue." So even when many audiences did sing the song, it had become detached from any program of racial justice.

In 1888 Republicans sought to contest the Democratic hold over the South by sending prominent representatives to speak in the region. In July two Republican congressmen, one from Chicago and the other from Ohio, headed up a rally in Charleston, South Carolina. A crowd of more than ten thousand African Americans assembled to hear them speak, preparing themselves beforehand by marching through the streets of the city singing "Hang Jeff Davis on a Sour-Apple Tree." A reporter noted that the fervor of the event recalled the early, radical days of Reconstruction. But the audience was disappointed by the representatives' campaign speeches, which confined themselves to the tariff question, even though the crowd had little interest in the issue. Speaking to a reporter afterward, one of the congressmen explained their decision: "I don't believe in the bloody shirt business any longer. . . . [It] has been folded up and quietly laid away."[27]

The African Americans who crowded the streets of Charleston that day, much as they had when the city fell into Union hands at the Civil War's end, turned to "John Brown's Body" to promote a particular understanding of the conflict. During Reconstruction and in the decades that followed, African Americans served as the primary custodians of the emancipationist memory of the war. No one protested the amnesia that seemed to overtake the nation in its abandonment of that memory more vigorously than Frederick Douglass. "There was a right side and a wrong side in the late war that no sentiment ought to cause us to forget," Douglass announced at a GAR meeting on Decoration Day 1878. The war had not been "a mere display of brute courage and endurance" by soldiers of each section. It was a battle of ideas and values, which pitted freedom against slavery.

Even more than the "Battle Hymn of the Republic," "John Brown's Body" was the song of protest against the betrayal of African American political and social rights after the war. At an 1876 mass meeting held by Chicago's African Americans to call attention to violence against Southern blacks, the proceedings opened with the John Brown song. In Portsmouth, Virginia, in November 1888 four hundred African Americans marched down the city's streets singing an improvised version of the song. It included the verse "Hang Grover Cleveland to a sour apple tree," referring to the first Democrat to occupy the White House after the Civil War. The singers were met by a group of white citizens, and the two groups clashed. More than forty pistol shots were fired, leaving three of the whites seriously injured.

"John Brown's Body" did more than just express frustration with the racial injustice that plagued that nation. By establishing continuities between the abolitionist battles of the antebellum period and the post-bellum and postemancipation struggles for African American political and social rights, the song could also serve as a statement of hope and resolve. In Meriden, Connecticut, in 1883 a racially integrated crowd came together to celebrate Lincoln's birthday in a room festooned with pictures of prominent abolitionists—Frederick Douglass, William Lloyd Garrison, John Brown, and others—and notable Republican politicians. The speeches offered that day combined reminiscences of the antislavery movement with calls to carry on its animating principles by combating "the color line." Those assembled ended the event by singing "John Brown's Body." Like those pictures on the walls, the song provided a bridge to the triumph of emancipation and offered assurances that future triumphs lay ahead.

Three decades later the song continued to inspire hope that the nation would soon embrace the principles of racial justice and egalitarianism. At the 1911 commencement ceremony at Ohio's Wilberforce University, the first private African American university in the nation, school trustees burst into "John Brown's Body" after relating recent indications of racial progress: Texas allowing black men to sit on juries and the insistence of a Georgia judge that no one speak of African Americans as "niggers" in his courtroom.

When considering these signs of advance, one trustee claimed, "It is entirely proper to sing, 'John Brown's soul is marching on.'" And yet given the countervailing evidence that confronted the singers—the routine violence perpetrated against African Americans, the system of racial segregation entrenching itself throughout the nation, and the public's indifference to such injustices—there must have been a hint of defiance even in their hopefulness.[28]

Indeed in the closing decades of the century, "John Brown's Body" held as strong an appeal to the persecuted, marginalized, and malcontent as it did to the hopeful. The song was a favorite of condemned criminals, those who followed Brown up the scaffold. It gave some comfort to an eighteen-year-old African American who had been convicted of rape and was executed in August 1879 in Austin, Texas. The young man made a speech protesting his innocence to the more than four thousand spectators who had come to watch him die and held his composure till the hood was placed on his head. Then he began to resist and only steadied himself by singing. The drop fell with "John Brown's Body" on his lips.

The song also occupied a prominent place in the trial of Charles Guiteau, the mentally unstable lawyer who assassinated President James Garfield in 1881. Insisting on addressing the court during the closing argument, Guiteau defended his actions as divinely inspired. He styled himself John Brown's heir, a bold and righteous martyr—though for what cause, other than his own vainglory, was never entirely clear. "You can put my body in the grave," he declared to the packed courtroom, echoing Brown's own gallows admonition, "but there will be a day of reckoning." Glancing heavenward and swaying, Guiteau worked the analogy in a sort of religious trance. "The jury may put my body in the ground, but my soul will go marching on. The slaveholders put John Brown's body in the ground, but his soul goes marching on!" Then, in case the audience had not entirely appreciated the comparison, he sang a verse of "John Brown's Body"—"most weirdly," according to one observer—and finished with two recitations of the "Glory, Hallelujah" chorus.[29]

★

IF THE SONG BECAME increasingly associated with the marginalized and maligned in the United States, across the Atlantic it continued to appeal to all strata of society. Just a few years after the war, one Chicago journal noted that "John Brown's Body" had become "one of the most popular songs among the laboring classes of the old world." In the postbellum decades, its popularity overseas had much to do with the touring of the Fisk Jubilee Singers, the singing group from the Nashville school for freedmen and women that popularized the slave spiritual. The Fisk singers granted the song, particularly a version that adopted many of William Patton's lyrics, a privileged place in their programs during their European fundraising tours of the 1870s.

Their 1873 trip began inauspiciously, when they could not find an American steamship willing to take them over. Finally the group's manager arranged passage on a British ship. Once they arrived in England, the singers were almost immediately embraced by British society. So too was their version of "John Brown's Body." According to one Manchester reporter, before the Fisk singers arrived, the British regarded it "almost as a comic song," the lighthearted kin of "Yankee Doodle Dandy." But after their trip, many British listeners considered the song one of the most moving and powerful expressions of African American spirituality.

The Fisk singers had initially hesitated to sing the song at all. They had secured arrangements that allowed them to perform at local British churches with the stipulation that they restrict their program to religious songs; overtly political songs were discouraged. The Fisk singers were not sure how to classify "John Brown's Body." In the United States, after all, the song was clearly identified with Republican and radical causes, and the singers' church sponsors had initially assumed it was a secular song; some even expressly forbade them to sing it. But after they had performed the song on a few occasions, the overwhelming public response led them to include it in their programs. They sang a distinctive version whose first verse, after announcing that Brown's soul was marching one, added another declaration: "Now has come the glorious jubilee, when all mankind are free. / Glory, glory hallelujah, when all mankind are free." Those verses heightened the song's millennial associations and linked it to the other slave spirituals that the Fisk singers performed (but by referencing emancipation, it did not disown its political overtones entirely). In fact one reviewer claimed that it was the "slavish feeling" with which the Fisk group sang the song that overwhelmed audiences.[30]

The song was an enormous hit. The Jubilee Singers performed "John Brown's Body" for Queen Victoria, who listened to it with "manifest pleasure." Prime Minister William Gladstone invited the singers to perform at a lunch he was hosting for the Prince of Wales and other members of the royal family; the group responded most enthusiastically to the John Brown song.

Gladstone in fact asked for an encore performance as a special favor to one of his guests, whose father-in-law, Czar Alexander II, had emancipated the serfs in Russia. As a finale the Jubilee singers sang "John Brown's Body" as they returned to the United States, just as their ship approached New York Harbor; the performance provoked grumbles from the Southerners on board. In fact the singers were particularly struck by the different receptions accorded to the song on either side of the Atlantic. In England, one of the singers noted, the song met with unbridled enthusiasm. "It sent a thrill through us to think that so many hearts beat in unison with ours on the subject of universal freedom," the singer recalled. "[But] in our own country there are many who think otherwise, and when we sang the same song there it was almost received with groans." Given the likelihood of such an unenthusiastic response, the group's manager often left the song off American concert programs.[31]

Indeed the specter of John Brown cast such a threatening pall over the reconciled Union that the "Battle Hymn" could present itself as conciliatory, and as fully national, in comparison. Thus when, in January 1895, Nicholas Smith, a captain of a Wisconsin regiment who after the war delivered a popular lecture on Civil War songs, set out to give his talk in Kansas City, the organizers of the event warned him that many in the audience would be ex-Confederates and asked him to refrain from discussing anything that might "open old sores." He denied that anything in his lecture was particularly incendiary, but he agreed that he would refrain from singing "John Brown's Body" and would instead sing the "Battle Hymn." It was a wise choice. When he began the hymn, the audience sang along "lustily."[32]

As the champions of sectional reunion removed slavery from the center of Civil War memory, and as they demoted "John Brown's Body" to the margins of American public memory, they required a revised explanation for the song's popularity during the war. By dismissing the song as a forgettable historical ephemeron, an unserious relic of an earlier generation, supporters of reconciliation could ensure that it survived only as a curiosity rather than as a vital expression of radical commitment. The revelations about the Scottish John Brown serving as the original inspiration for the song helped in this effort; one newspaper editorialist referenced the origins of "John Brown's Body" to argue that the song had never really carried an abolitionist message.

Others sought to reverse the causal relationship between the abolitionist Brown's renown and the song's popularity. It was not the force of

Brown's public esteem or widespread enthusiasm for his racial egalitarianism that fueled the song's spread throughout the North. Rather it was "the accident of the John Brown song," in the words of one early twentieth-century historian, that kept alive the memory of the misguided fanatic. A Philadelphia editorialist agreed, commenting at the fiftieth anniversary of Brown's execution, "It seems very probable that had it not been for that famous song about 'John Brown's Body' . . . the old man would never have had such a large place in the imagination of the American people."[33]

At the end of the century, Brown did in fact occupy an ambivalent position within the American imagination. Social reformers still claimed him as a revered predecessor; to the Socialist leader Eugene Debs, for instance, Brown was "history's greatest hero." Arbiters of middle-class, mainstream culture, on the other hand, were in the process of dismantling Brown's renown.[34] The model of his fierce and radical individualism proved out of sorts with the intense and coercive patriotism that had developed by the 1890s, the decade that witnessed the birth of the Pledge of Allegiance, the tradition of standing and removing one's hat for the playing of the "Star Spangled Banner," and the first push to celebrate Flag Day. Amid the social unrest that convulsed a decade marked by devastating labor violence and economic depression, many Americans sought security in the bonds of an aggressive nationalism. The rebuke that Brown's raid represented to a citizenry indifferent to the plight of its most exploited inhabitants had become deeply unfashionable. For many Americans, the nation's prerogatives, as articulated by its authorities, *were* the "higher law." By 1904 *Harper's Weekly*, a mouthpiece of respectable opinion, noted that the Northern public had seemed to sour on Brown. "John Brown's raid, which, at the time, was regarded with admiration by certain professed philanthropists of New England," an editor remarked, "would now provoke only wrath and indignation at the North."[35]

In the final years of the century, as the United States entered into a war with Spain, the patriotic pressures intensified. In 1895 Cubans rebelled against Spanish colonial rule, and the Spanish authorities, led by Governor-General Valeriano Weyler, ruthlessly quashed the uprising, herding the families of peasant farmers and plantation laborers into concentration camps and then decimating the land in order to starve the rebels of food and military intelligence. Soon reports of Spanish atrocities reached the United States, provoking a drumbeat of calls for humanitarian intervention, which, combined with the surging desire for the United States to assert itself more aggressively upon the world stage (and to claim a larger share of global markets), prompted much of America's popular press to call for military action. A purloined letter from the Spanish ambassador leaked to American officials that demeaned President William McKinley further enflamed the public. And when the *Maine*, a battleship that had been dispatched to Havana Harbor to protect Americans living on the island, sank under mysterious circumstances, those calls grew shriller still. "Worst Insult to the United States in Its History," shrieked the fire-breathing *New York Journal*. Although subsequent investigations determined that the disaster was an accident, only a decisive military response would seem to relieve the sense of wounded American honor that the daily newspapers so profitably stoked. A "sort of bellicose fury has seized" Americans, groused the French ambassador. The chant popular with crowds in cities across the nation seemed to capture the mood well: "Remember the *Maine*, to hell with Spain!"[36]

The jingoistic war frenzy only amplified the forces that had elevated the "Battle Hymn of the Republic" to the status of sacred civic anthem and relegated "John Brown's Body" to historical curiosity. In fact the famous concluding lines of the "Battle Hymn" served as the peroration for one of the speeches that galvanized the supporters of military intervention. In early March 1898 Senator John Thurston and his wife traveled to Cuba as part of a "special committee" assembled by the newspaper magnate William Randolph Hearst, owner of the *New York Journal*, to investigate conditions on the island. A day after visiting a prison camp, Mrs. Thurston suffered a heart attack and died. Her traveling companions claimed that the scenes of Cuban suffering she had encountered, especially the sight of a mother clutching a baby wasting away from starvation, had hastened her death and that her final request was that her husband do all he could to save Cuba and its people.

And so, ten days later, "by command of silent lips," Senator Thurston appeared on the Senate floor. Before a packed chamber he presented a devastating indictment of Spanish atrocities on the island and a rousing demand for American military intervention on behalf of a free Cuba. His voice held steady throughout the lengthy oration; only at the end did it begin to crack, when he offered his final appeal. "I believe in the doctrine of peace," Thurston insisted, but "men must have liberty before there can come abiding peace." And so he was indeed calling for force and for blood. "But it will be God's force," the same force that had sustained Union troops in their glorious battles for freedom three decades before. "The time for God's force has come again," he insisted. "Let the impassioned lips of American patriots once more take up the song:

In the beauty of the lilies Christ was born across the sea;
With a glory in his bosom that transfigures you and me.
As He died to make men holy, let us die to make men free,
For God is marching on."

Thurston ended by making one final reference to his wife's passing and then slumped into his chair, burying his face in his hands. A fellow senator ushered him out of the chamber while the galleries erupted in applause. The next day, like hothouse flowers of war, the "Battle Hymn" bloomed in scores of papers across the nation.[37]

Upon assuming the presidency, McKinley had resisted the increasingly vociferous calls to liberate the Cubans from Spanish tyranny through force of American arms. His restraint angered large swaths of an increasingly belligerent public, who interpreted it as cowardice. The president has "no more backbone than a chocolate éclair," Theodore Roosevelt, the young assistant secretary of the navy, declared, and in several cities crowds hung McKinley in effigy. Congress too began to make clear its patience was wearing thin. By April the president, subsisting on just a few hours of sleep a night and haunted by visions of American soldiers dying in battle, relented and requested congressional authorization for military intervention.

On April 19, 1898, after passing a resolution granting authorization, as members of the House waited for the Senate to do the same, fifty representatives gathered in the congressional lobby and sang the "Battle Hymn." Some ex-Confederate congressmen chimed in with a version of "Dixie." Then both Northern and Southern representatives joined together in an improvisation: "We'll hang General Weyler on a sour apple tree, as we go marching on." It was a public exorcism of the ghost of John Brown through a gesture of sectional amity, as America's latest arch-fiend took Jefferson Davis's place in the noose.[38]

The United States officially declared war on Spain on April 25. The actual fighting lasted only 109 days, but that was long enough for a number of Americans to snatch their morsel of glory—most famously, Theodore Roosevelt, who had resigned from his position in the Navy Department to assemble a motley crew of "Rough Riders," a volunteer cavalry regiment composed of Ivy League athletes, New York policemen, frontier scouts, cowboys, Native Americans, and European immigrants. At the sinking of the *Maine*, Roosevelt had ordered Commodore George Dewey, commander of the navy's Asiatic Squadron, to make preparations for an attack on the Spanish fleet stationed at the Philippine Islands. And so when war came, Dewey was ready. He had stockpiled coal and ammunition and, on May 1, achieved a stunning victory against the Spanish, crippling or destroying their entire fleet stationed in Manila Bay. When the news made it back to the United States, the public erupted in celebration. But the euphoria masked an uncomfortable fact: the republic now found itself poised on the brink of empire, with control of a chain of islands halfway across the globe in its reach.

The pro-imperialist camp pushed for retaining the entire archipelago. The Protestant establishment, especially its powerful missionary wing, united in its call to keep all of the Philippines under American sovereignty, invoking the need to bring freedom and "soul-liberty" to a backward people. McKinley wavered, unsure of how to proceed. He took to pacing the White House halls at night, dropping to his knees in prayer when the immensity of his decision overwhelmed him.

Then, one night, the answer came. The nation could not shirk its responsibility to "uplift and Christianize" the Filipinos by returning sovereignty to the Spanish or to the Filipinos themselves. That was a burden Americans must bear. For the first night in days he slept soundly, and the next morning called the War Department's mapmaker to tell him "to put the Philippines on the map of the United States."[39]

The Americans' refusal to grant them sovereignty shocked the Filipinos, who had initially welcomed the U.S. military as liberators. Filipino rebels had crafted a "declaration of independence" from Spanish rule, announcing that the new nation existed "under the protection of the Mighty and Humane North American Nation," and had designed a red-white-and-blue flag to celebrate their special relationship to the United States. But when it became clear that the United States would not grant them a degree of autonomy, the Filipino insurgency deployed the guerrilla tactics they had honed against the Spanish against the American forces. The Americans responded with a determined brutality that would have impressed General Weyler. They tortured prisoners (the "water cure," an early term for waterboarding, was a favored method) and summarily executed others; they cleared out entire territories by herding men, women, and children into concentration camps and then destroying everything—humans, animals, houses, crops—outside the camps' "dead lines." In one of the most infamous incidents of the war, after Filipinos massacred more than forty American soldiers in a surprise raid, Jacob Smith, an especially unhinged general who was sent to pacify the island on which the attack had occurred, ordered his officers to kill all male Filipinos over ten years of age. Revelations of such abuses soured some Americans on the war, but most of the public did not seem terribly troubled, and the faith of the Protestant establishment that the war represented a providentially sanctioned mission never wavered.[40]

The war with Spain, and the imperial yearnings it stoked, brought about the full convergence of the emancipationist and reconciliationist strains of Civil War memory. Many Americans believed that God had led the nation through the crucible of war so that, purged of the moral taint of slavery, it could pursue its mission to extend the blessings of freedom and establish the kingdom of righteousness throughout the globe. The millennial energies unleashed by the Civil War could not be contained within national boundaries, since they presupposed a total cosmic conflict between the forces of good and evil, between God and Satan.

Many leading Protestants had no difficulty embracing the imperialist mission. The foreign missionary movement, which underwent dramatic growth in the decades after the Civil War, frequently employed martial metaphors to describe its own efforts to spread the Gospel, and many missionaries regarded military conflict as a necessary precursor to evangelization. With the addition of a single letter, they incorporated this evangelical imperative into Howe's hymn: "In the beauty of the lilies, Christ was *borne* across the sea." The lines between military and spiritual conquest blurred, allowing supporters of imperialism to frame their refusal to grant Filipino independence as a sacred duty. Defending the administration's policies in the Philippines, Albert Beveridge, a young, ardent senator from Indiana, announced, "If this be imperialism, the final end will be the empire of the Son of Man."[41]

The Spanish-American War also cemented the sectional reconciliation that had begun soon after the Civil War's conclusion. McKinley, the last Civil War veteran to occupy the White House, had made Unionist tropes a centerpiece of his successful 1896 campaign for the presidency; the prominent Civil War generals who campaigned on his behalf argued that a vote for the Democratic candidate, William Jennings Bryan, whose populist appeals pitted the classes against one another, represented a threat to the Union's integrity just as dire as that which had been posed by the secessionists of 1861. McKinley's belief that a war would further the cause of sectional comity helped overcome his initial hesitation to support military intervention in Cuba.

The Reconstruction of the "Battle Hymn"

He would not be disappointed. The news that a Southern sailor was the war's first casualty prompted a torrent of reconciliationist sentiment. When Northern soldiers marched through the South on their way to Cuba, they were struck by the warm reception they received and by the prominent placement in the crowds of Confederate veterans, proudly applauding the Stars and Stripes. Such scenes allowed Northerners to speak of Southern bravery, honor, and patriotism without desecrating Unionist memories, while Southerners could join the North in a campaign to promote freedom without fear that their own social and racial hierarchies would be threatened. "For the first time for more than half a century," McKinley announced triumphantly to an audience in Tipton, Indiana, "North and South are united in a holy alliance, with one aim, with one purpose, and with one determination." For the president and many others, the fact that the war with Spain had fostered national unity was a key sign that the United States fought with divine blessing.[42]

The struggle to put down the Filipino insurgency brought Northerners and Southerners together by promoting what one historian has called "a racialization of American patriotism." Through selective invocations of the memories of the Civil War and Reconstruction, and through the global extension of their own racial attitudes, Americans linked the imperatives of white supremacy at home and imperialism abroad. Americans stationed in the Philippines incorporated Filipinos into their preexisting racial categories; according to one American observer, "Almost without exception soldiers and also many officers, refer to the natives in their presence as 'niggers.'" In fact the military commander of U.S. forces in the Philippines, General Elwell Otis, initially refused two regular "colored" regiments out of fear that the troops' "racial loyalties" would lead them to sympathize with the enemy. (In the end he relented, and approximately ten thousand black troops fought in the war.[43])

Americans' own racial preoccupations informed—and haunted—the debate over U.S. policy toward the Philippines. Imperialists argued that Americans' efforts to improve conditions for African Americans had prepared the nation for its global mission to "uplift the child races everywhere." The fight against a tyrannical Spanish Empire stoked the embers of the emancipationist fervor of the Civil War. Yet those who opposed the granting of home rule to the Filipinos, such as Secretary of State Elihu Root, could point to the failure of Reconstruction as proof that it would be "foolish" to enfranchise "any non-white people." The moral ardor that accompanied Reconstruction's beginnings and the cautious disillusionment that marked its conclusion achieved a sort of equilibrium when the military transferred authority over the islands to a civilian governor, William Howard Taft, in 1901. Taft had declared himself in favor of extending some autonomy to the Filipinos but had also assured McKinley that "our little brown brothers" would need "fifty or one hundred years" of American tutelage "to develop anything resembling Anglo-Saxon political principles and skills." The islands did not in fact achieve full independence until 1946.[44]

The "Battle Hymn of the Republic" served as the choice expression of wartime patriotism because it could express both the radical emancipationist and conservative reconciliationist strains. The song trumpeted the advance of a nation unified around its imperial ambitions, muffling lingering sectional animosities. A Baptist preacher in Atlanta addressed the men mobilizing to fight Spain in a "holy crusade" by invoking the "Battle Hymn": "Go forth from the north and the south, from the east and the west, without regard to creed or color or party. Go forth singing the old battle song of freedom." He closed by quoting the hymn's final verses urging Americans to "die to make men free," as if the poem was naturally his own cultural patrimony.[45]

The hymn's ability to express the glories of imperial uplift and sectional reconciliation was on vivid display during an 1899 Memorial Day meeting of the Grand Army of the Republic. That year the Boston GAR had invited Confederate General Joseph Wheeler, who had led the cavalry charge at Shiloh and more than three decades later had led troops in Cuba, to give the Memorial Day oration. McKinley had offered Wheeler the rank of major-general in the war with Spain as a gesture of sectional unity; it would demonstrate, the president insisted, "that the old days are gone." Yet champions of the Lost Cause had taken an immense satisfaction in Wheeler's appointment. Another ex-Confederate general congratulated Wheeler, declaring that through his military service he "honor[ed] again the Old Cause" and "captured that prize for the memory of the Confederate Army." (Wheeler had in fact taken his status as representative Confederate perhaps a bit too far; in the midst of battle, when the Spanish were retreating, he yelled, "We've got the damn Yankees on the run!")

The Boston Memorial Day meeting marked the first time a Confederate officer had addressed a major meeting of the GAR, and sectional balance to Wheeler's presence was provided by the event's second guest of honor, Julia Ward Howe, who shared an open carriage with the general and a gallery box with Wheeler's wife. Privately Howe had been somewhat ambivalent about the American annexation of the Philippines. "I don't quite see that we ought to," she wrote to her daughter Maud, "but think we shall." Many of the remaining members of the antebellum reform community, Howe's social peers, had in fact joined the anti-imperialist movement. Yet despite those attachments, and her growing association with the peace cause, Howe's belief in the existence of just and divinely sanctioned wars allowed her to lend her moral authority, as well as her most famous poem, to the nascent American imperium. Ambivalent or not, she viewed the military conquest of the islands as the first stage in a grand missionary project that would "sweep away the accumulated moral filth of ages, to make whole races free with the freedom of the 19th century, the freedom of intelligent thought, of just institutions, of reasonable religion." The "horrors of the battlefield" were real, she conceded. But they were the birth pangs of "the beginning of a new society, redeemed, [and] reformed."[46]

That afternoon in Boston, Wheeler was greeted by fifteen minutes of sustained applause before he could even begin his remarks. Howe was accorded just as impressive a reception. According to one contemporary account, as a noted bass singer began Howe's famous hymn, he bowed in the direction of its author, which resulted in a giant roar from the audience. "By the time he had reached the words—'As He died to make men holy, let us die to make men free'—the whole audience was on its feet, sobbing and singing at the top of its thousands of lungs. If volunteers were needed right there for the Philippines, McKinley could have had us all right there."[47]

ONCE WAR WITH SPAIN began, the "Battle Hymn of the Republic" appeared in scores of newspapers throughout the nation. The song seemed to serve as a cultural guarantor of American good intentions. "No more appropriate occasion than the present can appear for the republication of the [song]," one paper declared a few days after American troops first clashed with Spanish forces, "when after thirty-three years of peace, the American Nation takes up arms for the freedom of the oppressed in Cuba." A Louisville minister made the "Battle Hymn" the center of an address delivered when the United States declared war on Spain. "The issue is clearly defined," E. L. Powell declared. "It is humanity against cruelty; it is liberty against oppression. If ever there was a righteous war, we are now entering upon it." He then offered an extended gloss on Howe's hymn, which he insisted "express[es] the spirit of a Christian nation in waging a war of conscience and conviction." The YMCA clearly agreed. It distributed thousands of pamphlets to troops stationed in military camps preparing to head to Cuba with sanitary rules on one side and the "Battle Hymn" on the other.[48]

But as the battle shifted to the Pacific and as the United States became less a liberating than an occupying power, the "Battle Hymn" was wielded nearly as aggressively by the war's opponents. Anti-imperialists used the song to undercut the pretensions of those who claimed that the United States was acting as an emissary of freedom, even as it denied to the Filipinos the right to political autonomy. In January 1899 an Illinois senator who opposed the annexation of the Philippines recalled to his colleagues a speech given the year before by another senator who had defended American intentions in Cuba by quoting the final lines of the "Battle Hymn." Shall we now change those lines to read, "Let us die to make men slaves?" the senator demanded. After hearing the "Battle Hymn" sung at a patriotic rally in Chicago, Patrick Ford, the editor of the *Irish World and American Industrial Liberator*, called attention to the false note struck by that final line. "It appears to have been sung by the audience without a qualm or a wince," he noted icily. Ford, who had once served as a printer's apprentice at William Lloyd Garrison's *Liberator*, recognized that the war supporters' appropriation of the song presented American imperialism as an heir to abolitionism. But he quickly dismissed that lineage: "The way we went about freeing the negroes was not to kill them by the thousands."[49]

The prominence of the "Battle Hymn" in the patriotic furor surrounding America's war with Spain, and then its conflict with the Filipinos, made it an especially attractive instrument of parody. The "Battle Hymn of the Empire," composed by the editor of the *Helena (Montana) Independent*, began:

> In the beauty of the lilies
> Christ was born across the waves
> As he died to make men holy
> We will fight to make men slaves.

The *Baltimore Sun* offered its own version that targeted "Expansion Marching On." For a handful, the original song represented American bombast and millennial pretensions, and so a parody cheapened what was an already debased commodity. But for most others, the "Battle Hymn" represented the high ideals of the Civil War, and parody served as a form of musical jeremiad. Every war sermon that ended with the congregation singing the hymn, and every politician who invoked its lyrics in a jingoistic speech, increased the song's power to level a critique of American actions in light of American principles.[50]

The most powerful "Battle Hymn" parody was not in fact published during the conflict itself. In February 1901 Mark Twain inscribed in a book to a friend, "I have rearranged the 'Battle Hymn of the Republic' this afternoon and brought it down to date." "Mine eyes have seen the orgy of the launching of the Sword," Twain's poem began. It continued to track Howe's original and concluded by referencing the suspicion that behind lofty imperial rhetoric lay callous economic interest:

> In a sordid slime harmonious, Greed was born in yonder ditch;
> With a longing in his bosom—for other's goods an itch;
> Christ died to make men holy; let men die to make us rich;
> Our god is marching on.[51]

The poem was found in Twain's papers after his death; he had made no effort to publish it during his lifetime. This reluctance was not a function of Twain's timidity. He had been quite vocal about his opposition to the occupation of the Philippines and had been willing to disregard the advice of his friends to temper some of his more inflammatory compositions so as to avoid antagonizing his readers. Scholars have suggested he pocketed his parody out of respect for Julia Ward Howe. But he also might have been responding to his own conflicting attitudes toward the ideas of America's millennial mission heralded in the hymn. Twain was a devout admirer of the "Battle Hymn"; at a celebration of Lincoln's birthday in 1901, he declared it both "beautiful" and "sublime." And not long before he composed the parody, he believed that the hymn's call for a providentially blessed campaign on behalf of freedom could consecrate America's military conflict with Spain as well. As a self-declared "red-hot imperialist," he supported intervention in Cuba because he had assumed that the United States had been impelled by entirely humanitarian motivations: to save the island from Spanish depredations. "This is the worthiest [war] that was ever fought, so far as my knowledge goes," Twain wrote from Vienna to his good friend Joseph Twichell. "It is a worthy thing to fight for one's freedom; it is another sight finer to fight for another man's. And I think this is the first time it has been done." The war at the century's conclusion marked the fulfillment of the emancipationist promise of the Civil War, which the nation had neglected over the past decades in its headlong pursuit of material gain.[52]

But as he watched events unfurl from various European capitals at the conclusion of his decade-long world tour, Twain began to realize that the United States had no intention of ceding sovereignty of the islands to the Filipinos. "When the United States sent word that the Cuban atrocities must end, she occupied the highest moral position ever taken by a nation since the Almighty made the Earth," he declared. "But when she snatched the Philippines and butchered a poverty-stricken, priest-ridden nation of children, she stained the flag." His parody of the "Battle Hymn" allowed him to express that sense of betrayal; that is why he insisted he had brought it "down to date," an expression premised on a previous degree of elevation. The hymn had once rung true, and so it could provide a way for critics of American military engagement to confront the public with the nation's moral shortcomings without calling into question the nation's exceptional millennial promise.[53]

Twain was a willing promoter of the culture of reunion; at the same Lincoln event during which he praised the "Battle Hymn," he spoke as a Confederate veteran (he had served briefly with a Missouri militia unit before deserting), insisting that both Northerners and Southerners had fought nobly during the war, while celebrating the fact that "the blue and the gray" had become "one." Yet he also employed the "Battle Hymn" to challenge some of the primary tenets of that culture, specifically the belief that the emancipationist legacy of the Civil War could be redirected to America's imperial mission in a military campaign that would unite North and South.

In this respect he found a partner in another group that dissented from the place of the "Battle Hymn" in the culture of reunion: the jealous guardians of the Confederate Lost Cause. Members of organizations such as the Daughters of the Confederacy (DOC) and United Confederate Veterans (UCV) did not seek to rechannel the war's emancipationist legacy. Instead they denied it entirely by promoting a nostalgic vision of antebellum Southern society in which slavery was a positive good. They too rejected the culture of reconciliation's celebration of forgetfulness as an impediment to the full vindication of the Confederacy. And so they initiated campaigns to revise school textbooks to remove passages that affronted Confederate remembrance of the Civil War. Among the offenders most often cited was the "Battle Hymn."

Various branches of the DOC and UCV protested inclusion of the song in school readers used by Southern school districts. In 1904 the Louisiana branch of the UCV objected to the use by the state's school of the *Boston Music Primer*, which included the hymn. It was, a UCV member complained, "written exclusively from a Northern point of view." He especially protested an image that shared the page with the poem of U.S. troops advancing with flags flying. This, the Confederate veteran assumed, was a pictorial representation of "the fateful lightning of [God's] terrible swift sword." Union soldiers had not enlisted to "die to make men free," he insisted. The Emancipation Proclamation had been employed only as a war measure to defeat the South. In place of the "Battle Hymn," the UCV recommended singing "The Conquered Banner," a Lost Cause anthem that called on Southerners to retain their tattered battle flags and to resist the enticements of sectional reconciliation. The UCV's efforts proved a success, and the state discontinued its use of the reader.

The UCV and DOC waged similar campaigns in other Southern cities. For these sons and daughters of the Confederacy, the "Battle Hymn" could not transcend its sectional origins; it remained a song of Northern aggression and required an equally aggressive defense of Confederate memory in response. The "Battle Hymn" could sound the notes of national unity and cohesion, but it also exposed the fragility of a national culture built upon the fault lines of deep political and cultural divisions.[54]

And so, by the start of the new century, various currents of meaning coursed through the old camp meeting tune. The song's unionist associations were strongest, but they at times eddied with more radical and divisive emancipationist and sectional meanings. When the song was played instrumentally, these currents converged; without lyrics, listeners were forced to extract meaning from the competing resonances of "Say Brothers," "John Brown's Body," and "Battle Hymn of the Republic." The contest among these different incarnations of the tune was on display one Sunday evening in August 1905, when Montgomery's Capital City Guards, Alabama's only African American military unit, returned from a five-day encampment on the city's outskirts. As they marched down Montgomery's main thoroughfare on the way to their armory, their band played the "Glory, Hallelujah" tune. The music shocked those observing the procession, who assumed the band was playing "Hang Jeff Davis to a Sour Apple Tree." Soon officers of the Alabama National Guard circulated a petition denouncing the band for playing "the hateful tune . . . right in the heart of the Cradle of the Confederacy" and calling on the legislature and governor to muster the company out. The Guards, however, protested that they had simply been playing the "Battle Hymn of the Republic," certainly not a capital offense. "We are so sorry that our white friends of this city took the tune for one thing when our words were another," the Guards apologized in a letter published in a local paper.

The incident generated some chuckles in the Northern press; when an African American paper in Indianapolis explained that the band had likely been playing "a standard composition applicable alike to all sections of the country" and noted how easily the "Battle Hymn" was confused with "John Brown's Body," it was also issuing a warning. John Brown's spirit would continue to haunt the celebratory strains of the "Battle Hymn" and the culture of reunion it had come to celebrate. The Alabama officers, for their part, thought the distinction between the songs meaningless. Since Union armies had adopted the tune, it had always been a reproach to the South; it instantly conjured up the desecration of the memory of the Confederacy's leader. Julia Ward Howe's lofty revisions could do nothing to exorcise the spirit of John Brown, they insisted. The white officers' argument proved persuasive; a few months later the governor mustered the unit out of existence.[55]

A police band from Augusta, Georgia, found itself in a similar predicament several decades later, when it played at the 1932 annual convention of the Confederated Southern Memorial Association (CSMA), an organization composed of representatives of various women's associations throughout the South dedicated to the preservation of Confederate memory. The ladies of the CSMA had invited the Augusta Police Band to perform for the event, and they were quite satisfied with the music until they recognized an unwelcome tune. Backs arched stiffly and conversations abruptly halted when the music to "John Brown's Body" filled the hall. This time, however, the band had a ready answer that satisfied their hosts. They had not been playing "John Brown's Body" or Howe's "Battle Hymn" at all, they explained. They had been playing "Glory, Glory to Old Georgia," the University of Georgia fight song.[56]

V

★ ★ ★

THE PROGRESSIVE "BATTLE HYMN"

ON JUNE 15, 1912, Theodore Roosevelt, now a former president of the United States, arrived in Chicago, two days before the opening of the Republican national convention. Throngs of supporters greeted his train at the station. Thousands more lined the streets and crowded rooftops and elevated tracks, chanting "We Want Teddy" as his car sped by. When Roosevelt finally arrived at the Congressional Hotel, his admirers surged into the corridor outside his door. Eventually he moved out onto a ledge outside his window and addressed the mass of devotees congregated below. "The people have spoken," he declared, "and the politicians must learn to answer or understand."

Roosevelt understood: that was why he was running for president again, breaking an earlier vow not to pursue a third term. In fact he understood so well that he was willing to ignore another long-standing political tradition, one that stipulated that presidential candidates keep their distance from nominating conventions, letting the messy process of democratic deliberation grind on in their absence. But Roosevelt had little patience for demonstrations of stately reserve, not when the moment called for his own galvanic, charismatic presence.[1]

Four years earlier, after Roosevelt had left the White House, he had taken a dramatic leave from the political arena, embarking on an eleven-month safari in British East Africa and then on a triumphant tour of European capitals. Yet even as he felt himself "passing through stratum after stratum of savagery and semicivilization," he had been unable to escape his supporters' mounting fears that his hand-picked successor to the White House, William Taft, was squandering his presidential legacy. Most distressingly, while he was camped out in southern Sudan, a messenger brought him a telegraph from an American press agency informing him that Taft had fired Gifford Pinchot, one of Roosevelt's leading conservationist allies, as the nation's chief forester.

The drumbeat for Roosevelt to challenge Taft for the Republican presidential nomination steadily mounted, and by the time Roosevelt made his return to the United States in June 1910 it had reached deafening levels. A twenty-one-canon salute and a battleship accompanied by five destroyers met his ocean liner at New York Harbor, while no fewer than a million citizens waited on shore, packing the city's streets, to welcome Roosevelt as he joined a troop of dignitaries for a parade up Broadway. Many shared the sentiments of one man who shouted into a megaphone as Roosevelt's car crept by, "Our next president!"

Even as insurgent Republicans rallied to his side, and even as the rift between him and Taft continued to widen, Roosevelt spent the next few months on the sidelines, refusing to endorse Taft for renomination and yet also reluctant to declare his own candidacy. He had no difficulty dismissing his somewhat inconvenient promise, made when he was still in the White House, not to pursue a third term; he had issued that vow out of a fear of the dangers represented by the power of presidential incumbency, a threat that, as a political outsider, he no longer posed. More significantly the attraction of a life of leisure on his Oyster Bay estate pulled strongly on him. Yet stronger still was his congenital restlessness and his craving for power.[2]

By early 1912, convinced that a popular groundswell demanded his entrance into the race, he had made up his mind. "My hat is in the ring," he told reporters. "The fight is on and I am stripped to the buff." In the next several months he achieved some impressive victories in the handful of states that held direct primaries. But Taft's control of the Republican Party machinery guaranteed him the votes of a large portion of the delegates who would attend the nominating convention. Both camps raised charges of electoral fraud. Taft, however, could also claim the allegiance of the majority of the Republican National Committee, whose determination of the status of the more than 250 contested delegates would ultimately prove decisive. As it became clear that the powers of incumbency would tilt the nomination to the sitting president, Roosevelt's supporters cried foul, claiming that Taft had stolen the election. Roosevelt did little to tamp down these grievances.

In fact he stoked them, and at a speech delivered the day before the nominee would be officially determined, he endowed them with an apocalyptic grandeur. "What happens to me is not of the slightest consequence," he told his partisans, with his characteristic blend of self-aggrandizement and humble obeisance to a higher cause. "We fight in honorable fashion for the good of mankind; fearless of the future, unheeding of our individual fates, with unflinching hearts and undimmed eyes, we stand at Armageddon, and we battle for the Lord!"

But the next day the Lord's hosts did not have the votes. And so Roosevelt and his supporters bolted from the GOP to establish a new party that might serve as a worthy instrument of their political millennialism: the Progressive Party. The party would also channel Roosevelt's own outsized personality, and for that reason another name held more popular favor. Speaking to reporters at the Republican convention, Roosevelt had announced that he felt as fit as a "bull moose," and the Progressives embraced the animal (often depicted with TR's toothy grin) as the mascot of their nascent political movement.[3]

In early August Roosevelt returned to the Chicago Coliseum for the inaugural convention of the Progressive Party. The venue boasted a few novel touches since it had housed the Republican convention six weeks earlier, the most prominent of which was a giant stuffed moose's head that hung over the main entrance. Observers and participants alike were struck by other differences: the absence, for instance, of cigar-chomping party hacks on the convention floor, and of millionaires perched in the galleries, superintending their political investments below. Instead a motley (if largely middle-class) crew of professional reformers, reform-minded professionals, businessmen, farmers, sociologists, and suffragists gathered in a spirit of shared moral fervor. In fact many who witnessed the proceedings reached for the same analogy to describe the scene: the gathering had the buzz and enthusiasm of a "giant revival meeting." A reporter for the *New York Times*, a paper generally unsympathetic to Roosevelt, who had arrived in Chicago expecting to produce some breezily condescending copy, wired his editor apologetically that he could not "make fun of this convention. This is a religion." It did not seem like a partisan convention at all, he wrote in his dispatches. It seemed more like "a Methodist camp meeting done up in political terms," where "one thousand serious, earnest, almost fanatical men and women" met to "enlist" in a "contest with the Powers of Darkness." They marched behind Roosevelt in his effort to "usher . . . in the millennium in public and political life in this country." The "Battle Hymn of the Republic" served as a common expression of their enthusiasm. "The convention could not get enough" of the hymn, declared the *Times* reporter; the delegates sang the song at every opportunity during the proceedings.

On the convention's first day, the temporary chairman, Albert Beveridge, former senator of Indiana, delivered a rousing speech on the Progressive creed of ambitious social and political reform that he concluded by quoting the hymn's opening verse. The audience took this as a cue to stand and sing all but the final verse of the song. The following day, when Roosevelt addressed the delegates—the first time a presidential candidate did so at a nominating convention—and gave a "confession of faith" outlining his political beliefs, he appeared on stage as the band played the "Battle Hymn." Roosevelt ended his speech by reprising the lines that he had uttered so famously during his earlier visit to Chicago and which had given the Progressives' rendition of the "Battle Hymn" an additional resonance: "We stand at Armageddon, and we battle for the Lord." On the convention's final day, when Roosevelt appeared on stage to accept the party's nomination— again the first time a candidate did so in person—and the band struck up the song once more, Roosevelt joined his running mate, California's governor Hiram Johnson, along with the thousands of assembled Progressives, in a "fervent singing" of the song. As Roosevelt would later explain on the campaign trail, this was for him one of the convention's defining moments, representing not merely the delegates' religious enthusiasm but also, through the hymn's associations with Julia Ward Howe, the impressive number of women who took active roles in the proceedings.[4]

Over the next several months, the "Battle Hymn of the Republic" became something like the unofficial anthem of the Progressive Party; even Oscar Straus, the Jewish former commerce secretary who ran on the Progressive ticket for the governorship of New York, printed the "Battle Hymn" on his campaign flyers. As one Boston journal commented, at Progressive rallies the hymn was "creating the same patriotic thrill it created fifty years ago," during the Civil War.

Unspoken was the recognition that the hymn's prominence had dimmed somewhat in the early years of the new century, after its surge in popularity during the Spanish-American War. Julia Ward Howe's death in 1910 at the age of ninety-one once again pushed the song into the public's attention. Yet these remembrances functioned to associate the hymn with the glories of past campaigns; as the *Philadelphia Inquirer* noted in the midst of a glowing tribute to Howe, despite her many accomplishments, she would likely be remembered longest for her "Battle Hymn," though it had "ceased to appeal to the rising generation." Similarly, at semicentennial celebrations of the Civil War, veterans gave their full-throated endorsement of the hymn, yet this reception too contributed to the mustiness that clung to the song.[5]

Yet even before the Progressive campaign, there was evidence that the song could continue to speak to Americans, that it could be gently loosened from its historical moorings and receive fresh meanings in the twentieth century. In July 1911 the American Vitagraph Company, the nation's first major film company, released *The Battle Hymn of the Republic*, a fictionalized account of the hymn's creation. The film honored (while taking some liberties with) the hymn's Civil War origins as well as the timelessness of its millennial themes, while its technical and artistic innovations helped to revitalize the "Battle Hymn" for a modern age.

When the movie opens, a widow whose husband had been killed in the war is refusing to grant her son permission to enlist. The scene then shifts to an apocryphal encounter at the White House, where President Lincoln and Julia Ward Howe are looking mournfully at an empty recruiting center for Union troops. Soon after, the camera shows Howe rising from her sleep and, in a sort of somnambulistic trance, composing the hymn at a table near her bed. Her words flash by on the screen, accompanied by corresponding allegorical tableaux that detach the poem from its particular referents in the Civil War and grant the images a cosmic significance. The "coming of the Lord" is represented not with scenes of Union troops preparing for battle but the nativity of Christ; the "watchfires of a hundred circling camps" bring images of the Crusaders trooping through the Holy Land. To depict God sifting out the hearts of men, the audience is granted the perspective from the "judgment seat" itself, as a great procession of men from throughout history (Caesar, Dante, and Napoleon among them) troop toward the camera's eye, fill the screen as they approach, and then disappear to their fates. The lines calling for the hero to crush the serpent with his heel are matched with an image of Lincoln removing the chains from four cowering slaves, while the refrain "Our God is marching on" is accompanied by a scene of a great heavenly host marching toward the audience. Vachel Lindsay, the American poet and pioneer of film criticism, was particularly impressed with this last image. (He considered the movie itself to be a landmark of early cinematography.) "The celestial company," he noted, "is a thing never to be forgotten, a tableau that proves the motion picture a great religious instrument."

The poem complete, Howe returns to bed, where, the next morning, she finds her night's work. The audience watches as the poem spreads throughout the nation, including to the home of the widow from the film's opening.

After reading the hymn in a newspaper, she promptly takes her husband's sword from the wall and gives it to her son, bidding him to join the fight. "It is a holy war and a holy cause," she tells him. In the film's final scene, Lincoln and Howe are once again regarding the recruiting center, but this time it is teeming with men, who are all singing the hymn.

Vitagraph's *Battle Hymn* proved immensely popular, especially after the company hired full orchestras to play the song during the movie. Rave receptions and packed theaters greeted the film in showings in Fort Worth, Portland, Oregon, Hopkinsville, Kentucky, Savannah, and Trenton, New Jersey; it was "one of the greatest works of art ever filmed," according to one review. In 1912, in the midst of the presidential campaign, Vitagraph staged the first ever screening of a movie at the White House, featuring *The Battle Hymn*. According to one spectator, at the appearance of Lincoln on screen, President Taft seemed "visibly and deeply impressed."[6]

THE FIGURE WHO HAD most aggressively promoted the "Battle Hymn," even during its moments of waning popularity, was the man hoping to replace Taft in the White House. Teddy Roosevelt had been a sickly youth, born into a patrician New York family, who had willed himself into robustness with a strict regimen of calisthenics. From then on, he had dedicated himself to what he later glorified as the "strenuous life." After graduating from Harvard, he took a seat in the New York Assembly, at the time considered a rather ungentlemanly perch for someone of his social stature. Three years later he left for even rougher precincts after the deaths—on the same day—of both his wife during childbirth and his mother, taking refuge on a cattle ranch in the Dakota Territory. For the next several years he shuttled back and forth between East and West and between personas of gentleman scholar and "dude." He reentered Republican politics and was appointed New York City's police commissioner, and then assistant secretary of the navy in the McKinley administration. His performance as a Rough Rider in the Spanish-American War catapulted him into celebrity, and six months later into the New York governor's mansion. There he sparred with the bosses of the state's Republican political machine, who conspired to remove him from the state by installing him as a candidate to replace McKinley's deceased vice president. "Don't any of you realize that there's only one life between this madman and the White House," objected Senator Mark Hanna from Ohio, the leader of conservative forces within the GOP.

An assassin's bullet proved Hanna's worries prescient, and on September 14, 1901, Roosevelt became president of the United States.[7]

From early in his life Roosevelt embraced the "Battle Hymn" as a sort of personal anthem, a lyrical description of the "strenuous life." In 1890, when a reporter from an Ohio newspaper asked him to name his favorite poem, he selected two: Elspeth's ballad from Walter Scott's *Antiquary* and Julia Ward Howe's hymn. As Roosevelt recruited his motley band of Rough Riders to fight in Cuba, he insisted that the "Battle Hymn" be sung at every one of their meetings. He held Howe in the deepest esteem, and their families shared close social bonds; at Howe's death, Roosevelt wrote to her daughter Maud, "There was not a man or woman in America for whom I felt the same kind of devotion that I felt for your mother." Howe returned his affection. In the latter years of her life, she remained fiercely loyal to Roosevelt and refused to allow any criticism of him in her presence. After Howe's death, Roosevelt continued to lavish praise on her. He prefaced his 1916 best-selling brief for military preparedness, *Fear God and Take Your Own Part*, with the "Battle Hymn" and dedicated it to her. "In the vital matters fundamentally affecting the life of the Republic she was as good a citizen as Washington and Lincoln themselves," he wrote.

For Roosevelt, Howe embodied the trait most essential to a republic: "the valor of righteousness." This was an elusive quality, one that Roosevelt unceasingly invoked but never definitively defined. By yoking together righteousness and republicanism in Howe's exemplary person, he placed the fate of the nation beyond the mutual sacrifices citizens might make for the sake of the polity, as classical virtue would dictate, and in the workings of a transcendent order. In other words, Roosevelt laid claim to—and installed Howe as the presiding genius of—the tradition of civic millennialism.[8]

While president he even took up the cause of securing to the "Battle Hymn" the status of a national anthem. In the summer of 1908, while taking a new horse out jumping, Roosevelt shared a memorable conversation with one of his military aides, Archie Butt. Roosevelt began to praise the song "Dixie," which the men had recently heard performed at a White House function. He considered it the nation's "only piece of martial music." Butt agreed but pointed out that it did not rise to the level of a national anthem; only the "Battle Hymn of the Republic" could claim that distinction. There was not a sectional line in the hymn, Butt claimed, "not a word that could awaken a single unpleasant thought in the mind of any American, no matter where he lived and no matter on which side he or his father had fought in this great war." As they rode on, Roosevelt began to sing the song, and when he stumbled on a word, Butt would gently correct him. "Archie, I am so glad you know that hymn," the president remarked when he had made it through all the verses. It was the first time, Butt wrote to his mother soon after, that the president had addressed him by his first name.

Roosevelt was especially impressed that Butt, a man of Southern birth, should hold the song in high regard. (Their other riding companion, Roosevelt's military aide Fitzhugh Lee, nephew of the Confederate general, remained pointedly silent during the conversation.) He wondered how they might convince more Americans of the hymn's merits. They rode in silence for a few minutes. Then suddenly Roosevelt announced his solution: he would recruit Atlanta's Joel Chandler Harris, the author of the Uncle Remus stories and one of the leading literary figures in the cult of the Southern Lost Cause. The president was convinced that the movement to make the "Battle Hymn" the national anthem must originate in the South. Soon after, he wrote to Harris to solicit his support. Harris's response seemed favorable, and in the next issue of his monthly magazine, he called on his readers to forget the "partisan genesis" of the song and to embrace it as Northerners had taken to Dixie. "Acquiescence in President Roosevelt's proposition would mark to a greater degree than almost anything else could the fact that this is indeed a unified country," he declared.[9]

When informed of Roosevelt's campaign to promote her song, Howe expressed a full-throated endorsement of his efforts. "It would gratify a dear wish of my heart if the South would adopt my verses," she wrote to Butt, reminding him that she too could claim Southern blood.

Others were less receptive. After the *New York Times* published Roosevelt and Harris's correspondence, the paper received a steady stream of letters elaborating upon the song's faults and inappropriateness as a national anthem. The song was too sectional, stirring up "bitter memories" best left in the past, an editorial argued. Forever linked with the "John Brown tune," it "recalled the conqueror's boast." A Jewish critic argued that the "Battle Hymn," steeped in Christological imagery, was too sectarian; it was better suited to serve as a "church or Salvation Army ode." Another critic suggested that it was simply too abstruse for most Americans to comprehend. Unsurprisingly the reception to Roosevelt's proposal in the South was even less enthusiastic. It did not help the hymn's cause that Harris, who might have led the song's campaign in the region, died soon after publishing Roosevelt's plea. Typical of the Southern reaction was the response of one Biloxi newspaper that asserted that the "Battle Hymn of the Republic" would become the national anthem only when *Uncle Tom's Cabin* became a Southern best seller.[10]

Roosevelt was not so easily discouraged. In his incarnation as a Progressive presidential candidate, he once again promoted the "Battle Hymn" as an expression of national solidarity, a theme crucial to his campaign. He repeatedly denounced, for instance, the exploitation by party bosses of the sectional antagonisms that still lingered within the Republican and Democratic parties and insisted that the Progressives would unite Northerners and Southerners, Easterners and Westerners around the promotion of the public good. At the Progressive convention, delegates sang the "Battle Hymn" alongside other anthems of the Union and Confederacy; during Roosevelt's official nomination, whenever a Southerner ascended the podium, a Grand Army of the Republic fife-and-drum corps would accompany him by playing "Dixie." These songs were sacrificial offerings of sectional pride on the altar of an undivided, transcendent nationalism. The "Battle Hymn" amplified this message. Its apocalyptic imagery offered an even more powerful vision of the transcendence of partisan, parochial, and sectional affiliations.[11]

Roosevelt had rarely employed such images in the past. Indeed his adoption of them seems as surprising as the Unitarian Howe's embrace of the idiom. But Roosevelt was perhaps an even more unexpected holy warrior, since Howe could at least call upon her Calvinist upbringing and her deeply felt connection to a personal Christ. Roosevelt, on the other hand, had never shown much sympathy for orthodox evangelical Christianity or a political philosophy informed by it. Although throughout his life he had been a regular church-goer and a devoted Bible reader, his religious commitments were grounded more in duty and the promotion of decency and fellowship than in spiritual arousal. He believed in what one observer termed "sane religion," which promoted "courage, uprightness and broad serviceableness." His faith was essentially a social one, and yet it was also private; as president, he had spoken little of his religious convictions or of America's providential identity. He had even tried to remove the phrase "In God We Trust" from the nation's coinage, arguing that the association with commerce would only cheapen American religiosity.[12]

Like many Americans of the age, Roosevelt had regarded John Brown with a certain degree of ambivalence. In one sense, Brown represented that manly purposefulness with which Roosevelt hoped to endow the Progressive cause. In 1910 Roosevelt chose to unveil his postpresidential political philosophy, "the New Nationalism," at the dedication of a state park at Osawatomie, Kansas, near the site where Brown and a band of followers had famously skirmished with a much larger proslavery force. Thirty thousand citizens showed up for the ceremony, including several of the men who had fought with Brown more than five decades before. Standing on a kitchen table that served as a podium, for one and a half hours Roosevelt championed the need for a strong executive to protect the rights of the commonwealth against the aggressions of the special interests. If the reforms he endorsed—vigorous federal regulation of the railroads and of corporate consolidation more generally, workmen's compensation laws, graduated income and inheritance taxes, the prohibition of child labor—had not themselves done so, the association with Brown allowed Roosevelt to make clear his allegiance to the Republican insurgents and to thumb his nose at the conservative Old Guard establishment that backed Taft.[13]

Still, William Allen White, a prominent Kansas editor and Progressive stalwart who had helped write the speech, had convinced Roosevelt that it was best not to dwell too long on Brown himself, whom he considered "a bloody butcher and a fanatic." Doubting the contributions an "extremist" could make toward social progress, White had warned Roosevelt against forging too close an association with Brown or his tactics. Roosevelt responded that he held similar views about Brown and about extremism more generally, though he did think Brown had achieved some good with his raid: "The North needed a martyr and he gave the martyr." And so Roosevelt made only a passing reference to the abolitionist in his remarks, mentioning him twice and speaking obliquely of the impassioned protagonists of the Civil War generation whose actions mingled good and evil. For many who had assembled for the dedication of the John Brown Memorial Park, this lukewarm tribute seemed like a rebuke. As another editor recalled the event a few years later, with only slight exaggeration, the former president "dedicated a monument to John Brown without mentioning . . . Brown's name."

A few days later Roosevelt published another version of the speech, more conciliatory toward the forces of concentrated wealth but which discussed Brown and his legacy in greater detail. "John Brown stands to us now as representing the men and the generation who rendered the greatest service ever rendered this country," he wrote in the *Outlook*. "He stood for heroic valor, grim energy, fierce fidelity to high ideals." Progressives would need to apply those same qualities to the problems of the twentieth century, he insisted.

But Brown should serve as a warning as much as an inspiration. He represented the dangers inherent in acts of "heedless violence" that would only "invite reaction." It was the Socialists rather than the Progressives who were Brown's modern-day successors; Brown's "notion that the evils of slavery could be cured by a slave insurrection was a delusion analogous to the delusions of those who expect to cure the evils of plutocracy by arousing the baser passions of workingmen against the rich in an endeavor at violent industrial revolution." Progressives should not shun the John Browns of the current moment, and might even profitably cooperate with them, but should reject the "vindictiveness" that poisoned their works. Instead they must make sure that it was the spirit of Abraham Lincoln, marked by "patience and moderation in the policy pursued, and . . . kindly charity and consideration and friendliness to those of opposite belief," that inspired their efforts.[14]

From the beginning of his political career, Roosevelt had prided himself on his willingness to call out the excesses of reformers and reactionaries alike. He was familiar with the faults of each, he told a friend in 1894. He knew "the banker, merchant and railroad king" well enough to appreciate that they were in need of "education and sound chastisement," and was intimate enough with populists and radicals to take pleasure in the thought of a "mob [being] handled by regulars, or by good State guards, not over-scrupulous about bloodshed." In the 1912 campaign he continued to strike this balance. Before bolting from the Republican Party, he had hoped to take control of the potentially irresponsible insurgent forces within it and orchestrate a reconciliation with the GOP's more conservative wing. And while running as a Progressive, he sought to arouse *and* to restrain the reformist energies of his followers. He urged Progressives to wage a war against economic injustice in order to stave off the onslaught of less responsible radical marauders who would be tempted to raze the entire social and economic order. Progressives, he insisted, were fighting to *save* capitalism.

Thus the battle at Armageddon that Roosevelt foresaw would not really be a totalizing holy war, and there would be little place in it for the anarchic passion that the legacy of John Brown might unleash. "We want to say to those who vaunt their conservatism, that we are the real conservatives," he had declared during his "confession" at the Progressive convention. The crowd, which had erupted at his every word in frenzied enthusiasm, sat in "amazed silence" for a moment, before Roosevelt won back their cheers by explaining, "The only wise conservative is a wise progressive." If the millennial fervor of the "Battle Hymn" spoke to Roosevelt's own reformist enthusiasms, he was no doubt attracted as well by the hint of conservatism it had acquired over the preceding half century through its association with the nation's unification around its capitalist and imperialist ambitions.[15]

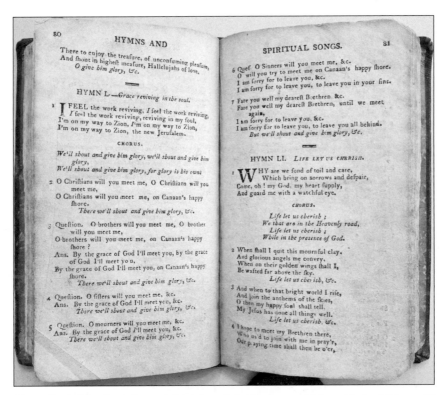

From Stith Mead, *A General Selection of the Newest and Most Admired Hymns & Spiritual Songs* (1807). Collection of Richard H. Hulan.

Martin M. Lawrence, *John Brown*, 1858. Salt Print. This is the last known photograph of John Brown and the basis of the engraving that appeared on the cover of *Frank Leslie's Illustrated* after his capture at Harpers Ferry. Collection of John Stauffer.

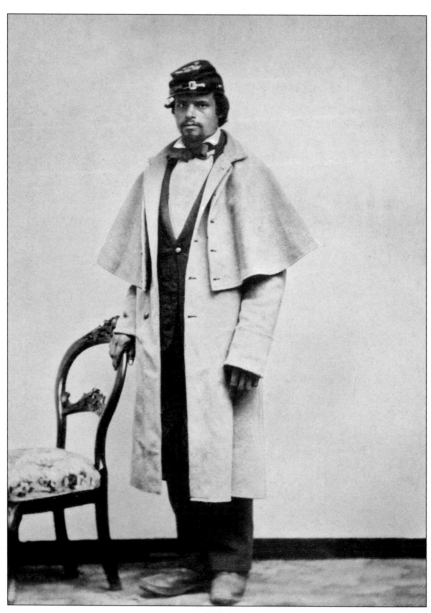

Sergeant John Brown of Boston, undated photo. West Virginia Memory Project.

"John Brown's Body" sheet music. Copy of the original, as written and sung at Fort Warren, May 1861, by James Greenleaf. West Virginia Memory Project.

"John Brown's Body" sheet music, 1861, arranged by C.B. Marsh. The first publication of the song with music. Courtesy Boston Public Library.

Josiah Hawes, *Julia Ward Howe*, ca. 1861. Schlesinger Library, Radcliffe Institute.

Facsimile of the first draft of the "Battle Hymn of the Republic," as written by Julia Ward Howe at Willard's Hotel, Washington, D.C. From Julia Ward Howe, *Reminiscences, 1819-1899* (Boston: Houghton, Mifflin and Company, 1899). Collection of John Stauffer.

THE

ATLANTIC MONTHLY.

A MAGAZINE OF LITERATURE, ART, AND POLITICS.

VOL. IX.—FEBRUARY, 1862.—NO. LII.

BATTLE HYMN OF THE REPUBLIC.

MINE eyes have seen the glory of the coming of the Lord :
He is trampling out the vintage where the grapes of wrath are stored ;
He hath loosed the fateful lightning of His terrible swift sword :
　　　　　His truth is marching on.

I have seen Him in the watch-fires of a hundred circling camps ;
They have builded Him an altar in the evening dews and damps ;
I can read His righteous sentence by the dim and flaring lamps :
　　　　　His day is marching on.

I have read a fiery gospel writ in burnished rows of steel :
" As ye deal with my contemners, so with you my grace shall deal ;
Let the Hero, born of woman, crush the serpent with his heel,
　　　　　Since God is marching on."

He has sounded forth the trumpet that shall never call retreat ;
He is sifting out the hearts of men before His judgment-seat :
Oh, be swift, my soul, to answer Him ! be jubilant, my feet !
　　　　　Our God is marching on.

In the beauty of the lilies Christ was born across the sea,
With a glory in his bosom that transfigures you and me :
As he died to make men holy, let us die to make men free,
　　　　　While God is marching on.

"Battle Hymn of the Republic," as published on the cover of *The Atlantic Monthly*, February, 1862. Widener Library, Harvard University.

"News in Libby Prison," engraving of the scene, made popular by Chaplain McCabe, when the inmates in the Confederate prison learn that Gettysburg was a Union victory and sing the "Battle Hymn" to celebrate. Published in Edward P. Smith, *Incidents of the United States Christian Commission* (Philadelphia: J.B. Lippincott & Co., 1869). Widener Library, Harvard University.

"The Dark and Trying Days," film still of Vitagraph's *The Battle Hymn of the Republic*, depicting Julia Ward Howe's visit to Abraham Lincoln, from *The Moving Picture World*, Vol. 8, No. 26 (July 1911). Baker Library, Harvard University.

Lone trumpeter performing "Battle Hymn of the Bulldog Nation" to the tune of the "Battle Hymn of the Republic" at a University of Georgia football game. University of Georgia Photographic Services. All rights reserved.

"Battle Hymn of the Republic," in Frederic H. Ripley and Thomas Tapper, *The Music Primer* (1895), whose use in Southern schools was protested by the United Confederate Veterans. Widener Library, Harvard University.

Teddy Roosevelt speaking at the 1912 Progressive Convention in Chicago.
Library of Congress Prints and Photographs Division Washington, D.C.

Oscar Cesare, "The
real Armageddon,"
political cartoon from
the *New York Sun*,
Thursday, June 1, 1919.

The real Armageddon

I.W.W.
SONGS

TO FAN THE FLAMES OF
DISCONTENT

We Are
In Here
For YOU

You Are
Out There
For US

Remember!

GENERAL DEFENSE EDITION
▼
PUBLISHED BY
I. W. W. PUBLISHING BUREAU
1001 W. MADISON STREET, CHICAGO, ILL.
U. S. A.

I.W.W. Songs: To Fan the Flames of Discontent. Known as the "Little Red Song-book," this 1918 edition includes on the cover the self-portrait Ralph Chaplin drew, first published in the Wobbly organ *Solidarity*, after he was arrested in the wake of the Espionage Act. Courtesy Washington State Historical Society.

"Billy Sunday, Playing Center Field for the Chicago White-stockings," Baseball Card, 1887. Library of Congress Prints and Photographs Division Washington, D.C.

Billy Sunday, Posed as if Preaching, ca. 1917. Library of Congress Prints and Photographs Division Washington, D.C.

Elliott Erwitt, "Billy Graham preaching in New York City, 1957." Courtesy Elliott Erwitt/Magnum Photos.

Addison N. Scurlock, Pilgrimage of the 23rd Annual Conference of the N.A.A.C.P. to Harpers Ferry, W. Va., May 22, 1932. Library of Congress Prints and Photographs Division Washington, D.C.

Martin Luther King Jr. addressing a crowd after the first aborted attempt to march from Selma to Montgomery, March 9, 1965. AP Photo/Charles Kelly.

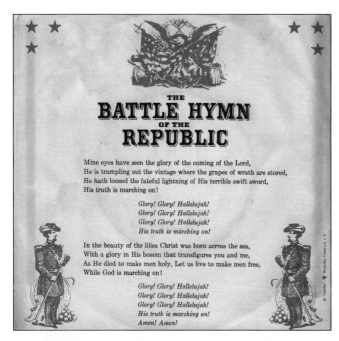

Record sleeve for the Mormon Tabernacle Choir's Grammy-winning 1959 version of the "Battle Hymn." Courtesy of the American Music Recordings Archive.

"The Spirit of American Youth Rising from the Waves," memorial for American dead at Omaha Beach, on which is inscribed: "Mine Eyes Have Seen the Glory of the Coming of the Lord."

"Battle Hymn of Lt. Calley." Cover of the 1971 album by Terry Nelson and C Company. The Lester S. Levy Collection of Sheet Music, Special Collections at the Sheridan Libraries of the Johns Hopkins University.

The Brooklyn Tabernacle Choir performs the "Battle Hymn" during the Presidential Inauguration of Barack Obama at the US Capitol, January 21, 2013. Photo by Jewel Samad, AFP/Getty Images.

Roosevelt's detractors were little impressed by his calls for patience and moderation. Taft's conservative supporters, who regarded Roosevelt as a dangerous, and very possibly insane, megalomaniac, did not tire of issuing warnings on the Bull Moose's radicalism. And many Socialists resented what they considered to be Roosevelt's poaching of a good part of their program—all in the name of the protection of capitalism. For Roosevelt did champion a number of bold policy prescriptions that anticipated the reforms and pre-occupations of the New Deal: worker safety regulations, minimum wage and child labor laws, the intelligent conservation and development of natural resources. As a recent historian of the 1912 election has declared, "In his party's platform and on the stump, Roosevelt pushed the boundaries as much as any major-party candidate did during the first four decades of the twentieth century."[16]

Those who shuddered instinctively at Roosevelt's rhetoric likely took some solace in the fact that it was a peculiar holy war against the forces of corporate malfeasance that could claim a partner of J. P. Morgan as one of its major financial backers. George W. Perkins had served as a major Republican donor for many years and had recently become enamored with Roosevelt's emphasis on regulation through a federal industrial commission (as opposed to Taft's reliance on statutory trust-busting), which Perkins believed would serve as a more predictable (and to his critics, more controllable) instrument of governmental policy. Perkins appreciated that Roosevelt proposed not to challenge corporate bigness but to regulate corporations through a compensatorily robust federal bureaucracy. He felt entirely comfortable navigating Roosevelt's Manichaean distinction between good and bad trusts; if those were the sides, he too could claim to be fighting for the Lord—from the boardroom. During the campaign Perkins was able to remove an endorsement of the Sherman Antitrust Law from the Progressive plank; when support for the law crept back in and was read to delegates during the convention, Perkins stormed out of the hall. He was mollified only when Roosevelt's press aide convinced most press agencies that the offending plank had been inserted by mistake and that they should leave it out of their transcripts of the platform's recitation.[17]

The power that Perkins wielded through his purse attracted the suspicions of the anticorporate and antimonopolistic reformers who had flocked to the Progressive Party. Explaining the high stock price of a mining company controlled by U.S. Steel (a trust consolidated by J. P. Morgan), one financial journal reflected these concerns by pointing to the market's belief that Roosevelt was "battling at Armageddon more for a chance to save the

Steel Trust's lease than for the Lord." More generally, in a review of Roosevelt's Progressive convention speech, the *Nation* suggested that in light of the candidate's "vague and . . . hesitating" policy prescriptions, his "holy zeal" should be heavily discounted and considered a product more of his fervor for the limelight than for progressive principles. The journal saw fit to repeat Prime Minister Benjamin Disraeli's ridicule of some overly exuberant political associates engaged in petty disputes: "They call it the Battle of Armageddon—but let *us* go to lunch."[18]

Roosevelt's moderation became even more pronounced when it was set off against the program of one of his three challengers to the presidency in 1912: that of Eugene Debs, the Socialist candidate, who would end up receiving more than 900,000 votes and who actually did champion a radical challenge to the capitalist, corporate order. Debs shared Roosevelt's predilection for millennial idioms but shaped them for his own ideological purposes. When the former locomotive fireman from Terre Haute, Indiana, shared his vision of working men and women establishing the kingdom of heaven in their own backyards and back alleys, he did so to communicate that his brand of socialism was not some noxious foreign import foisted on unsuspecting Americans but a set of ideas organically emerging out of an abiding faith in the American promise and nourished by the nation's traditions of democratic individualism. As he had written in 1893, the United States, "a country of boundless resources," was "the new earth and the new heaven of workingmen." In striving toward the realization of the nation's potential to become "the kingdom of heaven too long prayed for," American workers could honor their revolutionary heritage, handed down from the nation's Founding Fathers.[19]

Debs was also comfortable adopting apocalyptic images. Roosevelt's military service in Cuba lent his martial metaphors resonance, and yet Debs's past suggested an even closer link between electoral politics and millennial violence. Debs had at one time been a member of the International Workers of the World (IWW), a group that advocated direct action, including violence, as a means of achieving a Socialist revolution. He had since repudiated his early ties to the Wobblies, as the group became known, coming to believe that their embrace of violence would prove fatal to the development of industrial unionism. Sabotage and other IWW-endorsed tactics were "reactionary, not revolutionary," he insisted, for they simply played into "the hands of the enemy." Debs insisted that such tactics alienated the majority of American workers, who prided themselves on being "law-abiding." He took an active role in the campaign, brought to a head at the 1912 Socialist convention, to expel from the party the IWW and any group that advocated violence "as a weapon of the working class to aid in its emancipation."

Yet Debs also appreciated the extent to which the forces of capital themselves relied upon violence in order to preserve their own prerogatives, and at certain moments of crisis, he suggested that workers had little choice but to counter force with force. In a 1906 article, after mine owners kidnapped two union officials accused of murdering a former Idaho governor, Debs declared that if they executed the men, "a million revolutionists, at least, will meet them with guns." In 1910, in a midst of a bitter labor dispute between the publisher of the *Los Angeles Times* and his employees, a bomb exploded at the newspaper's headquarters, killing twenty-one workers; guilt soon fell upon the McNamara brothers, two members of a union constructing the *Times* building, which the paper's owner refused to recognize. Once the brothers confessed—one on the condition that his brother not be charged and the other on the condition that his brother not be executed—most of the political establishment, as well as the leaders of the non-Socialist labor movement, condemned them. "Murder is murder," declared Roosevelt. But though Debs did not endorse the bombing, he refused to join in the denunciation of the brothers. Murder was not always murder, he explained, for capitalists routinely and with impunity murdered laborers through unsafe working conditions or the brutal suppression of legitimate labor protest. Polite society tolerated some kinds of violence and not others, depending on which advanced their economic interests. "John Brown was an atrocious murderer in the eyes of the slave power, but today he is one of the greatest heroes of history," he pointed out in a 1912 article.

Instead Debs insisted on considering the "mitigating circumstances" that fed their violent act, the sense of desperation most other workers felt after years of capitalist exploitation. The brothers had "resort[ed] to the brutal methods of self-preservation which the masters and exploiters of their class have forced upon them," he argued. They were simply playing by the "moral code of the capitalist class," which was preferable to "cowardly surrender." Based on this acknowledgment of the state of belligerence that existed between workers and capitalists, Debs's rejection of violence could never be absolute. So when he spoke of waging a war—and even, occasionally, of waging a "holy war"—against the capitalist class, his millennial rhetoric carried perhaps a little more steel than Roosevelt's.[20]

There is yet another arena in which Roosevelt proved less than a holy warrior. Roosevelt hoped to challenge the Democratic stranglehold on the South, and if the Progressive Party was to woo Southern whites, it could not be regarded as the champion of Southern blacks. Explaining himself in a public letter to Joel Chandler Harris's son Julian, Roosevelt declared, "I believe that in this movement only damage will come if we either abandon our ideals on the one hand, or, on the other, fail resolutely to look facts in the face, however unpleasant these facts may be." Practically speaking, such equivocation translated into a policy of supporting the political participation of Northern blacks but not extending similar encouragement to Southern blacks. Instead Roosevelt would "appeal . . . to the best white men in the South" to protect the interests of both races in the region.[21]

So when competing white and black delegations from four Southern states made claims to be seated at the Progressive convention, he agreed with Southern whites that the Progressives should be a "lily-white" party and refused to accept his black supporters. The platform of the party made no mention whatsoever of racial violence or racism, and when an African American delegate interrupted Roosevelt during his convention speech to ask him about the issue, Roosevelt took the opportunity to chastise the "ignorant and debased" Southern blacks who had served as delegates to the Republican national convention and who had sold their votes to Taft's henchmen.

These slights led to a profound sense of betrayal among those African Americans whose millennial expectancy had been aroused by Roosevelt's call to arms. From his seat in the gallery, William H. Lewis, who through his friendship with Roosevelt had become the first African American to be appointed an assistant U.S. attorney, watched the Progressive convention proceed with a heavy heart. He was particularly struck by the incongruity between the countless speakers who trumpeted the principle of justice and their complete disregard of justice for African Americans. When the strains of "John Brown's Body" and the "Battle Hymn" reached his ears, the music seemed almost a taunt. Thinking of the Southern black delegates who had been barred from attending the convention, he could only conclude that if John Brown's soul was still marching on, it had bypassed the Chicago Coliseum. When the delegates sang the famous concluding lines of the "Battle Hymn," Lewis recalled, "I felt that human cant and hypocrisy could go no further; it had reached its fitting climax."[22]

YET FOR ALL THESE contradictions and counterpressures, Roosevelt's campaign style offered fertile soil for millennial themes. He had a penchant for self-dramatization and an affinity for political messianism that led him to view whatever battle he happened to be waging at the given moment in Manichaean terms. Both his admirers and especially his detractors appreciated this tendency and believed it to be especially pronounced as he pursued his third-party candidacy. According to Elihu Root, in leading the Progressives, Roosevelt considered himself a kind of "Moses and Messiah for a vast progressive tide of rising humanity." On the final day of the Republican convention, handbills were passed around Chicago announcing that, at "6 p.m. sharp," Roosevelt would walk on the waters of Lake Michigan and inviting "all unbelievers" to attend.

The providential underpinnings of millennialism appealed to Roosevelt, for they gave him a means of cloaking his personal ambition and his desire for individual glory with the mantle of service to some grander cause or some higher power. Julia Ward Howe had presented herself as an eager medium, yearning before her early-morning visitation for a way to serve her nation and then channeling that desire toward the composition of her hymn. Roosevelt posed as a more reluctant millennial agent. He would run for president, he told two old friends, only if it was "practically universally demanded." "I am not a candidate; I shall not become one," he informed California's governor (and his eventual choice as running mate) Hiram Johnson at the end of 1911. "But if the matter of my candidacy should appear in the guise of a public duty, then however I might feel about it personally, I could not feel that I ought to shirk it." Such statements did not merely express the slyness with which Roosevelt stalked power; they also served as coded instructions to his allies to gin up public support for his candidacy. In fact Roosevelt made such directives explicit, encouraging seven governors who were among his most prominent advocates to draft a written appeal for his candidacy. If the governors could demonstrate that they represented the "plain people" who had elected them, he coyly conceded that he would feel "honor bound" to comply.[23]

Events on the campaign trail conspired to heighten his sense of millennial agency, lending Roosevelt the nimbus of near-martyrdom. In October, while campaigning in Milwaukee, John Schrank, a demented former bartender, shot the Progressive candidate in the chest. The bullet passed through Roosevelt's heavy overcoat, a thick copy of his prepared speech, his vest pocket, his steel-reinforced glasses case, through his suspender belt and his shirt and undershirt, before lodging in his ribcage, pointing menacingly at his heart. Roosevelt insisted on going ahead and giving his planned remarks. "I have altogether too important things to think of to feel any concern over my own death," he insisted, speaking for nearly an hour and a half before being taken to the hospital. When the shooter was apprehended later that day, the authorities found a note in his coat pocket explaining that God had called him to serve as his "instrument" in preventing a third-term president and concluding with a reference to Luther's famous battle hymn, "A Mighty Fortress Is Our God," which also happened to be one of Roosevelt's favorite hymns. It was as if Roosevelt had encountered the distorted echo of his God-saturated rhetoric thrown back at him.[24]

The main reason Roosevelt could adopt such rhetoric so comfortably was because of changes in the nature of millennial thought more generally at the turn of the century. The dominant mode of thought among mainstream Protestants at the time of the Civil War was postmillennialism, which held that Jesus Christ's return to Earth would occur after the millennium, a period of peace and prosperity that could be advanced through the conversion of individual Christians. Yet by the beginning of the twentieth century, support for postmillennialism had begun to erode. This decline did not necessarily reflect the rise of the rival tradition of premillenialism, which held that Jesus Christ's return would *precede* the millennium, thereby encouraging a degree of fatalism and passivity about the world's condition since the works of human hands could do little to advance the coming of God's Kingdom. Instead postmillennialism became increasingly secularized, transformed into a hope for material and spiritual progress in *this* world through secular agencies and instrumentalities. God was not banished entirely, but His Kingdom was to be found less in the souls of men than in the world itself. He was immanent in improved living conditions and health standards across the globe, in advances of material well-being, and in the spread of humanitarian reform more generally.[25]

God's perfect Kingdom would arrive through the steady operation of moral and natural law and not through the traditional eschatological agents—the trumpeting angels and the spilt vials—that many mainstream Protestants had begun to regard with embarrassment. By the beginning of the twentieth century, to speak—or to sing—of the "coming of the Lord" meant something very different to the Protestant establishment than it had half a century before. Jesus' Second Coming would not inaugurate a radical apocalyptic rupture with secular time. Instead His return was ongoing, a continuous process of social and moral improvement, revealed in safe and productive factories and budding schools and hospitals, in a fairer distribution of wealth, and in the discovery of vaccines. Citing the "Battle Hymn" as the classic illustration of this progressive millennialism, the Presbyterian minister James Henry Snowden explained, "The fact is that God is coming at all points in history, for he is immanent in all creation. . . . Every act of judgment and justice and every new manifestation of sympathy and service is a coming of God and of Christ."

Their shared invocation of the "Battle Hymn" highlighted the strong affinities between the progressive Christianity championed by liberal Protestants at the turn of the century and the political gospel of the Progressive movement. The frequent use of martial and millennial imagery to describe reformist campaigns further solidified the connections. When Roosevelt spoke of battling for the Lord or his ally Gifford Pinchot, the chief forester whom Taft had fired, described such efforts as an "endless" "war for righteousness," they were infusing their work with the urgency of a military struggle. Progressives in a sense diffused the apocalyptic moment over time, vowing to function in a state of perpetual crisis and calling for unceasing service and sacrifice. Indeed one of the more striking elements of liberal theology was its secularization of Christ's atonement as a model for the "suffering love" that would animate the efforts of men and women to bring about the Kingdom of God on Earth. The final stanza of the "Battle Hymn of the Republic" became a favored expression of this mission. When progressive Protestants sang, "As He died to make men holy, Let us die to make men free," they were not merely analogizing to the crucifixion. They were making the bold claim that in a very *literal* sense the dedicated service and sacrifice of men and women would redeem the world.[26]

For the substantial number of Americans who resisted the offerings of religious liberalism, such claims smacked of heresy. As a prime expression of a secularized millennialism, the "Battle Hymn" often attracted the censure of the orthodox. The biblical scholar and professor at Princeton Theological Seminary, J. Gresham Machen, the leading theorist of fundamentalism and most robust critic of religious modernism, ended his influential defense of Christian conservatism, *Christianity and Liberalism*, with a swipe at the hymn and the crusading, progressive Protestantism it trumpeted. The Church, he lamented, had become consumed by the impulse to change the world and had thus been changed by it. It no longer served as a sacred refuge for spiritual pilgrims and no longer communicated the central Christian message that man's ultimate hope rested not in human goodness but in the grace of a transcendent God. It encouraged Christians to regard Christ as an "example for faith" rather than an "object of faith." It was no wonder that those who now gathered within her walls had forgotten the meaning of Christ's atonement and were unable to appreciate the radical difference between the blood spilled on the Cross at Calvary that redeemed mankind and the blood spilled on the battlefield. And so a Christian "weary with the conflicts of the world" and seeking "refreshment for the soul" would not find it within most churches. Instead of a sermon with "human wisdom pushed far into the background by the glory of the Cross," he would likely hear a preacher discourse on "the social problems of the hour." And then the service would conclude with some singing, with "one of those hymns breathing out the angry passions of 1861." Although Machen did not mention the "Battle Hymn of the Republic" by name, he had the song in his sights. "Thus the warfare of the world has entered even into the house of God," he protested.[27]

Yet for those who hoped to recruit the Church into the warfare of the world, using a song that could channel the passions of 1861 proved irresistible. Not surprisingly the "Battle Hymn" became a favorite at rallies for reform causes closely associated with the evangelical wing of the Progressive movement, especially the movements for temperance and world peace. As early as July 1872, a decade after the song had gained its popularity as a war anthem, the "Battle Hymn" was granted a central place in the program of the World's Peace Jubilee. Held in Boston to celebrate the ending of the Franco-Prussian War and organized by Patrick Gilmore—who ten years before, as a young bandleader, had discovered "John Brown's Body" at Fort Warren—the celebration featured a twenty-thousand-voice choir, accompanied by an orchestra of two thousand instruments, including, somewhat incongruously, field artillery. Many of those attending agreed that the event's most powerful moment occurred when the Fisk Jubilee Singers, an African American singing group composed largely of former slaves, fronted a 150-person chorus and performed the "Battle Hymn." As one of the singers recalled, "The audience of forty thousand people was electrified. Men and women arose in their wild cheering, waving and throwing handkerchiefs and hats. The twenty thousand musicians and singers behind us did likewise."

In the following decades the hymn continued to occupy a central place at peace conferences. At the opening of the twentieth century, as Congress debated which song should be designated the national anthem, evangelical Protestants lobbied for the "Battle Hymn" because, one of its partisans explained, it "expressed peace and the triumph of God, instead of war and hate." And in 1904 Julia Ward Howe herself telegraphed a youth meeting at an international peace conference held in New York, "Tell the children that mine eyes have seen the glory of the coming of the Lord."[28]

A song born of the nation's bloodiest conflict had become a peace anthem. Only occasionally did an awareness of this seeming contradiction intrude. In

Seattle in 1913, for instance, the school board banned the "Battle Hymn" from celebrations of Peace Day, determining it was more appropriate for Memorial Day. Perhaps some could hear in the song both enthusiasm and revulsion for war because Howe's shifting reform engagements seemed to encompass both. Just nine years after writing the "Battle Hymn," Howe composed "Appeal to Womanhood throughout the World," in which she called upon "Christian women" to marshal their collective maternal instincts to promote peace. Given that mothers bore the burdens of birth, they also carried a special responsibility to protest the wanton killing that war promoted. She wrote tirelessly on the topic and in the early 1870s sought to organize an international congress of women in behalf of world peace to be held in London. When her efforts failed to bear fruit, she turned her attention to planning a Mother's Day of Peace to be celebrated annually in early June. On June 2, 1873, celebrations were held in eighteen cities across the nation, a precursor to what would become Mother's Day.

In *Reminiscences* Howe traces her conversion to the peace cause to her revulsion over the outbreak of the Franco-Prussian War, a conflict many believed to be recklessly initiated by the leaders of both nations. But another tragic event likely carried just as much influence: the death of her three-year-old son, Sammy, of diphtheria in May 1863. Sammy had been Howe's favorite; the day after his funeral, sitting in the room where he died, she felt "almost strangled with grief." She struggled to find meaning in the tragedy. Neither the cold Calvinism of her youth nor the warmhearted evangelicalism of her adulthood gave her much comfort. Ultimately, much like the death of President Lincoln's son Willie had deepened the president's appreciation of the inscrutability of divine will, the loss of Sammy tempered some of Howe's millennial certainties. In the "Battle Hymn" she had written of warfare—and of the suffering it brought—from an abstracted, providential perspective. But now she had suffered a loss that linked her to those for whom the fallen were not nameless millennial agents but husbands, sons, and brothers. That shared grief pointed the way toward a campaign against warfare rooted in her status as a grieving mother rather than poetic visionary. This was the message of her proposed international congress of women. "Let them meet first, as women, to bewail and commemorate the dead," she urged. Then they may "solemnly take counsel with each other as to the means whereby the great human family can live in peace."[29]

How to understand the relationship between the Howe who wrote the "Battle Hymn" and the Howe who promoted world peace? Some regarded her two identities as markers of moral progression. At her death, an old

friend and colleague from the peace movement offered a few lines of verse
that depicted that dual identity:

> She sang the Battle Hymn that rings
> Down the long corridors of time;
> Her lifelong human service sings
> of Peace, an anthem more sublime.[30]

There is some evidence that Howe regarded her own reformist persona
similarly, which can perhaps explain her ambivalence to her hymn's overshadowing of all other elements of her public identity (though the endless
requests to recite the poem in every conceivable circumstance no doubt
contributed as well). In April 1908 she experienced a nighttime vision that,
much like her poetic visitation nearly half a century earlier, bequeathed to
her "various couplets of a possible millennial poem." Bedridden with a bad
case of bronchitis, she awoke in the middle of the night, her mind overwhelmed by a torrent of vivid images and ideas that updated, and perhaps
even gently disowned, the early-morning inspiration that had produced the
"Battle Hymn." The images that marched through her head and arrayed
themselves into verse were not depictions of a military struggle but scenes
that flowed from a single, pacific phrase: "Living, not dying, Christ redeemed
mankind." It was as if in her final years Howe allowed herself to subscribe
to the Hutchinson Family's revision of her hymn's concluding lines, which
called on Christians to *live*, not to die, to make men free. In fact rather than
illuminating the apocalyptic conflict that would usher in God's pacific kingdom, her vision took in the triumphs of that age itself. As she later recalled,
she saw the "glory" of "men and women of every clime working like bees to
unwrap the evils of society and to discover the whole web of vice and misery
and to apply the remedies." She saw them working together, with "a
common lofty indomitable purpose." And then, she wrote, she "saw the
victory. All evil was gone from the earth" and mankind stood ready to enter
"the new Era of human understanding, all-encompassing sympathy and
ever-present help, the Era of perfect love, of peace passing understanding."[31]

This was a millennium freed of apocalyptic ruptures and calamities. The
"victory" Howe witnessed—the millennial moment itself—blended seamlessly with the campaign of righteous human labor that preceded it. This
time the "glory" she witnessed was of a largely human manufacture.

The two visions were not entirely at odds. In the final decades of her life,
Howe's millennial hopes rested less on the combined efforts of mothers

worldwide to promote peace than on the marshaled power of a united Christendom to overthrow the forces of barbarism. She insisted that such an aim did not necessarily require bloodshed, only "armed authority." And yet, as her support for the Spanish-American War testified, she did not shy away from endorsing bloodshed in the cause of preventing further brutality. Many of her admirers had little difficulty reconciling her visions of cataclysmic war and perfect peace. At a celebration of Howe's eightieth birthday, for instance, her friend Richard Watson Gilder, an eminent poet and editor, dubbed her the "Priestess of righteous war and holy peace," with little sense of contradiction between those two personae. The poet could sight the era of perfect love and peace passing understanding through the scrim of righteous violence she was called on to witness.[32]

In fact, in the decade after Howe's death in 1911, the imperative of engaging in a righteous war that would lead to a holy peace became a prominent theme of Progressive discourse. Few championed this idea more aggressively than Theodore Roosevelt. When he invoked the principle of righteousness in the conduct of American foreign policy—as he did on almost every occasion in which he addressed the topic—he meant that the nation must not only forgo the comforts of isolation but be willing to forgo the comforts of a misguided and short-sighted pacifism as well.[33]

During the 1912 campaign Roosevelt expanded upon these views in challenging Taft and Wilson's embrace of arbitration treaties. Only the threat, and at times the prosecution, of credible force could protect American interests, honor, and ideals. Citing the Revolutionary, Civil, and Spanish-American Wars in a 1911 article titled "The Righteousness of Peace," Roosevelt declared that Americans, when faced with a choice between righteousness and peace, have "again and again . . . chosen righteousness" and, in doing so, had ultimately secured both. "The fact is," Taft joked to an aide after reading the article, "the Colonel is not in favor of peace." Roosevelt simply "loves war," he confided to another friend.

There was much truth to these remarks. Ultimately Colonel Roosevelt, as he preferred to be called after leaving the White House, did not merely endorse war as a means of promoting righteousness, international order, or national interests; he relished combat for its own sake, for the manly virtues it cultivated, for the sacrifices it demanded, and for its capacity to regenerate the vitality of combatants and civilians alike. When Mexico threatened to descend into civil war in 1911, Roosevelt immediately began fantasizing about the possibility of an American military intervention and sent an impassioned missive to Taft offering to raise a cavalry division. And as soon as war erupted in Europe, Roosevelt desperately sought the opportunity to join in the fight against German militarism. He lobbied the Wilson administration furiously. As the prospect of American intervention grew more certain, he became nearly frantic at the chance to lead a division of volunteers as part of an expeditionary force to France. He had no illusions that were he granted his wish, he would return home; he admitted he craved death in battle. And although he was spared this fate due to the immunity of the War Department to his entreaties, his son Quentin, an aviator shot down over the skies of northern France, was not.[34]

The defense of righteous war and the repudiation of unrighteous peace preoccupied Roosevelt in the years after his Bull Moose campaign. The 1912 election had resulted in a decisive loss for the Progressives. Although Roosevelt had won 64,000 votes more than Taft, Woodrow Wilson, the former Princeton University president and New Jersey governor, achieved an overwhelming victory in the electoral college. Roosevelt wore the loss lightly; if anything, he seemed a bit relieved by the outcome, as if the gallant charge, and not the actual conquest, had sufficed. As he had done after leaving the White House in 1908, he fled politics (and especially the importunate yelping of the Progressive activists birthed in the Bull Moose campaign) for foreign adventure, taking an arduous five-month journey down an uncharted river into the jungles of Brazil. The venture nearly killed him; he returned to New York having lost nearly sixty pounds. He quickly regained his strength, though, feeding off his fury at what he perceived to be President's Wilson's mollycoddling of German militarism. Wilson's support of a "principled neutrality" Roosevelt found unintelligible; according to his moral calculus, "weaklings" who opposed military intervention from a lack of will deserved greater contempt than the "wrong-doers" themselves. The "cold and timid hearts" of these "shivering apostles of the gospel of national abjectness," he remarked, "are not stirred by the surge of the tremendous 'Battle Hymn of the Republic.'" There could be no greater proof for him of their moral obtuseness.[35]

Roosevelt's friends noted a darkening of his personality after his return from South America. It was as if two prime elements of his persona, whose union the "Battle Hymn" expressed so powerfully, had sundered: he had lost the fervent millennial hopefulness and retained the apocalyptic stridency. The illustrator Oscar Cesare highlighted the more menacing elements of Roosevelt's persona with a cartoon published in the *New York Sun* in June 1916 titled "The Real Armageddon." It featured a fierce-looking Roosevelt holding a club in one hand and a tattered American flag in the other, with the Capitol in the background, under dark, foreboding clouds. With it, Cesare used Roosevelt's own apocalyptic imagery against him, suggesting that the former president's belligerent fulminations against German militarism carried as much of a threat as German militarism itself.

Roosevelt found himself increasingly alienated from many of his Progressive cobelligerents, who, he wrote to Quentin, continued to "drive [him] nearly mad." Progressive defeats and Old Guard Republican victories in the 1914 election convinced Roosevelt that "the country was sick and tired of reform." His own reformist enthusiasms had clearly flagged. In 1916 he declined the Progressive nomination for president, and in a move that led many delegates to tear off their "Teddy" badges and storm out of the convention hall, he recommended that the party nominate instead the conservative Republican stalwart Henry Cabot Lodge, who had steadfastly refused to follow Roosevelt into the new party four years earlier. Roosevelt's subsequent endorsement of the Republican candidate Charles Evans Hughes effectively demobilized the Progressive Party for good. Roosevelt in fact began to draw closer to some of the "malefactors of great wealth" whom he had once deplored, as he came to appreciate that many industrialists (especially those poised to profit from arms manufacture) were his allies in the push for military preparedness and intervention.[36]

Among his former Progressive allies, Roosevelt was by no means alone in pushing for military intervention as Europe descended into war. Many agreed with Lyman Abbott, a Congregational minister and the editor of the *Outlook*, a leading progressive journal that featured Roosevelt on its masthead, that Americans must "plant the seed of international brotherhood with swords at our side." Meekness and aggressiveness mingled awkwardly in their calls to arms. In an article on the duty of the Church in a time of war, for instance, Abbott merged the models offered by Christ and Lincoln as paragons of peace-loving militancy. In order to establish the Kingdom of God on Earth, he urged the Church to "lead Christ's followers forth, his cross on their hearts, his sword in their hands, with malice toward none and with charity for all, to fight, to suffer, and, if need be, to die for their oppressed and stricken fellow-men." The contradictions inherent in the calls to wield the sword charitably were resolved through the promotion of a war that would end wars. The phrase, initially popularized by Prime Minister Lloyd George (who likely borrowed it from a book by H. G. Wells) is often misattributed to President Wilson. Yet the sentiment the phrase expressed was widespread in the United States. Its prevalence startled the German ambassador to the United States. "The juxtaposition in the American people's character of Pacifism and an impulsive lust of war should have been known to us," Count Johann Heinrich von Bernstorff explained in 1920, "if more sedulous attention had been paid in Germany to American conditions and characteristics."[37]

Some of the more prominent veterans of the Bull Moose campaign sought to portray American military involvement in the Great War as the natural extension of the millennial conflict for which Roosevelt had rallied his Progressive troops four years before. Abbott issued a series of editorials in the *Outlook*, seeking to convince readers that the pursuit of righteousness demanded that the United States retire its policy of neutrality and that Christians renounce a misconceived devotion to pacifism. Just as Progressives had on the convention floor in Chicago, the *Outlook* quoted the "Battle Hymn," especially its final lines, as the most compelling expression of this duty. Soon after the United States did enter the war, in April 1917, Abbott issued an open letter "to a former Progressive" who opposed intervention. "In 1912, you and I were singing together 'The Battle Hymn of the Republic' and in imagination were fighting the battle of Armageddon," he wrote. "We had enlisted for life in the war against social injustice." Why had they since parted company? Abbott made clear that it was the antiwar Progressive who had betrayed his principles. Referring to German atrocities, Abbott demanded to know whether his former comrade believed child labor ought to be fought in America but that child murder ought to be condoned in Belgium. "Do you think that justice is worth voting for, but not worth dying for?" he demanded.[38]

Progressive religious leaders took up these themes with particular fervor. House Democratic Majority Leader Claude Kitchen, a North Carolinian who vehemently opposed American intervention, placed much of the blame for the nation's eventual entrance into the war on the drumbeating of "big rich preachers" serving metropolitan congregations, "whose petitions for more bloodshed are given the widest possible publicity by a war-mad press." A handful of ministers did protest against the proliferating calls to holy war. Harry Emerson Fosdick, a young but influential Baptist, insisted that Christians must regard war as a travesty of the will of God. Such resistance to the ascendance of Christian belligerence was rare, however. More often religious leaders promoted an image of Christ not as the peace-loving Galilean who turned the other cheek but as the prophet who swept the Pharisees out of the temple. In January 1917 sixty prominent clergymen signed a letter rebuking President Wilson for continuing to seek a mediated end to the conflict, as opposed to taking the nation boldly into the fight. "We need to be reminded that peace is the triumph of righteousness and not the mere sheathing of the sword," they intoned. Such pronouncements interpreted American military engagements as demonstrations of a self-sacrificial ethic. With their swords unsheathed, Americans would die—and kill—to make men free.[39]

★

BUT MOST AMERICANS DID not relish the prospect of either dying or killing on distant battlefields. Wilson, who during his first term vigorously defended a position of neutrality, served as their champion. Campaigning for re-election in 1916 under the slogan "He Kept Us Out of War," Wilson suggested an alternative understanding of American exceptionalism and millennial purpose, one detached from martial experience or imagery that seemed less welcoming to the "Battle Hymn of the Republic." Yet he had never subscribed to a doctrinaire pacifism or entertained the isolationism common among many Democratic loyalists. And he had supported the Spanish-American War. "When men take up arms to set other men free, there is something sacred and holy in the warfare," he had declared in May 1911, as if offering a prose translation of final verse of the "Battle Hymn."[40]

Counterposed to this imperialist streak in Wilson was a revulsion against the human cost of war, especially after the deaths of seventeen American servicemen who had been part of an expedition he had sent to occupy the Mexican port city of Veracruz. American intervention in the European war, he feared, would unleash a "ruthless brutality" on the home front that would jeopardize his ambitious program of domestic reform.

Finally, Wilson's commitment to neutrality was solidified by a deep personal conviction that the highest virtue—in an individual and in a nation—was self-control. In his first foreign policy speech as president, addressing the civil war in Mexico, he had linked American national greatness to its citizens' capacity for "self-restraint." And in his remarks discussing the conflict in Europe, he brushed aside the offenses committed against the United States by both the British and the Germans by championing self-possession as a form of disinterested service. By refusing to be pulled into the vortex of European carnage, the United States could preserve its potential as peacemaker. The nation could thus fulfill its providential mission not through combat but through the avoidance of combat. "The example of America must be the example not merely of peace because it will not fight, but of peace because peace is the healing and elevating influence of the world and strife is not," Wilson declared in a speech given on May 10, 1915, three days after the Germans sank the *Lusitania*, the British ocean liner, killing 1,198 passengers, including 128 Americans. "There is such a thing as a man being too proud to fight. There is such a thing as a nation being so right that it does not need to convince others by force that it is right."[41]

Although Wilson later came to regret these remarks, he continued to push back against a vocal corps of interventionists while also endorsing calls for military preparedness through a policy of "armed neutrality." He sought to ground the decision facing the nation in terrestrial terms without losing sight of the transcendent import of the decision. Shortly after the sinking of the *Lusitania*, Wilson received a telegram urging him, "in the name of God," to declare war on Germany. "War isn't declared in the name of God," he responded, "it is a human affair entirely." Yet he also recognized the limits of his own agency in the face of human folly and historical contingency. For all his efforts to keep the nation out of the war, he knew that he was at the mercy of "any little German lieutenant" who, by "some calculated outrage," could thrust the nation into the European maelstrom at any moment.[42]

Ultimately it was Germany's policy of unrestricted submarine warfare, formulated at the highest ranks of the German imperial government, that forced Wilson's hand. On the night of April 2, 1917, Wilson made his way to the House chamber to request a declaration of war. The assembled senators and representatives greeted the president with a sustained burst of applause, many waving small American flags they had brought for the occasion. When Wilson, reading somewhat impassively from his manuscript and rarely looking up at his audience, announced that the policy of armed neutrality had proved "impracticable" and that the nation would never choose the "path of submission," Edward White, the chief justice of the Supreme Court, raised his arms above his head and delivered a thunderclap of approval. His gesture broke the apprehensive silence that had reigned until then; the cheer that came from the Congress and galleries, according to one observer, "sounded like a shouted prayer." The applause grew even louder when, minutes later, Wilson affirmed the principle that would lead the United States to battle: "The world must be made safe for democracy."

Wilson intended his remarks to temper the celebratory mood. He emphasized "the solemn and even tragical character of the step" he was taking and the "distressing and oppressive duty" he was performing. In fact his address, with its evocation of war as an awesome yet unwelcome undertaking, echoed Lincoln's Second Inaugural. Like Lincoln, Wilson resisted notions of the nation's status as an exceptional millennial instrument. The United

States must fight for the vindication of "human right," Wilson insisted, "of which we are only a single champion." Lincoln had emphasized that an inscrutable providence had led the nation to war; Wilson implied that the United States had been pulled as much by human malice and recklessness. Germany's violation of Americans' right to enjoy freedom of the seas had necessitated intervention. But the United States would be fighting not merely to defend its own rights but those of all nations. For most of the speech, Wilson assigned to the United States a purpose that was circumscribed by the vicissitudes of national interest and yet whose heroism touched on the transcendent.

Only in the speech's final lines did he suggest God's hand in the course of events. After spelling out the nation's duty to defend democratic principles, he ended, "God helping her, she can do no other." Here he paraphrased the famous remark of the Protestant reformer Martin Luther at the Diet of Worms: "God helping me, I can do no other." Luther had insisted on the need for faith—and for action—in the face of the mysteriousness of God's will and the sinfulness of human nature. By evoking Luther's declaration, Wilson suggested that the United States would play a providential role in the conflict while also counseling a degree of humility. In doing so, he introduced a note of reserve and restraint rarely sounded in millennial calls to arm.[43]

Nonetheless the speech contained enough intimations of America's messianic purpose for many Americans to understand it within the context of a more triumphant millennialist tradition. A reviewer for the *Boston Transcript*, for instance, wrote that Wilson had framed America's entrance into the war in terms that recalled the boldness of the "Battle Hymn of the Republic": "Upon the last refuge left to autocracy, [the president] pronounced the judgment of mankind and 'sounded forth the trumpet that shall never [call] retreat.'" Several newspapers soon distributed free booklets containing Wilson's war message along with the words to the "Battle Hymn."[44]

The notion that the United States was embarking on a holy war gained even more prominence in the first few weeks after U.S. military intervention. The fact that the debates on Wilson's war resolution took place during Holy Week—with the House approving the resolution on Good Friday by a vote of 373 to 50—underscored the analogy between Christ's redeeming sacrifice and America's selfless military engagements. Indeed for many Americans, the war was transformed from a clash of terrestrial powers, each with its own interests and grievances, into a transcendent and apocalyptical struggle. The forces of good were arrayed against the forces of evil, the righteous armies of Christianity against Germany, a "pagan nation" whose militarism impeded the coming of the millennium. "If ever there was a holy war, it is this war," announced Teddy Roosevelt before an audience at the Harvard Club in New York.[45]

More militant and millennial strains began to creep into Wilson's own wartime rhetoric. In his war address, the president had vowed that the United States would conduct itself as a belligerent "without passion." Yet a year later he struggled to keep his own passions in check. There was only one response to German aggression, he announced during a speech commemorating the anniversary of America's entrance into the war: "Force, Force to the utmost, Force without stint or limit, the righteous and triumphant Force which shall make Right the law of the world and cast every selfish dominion down in the dust." It became increasingly difficult to marry the humility and restraint that he had urged on the nation's citizens during the period of neutrality with the fervor fueled by the understanding of America's military engagement in providential terms. Wilson, the son, grandson, and nephew of Presbyterian ministers, had long cultivated a keen sense of his own providential destiny and of God's superintendence of the United States. After his election he had confided to an aide that he believed God had ordained his victory, and he would tell a group of British Methodists and Baptists after the Armistice that only a belief in Providence had preserved him from despair during the darkest days of the war. Although he had rarely invoked God in his public speeches before the war, after the United States entered the conflict he increasingly portrayed America's military service as divinely directed. Speaking before a Confederate veterans organization on the day of national registration for the draft, Wilson insisted that God had shepherded the nation through the crisis of civil war so that it might, at this moment, serve as "an instrument in the hands of God to see that liberty is made secure for mankind."[46]

Wilson's adoption of millennial themes grew even more pronounced after the war ended, when he attempted to rally the public behind the establishment of the League of Nations, which he believed to be the only mechanism capable of preventing future bloodshed on an even greater scale. Delivering to the Senate the Versailles Treaty—which the United States would need to ratify in order to participate in the League—he framed America's support for the institution as a duty that would fulfill its providential mission: "The stage is set, the destiny disclosed. It has come about by no plan of our conceiving, but by the hand of God who led us this way." As he toured the country to defend the treaty against its antagonists in the Senate, he insisted that at stake was not merely international peace or prosperity but the spiritual redemption of mankind. He concluded a speech in Pueblo, Colorado, by insisting that the nation must be led by the "truth of justice and of liberty and of peace" represented by the League. The truth would lead the United States, he insisted, "and through us, the world out into the pastures of quietness and peace such as the world has never dreamed of before." It would prove his last major address. That night Wilson suffered a stroke that cut short his speaking tour and incapacitated him for the rest of his presidency.[47]

In the end Wilson came to regard the Great War through the prism of the "Battle Hymn." At times he did so explicitly. Speaking at the inauguration of a Red Cross fundraising drive in New York in May 1918, he expressed the hope that if the "oppressed and helpless" peoples of the world could listen to the "Battle Hymn" and could hear in its steady meter "the feet of the great hosts of liberty going to set them free, to set their minds free, set their lives free, set their children free," they would understand the spirit in which the United States entered the conflict.[48]

As it had during the Spanish-American War, the "Battle Hymn" became a favored means for many Americans to express certainty in the righteousness of their nation's cause. After Wilson delivered his war address to Congress, the *New York Times* published the hymn on its front page to register the solemnity of the occasion. Maud Howe Elliott, Julia Ward Howe's daughter, wrote a letter to the paper congratulating it for the selection and suggested that the poem be read from the pulpit the following Sunday. Over the next few weeks, in churches across the nation, religious leaders complied. American papers reported with pride that when the first U.S. troops landed in France, they sang the "Battle Hymn" as they made their way to the front. On the home front, versions of the hymn put out by the major recording studios became best sellers. And Vitagraph, detecting yet another commercial opportunity, reissued its cinematographic interpretation of the hymn's inception.[49]

Americans weren't the only ones to embrace the "Battle Hymn." On April 20, 1917, a day on which for the first time in British history a foreign flag—the Stars and Stripes—flew above the Houses of Parliament, the hymn was granted a privileged place in a ceremony held at St. Paul's Cathedral to honor America's entrance into the war. In front of an audience that included the king and queen, the Welsh Guards performed what one journal termed "the American national hymn." The same description of the "Battle Hymn" was used in the program for a notable service held at the Lowtherstreet Congregational Church, in Carlisle, England, where

President Wilson's grandfather had once preached. When Wilson made his triumphant return to the church after Germany's surrender, in December 1918, the organist launched into the hymn as the president walked into the church and was escorted to the front pew.[50]

Once again the "Battle Hymn" established lines of continuity between the current conflict and the Civil War. The capaciousness of its millennial imagery provided enough slack for the images to stretch across the decades—and across the Atlantic. The Great War could also be regarded as a struggle against the evil of slavery, this time embodied not in the system of human bondage but in German tyranny and autocracy. Lyman Abbott made this point after hearing the "Battle Hymn" sung at a patriotic meeting in the weeks before the United States entered the war. Reading the poem again, Abbott was struck by its universality; it was, he noted, "wholly without local color. Not only the words 'slavery,' 'secession,' 'rebellion,' 'North,' 'South,' 'the Union,' do not occur; but not even the word 'America' appears." Its appeal was global. The "Battle Hymn," he declared, could become an "international hymn of liberty," a song "not merely for our Republic; it is for all republics."[51]

In the cultural chauvinism implicit in Abbott's suggestion that France, Russia, and Belgium adopt a Bostoner's composition to express their own yearnings for freedom and self-determination, Abbott revealed one of the tensions at the heart of American millennial thought: it promoted the idea of the United States as a chosen nation but also tapped into a powerful Christian universalism that could transcend national particularism. Ultimately such tensions would doom Wilson's dream of zealous American support for the League of Nations.

During the war the hymn's lack of "local color" also solidified its status as a fully *national* anthem. As it had during the Spanish-American War, the hymn served as a rallying cry for both Northerners and Southerners, united by a common enemy. In June 1918 the *Confederate Veteran*, which had served as the leading organ of the Lost Cause ideology, reprinted an editorial from a Georgia newspaper that celebrated this fact. The patriotic inspiration the "Battle Hymn" provided Americans during the war had removed the song's residual taint of bitter sectionalism, the *Macon Telegraph* argued. At a moment when "the sons of the grey and the sons of the blue battle as brothers . . . on the fields of Flanders and Picardy," the paper noted that Southern editorial writers often quoted the song in their pro-war dispatches. Half a century after its composition, the "Battle Hymn" could no longer be said to belong exclusively "to the sons of the hating abolitionists, the worshippers of [the prominent Radical Republican] Thad Stevens, and the spawn of the carpetbaggers." It belonged now to the entire nation.[52]

The hymn's power to inspire nationalistic sentiments was not lost on those officials charged with bolstering support for the war. The Connecticut State Council of Defense, one of the voluntary state councils that sought to maintain community morale, recommended giving the "Battle Hymn" a prominent place in war rallies. The relationship the poem established between military struggle and the cause of Christ, the Council declared, "applies to the present crisis even more poignantly than it did to the situation for which it was composed." The Committee on Public Information, the propaganda bureau set up by the Wilson administration to sell the war to the American public, also mined the hymn. On July 4, 1918, the Committee organized an Independence Day ceremony at Mount Vernon, at which representatives from thirty-three ethnic groups, having made the pilgrimage to George Washington's home, would affirm their loyalty as American citizens. A piano, discreetly hidden behind a bunch of cedar trees near the house, struck up the famous opening chords. As the Irish American tenor John McCormack began to sing the "Battle Hymn," each immigrant walked into Washington's small brick tomb, laid down a wreath, offered a prayer, and was greeted by President Wilson, who afterward delivered a stirring speech on the nobility of the nation's war aims.[53]

Progressives had long sought to use music education as a means of inculcating civic-mindedness and morality in working-class Americans, and especially in recent immigrants. As the advertising campaign of a company that sold music books to schools announced, "Good music makes good citizens." Military training camps, with their emphasis on discipline and their tradition of public singing, provided the perfect forum for demonstrating the edifying power of song. Reformers hoped that these camps would Americanize troops from disparate ethnic backgrounds and that song instruction could encourage national unity—and a degree of cultural homogeneity. The "Battle Hymn" was among the seven songs that the National Committee on Army and Navy Camp Music designated as essential for all troops to learn. Some pared the repertoire even further. One song leader explained that he taught immigrant soldiers, many of whom did not speak English, only three songs: "America," "The Star Spangled Banner," and the "Battle Hymn of the Republic." He would repeat the lyrics slowly to them and, in between their attempts to answer back, would add a few words "of loyal exhortation." As their commanding officer exclaimed with astonishment, his men were soon "made Americans through song."[54]

As an instrument of Americanization, the "Battle Hymn" carried a special weight, for it enabled the instructors to frame the war as a battle of absolutes, one in which there was little room for dissent or even conditional support. Dissent became treasonous, even heretical; to oppose the war was to reveal oneself as an enemy of freedom, as an accomplice to a diabolical conspiracy that jeopardized the coming of the Lord. Shailer Mathews, dean of the University of Chicago Divinity School, declared that since an Allied victory would lead to a "better humanity," for an American citizen to oppose intervention in the war was simply "not Christian." So if the "Battle Hymn" stoked wartime enthusiasm it also sponsored wartime repression. At the urging of the Wilson administration, Congress passed legislation criminalizing speech that cast "contempt, scorn, contumely or disrepute" on the "form of government" or that encouraged interference with the war effort. Under its authority the Justice Department convicted more than one thousand Socialists and other radicals who had opposed the war. Among them were Eugene Debs, arrested after delivering a speech in Canton, Ohio, in which he barely mentioned the war but did point out the contradiction of a nation attempting to make the world safe for democracy while denying the rights of its own citizens to speak freely. He received a ten-year prison sentence for his remarks.[55]

While the Wilson administration's strong-arm tactics muzzled wartime protests, after the Armistice even the most soaring patriotic appeals could do little to move the staunch opposition within the Senate to America's involvement in the League of Nations. When Wilson delivered the Versailles Treaty to the Senate and urged its members to ratify it with invocations of the nation's providential destiny, Senator Frank Brandegee of Connecticut dismissed the remarks as "soap bubbles and a soufflé of rhetorical phrases."[56]

The resurgent isolationism that ultimately triumphed in the Senate tapped into its own stream of millennialism, one that nourished the long-standing fantasy that the United States could shut itself off in its continental paradise and that its mission was linked to the pristine, edenic model it held out to the world. But the defeat of the League also could be interpreted as a symptom of millennial exhaustion. Whatever hopes Americans had harbored that the cataclysm of world war would usher in the Kingdom of God quickly dissipated in the months after the war ended, when the victorious Allies cynically divided up the spoils in the same spirit of aggrieved nationalism that had sparked the conflict. This war would clearly not end war; it would pave the way for new ones to come.

President Wilson had in fact been acutely aware of the danger of oversized expectations, even as he stoked them. During the 1912 presidential campaign, he had taken Roosevelt to task for "promis[ing] too often the millennium." "You have no right to promise Heaven unless you can bring us to it," he told a group of journalists after the Democratic convention, "for, in making promises, you create too much expectation and your failure brings with it only disappointment and sometimes despair." Seven years later, as he paced the deck of the *George Washington* with an old Princeton friend on the way to the Paris Peace Conference, he reprised the theme. The grand hopes invested in the United States by "the common people of the world" frightened him, he confided. "People will endure their tyrants for years, but they tear their deliverers to pieces if a millennium is not created immediately." And yet, their "present unhappinesses," fed by "ancient wrongs," could not be swept aside "in a day or with a wave of the hand." He foresaw "a tragedy of disappointment" ahead.

What worried Wilson on deck that day—and what his own utopian pronouncements and stroke-induced obstinacy in his negotiations with the Senate hastened—were the stirrings of a dialectic at the heart of millennial thought. Predictions of the imminence of an age of perfect peace ignited waves of expectancy and activism; these would recede when the millennium failed to arrive, leaving behind a pall of disillusionment that would be swept aside by the next period of millennial fervor. After the war some chastened Christian leaders maintained their commitment to progressivism by using a newfound appreciation of the depth of human sinfulness to fuel a renewed project of Christianizing the United States. A corps of young writers honed their literary modernism on the lodestone of the tarnished ideals that had led the nation into war. As Frederic Henry declares in Ernest Hemingway's *A Farewell to Arms* (1929), he had become embarrassed by words like *sacred*, *glory*, and *sacrifice*: "The things that were glorious had no glory and the sacrifices were like the stockyards at Chicago if nothing was done with the meat except to bury it." Most Americans, however, could not sustain this level of disillusionment. More preferred simply to redirect their faith in the United States as a chosen nation inward, toward visions of material abundance and technological sophistication.[57]

And so even as the dream of America's messianic mission momentarily faded, Americans did not stop singing the "Battle Hymn"; they simply invested it with an alternative meaning. The song increasingly was embraced as a celebration of traditional American values, calling on the nation's citizens to defend and conserve the institutions and social mores that allowed those values to flourish. At the 1920 Republican convention, held in the same Chicago Coliseum where Progressives had chanted the "Battle Hymn" eight years earlier, the song once again rang though the halls. But now it carried a different meaning, given that the Republican delegates nominated Senator Warren Harding of Ohio, who would campaign under the promise of delivering a "return to normalcy"—hardly a millennial call to arms. In fact by the 1920s the "Battle Hymn" had become so closely associated with a defense of traditional American values—and so disassociated from calls for transformative change—that even the Ku Klux Klan could ignore the song's abolitionist lineage and embrace it as a celebration of the America they sought to preserve from contamination by blacks, Jews, Catholics, and radicals. One historian has recently counted at least nine early twentieth-century Klan songbooks that include the hymn.[58]

In the decades after the Great War, the song came to express confidence in the promise of American life, while its martial imagery highlighted the defensiveness that underlay that confidence, reminding citizens that this promise required active vigilance from its enemies, domestic and foreign. At the same time, the "Battle Hymn" continued to hold a special meaning for those who believed that the United States was failing to fulfill its promise and who sought to call its citizens to account or to stir them to battle. No one appreciated these interwoven strains more acutely than John Steinbeck, whose novels chronicled the human costs of the failure of the American promise. As he worked on *The Grapes of Wrath* (1939), his wife, Carol, suggested the image from Howe's song, and from Revelation and Isaiah before that, as the title. He declared the suggestion "marvelous" and exulted to his diary, "The book has being at last." He considered the hymn "one of the great songs of the world," one that most Americans were familiar with. "People know the Battle Hymn who don't know the Star Spangled Banner," he explained to his agent.[59]

In its account of the Joad family's doomed trek from Oklahoma's Dust Bowl to California, Steinbeck's novel portrays an American landscape devastated by human avarice, economic depression, and environmental disaster, as well as the spirit of brotherhood and mutual redemption that might emerge from the dust. For Steinbeck, the reference to the "Battle Hymn" suggested the nation's "own revolutionary tradition," which he believed an indigenous movement of small farmers and workers had honored as they battled against their moneyed oppressors during the Depression. The title, he claimed, would blunt attacks from those who would try to smear his book and its portrayal of American poverty as inspired by communists or other foreign ideologues. The truths he delivered, Steinbeck's title testified, were as American as Julia Ward Howe—or as John Brown.[60]

Steinbeck insisted that the hymn be printed, in its entirety, at the beginning of the novel. He wrote to his publisher, Pascal Covici, "The fascist crowd will try to sabotage this book because it is revolutionary. They try to give it the communist angle. However, the Battle Hymn is American and intensely so. . . . So if both words and music are there the book is keyed into the American scene from the beginning." Even the title of the song itself, Steinbeck claimed, had "a special meaning in the light of this book." In its union of militancy and thanksgiving, wrath and reverence, the "Battle Hymn" spoke to the nation's hopes and fears, much as Steinbeck himself had attempted to do. When, in an early proof, the book contained only the hymn's first verse as a prologue, the writer objected. All the verses were necessary, and the music as well, "in case anyone, any one forgets."[61]

Ultimately Viking Press published *The Grapes of Wrath* with a song sheet of the "Battle Hymn of the Republic" printed diagonally on the endpapers at the front and back of the book. Steinbeck was satisfied, writing to Covici that the layout was "swell." In the decades to come, many *would* remember—and many would forget.[62]

VI

★ ★ ★

"SOLIDARITY FOREVER"

The Workers' "Battle Hymn"

SUNDAY, JANUARY 17, 1915, was another day of hunger for many Chicagoans, and the gray sky and biting wind further drained them of energy. But the League of the Unemployed had vowed to brave the weather. They had organized a "hunger march," collecting at Hull House, the famous settlement run by Jane Addams. The League's members ranged from young girls to old men and included blacks and whites, unskilled needle workers and white-collar clerks, immigrants who spoke little or no English and Puritan descendants. They carried placards that read, "We Want WORK, Not Charity"; "Hunger Knows No Law"; and "Give Us This Day Our Daily Bread." What united them was their hunger for work and sustenance.[1]

Signs of poverty were everywhere. Almost half of the nation's population lived at "a near-starvation level," according to a 1915 federal report on industrial relations, whereas the wealthiest 2 percent owned about 60 percent of the nation's assets. Most of the working classes were propertyless and living in unsanitary conditions; death rates from tuberculosis and injuries on the job were exorbitant. Every incoming freight train brought more jobless workers. Destitute families found shelter under bridges, only to be forced out. Unemployed clerks and secretaries besieged newsboys in the Loop district, hoping for a job from the "Help Wanted" columns. People even sought food and shelter at police stations. But the police viewed the poor and jobless as a threat to the existing order and did little to help. In fact they regularly raided the riverfront, clubbing "wharf rats" to keep them away from the lumber and freight yards.[2]

These stark conditions highlighted to labor radicals the failure of progressivism to lift the poor out of the quagmire of capitalism. To many Americans in 1915, the "Battle Hymn of the Republic," co-opted by Progressives and preachers to sing conservative values, no longer resonated. The song needed to be reenergized, reinfused with its original, revolutionary note of universal freedom amid apocalyptic war. The result was "Solidarity Forever," the hymn that has long served as the nation's leading labor anthem. The hunger march was central to this transformation.[3]

It began with music and speeches in Hull House's Bowen Auditorium. Demonstrators sang "The Internationale," the French labor song that the Chicago Socialist Charles Kerr had translated into English: "Arise, ye prisoners of starvation! / Arise ye wretched of the earth." But there was little support for it among the workers that day, and the singing "petered out" before the last stanza. An immigrant Russian baker received generous applause for his speech highlighting the contradictions of hunger in a land of plenty: "I am expected to starve because I cannot get work baking the bread you people need and cannot buy!"[4]

The principal speaker was Lucy Parsons, the widow of Albert Parsons, who had been hanged for his alleged complicity in the Chicago Haymarket Square bombing in 1886 that killed seven policemen and four civilians. Parsons accused the government of denying labor radicals the rights of free speech, petition, and assembly. It was as though the First Amendment did not exist, she said.[5]

Parsons stood near a big black banner with the word "HUNGER" written across it in large white letters. The banner recalled for her and many others the fight against working conditions thirty-one years earlier at Haymarket Square and the trial that had led to her husband's execution. She had carried a similar black banner at the Haymarket parade that preceded the bombing, and she hoped she "could carry such a flag again," she now told the crowd at Hull House.[6] Two undercover detectives, wearing ragged clothes and passing themselves off as unemployed workers, listened carefully to Parsons's speech. They had been ordered to report on the proceedings and look for any evidence to incite violence. They later said that Parsons told the crowd to "go out and break windows and take food if they didn't have money to buy it." No one else, including a University of Chicago dean who was in the audience, heard such incendiary rhetoric.[7]

After Parsons's speech the marchers assembled outside on Polk Street, just west of Halsted Street, and formed rows six abreast. They planned to parade north up Halsted with their "HUNGER" banner and placards. The undercover detectives immediately sent word to Assistant Police Chief Herman Schuettler. "They are going to march. It looks like trouble." Schuettler had been an officer on duty at the Haymarket bombing, had arrested one of the conspirators, and hated Lucy Parsons. He ordered his men to break up the march. "If any crowd . . . headed by Lucy Parsons . . . attempts to parade on the streets of Chicago, I will order them arrested," he said. "I have had experience with mobs, and I know that they are stopped much easier at the start than after they have developed momentum." He ordered several squads to Halsted Street to stop the parade.[8]

With policemen lining the curbs down the block, a handful of officers accosted the marchers and demanded to see a permit to march. They had no permit, they replied, because the police had refused to grant them one. "Then you will have to disperse," said an officer. The police had no legal authority to require a permit to march on city streets. It's unclear, however, whether or not the marchers knew this. In any event, they ignored the police order and continued their march, walking around the officers who had stopped them. As one demonstrator phrased it, "Nobody turned back and nobody dropped out of line. We walked into the police trap like lambs to the slaughter."[9]

The march descended into "a maelstrom of fists and clubs." According to the *Chicago Tribune*, girls and women joined the fray, biting officers, "tearing their faces with fingernails," yanking out clumps of hair, and slugging them. One officer testified that a man named Laughman hit him in the face, knocked him down, and kicked him in the side, prompting him to fire three shots into air. But ten other witnesses testified that at the time of the riot, Laughman was sitting in the front row of a peace meeting. The most graphic description of the battle came from one of the marchers:

Plain-clothesmen charged with upraised "billies," smashing right and left through the crowd. . . . Detectives, wearing brass knuckles, rushed the crowd, sending men and women sprawling in all directions with their fists. . . . Ragged figures slumped under the impact of slugshots (metal balls attached to clubs). . . . An old man tumbled into the gutter and was trampled by many feet. Another old man had one side of his face bloodied with a "billy." . . . Blood spurted over hands, clothing, and paving stones.

The battle lasted half an hour, ending when mounted police rounded up the remaining marchers in "Black Marias" (police vans). Halsted Street looked like "an armed camp." Surprisingly no one was killed or critically injured, despite the use of guns, billies, and slugshots. "I am satisfied that it came out as well as it did," Captain James O'Dea Storen announced. Twenty-one people were arrested for inciting a riot and jailed, but the charges were eventually dropped.[10]

The Chicago hunger march inspired Ralph Chaplin to finish writing "Solidarity Forever." An editor and artist aligned with the International Workers of the World (IWW, the Wobblies), Chaplin participated in the march and considered it "pretty much of a flop." That same day he scribbled "stanza after stanza" in his living room. He wanted "the song to be full of revolutionary fervor and to have a chorus that was ringing and defiant." He walked down Seventy-second Street and tried it out:

Solidarity forever,
Solidarity forever,
Solidarity forever,
For the Union makes us strong.

It seemed to have the right ring of defiance, so he kept it.[11]

Chaplin had begun writing the lyrics a few years earlier, during the 1912–13 coal miners' strike in Kanawha County, West Virginia. The strike had been far bloodier than the Chicago march. At one point Chaplin was en route to give a speech to the miners when he was hit in the back of the head with a slugshot and knocked unconscious. He came to hours later, lying beside some railroad tracks near the Virginia border, his head throbbing. Soon after that, an armored train called the Bull Moose Special stopped beside a tent colony of miners in the dead of night and opened fire with rifles and a machine gun. One man was killed and a woman had both legs broken "by a rain of lead." Another miner ran for cover with an infant in his arms but got hit and fell. Three bullets pierced the baby's calico shirt, but it was somehow unhurt.[12]

The plight of the miners resembled that of the abolitionists a half-century earlier, Chaplin concluded. When one of the strike's leaders, a Socialist named John Brown, was arrested on trumped-up charges and thrown into a bull pen, Chaplin wrote an editorial titled "The Two John Browns." Likening the Socialist Brown to the abolitionist Brown, he advocated direct action to rescue the labor leader, much as abolitionists had planned to rescue Brown during his imprisonment at Harpers Ferry.[13]

"Solidarity Forever"

Likewise the miners' strike in West Virginia and the hunger strike in Chicago both inspired Chaplin to write "Solidarity Forever," for together they demonstrated that another civil war was raging in America, this one over "wage slavery" rather than chattel slavery. "My 'Battle Hymn of Industrial Democracy' was tailored to meet the unique requirements" of Americans who resented "unresisting wage slavery," Chaplain wrote. Much like Northern opponents of chattel slavery, from Lincoln to John Brown, Chaplin argued that liberty and slavery could not coexist. He paraphrased Lincoln: "Man's last, best hope of freedom is at stake." Therefore he wrote and published his lyrics "to the tune of 'John Brown's Body.'" In essence Chaplin sought to purge the conservative strains of the "Battle Hymn" by recoupling it to the radical impulses of the earlier song. The new lyrics were needed to inspire people to fight and die in this new civil war for a new transcendent union.[14]

In six hard-hitting stanzas, "Solidarity Forever" upends bourgeois values. The first stanza highlights the transcendent power of "one big Union," an IWW motto:

When the Union's inspiration through the worker's blood shall run,
There can be no power greater anywhere beneath the sun.
Yet what force on earth is weaker than the feeble strength of one?
But the Union makes us strong.

The second stanza emphasizes capitalists' greed and recalls John Brown by invoking the lash and evoking slaves' desperation and a vision of insurrection:

Is there aught we hold in common with the greedy parasite,
Who would lash us into serfdom and would crush us with his might?
Is there anything left for us but to organize and fight?
For the Union makes us strong.

The fifth stanza calls corporate capitalists thieves who have stolen workers' labor and hence their freedom:

They have taken untold millions that they never toiled to earn.
But without our brain and muscle not a single wheel can turn.
We can break their haughty power; gain our freedom when we learn
That the Union makes us strong.

What is most surprising about the song, given the common association of labor radicals with secularism, is that it ends on a millennialist note. Chaplin retains Julia Ward Howe's imagery but revises the "Battle Hymn" by associating the inauguration of the new age with a transformation of labor relations:

In our hands is placed a power greater than their hoarded gold;
Greater than the might of armies, magnified a thousand fold.
We can bring to birth the new world from the ashes of the old,
For the Union makes us strong.[15]

"Solidarity Forever" became a sensation. It was a favorite on picket lines, often with a dozen different native tongues joining in. Defendants would sing it as they filed out of a courtroom, after being sentenced to years in prison, and prisoners would sing it to rally their cellmates. The song became so popular that most hoboes riding the rails knew it by heart. Often it erupted spontaneously, and given the contexts in which it was sung there were rarely accompanying instruments. It became the anthem not only of the IWW but of the labor movement more generally. The musicologist John Greenway called it "unquestionably the greatest song yet produced by American labor."[16]

Chaplin attributed the song's success to the power of solidarity: "I wrote it . . . for a bunch of 'timber beasts,' 'gandy dancers' [railroad workers] and 'harvest stiffs' who wouldn't have had a full belly or a place to flop if they hadn't learned to become the 'stick-together guys that organize.'. . . It was they, rather than any special skill on my part, that breathed the breath of life into whatever it was that made the words and rhythm click." Much like Howe had, he disclaimed exclusive authorship of the hymn. And he downplayed his position as a leader of Wobblies: "There were no supermen among us—and none would have been tolerated." Wobblies were "we guys," not "I guys."[17]

Chaplin's hymn highlights the spiritual nature of worker solidarity and the "one big Union" that Wobblies fought for. The "one big Union" of the "Battle Hymn" was defined explicitly in providential terms; in contrast, one might conclude that since "Solidarity Forever" never directly invokes God, it points to a secularization of the millennialist fervor of the original. But it would be a mistake to interpret Chaplin, his song, or the Wobblies as secular or atheistic.[18] "Solidarity Forever" enabled workers disenchanted with the "Battle Hymn," which obscures material conditions, to couple their millennial aspirations with social and economic transformation. It fed the civil religion of America's working class and radicals. Chaplin suggested as much when he wrote, in an essay on why he composed "Solidarity Forever": "Nothing less than the solidarity of freeborn, God-guided men can make the 'final conflict' anything other than Armageddon."[19]

★

RALPH CHAPLIN WAS NOT merely a song writer; he was also a central figure in the IWW.[20] His life highlights the degree to which the Wobblies' commitment to their cause was a religion, much like the "sacred vocation" of the abolitionists, whose millennial vision of universal freedom the IWW sought to emulate.[21] Chaplin was born on a farm in Cloud County, Kansas, in 1887, the year the Haymarket conspirators were hanged. His parents had moved there from New England. His mother was a direct descendent of William Bradford, the founder of Plymouth Colony. His paternal great-grandfather fought as a patriot in the Battle of Saratoga, and his grandfather served under General George Armstrong Custer in the Civil War. Chaplin's impressive ancestry suggested to him the indigenous nature of labor radicalism, an aspect of America's pioneer spirit: "My ancestors . . . were at war with their generation just as I have been at war with mine. My father and mother . . . did their pioneering in the good black soil of Kansas. I did much of mine on the soapbox, on the picket line, and in prison."[22]

Even as a young boy Chaplin learned that a distinguished ancestry had little value in the new age of industrial capitalism. He spent his youth shuttling between a series of failed midwestern farmsteads and Chicago, a rapidly growing city and a center of union organizing and radical ferment. His father got a job as a freight-yard tower man, which he then lost during the Pullman Strike of 1894, when the American Railway Union that he joined struck in support of the Pullman strikers, prompting his employer to call in strikebreakers. The experience had a profound effect on the young Chaplin: "I had thought a job was something that was always there. Now, I knew otherwise. And a feeling of panic got me."[23]

Perhaps as a result, young Chaplin frequently fought other boys, threw brickbats at posters of politicians he didn't like, and did poorly in school, despite his love of art, literature, and music. His mother, a devout Methodist and talented musician who played the organ at church, worried that he would "become a hoodlum or a clodhopper."[24]

Things improved a bit when the Chaplins moved back to a farm, this one in Iowa. It was there that Ralph had his first religious experience. One morning at family worship his mother recited the line from Song of Solomon, "terrible as an army with banners." "[The words] gripped my imagination . . . [and] set me on fire," Chaplin recalled. But he didn't know why. Later that day "the sky darkened and the earth was shaken with thunder." He suddenly understood that faith could blot out fear. "All I had to do was keep that inner glow alive—be ablaze with it, and all other things would shrink to insignificance." Music brightened his divine "inner glow"; when hymns were sung "the heavens seemed to open." Eventually he would express his faith through art and politics.[25]

The Iowa farm proved another failure, and the family returned to Chicago. His father was forced to become a day laborer, wandering the streets every morning in search of employment. The family became "migratory tenants," moving from one cheap tenement to another. Ralph began reading Socialist pamphlets shoved under the door. Increasingly his world seemed an epic battle between capital and labor, jobs and layoffs, strikes and strikebreakers.[26]

Then he had another conversion experience, this one in the form of a prophetic dream. It happened on Independence Day in the late 1890s. An old revolver he was cleaning exploded in his hand, almost severing his thumb and index finger. Dr. Gentry, a faith healer and Christian Socialist, tended the wound. He kneeled at Ralph's bedside, laid on his hands, and prayed for Ralph's recovery. He refused to accept a fee, saying, "God's healing is free to all." Ralph fell asleep and dreamed that he "was standing on a hill overlooking an unfamiliar city": "It was very dark, and my hand was hurting. There was a blinding flash of lightning and a roar of thunder. Each of the tall buildings in the distance curved like the letter S and crashed horribly to the ground." The message of the dream suggested that God and socialism could smite these shrines of capitalism to the ground.[27]

Ralph's hand "healed perfectly," and soon he was standing on soapboxes on the streets of Chicago, lecturing on socialism and the power of God to passersby. On January 1, 1900, he wrote in his black notebook, "A new century is being born, the Century of Socialism." He was thirteen years old, filled with visions of a new age.[28]

A few years later Charles Kerr, his Socialist mentor, recommended he read Walt Whitman's *Leaves of Grass*, calling it "rebel poetry of the highest order." Chaplin had been reading Karl Marx and Peter Kropotkin and had almost convinced himself, despite his religious experiences, that he had "outgrown both God and country." Decades after its first appearance in 1855, *Leaves of Grass* was becoming popular among labor radicals and other reformers. "It was a revelation," Chaplin said. The poems offered him a vision of society defined by an ethos of comradeship, equality, and respect for all people. And it rejuvenated his spiritual faith. Whitman became for Chaplin—and many other Socialist leaders, including Eugene Debs and Horace Traubel—a prophet whose poetry embodied their vision of a new age in which the transformation of labor relations was the material manifestation of Christ's Second Coming.[29]

Whitman's poetry also offered Chaplin a model of "grassroots frontier" activism that looked askance at too much power held in the hands of a few. The bureaucratization of labor was one of the major evils of capitalism, Chaplin concluded. The poet had warned against such bureaucratic and tyrannical power in "Walt Whitman's Caution," and Chaplin quoted him:

> To The States, or any one of them, or any city of The States, *Resist much,*
>   *obey little,*
> Once unquestioning obedience, once fully enslaved;
> Once fully enslaved, no nation, state, city, of this earth, ever afterward
>   resumes its liberty.[30]

Chaplin also invoked Thomas Jefferson in his struggle against bureaucracies: "The government that governs best is the government that governs least" became a sort of mantra. For the rest of his life he would oppose powerful bureaucracies in any form, from corporations and communism to the corporatist labor unions emerging out of the New Deal. He was convinced that bureaucratic power threatened human relationships and undermined the sacred nature of solidarity and democracy.[31]

In 1910 Chaplin became a convert to the IWW's grassroots system of organizing and vision of industrial democracy. He was working in Chicago as an illustrator, had married Edith Medin, a Swedish immigrant and fellow artist, and had befriended William ("Big Bill") Haywood, an IWW founder, and Vincent St. John, its secretary-treasurer. That year his employer, the Chicago Portrait Company, cut employee rates. Chaplin organized the city's commercial artists, spearheaded a strike, and was fired. Already a Socialist and an admirer of Debs, he now became convinced that the IWW's "program of revolutionary industrial unionism," coupled with its strategy of direct action—meaning any action "at the point of production" that could improve workers' conditions—"answered the needs of the world's downtrodden proletariat."[32]

The Wobblies were the most inclusive labor organization in the country. Unlike the American Federation of Labor (AFL) and trade unions, which organized by craft, Wobblies sought to undermine corporate capitalism by organizing *all* industrial laborers. They welcomed everyone—blacks, Asians, Indians, women, foreigners, and natives—into "One Big Union." Their goal was to achieve universal solidarity, followed by a general strike and the ultimate abolition of the wage system. The result would be the material analogue of Christ's Second Coming, in which all workers would live in a new age of peace and prosperity.[33]

What this new age would look like was not entirely clear, even to the most devout Wobbly. Most agreed that the state would cease to exist. "There will be no such thing as the State or States," Haywood said. "The industries will take the place of what are now existing states." Each worker would receive an ownership share of the industry and an equal vote and enjoy the fruits of his or her own labor. But while preaching revolution, Wobblies also practiced "pork-chop unionism," seeking full employment with fair pay, safe conditions, and reasonable work hours. "We can talk of Utopia afterwards," Haywood said. "The greatest need is employment."[34]

The tactic of direct action reflected the Wobblies' belief that political power was a reflection of economic power. When the IWW was founded in 1905, its members forged an alliance with Debs's Socialist Party. The goal was that Wobblies would represent the "economic expression" and the Socialists the "political expression" of the working class in its war against capitalism. But by 1908 that alliance had already been severed. West Coast Wobblies in particular had little faith in political action. As one itinerant Wobbly lumberjack put it, "The fellow who owns the property makes the law." Wobblies' frustration with political power also reflected their makeup; they consisted of large numbers of migratory workers, who could not establish legal voting residence because they moved too often, along with immigrants, blacks, women, and child laborers who were denied the vote.[35]

Direct action included strikes, slowdowns, civil disobedience, and "sabotage," a loaded term that Chaplin and other Wobblies tried to soften by emphasizing its origins from the French *sabot* (wooden shoe), which referred to an era in which workers dropped their shoes into machines to protest conditions. While most Americans interpreted sabotage as a violent attack on property or persons, most Wobblies viewed it as a form of nonviolent civil disobedience—tampering with machines without destroying them, for instance. To be sure, they often employed militant rhetoric, such as Haywood's statements, "I despise the law" and "I am not a law-abiding citizen." But IWW pamphlets downplayed violent aggression: "We do not advocate violence; it is to be discouraged." In short, most Wobblies believed that "neither bullets nor ballots" but rather nonviolent direct action could achieve economic justice and usher in the millennium.[36]

In certain respects the IWW's industrial unionism resembled European syndicalism (or anarcho-syndicalism). Both groups believed in decentralized power and equal representation throughout the rank and file. Both emphasized that "the working class and the employing class have nothing in common" and that the concentration of industrial power into "fewer and fewer hands" was inherently corrupt, as the IWW Preamble stated. Both sought the abolition of the capitalist system. And both imagined that in the new order the political state would cease to exist, replaced by worker-run industries. But Wobblies emphasized the democratic and indigenous nature of their organization. Theirs was a bottom-up vision reflecting a pioneer spirit and an American-style millennium.[37] They based their understanding of economics on felt experience, not the writings of European philosophers and theorists. In fact many ignored revolutionary writings even if they knew of them. "I've never read Marx's *Capital*, but I have the marks of capital all over me," Haywood said. Music, not philosophy, spoke directly and powerfully to Wobblies' experience.[38]

In fact, in the eyes of most Americans, who likely did not appreciate the nuances of the Left, what most distinguished Wobblies from other labor organizations was the variety and intensity of their music. It was through their songs that they disseminated their vision of solidarity, hope, revolution, and millennium. Their songbook was their bible. Entitled *I.W.W. Songs: To Fan the Flames of Discontent*, but better known as the "Little Red Songbook," it was more widely distributed than any other IWW publication. First published in 1909, it went through thirty-five editions, with several printings per edition, and many translations. Millions of copies were distributed, and in the late teens multiple editions were published in a single year. It had a standard format: the IWW Preamble appeared on the first page; the rest of the book consisted of song lyrics that imparted to listeners the message of the Preamble.

Joe Hill, the Wobbly who became one of the most influential writers of protest music in the twentieth century—and a legend in his own right—explained the power of these songs: "A pamphlet, no matter how good, is never read more than once, but a song is learned by heart and repeated over and over; and I maintain that if a person can put a few cold, common sense facts into a song, and dress them . . . up in a cloak of humor to take the dryness off them, he will succeed in reaching a great number of workers." Hill's maxim helps explain the power of "Solidarity Forever." As one organizer said of Chaplin's song, "If you will analyze [its words], you will see it is practically a restatement of the IWW Preamble."[39]

Several writers invested Wobbly songs with spiritual power. Chaplin explicitly called the IWW a religion and its songs "hymns": "It was the fanatical Religion of Rebellion at whose shrine . . . we chanted hymns of hope and hate." The writer Wallace Stegner echoed this sentiment. The IWW was a "militant church," which "enlisted all the enthusiasm, idealism, rebelliousness, devotion, and selfless zeal of its members. . . . It had its legendry, its lore, its songs." But the richest description of the significance of Wobbly songs comes from James Jones's novel *From Here to Eternity* (1951), in which an imprisoned World War II soldier recalls the Wobblies of his boyhood days: "What they really were was a religion. They were workstiffs and bindlebums like you and me, but they were welded together with a vision we dont possess. It was their vision that made them great. And it was their belief in it that made them powerful. And sing! you never heard anyone sing the way those guys sang! Nobody sings like they did unless its for a religion."[40]

Like many religious groups, the IWW appropriated music from other denominations and sects. The majority of songs in the "Little Red Songbook" are based on tunes from religious and patriotic songs. Joe Hill, Jack Walsh, and Harry ("Haywire Mac") McClintock all parodied gospel tunes of the Salvation Army (Wobblies called it the "Starvation Army") while competing for attention with the Army's missionaries and brass bands on street corners in Spokane, Portland, and San Pedro (Los Angeles Harbor). The best-known such song, now a classic, is Hill's "The Preacher and the Slave." It parodies the Salvation Army's hymn, "Sweet Bye and Bye":

Long-haired preachers come out every night,
Try to tell you what's wrong and what's right;
But when asked how 'bout something to eat
They will answer with voices so sweet:
     Chorus:

You will eat bye and bye,
In that glorious land above the sky;
Work and pray, live on hay,
You'll get pie in the sky when you die.[41]

One Wobbly defended these parodies: "We liked to steal the old Christian hymns because everyone knew the tune. We just changed the words so they made more sense." Wobblies bore from within mainstream culture. Their songs gave resonance to the IWW Preamble, which told members to form "the structure of the new society within the shell of the old."[42]

Wobblies preferred hymns over other musical forms not merely because of their popularity and accessibility but because appropriating them allowed for a singing style that, in the words of one scholar, possessed a "singular combination of didacticism and parody." A common theme was the hypocrisy of mainstream moral and religious authorities who sided with the powerful against the powerless. Employing religious music heightened the critique. By harnessing a radical message to the "Battle Hymn," for example, Chaplin highlighted the ways it had strayed from its abolitionist past and had come to serve those celebrating the status quo. In changing the lyrics he recovered their original radicalism.[43]

★

THE COMPOSITION OF "SOLIDARITY FOREVER" in January 1915 coincided with the beginning of four years of extraordinary growth for the IWW. In one year alone (1916–17) membership more than doubled, from 40,000 to over 100,000. But perhaps the best gauge of the IWW's vitality was in the countless "acts of mass singing," which emboldened workers to unite and fight for industrial democracy. In Everett, Washington, fifty thousand striking loggers "bellowed out" "Solidarity Forever" to call for an eight-hour day, which they eventually won. One observer noted that even workers who had "never heard the song before . . . felt that this was their song, and that it was as closely allied to their strike . . . as a hymn is allied to religion. . . . The singing went straight to their heart."[44]

Chaplin acknowledged the importance of songs to the IWW's rapid growth. Beginning "around 1915," he said, "the rebel songs of the IWW resounded from every threshing rig, every freight train, and not a few hoosegows [prisons]." "Solidarity Forever" was by no means the only song contributing to the swelling rebel chorus. In fact Chaplin credited Joe Hill most of all with making the IWW a "singing organization." Indeed Hill had created the "Little Red Songbook," illustrating and publishing the first edition at his own expense. Hill's most popular songs, "Casey Jones," "Rebel Girl," "Workers of the World Awaken," and "The Preacher and the Slave," remain folk classics. Although Chaplin never met Joe Hill, he felt "a spiritual kinship" with him. "Solidarity Forever" was published in between "Casey Jones" and "The Preacher and the Slave" in the 1915 edition of the "Little Red Songbook."[45]

Music was not the only impetus of Wobbly growth and visibility beginning in 1915. That same year Chaplin created IWW "stickerettes," small two-toned (red-and-black) adhesive stickers that could be applied to everything from boxcars and bunkhouses to billboards and factory gates. With the stickerettes, called "silent agitators," Chaplin and other illustrators parodied patriotic and bourgeois clichés in their war on capitalism. One had "Sabotage" in large letters with the image of a wooden shoe, followed by a quote by "Big Bill" Haywood: "Sabotage means to push back, pull out, or break off the fangs of Capitalism." The first print run of 500,000 stickerettes sold out quickly. Wobblies loved them. One harvest stiff estimated that a dime packet of stickerettes could reach more than one thousand people. It was said that at the height of the stickerette campaign, almost every boxcar in the country advertised the IWW. In April 1917, following America's entry into World War I, four million stickerettes were sold in less than a week.[46]

The war itself greatly contributed to the IWW's surging popularity. Large numbers of Americans essentially agreed with the IWW that the United States had entered the war in order to enrich its business interests. The war also boosted the economy and created labor scarcities, making it more costly for employers to fight unions. The IWW struck in those industries that were considered vital to the war effort—agriculture, lumber, and mining—and achieved significant concessions from employers.[47]

The backlash against Wobblies was intense, however. Even before the war they were called "America's most damnable enemy" and "America's cancer sore," and systematically denied the rights of free speech, assembly, debate, and fair trials. Governing authorities generally refused to tolerate dissent against capitalism, much as the antebellum South had silenced antislavery agitation. As the radical economist Scott Nearing noted, "The advocate of a labor state is as unpopular in a capitalist society as the abolitionist was in the Carolinas before the Civil War." Wobblies were arrested simply for reading the Declaration of Independence or the

Bill of Rights on street corners. And with the onset of war, they were accused of aiding the enemy. IWW "means simply, solely, and only 'Imperial Wilhelm's Warriors,'" declared Senator Henry Ashurst of Arizona. In November 1916, when three hundred Wobblies tried to establish free speech in Everett, Washington, by singing "Solidarity Forever," police and vigilantes started shooting, killing five workers and wounding scores more.[48]

Persecution against the IWW during the war produced a host of martyrs. Frank Little, an outspoken antiwar Wobbly and a close friend of Ralph Chaplin, was lynched outside of Butte, Montana, for organizing metal miners. In August 1917 company guards broke into his room in the middle of the night, beat him up, tied him to the rear fender of their car, and dragged him several miles to a railroad trestle, where they hanged him and pinned a sign on his body: "First and last warning."[49]

Joe Hill, of course, became the most famous Wobbly martyr. Convicted of murdering a Salt Lake City grocer—on the "wispiest of evidence," according to the definitive biography by William Adler—he was executed by a firing squad in November 1915. The state could produce neither motive, murder weapon, nor positive identification. The most damning piece of evidence against him was an IWW red card found in his pocket.[50]

Five thousand Wobblies attended Hill's funeral in Chicago. Jim Larkin gave the final speech over Hill's grave at Graceland Cemetery and saw in him—and in all Wobblies—the legacy of John Brown, a warrior willing to die for the cause of freedom: "[Let] our slogan for the future be: Joe Hill's body lies mouldering in the grave, but the cause goes marching on." John Brown's soul was indeed marching on, for Joe Hill was soon commemorated in song as "the man who never died":

> "Joe Hill ain't dead," he says to me.
> "Joe Hill ain't never died."
> Where workingmen are out on strike,
> Joe Hill is at their side.[51]

★

PATRIOTIC WAR HYSTERIA ULTIMATELY crushed the IWW and "Solidarity Forever" as a Wobbly song. The IWW opposed the war as inhumane and America's entry into it as a capitalist conspiracy. One large stickerette encouraged draft resistance by proclaiming, "YOUNG MAN: The lowest aim in your life is to be a good soldier. . . . A good soldier is a blind, heartless, soulless, murderous machine. . . . Don't be a Soldier—Be a Man." Chaplin, now editor of *Solidarity*, the Wobbly organ, advised members to register for the draft but to write on their draft card, "IWW opposed to war." This kind of dissent, coupled with the Wobblies' phenomenal growth and fears about the rise of Bolsheviks in Russia, prompted the government to strike back. The Wilson administration passed the Espionage Act, prohibiting any interference with the war effort, including strikes. Thousands of immigrants were deported.[52]

Then, on September 5, 1917, federal agents raided every IWW branch office and union hall in the country, as well as the homes of Wobbly officials, and seized everything they could find. They took Chaplin's artwork, a bundle of love letters to his wife, and his son's toys. On September 29 a grand jury indicted 166 Wobbly leaders on five counts of obstructing the war effort. A U.S. attorney summed up the government's objectives: "Our purpose . . . [is] to put the I.W.W. out of business."[53]

The arrests turned into a patriotic parade. As part of "their contribution to winning the war," Chicago debutantes chauffeured Chaplin, Haywood, and other leaders to the courthouse for their trial. Across the street from the courthouse, a movie theater marquee announced, "Special Feature—The Menace of the I.W.W." On another line, "The Red Viper" flashed on and off spasmodically. A large crowd, screaming, cursing, and raising their fists, surged toward the defendants as they were led into the courthouse, handcuffed in pairs. Two rows of police were needed to hold back the mob.[54] As Chaplin awaited arrest, he sketched an image of himself behind bars, pointing to the viewer. Underneath the image he wrote, "REMEMBER: We are in here for you. You are out there for us." The image would appear on the cover of the 1918 edition of the "Little Red Songbook" in hopes of raising money for the defense fund.

It had little effect. The government had succeeded in its effort to suppress the IWW. Every defendant was found guilty of obstructing the war effort. On August 30, 1918, Chaplin's thirty-first birthday, Judge Kenesaw Mountain Landis—later commissioner of baseball—sentenced him and fourteen other Wobbly leaders, including Bill Haywood, to twenty years in prison, the legal maximum.[55] The court found no evidence of violence or destruction of property and ignored the fact that over 90 percent of eligible Wobblies had registered for the draft. Indeed prosecutors could not identify a single crime committed by a Wobbly

"Solidarity Forever"

defendant. So they drew attention to "the seditious and disloyal *character and teachings* of the organization." They used Wobblies' own publications against them as evidence, including "Solidarity Forever" and the "Little Red Songbook." As Haywood wryly noted, "I always thought it was against the law to force American citizens to give testimony against themselves."[56]

Chaplin experienced something of an awakening in prison. While serving one year in Cook County Jail and almost four years in the penitentiary at Leavenworth, Kansas, his hair turned white. He saw friends go mad and inmates get murdered. And countless times he heard hardened, unregenerate men cry out in agony, "Oh, God!" From their anguished pleas he acquired a newfound appreciation of prayer: it offered hope amid helplessness and "shut out the cruelty and ugliness of the world," if only for a moment. A similar sensation occurred when he agreed to paint a life-size portrait of "Fellow-Worker Jesus" for the Catholic chapel, using stolen materials. He was punished for this "impertinence," as he knew he would be, but the spiritual reward overshadowed the cost: being transferred to a much smaller cell. Then, too, he found inspiration among Menonite conscientious objectors, fellow inmates who refused prison work because officials had cut off their beards and had forced them to wear buttons, which violated their religious principles. The guards tried to "break" them, as Chaplin recalled, by handcuffing them to their cells eight hours a day for two weeks. The handcuffs cut into their wrists, their fingers turned blue and cracked open, and blood trickled down their upraised arms. But they remained unbroken. Chaplin realized that Wobblies and Mennonites "met on common ground" in their adherence to faith and principle.[57]

Writing helped him feel free amid "hell's forty acres," as he called prison. His friend Scott Nearing orchestrated the publication of his prison poems, *Bars and Shadows*. Several are sonnets, evoking the sensations of captivity and the possibilities of rebirth. He also wrote epistles in the hopes of becoming free. His "Open Letter to President Harding" helped spark public interest in the release of all political prisoners. And his wife, Edith, appealed to First Lady Florence Harding: "When Ralph was taken to prison our little boy was eight years old," she wrote. "He is now thirteen. It is my boy that is paying the greatest price. . . . To us, Mrs. Harding, [prison] has been an eternal nightmare." Her letter helped Chaplin's case, according to the White House secretary. In June 1923 Harding commuted Chaplin's and other

Wobblies' sentences on the condition that they henceforth act as loyal and law-abiding citizens.[58]

After his release, Chaplin went back to the IWW, but the organization no longer enjoyed the same degree of cultural influence. Haywood had jumped bail and fled to Russia to avoid imprisonment, and owing to the incarcerations of other organizers, IWW membership declined from over 100,000 in 1917 to 38,000 in 1924. Increasingly Communists rather than Wobblies were seen as the greatest threat to capitalism, even though membership in the Communist Party USA, and other radical labor organizations, also declined dramatically. To Chaplin, Communists were "militaristic and coldly political," more interested in gaining power than in securing freedom for workers. "All I could see in [them] was the replacement of unions by a totalitarian Labor Front." He and other Wobblies increasingly feared that Communists overshadowed "our One Big Union" with their top-heavy militancy.[59]

Through this transition, "Solidarity Forever" remained as popular as ever.[60] The Communist Party "cherished" it and called it their own. On May Day 1930 in New York City, some seventy thousand Communists sang "Solidarity Forever" as they marched "against imperialism." They joined millions of Communists throughout the world who took to the streets in solidarity, crossing "frontiers of race and nationality," according to one sympathetic reporter. Four years later fifteen thousand antiwar and anti-Fascist demonstrators, mostly Communists and including three thousand blacks, marched from Columbus Circle to Madison Square Park, singing "Solidarity Forever." And in 1935 twenty thousand Communists and left-wing Socialists fraternized at Madison Square Garden. They debated their respective tactics of "parliamentarism" and "armed insurrection" and, of course, sang "Solidarity Forever."[61]

Communists, however, stripped "Solidarity Forever" of its millennialist punch. In 1937 the Manhattan Chorus recorded a version of the anthem for Timely Records, a Communist label. They reduced Chaplin's song to four stanzas and replaced his apocalyptic last stanza with a more tepid and secular one:

The workers learned their lesson now as everyone can see
The workers know the bosses are their greatest enemy
We'll fight and fight until we win our final victory
For one big solid union!

Even before this recording, Communists had secularized Chaplin's song, for in borrowing and adapting folk songs, it was common to retain the first stanza and the chorus and replace subsequent stanzas with language that spoke more directly to the new group of singers.[62]

One leftist minister bemoaned the new secular nature of "Solidarity Forever." In 1933 Wilbur Patterson Thirkfield, a bishop of the A.M.E. Church and former president of Howard University, described the cultural decline of the black church and the rise of "infidel leadership." He cited a recent demonstration of four thousand black and white Communists who had marched together through Harlem to protest the killing of a black comrade by the police. While acknowledging the significance of this integrated event, he lamented its message: the black band leading the marchers sang "Solidarity Forever" instead of "'John Brown's Body,' with its old religious refrain."[63]

Chaplin witnessed a similar apostasy in his song and in the labor movement. At one open-air labor meeting in Chicago in the early 1930s, a group of Young Communists interrupted his speech, shouting, "Don't listen to that reactionary!" He ignored them, and so they tried to drown him out by singing "Solidarity Forever," unaware that Chaplin was the song's author. Chaplin said he felt like Dr. Frankenstein, "when the monster he'd created rose to threaten those he loved."[64] He seemed happier speaking at Walt Whitman Fellowship dinners than at labor meetings. Instead of contending with shrill and dogmatic Communists, he met in fellowship with other Whitman disciples such as Carl Sandburg. They read from *Leaves of Grass*, their new bible, and studied its gospel of poetic and mystic union.[65]

Finally, in 1936, Chaplin left the IWW. The break occurred after he was fired as editor of *Industrial Worker*, a Wobbly organ, owing to cost-cutting measures and internal politics. In his resignation letter he lashed out at the "would-be dictators" who now controlled the IWW. He also blamed the rank and file for permitting "itself to be shoved around by designing and ambitious politicians." Wobblies had become "just like . . . any other top-heavy outfit," he concluded. He ritualized his resignation while attending the funeral of Nina Spies, an "old faithful" (non-Communist) labor radical. He was asked to speak, and as he did the history of America and its labor movement suddenly "became clear to [him]." It was marked by division, strife, and warfare; he yearned for union, harmony, and peace. He felt as if he gave one of the best speeches of his life: "I spoke as a human being to another human being—not as a dogmatist." Then, as he watched the dirt being shoveled onto the grave, he removed his red-and-black Wobbly ribbon from his buttonhole and dropped it in. "[This] belongs to the past," he said. "Let it too be buried."[66]

★

THE TRIPLE THREAT OF communism, capitalism, and New Deal unionism led Chaplin to abandon his revolutionary idealism and seek rapprochement between capitalists and laborers. Initially he viewed the passage of the Wagner Act and the launching in 1935 of the Congress of Industrial Organizations (CIO) as part of the same old "pattern of slavery" that emerged with the rise of corporate America. "Organized labor was now big business," he said. But he was even more distraught to see so many "neo-liberal friends" embrace the "Marxist jargon" of communism and look to Moscow as the Promised Land. There were thus three enemies—capitalism, communism, and New Deal unionism—each one an evil bureaucracy that consolidated power into the hands of a few. But communism overshadowed these other two enemies in its threat to America. Chaplin said he personally knew over a hundred people who had become victims of Communist purges. And so beginning in the late 1930s he concluded that the established labor unions he had criticized, the organized Christianity he had rejected, and the capitalism he had rebelled against together offered "the last remaining bulwark against communism, history's blackest form of tyranny." Better to fight the devil with his own fire than to lose the last, best hope of freedom.[67]

Chaplin also felt that his former "revolutionary idealism . . . had backfired." Only totalitarian regimes profited from the kind of "hell-raising" that he had encouraged as a Wobbly organizer, editor, and songwriter: "I resolved to dedicate what remained of my life to more rational relationships between American employers and wage-earners." He renounced the axiom, embraced by Robber Barons, Wobblies, and Communists, that the end justified the means.[68]

Chaplin's postwar writings and speeches reflected his resolve to create a healthy union between employees and employers. His essays shared much in common with Peter Drucker and John Kenneth Galbraith, who articulated the concept of "countervailing power." Unions and corporations *needed* each other; their relationship constituted a healthy partnership, a union that vitally contributed to American affluence and the fight against communism. He contributed to a magazine dedicated to this vision: *Partners: The Magazine of Labor and Management.* This vision of partnership between labor and management was a far cry from his utopian Wobbly vision, as he acknowledged. But he preferred it to "any other earthly system." Significantly he retained his millennialist vision. He reimagined Armageddon in light of the cold war: the "final conflict" was no longer between workers and capitalists, but between Americans (and their allies) and Communists.[69]

Chaplin's worldview had shifted profoundly from his Wobbly days. Indeed the change was as dramatic in his mind as the Communists' appropriation of "Solidarity Forever." He now realized why his song was so popular with the Communists: they loved its martial beat and militant language but transposed his vision of sacred solidarity into secular "monolithic statism," as he put it.[70]

More than ever, Chaplin felt like Dr. Frankenstein lamenting his creation. He remained proud of the anarchic, American pioneer spirit that had spawned "Solidarity Forever" and the "working stiffs" for whom he wrote it. But he was revolted by its use by Communists and winced when he heard it sung by New Deal unions and politicians looking to win elections: "All of us [old Wobblies] deeply resent seeing a song that was uniquely our own used as a singing commercial for the soft-boiled type of post–Wagner Act industrial unionism that uses million-dollar slush funds to persuade their congressional office boys to do chores for them."[71]

These new bureaucracies had commercialized "Solidarity Forever," making it more popular than ever among left-of-center Americans. In 1936–37 auto workers in Flint, Michigan, sat down inside General Motors' plants to fight for recognition of the United Auto Workers (UAW), a CIO affiliate. Singing "Solidarity Forever" kept up the workers' morale and contributed to a remarkable victory that opened the doors to union contracts throughout the auto industry and also in steel, rubber, and glass. General Motors and the UAW signed a "peace pact" and viewed themselves as partners rather than enemies. A few years later "Solidarity Forever" came to be identified with General Motors the company, not just its unions. Company officials even let workers sing the song at corporate-sponsored events. "Never did I expect to hear General Motors play 'Solidarity Forever,'" wrote the eminent black leader and labor radical W. E. B. Du Bois. "Now anything can happen."[72]

Not surprisingly the UAW adopted "Solidarity Forever" as its anthem. It dropped the three stanzas that evoked the transition to an industrial society ("It is we who plowed the prairies / built the cities where they trade"). But it retained Chaplin's lyrics in the other three stanzas.[73]

Some New Deal unionists were "originalists," preferring "John Brown's Body" to "Solidarity Forever." In 1936 at the Firestone Tire and Rubber Company in Detroit, workers collectively sat down on the job after learning that their employer would not reconsider its suspension of a union committee man. The machines stopped and the shop suddenly became very quiet. The silence terrified some of the workers, prompting a tire builder near the window to declare, "Jesus Christ, it's like the end of the world." His outburst provoked wild cheering. Above the cheers someone started chanting "John Brown's Body," and others joined in the chorus. Workers "were nearly weeping, racked with sudden and deep emotion" as they sang "but his soul goes marchin' on." Like the Wobblies, New Deal unions recalled John Brown's martyrdom to stiffen workers' resolve. Some organizers even compared the sit-down strike to Brown's raid on Harpers Ferry.[74]

Chaplin's resentment of the big unions singing "Solidarity Forever" softened when his song received proper tribute. In 1960 the AFL-CIO published its own songbook and borrowed several tunes from the IWW's "Little Red Songbook."[75] "Solidarity Forever" is the first song in the collection, the editors calling it "the most popular union song on the North American Continent." "If a union member knows only one song, it is almost sure to be this," they continue. "It has become, in effect, the anthem of the labor movement." Chaplin was flattered by the praise, just as he was when he overheard a labor professor tell a student that "the story of 'Solidarity Forever' is one of the great success stories of our day." It was hard to feel resentful in the face of such accolades.[76]

Still, Chaplin believed that the bureaucratization of unions had stripped labor songs of their former power. "Highly efficient public relations experts . . . have taken over the field of spontaneous mass singing that once inspired better proletarian songsters than myself for something more rewarding than notoriety, fame, or coin," he wrote in 1960. Wobblies had sung "Solidarity Forever" for a higher cause, and they "roared it out to the cockeyed world." Today's workers sang for themselves, and their songs "lacked the old wallop." The critic Ed Marciniak agreed with Chaplin. Writing in 1958 for *Work Magazine*, he lamented that there was too much "business unionism" and not enough "revivalism." As a result, "unionists don't sing anymore." Marciniak described a large labor dinner where the pianist played "Solidarity Forever." Half the audience had never before heard the song, he estimated.[77]

Chaplin was even more troubled by politicians who sang his song for votes. During the 1960 presidential campaign Hubert Humphrey stopped his campaign bus beside a UAW picket line and sang "Solidarity Forever," while Joe Glazer, who had edited the AFL-CIO's songbook and was now serving as "Humphrey's Elvis Presley," played guitar. Chaplin wondered "what kind of solidarity" the duo had in mind. It was not the solidarity he had envisioned when he wrote the song.[78]

Chaplin's criticism of politicians and post–New Deal unions was mild, however, compared to his former revolutionary idealism. From the 1940s until his death in 1961 he acted on his resolve to seek rapprochement between employers and wage earners. "I think every song . . . should be a song of solidarity, rather than a song of division and discord," he wrote in his article criticizing Humphrey and Glazer.[79]

But he recognized that over the years his song had served simultaneously to unite and divide. It united workers against capitalists. It united Communists against capitalists. It united unions and their politicians against conservatives. And it united "big" business and "big" unions against Communists. Here, then, was another reason he sometimes felt like Dr. Frankenstein: in an ethos of conciliation, "Solidarity Forever" sounded cacophonous.

★

IF THE THREAT OF communism was a central factor leading Chaplin away from his revolutionary idealism, religion was another. World War II brought back memories of his religious awakening while in prison during World War I. He remembered being "deeply moved" by a mural of Christ breaking bread that hung above the altar in the Catholic chapel. He recalled the inmates who "devoutly raised their eyes to [his] portrait of 'Fellow Worker Jesus.'" And he thought about the prisoners' plea, "Oh, God!," along with their far more frequent curse, "God damn you!" What if, he now asked himself, "we just as freely God-blessed those around us? Here was the instrument of true solidarity, the real clue to Man's salvation, and the best weapon against totalitarianism. We must love one another, or, in the end, we'd destroy ourselves." He began to articulate a new civil religion that blended the "Bill of Rights with the Sermon on the Mount." Instead of placing his hopes in one big union to make workers strong, he looked to a union of all Americans that would make the nation strong—strong enough to fight communism.[80]

Until this point Chaplin's only religion had been his Whitman-like faith in "the dignity and worth of the working man" and woman, as he said. He now yearned for a religious community with more institutional support than Walt Whitman Fellowship dinners. During World War II he and Edith joined the First Congregational Church of Tacoma, Washington, where they lived. He was uninterested in sectarian debates. What he expected from his church was "affirmation of the reality of God and guidance in a basic faith on which men of differing opinions and interests might agree."[81]

Chaplin ends his autobiography, *Wobbly* (1948), with his joining the church and articulating his new civil religion. Soon after it was published, he received a letter of praise from Father Paul Murphy, a Jesuit priest and the director of St. Joseph's Retreat League for workers in Boston. Father Murphy had never met Chaplin but read and admired *Wobbly*, saying it "should do immense good for the workers of this country." He was deeply interested in Chaplin's spiritual growth and urged him to study Catholic doctrines: "You have seen so little of the mighty truths that establish the validity of Catholic Faith. Every conclusion you came to at the end of your book was so much in the right direction. But you are still short of the full sunlight. One who has fought so honestly and bravely for justice and truth, as you have, must keep searching for the full answer that God so surely has provided to 'men of good-will.'"[82]

So began a rich epistolary mentorship. Over the next year Father Murphy guided Chaplin toward the Catholic Church. He sent him books, arranged to have a Tacoma priest meet with him, and answered doctrinal questions. Father Joseph McSorley, a Paulist priest from New York City who had helped Dorothy Day establish the Catholic Worker movement in 1933, also encouraged Chaplin to join the Church. McSorley had never met Chaplin but, like Murphy, had read and enjoyed *Wobbly*. Chaplin expressed an interest in meeting him. He probably knew of McSorley's friendship with Day and their efforts on behalf of workers. Day had been a Wobbly in the late teens and in the early twenties had worked as a journalist in Chicago, where Chaplin lived. In fact in 1922 she roomed at a Chicago Wobbly house that Chapin knew well. While there she was arrested for prostitution and "treated as a whore" until charges were dropped for lack of evidence.[83]

Working together, Murphy and McSorley led Chaplin into the Catholic Church. He was baptized in December 1949 and confirmed three years later. His faith was soon tested, for in 1950 his only child, Vonnie, committed suicide. Chaplin took this as his failure, according to his friend Roger Baldwin, the founder of the American Civil Liberties Union. Chaplin's faith held and the support from his spiritual mentors sustained him. His only written response to his son's death was in his calendar. On the October 1950 page he circled the box that said "Tues 3" and in the upper left corner, in a very shaky hand, wrote "Vonnie died."[84]

Although Chaplin was sympathetic to Day's Catholic Worker movement, there's no evidence that he joined it. Nor did he contribute to its organ, *Catholic Worker*. But at the request of Father McSorley he did write an article for *Catholic World*, the general magazine for Catholics. Published a month before Vonnie died and titled "Religion and the Workingman," it is a jeremiad that ends with a call to faith. Faith in material progress has replaced faith in God, he argues, and as a result an "all-powerful state" has replaced the church of God in "matters of ethics, morals and education." He warns readers not to succumb to these material idols. Seek the living Christ, he urges, "the only principle on earth transcending that of godless destructiveness." Only through Him and His Church—the Catholic Church, he implies—can Americans vanquish godless communism and check the power of a secular state.[85]

In 1955 Chaplin subscribed to William F. Buckley Jr.'s *National Review*, the organ of a resurgent conservative movement, and wrote an admiring letter to the editor. "Congratulations to *National Review*! May it live long and serve worthily as the long-needed house organ of the out-numbered, but still dynamic, American underground that refuses to bend with the prevailing winds of Regimentation, Monopoly, Conformity and Ideological Sleep-walking." Buckley published the tribute and thanked Chaplin.[86]

Most scholars have concluded that Chaplin made a hard right turn and became a neoconservative. After all, he endorsed Buckley's *National Review*, he bemoaned New Deal unions, and in 1947 he lauded Senator Joseph McCarthy's efforts to expose and root out American Communists. But this conclusion is simplistic. Chaplin's endorsement of McCarthy occurred seven years before the senator was censured and publicly disgraced and three years before McCarthy egregiously lied by claiming that he had a list of 205 names of State Department employees who were Communists.[87] Chaplin's admiration for Buckley stemmed from their shared disdain of communism, bureaucracy, regimentation, conformity, and "bigness" in any form. They preferred anarchy (or libertarianism) to statism, and they embraced the tradition of the American pioneer. Buckley emphasized these themes in the early days of the *National Review*. But Chaplin parted company with Buckley's faith in the virtues of untrammeled capitalism and his belief in a "natural" hierarchy based on race and gender.[88]

Throughout his life Chaplin remained loyal to common workers. His closest friends were former Wobblies and inmates. They visited frequently, often without advance notice. His efforts to improve the lot of fellow workers remained remarkably stable, surviving his prison term, the collapse of his Wobbly dream, and his son's suicide. And he remained a "disciple" of Whitman's poetry, which reflected an ethos of empathy and connectedness that included blacks, women, minorities, and Indians. Indeed one of Chaplin's last publications was a protest on behalf of Native American rights. An epic poem, *Only the Drums Remembered* honors the patriotic Nisqually chief Leschi, who was falsely accused of killing a militia soldier in 1855 and hanged.[89]

Chaplin's battle hymn accommodated his changing worldview, from Wobbly radical to anti-Communist reformer to devout Catholic. His evolution resembled the path of many other working-class whites, writers, and artists in the twentieth century. Disdainful of bureaucracy, they distrusted what were called progress and efficiency. Cherishing freedom, they hated communism. Preferring anarchy to statism, they were suspicious of politicians. Forced to choose between big government and big business, they chose the latter because it seemed the lesser of two evils. The specter of communism in an atomic age pulled them out from the radical fringe toward the center.

EVEN AFTER THE DECLINE and obsolescence of the IWW, "Solidarity Forever" remained a Wobbly anthem in drama and fiction, where it enjoyed a vibrant afterlife. Two of the most influential writers in the first half of the twentieth century, Upton Sinclair and John Dos Passos, captured the richness of the Wobbly aesthetic and the power of their anthem.[90]

When Sinclair published his Wobbly play, *Singing Jailbirds: A Drama in Four Acts* (1924), he was one of the most famous writers in America. He had already published over twenty books, most notably *The Jungle* (1906), the novel whose impact prompted the passage of the Pure Food and Drug Act. He wrote as a documentarian, bearing witness to atrocities in the hopes of changing society. Most of his fiction and drama is based on eyewitness reporting and contextual research, and it was read as a "people's history" or narrative nonfiction. In this sense he borrowed from Harriet Beecher Stowe and the abolitionists, who authenticated their fictional characters, plots, and settings with supporting evidence. Sinclair also followed most abolitionists by stressing an immanent or indwelling God and the power of religious faith to change society. As a Christian Socialist, he imagined the Socialist revolution as the material manifestation of Christ's Kingdom on Earth. In *The Jungle* the narrator explains the Socialist movement in just these terms: "It was the new religion of humanity—or you might say it was the fulfillment of the old religion, since it implied but the *literal* application of all the teachings of Christ."[91]

The impetus for *Singing Jailbirds* was Sinclair's involvement in the IWW's Marine Transport Workers strike at San Pedro, California, in 1924. Though not a Wobbly himself, as he disagreed with their indifference to party politics and their strategy of direct action, he was nevertheless "infatuated," as he put it, with their creative use of art in the service of rebellion. And he was a friend of many Wobblies, including Chaplin. During the Marine Transport Workers strike, six hundred Wobblies were jailed one night for singing "Solidarity Forever" and other songs, and several were badly beaten. Outraged, Sinclair decided to join the strikers. He was arrested for reading the Constitution and "held in jail 'incommunicado'" for eighteen hours. In a "Postscript" to the play, he describes his arrest and authenticates the conditions he describes in the play.[92]

Singing Jailbirds dramatizes the Wobblies' millennialist vision, the power of their anthem, and the efforts to silence them. The first act depicts a scene in jail that in his postscript Sinclair calls "an exact account of what happened in the police station at San Pedro." The Dominie, an Episcopal minister based on the Reverend George Chalmers of Philadelphia, gives a sermon from jail. He calls Christ "the working-class revolutionist, the rebel carpenter, the First Wobbly of the World." He prophesies a new dispensation: "In the name of Jesus Christ the Redeemer I prophesy and ordain the downfall of World Capitalism, and the Second Coming of the Saviour in the Social Revolution!" And he describes a new church and a new covenant "sealed with the blood" of Wobbly martyrs. His sermon electrifies the prisoners, who affectionately call him "sky pilot." The police remove the Dominie from the holding cell to silence him, prompting the prisoners to sing "Solidarity Forever." Feeling even more threatened, the police try to gag the singers by closing off the ventilation and turning on the steam heat.[93]

"Red" Adams is the hero-martyr of the drama. He is thrown in the "hole" (solitary confinement) for his role in the strike but continues to protest with a hunger strike that eventually kills him. Red accepts death calmly, however, because he prophesies that his martyrdom will unite the workers. His prophecy is fulfilled. Like John Brown and Joe Hill, Red Adams's soul marches on, inspiring his comrades to keep fighting. "They'll punish you—they'll torture you," Red tells them in death. "But the soul of the working-class is unbreakable; there are no chains, no prison-walls, that can bind the will of the masses." The workers respond by singing Chaplin's hymn.[94]

The play ends with the Dominie giving another sermon and casting Red as the new body of Christ, who has returned to usher in a millennial age: "Upon this hallowed spot, where first His [Red's] spirit appeared to His disciples, and where His message of brotherhood was handed down to posterity— here we assemble with prayer and hymns, to pledge our loyalty to the new dispensation." When the Dominie finishes, he asks his congregation to bare their heads "and join together in singing." The song they sing is, of course, "Solidarity Forever," and the sound penetrates into the "hole," where jailors have just realized that Red is dead. The song terrifies them; they "put their fingers into their ears and run out of the cell in a kind of panic, slamming the door." The singing continues as the curtain falls.[95]

Some critics attacked *Singing Jailbirds;* the *New York Times,* for instance, dismissed its very premise: "The idea of the manual laborer as an oppressed creature . . . is so patently absurd that all the art of stagecraft . . . [is] wasted in the effort to give it the similitude of truth." Overall, though, the reception of the play was surprisingly positive. Even before it was staged, the influential critic Max Beerbohm reviewed it, arguing that Sinclair had visualized "the soul of the working man" to reveal "a fierce and revolutionary folk-spirit." He displayed "a genuine and impressive power of interior revelation."[96]

Most of all, the play appealed to labor radicals. And it highlights, more than any other single document, the power of "Solidarity Forever" and the Wobblies' millennial vision. Although the structure of *Singing Jailbirds* made it challenging to stage, there were productions in New York City in 1926 and 1927 and one in Berlin in 1928 that a reviewer said "did American drama all honor." The play received considerable notice when it opened the 1929 season at the Provincetown Playhouse in New York. It premiered in London in 1930, and it had a revival in New York City in 1934.[97]

★

WHILE SINCLAIR EMPHASIZED "SOLIDARITY FOREVER" as a force for uniting workers, Dos Passos used it to highlight a nation dividing along the lines of class. The song and its Wobbly singers constitute a leitmotiv of *U.S.A.,* a trilogy consisting of *The 42nd Parallel, 1919*, and *The Big Money* (1930–36). The trilogy tells the story of "the decline and fall of the Lincoln republic" from 1900 to the stock market crash of 1929, in which small-scale artisans and entrepreneurs are destroyed by robber barons and their followers.[98]

U.S.A. was a commercial and especially a critical success. Dos Passos became one of the preeminent living novelists, often placed in the same league as Joyce, Hemingway, and Faulkner. When *The Big Money* was published in 1936, he appeared on the cover of *Time*, which compared *U.S.A.* to Tolstoy's *War and Peace* and Balzac's *Comédie Humaine*. Jean-Paul Sartre declared Dos Passos "the greatest writer of our time." And in 1965, three decades after the trilogy was first published, the *New York Times Book Review* referred to *U.S.A.* as "the great American novel."[99]

The trilogy takes the form of documentary nonfiction. In this sense it resembles *Singing Jailbirds* but anticipates more the nonfiction novels of Norman Mailer and the historical fiction of E. L. Doctorow. Its structure is a four-part montage, consisting of fictional sections whose characters dramatize the worker-capitalist divide; biographies of contemporaneous Americans, who are occasionally mentioned by the fictional characters; "newsreels" containing headlines, news excerpts, and popular song lyrics; and "Camera Eye," a modernist autobiography in which Dos Passos recalls events from his life that roughly coincide with the chronology of the newsreels and the fiction.[100]

The Wobblies radicalized Dos Passos, according to his account in *U.S.A.* He was a freshman at Harvard during the famous IWW Lawrence strike of 1912–13, and he describes its effect on him in *The 42nd Parallel*: the "millworkers marching with a red brass band through the streets of Lawrence Massachusetts . . . was like the Magdeburg spheres[;] the pressure outside sustained the vacuum within." Wobblies pressure his protective "bellglass," and by the next "Camera Eye" the bellglass has cracked. He attends an antiwar rally at Madison Square Garden, where he "clapped and yelled for the [Russian] revolution and hissed for Morgan and the capitalist war."[101]

Though never an IWW member, Dos Passos got to know Ralph Chaplin and other Wobblies and at times joined in solidarity with them. In 1927 he and Chaplin marched together through the Charlestown section of Boston to protest the execution of Nicola Sacco and Bartolomeo Vanzetti, immigrant radicals who had been convicted—wrongly, they believed—of murder. On August 22, the night of the execution, Chaplin spoke at a mass meeting, and then he, Dos Passos, and thousands of others encircled the Charlestown Prison and "kept up a constant chant of 'Solidarity Forever.'"[102]

In *U.S.A.* Wobblies and "Solidarity Forever" highlight the degree to which the nation is engaged in another civil war, this one between workers and capitalists. Throughout the trilogy, Wobblies are beaten up and arrested for protesting the capitalist order. The major characters of Mac, Charlie Anderson, Daughter, and Ben Compton participate in a Wobbly strike, while J. Ward Moorehouse and Richard Ellsworth Savage repress Wobblies. During one strike, Wobblies sing "Solidarity Forever," a cop kicks a young woman, and Daughter punches the cop and is arrested, making headlines. The first three biographies feature leaders on both sides of this civil war: Eugene Debs; Luther Burbank, the botanist who industrialized agriculture; and "Big" Bill Haywood. Two other memorable biographies are of the Wobbly martyrs Joe Hill and Wesley Everest, a World War I veteran who was lynched on Armistice Day 1919 after a deadly clash between the IWW and the American Legion in Centralia, Washington.[103]

The trilogy's opening fictional sections also foreground the labor-capital divide. Mac evolves from apprentice printer to Wobbly printer and sacrifices his family for the cause. "A wobbly oughtn't to have any wife or children, not till after the revolution," his Wobbly mentor tells him. Mac marries anyway, and his wife, Maisie, burns every radical paper she finds in the house. She wants Mac to work hard and get rich; "Talk about money made her drunk." But Mac remains loyal to his Wobbly ideals. He leaves Maisie and their children for Mexico to support the revolution there, and when he stands to give a short speech, someone honors him by yelling "Solidarity Forever." He ends his speech "with the Wobbly catchword about building the new society in the shell of the old." His speech "went big," and "Mac felt pretty good." It's one of the only times he feels "pretty good." Devoting himself to the IWW gives him a sense of pride and dignity that he cannot find elsewhere.[104]

Near the end of *U.S.A.*, in his "Camera Eye" response to the execution of Sacco and Vanzetti, Dos Passos makes explicit his larger theme of a nation divided: "America our nation has been beaten by strangers who have turned our language inside out who have taken the clean words our fathers spoke and made them slimy and foul." They "have built the electricchair and hired the executioner to throw the switch." "[A]ll right we are two nations," he emphasizes. Using new language to reclaim national ideals and expose the "slimy" language of the enemy, Dos Passos has stripped "Solidarity Forever" of its millennial power. He casts the new civil war in wholly secular terms.[105]

In certain respects Dos Passos's career resembled Chaplin's. Both men disdained bureaucracy, sympathized with individual workers, and found inspiration in Walt Whitman and Thomas Jefferson. Both had friends killed by Communists, became virulent anti-Communists, and came to view the rise of the post–New Deal federal government as a greater threat to liberty than corporations. In 1959 Dos Passos summed up his faith in individuals and his hatred of institutions in words that Chaplain might have written himself: "The basic tragedy my work tries to express seems to remain monotonously the same: man's struggle for life against the strangling institutions he himself creates." In essence Chaplin and Dos Passos both evolved from quasi-anarchists to quasi-libertarians who admired Buckley's *National Review*. (Dos Passos wrote frequently for *National Review* from the late 1950s through the 1960s and became a friend of Buckley.) And like Chaplin's, Dos Passos's career suffered because of a perceived swing to the political Right.[106]

But unlike Chaplin, who always defined himself as a "radical," Dos Passos repudiated his earlier radicalism, viewing it (again in 1959) as a vain attempt to "conserve" the dignity of workers against the threat of "organized money." Also unlike Chaplin, Dos Passos seems to have endorsed a form of social Darwinism. "I had great sympathy for the Anarchist movement," he said in 1968, two years before his death. But with age he came to understand "the way the human race works: in simple terms, top dog always gets to the top, no matter what the system is. . . . No change in ideology changes that basic fact."[107]

While developing this understanding, Dos Passos effectively exchanged "Solidarity Forever" for the "Battle Hymn of the Republic" as the song that could restore national ideals. In 1962 he attended a Young Americans for Freedom celebration at Madison Square Garden, organized by the Republican senator Barry Goldwater. Amid the singing of the "Battle Hymn" he walked on stage to receive the Freedom Award, along with Senator Strom Thurmond, the Southern champion of segregation, and other "redeemers" of American conservatism. Forty years earlier Dos Passos had stood in the same arena with Wobblies and anarchists, clapping "for the revolution and [hissing] for Morgan and the capitalist war."[108]

"Solidarity Forever" has followed a similar trajectory. For decades it was interpreted chiefly as a post–New Deal union song, but quite recently it seems to have turned back toward its anarchic and millennial roots, celebrating a transcendent Union. The Occupy Wall Street movement is a direct successor to the IWW in its approach to protest. Like the Wobblies, it sees itself as a "leaderless movement," out of which intensely dedicated and gifted representatives emerge. Like the IWW Preamble, the Occupiers' "Declaration of Occupation" is more a worldview than a list of demands. It echoes the IWW Preamble in declaring, "No true democracy is attainable when the process is determined by economic power." The Occupy movement's website invokes "Solidarity Forever" as a foundational principle, Chaplin's version of the song appears on its song lists, and there are numerous instances of occupiers singing it, with help from lyric sheets.[109]

And yet there are still residues of "Solidarity Forever" as a union song, that is, a song that does not offer a transformative vision of society but pushes for gaining the best deal possible in the existing order. In the fall of 2011, as the Occupy movement grew rapidly and gained worldwide visibility, its general assembly held a planning session at New York's Zuccotti Park. Nelini Stamp, a facilitator, began a session with four hundred to five hundred occupiers by shouting, "High hopes! High hopes!," which the crowd repeated. She then led the assembly in singing "Solidarity Forever." A dissenter in the front row yelled out, "Not everyone here is into your narrow union politics." "It's not a union song." Stamp responded. "It's union like 'unity.'"[110]

But it was too late; the singing had already died out. And the religious fervor, which had allowed the Wobblies' version of the "Battle Hymn" to evoke transcendent unity while also reinforcing divisions between the forces of good and the forces of evil, also seemed absent. Perhaps the Occupy movement needed a new workers' battle hymn to reenergize the original, revolutionary note of freedom amid apocalyptic war. Or perhaps, like Chaplin in his later years, the movement would judge the costs of such warfare too dear.

VII

★ ★ ★

THE EVANGELICAL "BATTLE HYMN"

ON APRIL 7, 1917, the day after the United States declared war on Germany, Billy Sunday arrived in New York City. Sunday was considered by many the greatest revivalist in American history, some said "the greatest since the days of the apostles." He had been preaching for twenty years, his audiences rapidly growing from whistle-stop towns in Iowa to the wicked cities, which were, he believed, polluting the surrounding countryside and threatening the nation's spiritual fabric. He had recently achieved extraordinary successes in Boston and Philadelphia, where he filled ten-thousand-seat tabernacles built especially for his two-month campaigns. But New York, that "modern Babylon" and "capital of Satan," was considered the graveyard of evangelists. The revival there would be the most important of his career.[1]

Billy Sunday (his true name) was well prepared for it. His advisors included John D. Rockefeller Jr. ("old chap," Sunday called him); Major General Leonard Wood, a Congressional Medal of Honor winner who had captured Geronimo during the Indian wars and commanded the Rough Riders in Cuba; and former president Theodore Roosevelt, who once told Sunday, "There is no man, in recent years, who has done better work than you, in this country." A massive wooden tabernacle that held twenty thousand had been built on the corner of Broadway and 168th Street, the largest public venue at that time erected in New York. And Sunday had an army of some fifty thousand volunteer organizers to help with his campaign. They built the tabernacle, reached out to the city's churches, held prayer meetings and choir rehearsals, raised money, and aggressively advertised Sunday's campaign to "save New York."[2]

At the first service, on April 8, the tabernacle was filled to capacity hours before its 2 P.M. start. There was a two-thousand-voice choir and a professional orchestra with two grand pianos. But the crowd was there to hear and watch Billy Sunday, who was famous for his theatrical, athletic sermons. For eight years before turning to God he had played professional baseball, and his record for bases stolen in one season (ninety-five) stood until Ty Cobb broke it twenty-five years later. He began his sermon by comparing the tabernacle crowd to those at the ballpark when he had played in New York: "You're the same warm-hearted, enthusiastic bunch you used to be when you sat in the grandstand and bleachers when I played at the old Polo Grounds."[3]

His sermon emphasized the evangelical tenet of repenting one's sins and accepting Jesus as one's personal Savior, in contrast to the teaching of religious liberals (or modernists), who believed that all humans could be saved without a conversion experience. "I don't believe in the universal Fatherhood of God and the universal brotherhood of man. You're a *creature* of God. So is a hog eating slop out of a trough. You've got to be a *child* of God." Only conversion through the Holy Spirit could make men and women children of God.[4]

After that warm-up, Sunday paced across the stage, pointing at the crowd and railing against sin and the devil. He singled out the liquor business, his best-known target. It was "damnable, hellish, vile, corrupt, iniquitous." The "whiskey-gang" had raised half a million dollars to destroy his reputation, he told the crowd. "I say to them, 'Come on, you God-forsaken, weasel-eyed, white-livered, black-hearted gang of thugs. Come on. I defy you. . . . I ask no quarter and I give none." He proceeded to shadowbox the whiskey gang—or Satan (it was hard to know the difference)—and he shuffled across the floor as he jabbed away, throwing occasional hooks and knockout punches. He jumped on chairs and waved his arms. And he sprinted across the green-carpeted platform and slid home to Jesus. The crowd watched with rapture, laughing, cheering, applauding at every pause in his dazzling performance.[5]

Then he stood up, wiped the sweat from his face and the imaginary dirt off his pants, and made an announcement. The press had been accusing him of exploiting religion for financial gain, turning God's message into spectacle. In fact Sunday had received over $50,000 in "free-will offerings," as donations were called, from his recent ten-week campaign in Philadelphia and more than that in Boston. Now there were rumors that he would make $100,000 during his New York campaign. He put the allegations to rest by announcing that he would donate all the free-will offerings from his New York campaign, after expenses, to the Red Cross and the YMCA to help American soldiers and sailors. "I don't want your money," he said. "I want you; I want to win your soul to Jesus." Twenty thousand spectators erupted in applause. And then, without any prompting by either the choir or the orchestra, they burst into the "Battle Hymn of the Republic."[6]

The evening performance was even more spirited. Again the tabernacle was filled to capacity. Sunday's sermon, "God's Grenadiers," written especially for this occasion, singled out Germany's militarism as the source of evil. The German people had long been inculcated with the doctrine that "might makes right and that the ends justify the means." Americans would save the Germans from Germany: "[We will] set them free from the militarism that has enslaved them for generations. . . . We will destroy it or it will destroy the world." American patriotism and Christianity were synonymous: "You are patriots *or* traitors to your country and the cause of Jesus Christ." The battle lines were clearly drawn; there could be no fence-sitting or middle way. Militarism would be fought by militarism.[7]

At the climax of his sermon, Sunday climbed onto the large oak pulpit and waved an American flag back and forth in dramatic sweeps. As he did so, the choir led the crowd in another rendition of the "Battle Hymn." The verses swelled to a deafening crescendo. Men openly wept, and wives clung to their husbands. After the final "Glory, glory Hallelujah," he leaped from the pulpit onto the carpeted floor, mopped his face and collar, said good night, and marched off in triumph.[8]

Sunday's New York revival was the high point of his career. During the seventy-one-day campaign, he preached at least twice a day, six days a week (Mondays were his day of rest), and each day was as lively as his first. The tabernacle filled up before the service began. Total attendance surpassed 1.5 million, one quarter of the city's population. Sunday's gift to the Red Cross and YMCA totaled $120,000. And 100,000 New Yorkers "hit the sawdust trail": they walked down the aisles, covered with wood shavings to dampen the sound, as the band played "Onward Christian Soldiers," "The Star-Spangled Banner," "Just As I Am," and, of course, the "Battle Hymn." They shook Sunday's hand, signifying their acceptance of Jesus as their personal Savior and their vow to resist sin and lead better lives. One of his first converts was his former baseball trainer, who told him, "I helped you get into shape to play baseball. Now, Bill, get me into shape to meet God."[9]

The "Battle Hymn of the Republic" was the perfect anthem for Sunday's revivals, especially his New York City campaign. He loved old gospel songs such as "Brighten the Corner Where You Are," but he believed, "The church must be martial and we need martial music." The "Battle Hymn" fit his militant, triumphant, and patriotic style of sermonizing, and his audiences often sang it without any prompting. Sometimes he embellished his sermon by telling his choir director, "Give us a verse of the 'Battle Hymn.'" He often concluded a service with the hymn, as he did on the opening day of his New York campaign. During his Boston campaign, he ended one service by picking up a chair for a weapon, climbing atop the pulpit, and yelling, "Let's show the devil we don't know how to retreat," a reference to the line "He has sounded forth the trumpet that shall never call retreat." On cue, the choir sang the "Battle Hymn." It was in effect his theme song.[10]

It also resonated with the tenor of the times. With America's entry into World War I, Sunday and countless other Americans viewed the threat from Germany as an apocalyptic sign. Sunday read and took notes on one of the many prophetic tracts identifying the war in Europe as the realization of the Book of Revelation. "'Armageddon' has now become a household word," declared one religious writer with pride. After British forces led by General Edmund Allenby captured Jerusalem, many evangelicals felt heartened by the prospect of a Jewish restoration of Palestine, another sign, based on biblical readings, that end-times were at hand. Cyrus Scofield, whose Reference Bible fueled these beliefs, noted that even victory and peace could not stave off the Day of Judgment; there were too many signs that the Tribulation was at hand. The "Battle Hymn" both reflected and inspired millennialist fervor among evangelicals. Sunday and his favorite hymn rallied Americans to destroy the enemies of Jesus and the Bible and to define their faith in patriotic terms.[11]

Sunday dedicated at least one sermon in each campaign to the imminent Second Coming, summarizing Revelation in premillenialist terms. At the moment of Christ's return, the saved and the unsaved would be separated, the former sent up to heaven and the latter left to live for seven (or seven hundred, Sunday said he didn't know which) years under Satan's rule. Then Satan would be locked up in a pit, and Christ and his saints would return to rule Earth for a thousand years. "Think of coming here and reigning over people who used to slander and vilify you," Sunday told his audiences. "Think of coming back to this world as a ruler where you have been reviled." At the millennium's end, Satan would be released, the battle of Armageddon would ensue, and Satan would be defeated and sent back to hell forever. Then God would issue his Last Judgment, dividing all souls between those who would spend eternity in heaven and those consigned forever to hell. He ended the sermon by predicting that Christ would come back soon, perhaps "this very moment."[12]

Sunday hoped his millennial sermon, and the hymn that invariably accompanied it, would inspire people to repent and open their hearts to Christ. Though he believed that conversion led to social reform, his chief aim was to swell the ranks of the saved. The perception of America as a modern, secular state was widespread, especially in the cities. The nation had purportedly turned away from God and the Bible. "Christendom may be defined briefly," wrote H. L. Mencken, "as that part of the world in which, if any man stands up in public and solemnly swears that he is a Christian, all his auditors will laugh."[13]

In the first half of the twentieth century Sunday and the "Battle Hymn" helped make evangelical Christianity not only acceptable but dynamic and vibrant. His success paved the way for the only revivalist to outstrip him in influence and popularity: Billy Graham, who borrowed many of Sunday's techniques during his worldwide crusades after World War II, including the use of the "Battle Hymn" as his anthem. By coupling the song with evangelicalism, Sunday and Graham helped expand the nation's political and religious center, uniting progressives and populists, liberals and conservatives, rural and urban populations, men and women, the powerful and the poor, Northerners and Southerners, as well as, to a lesser degree, Catholics and Protestants and blacks and whites into an uneasy alliance dedicated to defending traditional Christian values. Sunday, Graham, and the "Battle Hymn" ensured that evangelical Christianity wouldremain a vital force in twentieth-century America.

IT IS APPROPRIATE THAT Billy Sunday adopted the "Battle Hymn" as his anthem, for his life was irrevocably shaped by the Civil War. He was born on a farm in Story County, Iowa, near Ames, on November 19, 1862, exactly a year after Julia Ward Howe wrote her hymn. Three months earlier, his father, William Sunday, had enlisted in Company E of the Iowa Twenty-third Volunteer Infantry Regiment. He died of disease in Missouri a month after Billy was born, having never seen his son.[14]

Illness and death were the dominant realities of Billy's young life. According to family lore, he was sick and unable to walk for his first three years, until a traveling doctor cured him with a potion of local berries, roots, and leaves. His mother, Mary Jane Corey (known as Jennie), remarried and had two more children. But tragedy overshadowed these births. In his autobiography Sunday cites eleven deaths in the family during his first ten years, including his half-sister, who burned to death in a bonfire accident, his stepfather, four aunts and an uncle, and his grandmother, to whom he was so attached that he had to be pulled away from her coffin during the funeral, and after she was buried he wept over her grave in the snow for hours and almost froze to death. His oldest brother, Albert, almost died when he was kicked in the head by a mule; he had to be institutionalized.[15]

Alcohol was also pervasive, which helps explain Sunday's later hatred of it. His stepfather drank too much, confiscated his father's Civil War pension, and abandoned the family when Billy was nine. His maternal grandfather, who lived nearby, also drank too much, abused him, and then felt remorse after sobering up. In 1874 his mother, unable to support the family, sent Billy and his older brother Ed to an orphanage in Glenwood, Iowa. Two years later it was shut down and they were sent to an orphanage in Davenport. Billy received about two years of schooling, but the superintendents, a Mr. and Mrs. Pierce, taught him a work ethic to which he attributed his later success and would often invoke as a preacher.[16]

Baseball defined Billy's formative years. He was extremely fast, could beat every other boy in a race, and became known for his speed around the bases and in the outfield. In 1876, when he was fourteen, he and Ed returned to Story County to work as field hands. Sunday soon moved to Nevada, Iowa, a few miles east of Ames, to work as a factotum for a Civil War veteran, attend high school, and play baseball for the local team. Though he never finished high school, he gained respect as an athlete. One Fourth of July he raced against an Iowa State professor in a hundred-yard dash. The professor wore a rose-colored silk suit and running shoes. Billy ran barefoot and shirtless with his calico overalls rolled up to his knees. He won the race and $3 in prize money. His friends carried him on their shoulders and yelled, "Bring on your college professors! We can beat the bunch!"[17]

In 1880 Sunday moved to Marshalltown, Iowa, to play for its team. Over the next two years he helped make the Marshalltown Nine one of the best in the state. His performance attracted the attention of Adrian "Cap" Anson, the captain and manager of the National League's Chicago White Stockings (forerunner of the Cubs). Anson invited Sunday to try out for the team.

When he arrived at A. G. Spalding's Sporting Goods Store in Chicago, the team's headquarters (Spalding owned the team), he had a dollar in his pocket and felt "like the hayseed that [he] was." But that didn't matter to Anson, who wanted a fast base runner to complement his roster of heavy hitters. In the tryout Sunday raced the team's fastest runner and "ran rings around him, beating him by fifteen feet," Sunday recalled. Anson gave him a $20 gold piece to help him get settled, a gesture that Sunday never forgot and frequently retold in his sermons.[18]

Sunday began playing professional baseball just as the game was becoming a national pastime and a viable business. New urban ballparks were being built that could seat thousands. Players were well paid compared to other industrial workers, and fans followed their careers and at times idolized them, collecting their baseball cards, including Sunday's. Anson helped grow the sport. He made the game exciting by recruiting power hitters and speedy base runners like Sunday, and he led the White Stockings to five pennants during his coaching years. Sunday played five years in Chicago (1883–87), including one pennant-winning season, and another four years for the Pittsburgh Alleghenies and Philadelphia Phillies. Through Anson's mentoring he became nationally known, renowned for his base running and fielding. Anson called him "the strongest man in the profession on his feet."[19]

Midway through his professional career, an event occurred off the field that would transform Sunday's life. One Sunday afternoon in Chicago in the summer of 1886, he and his teammates got "tanked up" in a downtown saloon. Sunday was not a heavy drinker, but drinking was part of the culture of pro ball, an occupational hazard. When the players finished their rounds, they sat on the curb at the corner of State and Van Buren Streets to listen to hymns from a Gospel Wagon. It was the kind of gospel music that the Wobblies would later appropriate for their "Little Red Songbook." Men and women played cornets and trombones and sang hymns that Sunday had heard his mother sing in their Iowa log cabin. They were simple songs, which modern churches often ignored for being "too crude," as Sunday noted. But while he was sitting there on that curb they had a profound effect on him. "These hymns stir memories that drive folks back to their mother's God and Christ," as he put it later. The singers, who worked for the Pacific Garden Mission on Van Buren Street, invited the group to come hear "stories of redeemed lives that will stir you." Sunday visited the mission that night and soon became a regular. One night he stepped forward and publicly accepted Christ as his Savior.[20]

He never forgot the moment of his conversion. He didn't sleep for three nights afterward. Forty years later he said, "If the same floor is in that old building, I can show you the knot hole in the board upon which I knelt that dark and stormy night." Neither did he forget his debt to the mission. During a revival campaign in Chicago in 1918, he received $63,000 from the free-will offering and gave it all to the mission. He never passed the corner of State and Van Buren Streets without taking off his hat, bowing his head, and thanking God for saving him.[21]

An additional factor possibly motivated Sunday's conversion. He was courting Helen ("Nell") Thompson, the daughter of a Chicago dairyman and ice cream manufacturer. Six years younger than Sunday, Nell had converted to Christ at fourteen. Her family were staunch, middle-class Presbyterians, and her father did not like the idea of a professional ballplayer and high school dropout wooing his daughter. While businessmen enjoyed watching baseball, they didn't want players as sons-in-law. Sunday attended the Thompsons' Presbyterian Church, and his conversion helped compensate for the social gulf separating him from the family.[22]

His conversion also apparently improved his baseball. As a revivalist Sunday frequently told the story of his first game after accepting Christ. Chicago was playing Detroit and was ahead by one run in the bottom of the ninth with two outs. Detroit had two men on base—the tying and winning runs—and Charlie Bennett, a power hitter, was at the plate. With a full 3-2 count, Bennett hit the next pitch "square on the nose." Sunday was in right field and knew the ball was going over his head and into the crowd. (There was no outfield wall in those days.) As he turned and ran he offered up a prayer: "God, if you ever helped mortal man, help me to get that ball!" He yelled at the fans to get out of his way, and "they opened like the Red Sea for the rod of Moses." He leaped in the air, shot out his left hand, "and the ball hit it and stuck." One fan got so excited he gave Sunday a $10 bill and the next day bought him his first tailor-made suit. "Greatest thing I ever saw," the man said of that catch.[23]

After his conversion, Sunday gave up drinking, gambling, and going to theaters and began giving talks to boys at the YMCA when he was on the road. The boys came to hear about baseball, but they learned about being a Christian. The press began covering his talks, and one journalist favorably compared him to ordained clergymen his age. To improve his oratory he studied rhetoric at Northwestern University's prep school, in return for coaching the college baseball team. And he took Bible classes at the Chicago Y, becoming a zealous student.[24]

His self-improvement regimen helped him win Nell's hand. He proposed on New Year's night 1888, and he would always remember how beautiful she looked in her oxblood cashmere dress and lynx shawl as she said, "Yes, with all my heart." Initially Nell's father tried to prevent the marriage, declaring that "no daughter of his would ever marry a ballplayer," but he soon relented, and they were married the following September. Earlier in 1888 he had been traded to Pittsburgh with a large salary increase. He sent his savings to Nell, who had studied business in college, and she began her career as his banker, bookkeeper, and manager. Their marriage became a brilliant business partnership.[25]

In the winter of 1890–91 Sunday was traded again, this time to Philadelphia, with a three-year contract at $400 per month, more than a year's salary for the average industrial worker. Soon after he signed, the Chicago Y offered him a job as an evangelist and Bible teacher for $83 per month. He felt called to work for Christ, but he also needed to support a wife, a one-year-old daughter, and an invalid brother. After consulting with Nell he decided to accept the Y's offer. The Phillies, however, would not release his contract. Feeling "greatly troubled," he entered into a covenant with God. If he did not receive a release by March 25, he would take it as a sign that God wanted him to continue playing ball; if a release came before that date, he would accept it as evidence that God wanted him to serve Him. The release came on March 18, St. Patrick's Day.[26]

Then he faced his first temptation as an evangelist. The Cincinnati team offered him $5,000 for the season. It was, by any measure, a princely amount of money, and he didn't know what to do. Nell set him straight. "There is nothing to consider," she told him. "You promised God to quit." The incident established a pattern that would persist for the rest of his career: being tempted by money—and indeed in the 1910s he got rich through the free-will offerings—but always getting back to the essentials: conversion, self-improvement, and social reform, and in that order. For Sunday and other evangelicals, the current of reform flowed outward, from self to society. Hence the importance of checking personal vices such as sloth, intemperance, lust, and greed before attacking social ills.[27]

Sunday left baseball at a time when American evangelicals were under siege. Religious modernists, or liberals, who dominated American churches, emphasized the here and now rather than the hereafter. They believed that the road to salvation led through progressive reform. Salvation began with society, not the self. As Walter Rauschenbusch (1861–1918), a leading theologian of the movement known as the Social Gospel, put it, "Jesus' end was not the new soul, but the new society." The Kingdom of God on Earth could be realized by human hands.[28]

In contrast, evangelicals embraced "old-time religion" and emphasized salvation in the hereafter rather than the here and now. All humans were innately depraved, in their view, and only by repenting and accepting Jesus as their Redeemer and personal Savior could people find true happiness. While most modernists embraced universal salvation, believing that Christ's death redeemed all mankind and that no one went to hell, evangelicals emphasized the stark differences between the bliss of heaven and the fires of damnation. They emphasized the power of sin. As Sunday would often say, sin triumphs "because it is treated as though it were a cream puff instead of a rattle snake." For evangelicals, God had given humans free will to choose sin or salvation. But only God could effect His Kingdom on Earth, and so they rarely embraced radical programs of social reform.[29]

The rift between evangelicals and modernists widened beginning in 1910, when conservative evangelicals began calling themselves fundamentalists, after a series of pamphlets called "The Fundamentals" that vigorously attacked religious modernists. Fundamentalists embraced those doctrines rejected by modernists, including the Bible's infallibility, the virgin birth of Jesus, and Christ's imminent return to Earth. They increasingly rejected society and worldliness, focusing instead on individual salvation. And they began treating those who did not subscribe to these tenets as heretics.[30]

The upshot of the theological rift between evangelicals and modernists was that many Americans increasingly worried about their nation becoming secular as it became modern. Among educated and urbane Americans, it became vogue to question the veracity of Scripture and embrace universal salvation. Robert Rauschenbusch interpreted Scripture through a pragmatist's lens of contingency and skepticism. "We see in the Bible what we have been taught to see there," he gleefully announced. "We drop out great sets of facts from our field of vision. We read other things into the Bible which are not there." This perspective allowed him to explode long-standing doctrines. God's Kingdom concerned Earth, not heaven, and religious duties served men, not God, he argued. Such radical interpretations, and the theological rifts caused by them, threatened to stifle Christianity, Sunday maintained, resulting in the decline of faith and the closing of thousands of churches.[31]

When he quit professional baseball, Sunday had to decide which road to take: the evangelical or the modernist. His new employer, the YMCA, had been founded on an evangelical basis, but it was also ecumenical and employed numerous modernists whose chief focus was social reform rather than individual salvation. Owing partly to his deprived youth, Sunday identified closely with the poor and downtrodden and was sensitive to the ways society shaped the self. At the same time, his rise from orphan to professional ballplayer with a comfortable salary had not sustained him. It was his conversion and Christian marriage that gave meaning to his life. Unsurprisingly he took the evangelical road.[32]

For three years Sunday worked for the YMCA, distributing tracts and Bible study announcements to saloons, preaching on street corners, creating an evangelical speakers' series, and leading prayer meetings. He also provided pastoral care, visiting the sick and destitute, comforting the afflicted, and burying the dead. He worked six days a week, fourteen hours a day, and to save money he walked to work, skipped lunch, dyed his clothes to make them look new, and wore cheap collars to cut down on laundry bills. In most social circles, his new job was considered a dramatic step down from professional baseball, where he had earned four times as much and had his name regularly in the papers. Nonetheless he loved the work and was unwavering in his conviction that the wages of sin were death and salvation could come only through Christ.[33]

His work at the Y attracted the attention of J. Wilbur Chapman, a respected evangelist who had trained with Dwight Moody (1837–99), perhaps the most influential preacher of his day. In 1893 Sunday became Chapman's assistant and advance man. His job, put simply, was to make Chapman look good. He visited midwestern towns, and occasionally cities, well in advance of Chapman's visit and oversaw all aspects of the revival. He met with the local pastors and listened to their needs, rented an appropriate hall, and organized the choir, ushers, fundraisers, prayer meetings, and publicity, all of which was handled by volunteers whom he trained. On the day of the revival, he served as factotum. If he did his job well, Chapman needed only to give a good sermon for the revival to be successful. Occasionally Sunday himself preached, and the reports were enthusiastic. "He goes straight to the point in a most practical way that is all his own," wrote an Indiana reporter. "He demonstrated that he was quite as efficient with the Bible as with the bat," said an Illinois editor.[34]

In 1896, after Chapman took a job as the pastor of the Bethany Presbyterian Church in Philadelphia, Sunday started out on his own. His first revival was in Garner, Iowa, a small farm community near the Minnesota border, where he preached for a week and gained 268 converts. Before leaving Garner he received another offer to preach at Sigourney, Iowa, a farm town twice Garner's size. Thus began a decade of what Sunday called the "Kerosene

Circuit," preaching in whistle-stop towns in Iowa, Illinois, Indiana, Minnesota, and Colorado, places often lacking natural gas and electric light. These were farm-service communities along railroad lines, usually with populations in the four digits. He stayed at local hotels or rooming houses and ate with the local pastors. As the crowds grew, he began renting tents. In Perry, Iowa, he experimented with a wooden tabernacle, which was far more expensive. But after his tent collapsed during a snowstorm in a Colorado town in 1906, ending the revival, he insisted on a wooden tabernacle unless the town had a large-enough venue to offer.[35]

Sunday participated in every aspect of his ministry. He erected the tents himself, helped build the tabernacles, and got to know the townspeople, who were trying to survive the new industrial order. At every revival there were Civil War veterans, and for that reason he began having the choir accompanying him sing the "Battle Hymn," either during the warm-up prior to the sermon or, as was more usual in later years, as a finale to the service.[36]

While Progressives embraced the "Battle Hymn" as an anthem of activist social reform, it also fit Sunday's message of battling sin and accepting Christ as one's personal Savior. After all, it is God, and not man, who is the central agent of change in its stanzas. Moreover the song trumpets the notion that national redemption must be based upon individual redemption. Fundamentalists could interpret the hymn's final lines, urging listeners to emulate Christ and die to make men free, as affirming their belief that the current of reform flowed from the self, redeemed through Christ, to society. Sunday preached much the same thing. His sermons focused on individual salvation. "Surrender to Christ and stop drinking up your paycheck," he told his audiences. "Get right with God and spend more time with your wife and children." But his message of self-help would, he believed, lead not only to greater fulfillment in this life and salvation in the next but to national salvation.[37]

One needed to get right with God. It was a simple message, but it was what his audiences wanted to hear. The crowds, and the numbers of converts, steadily increased. And his revivals energized the communities. Church attendance spiked in their wake, saloons closed down, and people sent him letters thanking him for helping them quit smoking. He was frequently broke during his Kerosene Circuit days and away from his family for weeks at a time. Had it not been for his father-in-law's financial support and Nell's financial acumen, he would have had to quit the new career that he found so fulfilling.[38]

Although by this point Sunday had been away from pro ball for over a decade, he continued to use baseball metaphors to describe religious work. In 1903 he sat for his ordination as a Presbyterian minister. He was unprepared for the exam and recounted, "[I] muffed the first ball they threw at me. I tried to steal second, but they caught me between the bases." When asked a question about St. Augustine, he said he didn't know because Augustine "didn't play in the National League." Finally the "umpire" moved that the examination come to an end, reasoning, "God has used him to win more souls to Christ than all of us combined."[39]

The story suggests the similarities Sunday saw between baseball and evangelism. Both were crafts in an age that emphasized managerial skills. Each involved an apprenticeship system or its equivalent: playing for the Marshalltown Nine and acting as a warm-up for Chapman. Success and salary were based on performance that could be quantified on a scorecard: runs, hits, errors, batting average, bases stolen, and so forth, and number of converts. In fact by 1906 local papers often published on the front page Sunday's "box scores" of converts and collection totals. A good coach or manager, Anson and then Nell, was important to his success. In each vocation Sunday excelled through daring and originality. Anson characterized his baseball playing as driven by audacity, sometimes to a fault: "He was altogether too daring, taking extraordinary chances because of the tremendous turn of speed he possessed." With its theatricality and athleticism, his preaching was unlike anything audiences had ever seen. And his formula was wildly successful. In no small part thanks to him, revivalism—much like baseball—started to evolve into a big business. Sunday made old-time religion appeal to modern audiences, and the numbers proved it.[40]

On the Kerosene Circuit, Sunday developed a preaching style and arsenal of sermons that he would use for the rest of his career. He combined homespun humor with flights of oratory, and he developed a form of friendly derision that made people laugh. Reporters and ministers were surprised to see more smiles than tears among his converts. As Sunday himself said, "God wants people to be happy." He also used modern business methods to attract audiences—to whom he denounced modern culture and theology. As he began making money, he wore expensive suits and hired a full-time managerial and marketing staff. Dressing like a highbrow, he attacked highbrow pretensions. And he loved to poke fun at intellectuals and pompous college students:

> I'm a dandy, I'm a swell,
> Just from college, can't you tell,
> I'm the beau of every belle,
> I'm the swellest of the swell.[41]

Many, both in his day and later, have dismissed Sunday as a buffoon, demagogue, and consummate salesman. In his Pulitzer Prize–winning book, *Anti-Intellectualism in American Life*, Richard Hofstadter wrote that Sunday resembled "a hardware drummer out to make time with the girls," and he blamed him for destroying the New England tradition of scholar-preachers. But what Hofstadter and others have missed is that Sunday's style was very much part of the tradition out of which he, Twain, and Lincoln emerged: midwestern humor, characterized among other things by the tall tale. The tall tale masked the insecurities of living in backwoods communities and, by turning these into art, enabled audiences to confront and critique society in a way that was appealing and deeply reassuring. Audiences smiled or laughed when Sunday ranted at the "whiskey gang" and shadowboxed the devil; they were also laughing at themselves and taking stock of their spiritual and moral codes. By the turn of the century, as both Twain's and Sunday's careers suggest, midwestern humor appealed to all corners of the country, from East Coast city slickers to country bumpkins.[42]

In 1907 Sunday's career took off, propelled partly by a cover story on him in the influential *American Magazine*. The article summarized both his baseball and preaching careers, included several photographs, and detailed his preaching methods: "Billy Sunday talks to people about God and their souls just as people talk to one another six days in the week across the dinner table or on the street." The results were "incredible," the magazine declared, estimating that in twelve years he had converted over 100,000 people with little backsliding. Sunday was "making more church members than all the ministers in the middle west working together." Two years later the *New York Times* began covering his career. His reputation as a performer and his message of self-help, which connected spiritual salvation to moral improvement, attracted the notice of businessmen, who saw in his revivals the spirit of civic reform and future profits. They began working with local clergy to raise money and organize revivals.[43]

The upshot was a change in venue, from the midwestern Kerosene Circuit to major cities in an ever-widening geographic range. The documented number of converts, the scorecard of a revival's success, reflects Sunday's rise to fame:

1906: between 600 and 3,000 converts per revival
1909: between 1,000 and 6,000 converts per revival
1912: between 3,000 and 10,000 converts per revival
1915: between 13,000 and 39,000 converts per revival
1917: between 15,000 and 100,000 converts per revival

Given that a conversion rate of 2 percent of the attendees was considered a success, these numbers convey something of his influence. The free-will offerings he received also skyrocketed, from $24,000 in 1907 to $200,000 in 1917. In 1914 *American Magazine* asked its readers, "Who is the greatest man in the United States?" Sunday ranked eighth, in a tie with Andrew Carnegie. By 1920 he was a millionaire.[44]

There are several reasons for Sunday's ascendance. Perhaps most important, his revivals tapped into a rich vein of ideological yearning in the early twentieth century. There was, as discussed, the acute sense that rapid industrial progress had come at the cost of the American soul and a growing awareness of the gaps separating urban and rural populations. Sunday saw himself as a bridge, offering audiences nineteenth-century beliefs in twentieth-century forms, antimodern values in a modern mode. He preached old-time religion as modern spectacle. He urged "old-time modesty" in dress while sporting the most fashionable suits and would further shock traditionalists by removing his suit coat, tie, and occasionally even his dress shirt as he sweated through his sermons. He emphasized individual conversion and self-help as pathways to reform in an age when many, if not most, ordinary Americans were considered—or thought themselves—irrelevant to the structures of the new society. And he embraced the ethic of the artisan-athlete in an industrial age, offering up himself as the exemplar. He thus united strains of progressivism and populism, conservative and liberal values, modern and antimodern thought.[45]

Sunday's use of the "Battle Hymn" echoed and reinforced this merging of old and new, emphasizing the sentimental ideals of faith and courage that were under assault in a modern age. The hymn's lyrical, symbolic, and allusive language had freed it from its abolitionist context during the Civil War, permitting it to be adapted and constantly updated and appropriated by Sunday—and many others, as we have seen—in fighting new conflicts and vanquishing new evils in yet another impending Armageddon. By helping people define themselves against their enemies, the song helped clarify individual and national values and identity.

The "Battle Hymn" also reinforced Sunday's image as a muscular Christian and his efforts to turn back the feminization of the Church. Countless observers linked the Church's institutional decline to the dominance of women as members and to a feminized understanding of Christ that their prominence encouraged. One English traveller described America as unlike any other place on earth, because religion had such a "strong a hold upon the women" and such a slight "hold upon the men." Sunday countered the feminization of the Church by casting Christ as "the greatest scrapper that ever lived," as he said. He rejected the notion that a Christian must be "a wishy-washy sort of galoot that lets everybody make a doormat out of him." "The manliest man," he insisted, "is the man who will acknowledge Jesus Christ." He offered himself as the perfect example, making sure that audiences would not forget his former prowess as a baseball player or his athletic approach to preaching, even if they forgot the content of his sermons. After his preaching day ended, he continued to present himself as a preacher-athlete. After every evening service, his personal masseuse, the ex-boxer Jack Cardiff, rubbed him down in the tabernacle's locker room, and Sunday advertised this ritual by holding interviews there. "His virility is his chief stock-in-trade," declared a *New Republic* reporter in 1917. "No one, not Mr. Roosevelt himself, has insisted so much on his personal militant masculinity."[46]

Sunday called himself the champion of "progressive Christianity" or "progressive orthodoxy," and in so doing he endeared himself to both liberal and conservative reformers while affirming the status quo. His signature sermon on Prohibition reflected his theology and reform views. Spiritual purity would lead to moral and social purity, but government needed to encourage this by removing the temptation to sin, much as it outlawed robbery and murder. Prohibition offered a concrete solution to individual and national sins, just as the "Battle Hymn" connected individual and national redemption.[47]

Sunday's muscular Christianity and attacks on liquor trafficking endeared him to Teddy Roosevelt and other progressive leaders. They saw in him a virile antidote to a feminized and intemperate culture that, in their view, had become soft, wasteful, and disorderly, resulting in untold social and economic costs. When Roosevelt told Sunday, "there is not a man in this country for whom I have greater respect and admiration than I have for you," it was because he believed that Sunday's evangelizing would make the nation stronger, more strenuous and robust, and consequently more productive, efficient, and orderly.

Then, too, Sunday's manliness and liquor crusade helped unite religious modernists and evangelicals in the Progressive era. Modernists were as concerned as evangelicals about the feminization of the Church, and they too championed Prohibition. The young Reinhold Niebuhr, who articulated a "neo-orthodox" theology, cautioned modernists against a too exuberant embrace of Sunday's evangelical reform efforts. "There is much in [Sunday's] theology to recommend it," Niebuhr declared in 1916, including the

Christian paradox that God is both righteous and merciful, judgmental and forgiving. Sunday's emphasis on divine judgment, added Niebuhr, "is a wholesome antidote against the 'tender-mindedness' of modern Christianity." But modernist ministers who tolerated Sunday's theology simply because they liked his temperance cause and muscular Christianity were practicing "a form of dishonesty that we do not tolerate in politics and ought not to be tolerated in the church."[48]

If Sunday was an exemplar of muscular Christianity, he also blurred traditional gender roles. He frequently acknowledged Nell's brilliance as a businesswoman and manager and his dependence on her for his success. He endorsed female suffrage and sex education for women and children. Women adored him, often pinning up his photograph as they later would pictures of movie stars. He held "women's only" services, which traditionalists called shocking, and they were among his most popular. No other man was allowed into these meetings, prompting one Boston journalist to marvel, "One man, all alone with 17,000 women. Can you beat it?" At these meetings Sunday preached old-fashioned domestic values while championing "new women" as independent and capable of supporting themselves. He denounced divorce, dancing, gold-digging, promiscuity, birth control, and abortion, roughly in that order. But he also told women that they shared in Adam's sin and needed to know about sin's power and thus sex. "I would rather have my children taught sex hygiene than Greek and Latin," he said. His talks inspired and empowered women without challenging patriarchy. Great women should be satisfied with their "common sphere in life . . . as wife and mother," he told them.[49]

Sunday also reached out to blacks without threatening white supremacy. He integrated his services in Wichita and Kansas City—the first time an evangelist had done so—and in Wichita the black turnout was especially strong. His Atlanta campaign in 1917 was his first revival in the South, partly because of his opposition to Jim Crow segregation. In Atlanta he preached in black churches, held special services for blacks, and recruited a black choir to sing at white services. His vision of race relations resembled that of Booker T. Washington, whom he consistently praised. He endorsed a segregated but civil society in the South and encouraged blacks to remain there among their white "friends," in a spirit of cooperation. At least one black evangelist called himself "the black Billy Sunday." He avoided the anti-Catholic sentiment so prevalent among Protestants at the time, and he tried with limited success to build bridges with them. At one point he said that had Nell been a Catholic he would have become one too. And he lashed out at Christians who called Jews "Christ killers": "It makes my blood boil to hear a man speak of the Jew as a sheeny or Christ-killer. If ever you walk the streets of glory and are kept out of hell it will be because of your repentance and faith in the shed blood of a Jew."[50]

Organizational changes also contributed to Sunday's striking success. Not only did the support from businessmen increase his visibility, but beginning in 1908 Nell took a far more active roll in managing his career. She traveled with him, hired governesses to care for their daughter and three young sons, and chose administrators to organize the revivals. According to the religious scholar Lyle Dorsett, "There is no way that [Sunday] could have vaulted himself and his infant organization to national fame, material wealth, and numerical success without Nell's administrative skills."[51]

Another important change occurred in 1910, when Homer Rodeheaver replaced Fred Fischer as Sunday's music director. Fischer, who favored stiff collars and sported a pince-nez, was out of place in Sunday's modern revivals. Rodeheaver, by contrast, was a showman—confident, jovial, suave—as well as an immensely talented trombonist, choirmaster, and hymnodist. In the warm-up to Sunday's sermons, he created an atmosphere that rivaled secular forms of entertainment. "All was laughter, excitement—like a circus," one journalist noted. He led the choir with his trombone, "waving it up and down as he played." He got men who considered hymns effeminate to sing boisterously. Reporters called him "one of the greatest adjuncts a revivalist ever had." Whereas traditional revival music had sounded like a forlorn and lonely wail, a cry for help, Rodeheaver made it sound like an army marching to victory. It was the perfect complement to Sunday's preaching style, and he played the "Battle Hymn" at almost every service.[52]

In essence, Billy Sunday and the "Battle Hymn" worked together to create a broad coalition of Americans at a time of intense fragmentation and polarization. He sought to unite moderns and antimoderns, progressives and populists, conservatives and liberals—all living in harmony, if not equality, in a Christian nation. What held this vital center together was his belief that the spread of evangelical Christianity depended upon patriotism, capitalism, and Prohibition.[53]

This framework created contradictions for which he admitted that he had no answers. Indeed the three pillars supporting the spread of evangelicalism perpetuated polarization, much as the "Battle Hymn" promoted both unity and divisiveness. Sunday was unsparing in attacking religious and social radicals. He frequently proclaimed that Unitarians (who denied or were silent about Christ's divinity) "will be in hell along with thugs and

The Evangelical "Battle Hymn"

thieves," and he made up a list of notable American Unitarians who were burning in hell, including Julia Ward Howe. He approved of the Wilson administration's detention of antiwar radicals and its draconian Espionage Act and "Red Scare"—the raids, arrests, and prosecutions of Wobblies, Socialists, and Anarchists (including Ralph Chaplin, Bill Haywood, and Eugene Debs). "I would stand every one of the ornery, wild-eyed I.W.W.'s, Anarchists, crazy Socialists, and other types of Reds up before a firing squad," he announced. And he was xenophobic, condemning foreigners as perpetrators of the liquor business and radical politics.[54]

After the war Sunday's influence waned. His audiences and converts dropped dramatically, to levels he had not seen since 1906–12. He turned sixty in 1922 and could no longer shadowbox and slide home to Jesus with the same vigor. Then too his sons, George, Billy Jr., and Paul, publicly embarrassed him with their drinking, philandering, divorces, and reckless- ness. Paul spent money extravagantly, causing bill collectors to harass his parents. Billy Jr., while working on his father's campaigns as a piano player, flaunted his profligacy by drinking in speakeasies, dancing, having affairs with floozies, and landing in jail, all of which made headlines. His oldest son, George, married and divorced multiple times and lost enormous sums speculating in real estate, leaving his parents to clean up the mess. After first attempting suicide in 1923, he killed himself ten years later. "Where did I go wrong?" Sunday often wondered as he thought about his children.[55]

Additionally there was fierce competition from other revivalists and from the movies and radio. Consumerism was in full swing and organized sports had become so sophisticated that the White Stockings seemed amateurish. Sunday broadcast some of his revivals on the radio, but they didn't have the same effect as seeing him perform in a tabernacle. Other performers enjoyed far more popularity on the radio, where the "Battle Hymn" enjoyed im- mense circulation. The performer Fred Waring, who eventually earned three stars on Hollywood's Walk of Fame for his contributions in radio, movies, and television in the 1920s, ended each performance with a rousing rendition of the "Battle Hymn." Waring recorded the hymn for Decca Records, expanding the melody notes in order to give "the wonderful words a chance to express themselves," as he recalled. His recording soon became a gold record. Maud Howe Elliot, Julia Ward Howe's last living child, heard Waring's recording and told him, "Your performance was the finest and most moving rendering of the hymn I have heard in my long life."[56]

But the main reason for Sunday's decline was that the vital center he had erected could not hold. His crusades against liquor and Germany had united him with modernists and progressives who, after his support for war-time repression, distanced themselves from him. Moreover he had believed that once the war was won and Prohibition the law of the land, social problems would vanish. But the new age was nowhere in sight. As a result, Sunday lost faith in progress and reform. And he lost his wealth as well, giving most of it away. As his biographer William McLoughlin noted, in the 1920s Sunday began "to lose his grasp on the American public." People were tired of personal salvation, civic cleanups, and saving the world, "and they were tired of professional evangelism."[57]

Finally, in the 1920s fundamentalists and modernists feuded bitterly, making it impossible to achieve the kind of harmony underpinning mass revivals. Sunday's sermons became more extremist; he sometimes sounded more like a demagogue than a midwestern humorist. His audiences smiled less frequently. But he continued using the "Battle Hymn," principally now for its apocalyptic chords, which, to Sunday, sounded clearer than ever. This was the "Battle Hymn" of omen and threat, not common purpose. He increasingly believed that the Apocalypse was at hand; at one point he set the date for the end of the world at 1935. It was the year he died.[58]

★

IN 1934 A SIXTEEN-YEAR-OLD boy entered a Billy Sunday–style tabernacle in Charlotte, North Carolina. A few years earlier he had heard Sunday preach, and now he listened to the revivalist Mordecai Ham give a sermon on the wages of sin and the promise of salvation to the four thousand in the tabernacle. At the end of his sermon, Ham, a fundamentalist, invited his audience to hit the sawdust trail, and the congregation sang an invitation hymn. Though not a particularly memorable sermon, it convinced the teenager that he had not adequately accepted Christ as his Savior, and as the hymn neared the end, he went forward and made a decision for Christ: "It was as simple as that, and as conclusive." Revivalism had declined since Billy Sunday's popularity waned in the 1920s, and many wondered when the next warrior for Christ would emerge. No one could have predicted that in a few years this teenager who had just given his life to Christ would not only follow in Sunday's footsteps but also become the most famous American preacher of his time.[59]

A spiritual advisor to eleven presidents, from Harry Truman to George W. Bush, Billy Graham has preached to more people around the world than perhaps anyone else in history. Like Billy Sunday, he organized his crusades, as he called them, as a big business and advocated gradual reform from within existing social structures. But there are also notable differences between the two men. While Sunday's chief target of reform was traffic in liquor, Graham's has been communism. And while Sunday began his career in the political and theological center and then moved to the right as he became a fundamentalist, Graham began his career as a fundamentalist and has moved toward the center.

The "Battle Hymn of the Republic" remained the favorite anthems of both men, but they teased out its millennial implications differently. For Sunday, the enemy—the "serpent" of Howe's song—lay within, associated especially with the nation's saloonkeepers and their patrons, labor radicals, and subversive immigrants. For Graham, the "Battle Hymn" was fundamentally an expression of cold war patriotism, appealing especially to middle-class constituencies; his enemy was chiefly Communists, with their base in the godless USSR, which threatened the United States both morally and militarily. Sunday understood the millennium in national terms; the new age would emerge out of America. Graham's millennium was far more global in scope, based on the political economy of the cold war.

Billy Graham grew up haunted by the Civil War. Both grandfathers had been wounded as Confederate soldiers. Ben Coffey, his mother's father, had lost a leg and an eye at Seminary Ridge on the first day at Gettysburg, and Cook Graham died in 1910 with a Yankee bullet still in his leg. Billy's father, Frank Graham, became a successful farmer, and as a boy Billy dreamed of playing professional baseball. But after his conversion he set his sights on the ministry. In 1936 his parents sent him to Bob Jones University in Cleveland, Tennessee, which even then was a standard-bearer of fundamentalism. But he suffered from respiratory problems and transferred after a semester to Florida Bible Institute in Tampa, which his doctor said would be better for his lungs. In Tampa he met Homer Rodeheaver, Billy Sunday's choir director, participated in student-led revivals, and was ordained as a Baptist minister. After receiving a bachelor's degree at Wheaton College in Illinois, he served briefly as pastor at a small, nearby church and then began his career as an evangelist with Youth for Christ, a fundamentalist youth movement.[60]

One of his first major crusades was a Youth for Christ rally at Chicago's Soldiers Field on Memorial Day 1945. The crusade drew seventy thousand, and the revivalists used "every means to catch the attention of the unconverted—and then . . . punched them right between the eyes with the gospel," Graham recalled. The program ended with the choir singing and band playing the "Battle Hymn of the Republic" as four hundred nurses formed a white cross on the field.

Four years later Graham's breakthrough came during a revival in Los Angeles, where he converted some notables, including a gangster, and Louie Zamperini, an Olympic runner who had endured especially savage treatment as a prisoner of the Japanese during World War II. Graham's revival attracted the attention of William Randolph Hearst, who urged his reporters to promote the young evangelist, purportedly wiring his staff, "Puff Graham." What appealed to congregants were Graham's straightforward preaching style and heartfelt message of hope and redemption. Displaying none of Sunday's histrionics, he stood still at the podium, looked his listeners "in the eye," as he put it, and told them simply, "You're a sinner, . . . but God so loves you that he's given you a way to save yourself, if you'll only say yes." The effect was extraordinary; his conversion rates have purportedly never been matched.[61]

In 1950 Graham incorporated as the Billy Graham Evangelical Association and began launching a weekly half-hour radio program, *Hour of Decision*, which was instrumental in disseminating his name and message. Cliff Barrows, who had been a close friend and mentee of Rodeheaver, became his director of music, and Beverly Shea became the vocalist. Graham's mother recommended the "Battle Hymn" as their theme song. Despite, or perhaps because of, her father's war wounds, the "reconstructed" hymn was one of her favorite songs. Coupled with his decision to headquarter his association in Minneapolis, the hymn helped Graham transcend his Southern identity and become a fully national evangelist. And his team agreed that it was also "a singable tune, and pretty well known," as Barrows recalled. Moreover the stanzas' final lines, "His truth is marching on," "Since God is marching on," and "Our God is marching on," "exemplified the heart of Billy's crusades." Graham preached "the truth of God," Barrows noted. The music "framed the theme" of what they were trying to do. *Hour of Decision* played the hymn's chorus at the beginning and end of each program. The "Battle Hymn" quickly came to be identified with Graham's crusades, echoing his evangelical message.[62]

The "Battle Hymn" also fit Graham's vision of what Americans were up against. Throughout the cold war he proclaimed that the world was hurtling toward an apocalyptical nuclear war, and he increasingly emphasized the need for disarmament. The world was divided between two camps—Communist and Christian—and both the Communists and Jesus Christ demanded the same zealotry, "everything," from their disciples. In the coming battle over the hearts and minds of men, Americans were "going to have to have the same fanaticism for Christ as Communists have for Communism." He believed, with millions of other Americans, that Communist Russia, if left unchecked, would "lead all of the other powers of darkness against Israel" and precipitate "the battle of Armageddon and the Second Coming of Christ." This interpretation, which identifies Gog (in Ezekiel 38) as the Soviet Union, was widespread and stems from the writings of Scofield and other fundamentalists. The "Battle Hymn," and Graham's crusades, thus inspired Americans in their apocalyptic battle against international communism. As he put it in a 1953 *Hour of Decision* sermon, "When you turn from your sins to Christ, you redeem America."[63]

During the 1950s Graham's anticommunism led him away from his fundamentalist roots toward the nation's ideological center, much as it did for other Americans, who believed that a united front was the only way to confront the Communists. In 1952 he planned a crusade in New York City and reached out to its ministers, but the liberal clergy spurned him for his fundamentalism. But by the end of the decade he had positioned himself as a conservative leader who could reach out to both fundamentalists and modernists. In 1957 he united liberal and conservative clergy to organize a crusade at Madison Square Garden. In his sermons he said that fundamentalism had gone too far to the right, liberalism too far to the left. He urged people to "come together," as he phrased it, in the fight against communism. This first New York City crusade constituted his final break with fundamentalism and the advance of a "new evangelicalism that would survive, even thrive, in the cultural mainstream," as the religious journalist Peter Boyer noted. Like Billy Sunday before him, Graham's New York City revival was a high point in his career, and the "Battle Hymn" was the keynote of his services.[64]

By the end of the 1950s Graham was reaching millions with his sermons and his hymn. He had become a mass-media personality, establishing, in addition to the *Hour of Decision*, a television show, his own movie company, and revivals on an unprecedented scale. He served as a state-sponsored evangelist to China and India, and in doing so, helped spread the "Battle Hymn" to those countries. Eventually he led 450 crusades in 185 countries. Barrows estimated that local choirs performed the "Battle Hymn" during roughly 150 of these crusades and in all of the English-speaking countries. In the non-English-speaking countries it was difficult to adequately prepare local choirs to sing it in English, and there were even more problems obtaining a timely translation. Nevertheless Graham's team carried recordings of the "Battle Hymn" on tape, airing it on the radio and in local congregations, disseminating American Christianity and the "Battle Hymn" throughout the world.[65]

With America's victory in the cold war, by the final decades of the twentieth century, the "Battle Hymn" served as a source of reconciliation between America and Russia, much as it had helped reunite North and South after Reconstruction. In 1992 Graham evangelized in Moscow, using the massive Olympic Stadium as his church. He later described the last night of his revival, with seventy thousand people in attendance: "The soaring voices of a magnificent men's chorus resounded through the huge, overflowing stadium, triumphantly echoing the familiar strains of America's best loved hymn of faith, the 'Battle Hymn of the Republic.'" The singers were the Russian Army Chorus, formerly the Red Army Chorus, who presented the hymn as a surprise (it was not listed in the program) and dedicated it to Graham. Cliff Barrows was so moved that tears coursed down his cheeks. He said, "I just praise God that in that place, at that time, our God *is* marching on, with the band and the cymbals and the drums."[66]

It was one of Graham's proudest moments. He felt that he had played a role in America's victory over Russia and then in the subsequent efforts at reconciliation. Indeed the Moscow moment has been enshrined in his forty-thousand-square-foot Billy Graham Library in Charlotte. One of the most striking displays is footage from the 1992 Moscow revival, with the Russian Army singing Howe's song.

As early as the 1970s, with the rise of the Christian Right as a force in politics and social reform, Graham used the "Battle Hymn" as a means of saving souls and preserving "freedom," defined in both individual and national terms. In the 1970s he frequently invoked the "Battle Hymn" as an antidote to what he called "the gathering storm of moral decadence in the country that threatens our survival." Instead of wallowing in the darkness of sin and decadence, he instructed Americans to heed Jesus' injunction "Let your light so shine." At the same time, he criticized the conservative Right for becoming so absorbed in political concerns "that they los[t] sight of the priority of the Gospel."[67]

Graham similarly endorsed desegregation without burning conservative bridges. "Growing up in the rural South, I had adopted the attitudes of that region without much reflection," he acknowledged in 1997. A racial moderate, he held his first desegregated crusade in the upper South in 1957 and in the lower South beginning in the 1960s. Indeed in his 1957 New York City crusade, Martin Luther King Jr. offered the opening prayer, and Graham introduced him as the leader of "a great social revolution going on in the United States today." As a boy Bill Clinton attended one of Graham's desegregated crusades in Little Rock. It had a powerful affect on him: "When he [Graham] gave the call—amid all the civil-rights trouble, to see blacks and whites coming down the aisle together at the football stadium . . . it was an amazing, amazing thing. If you weren't there, and if you're not a Southerner, and if you didn't live through it, it's hard to explain. It made an enormous impression on me."[68]

Desegregation was also consistent with Graham's efforts to unite Americans in the fight against communism. Secretary of State Dean Rusk made the connection between desegregation and anticommunism explicit in 1963: "The Communists clearly regard racial discrimination in the United States as one of their most valuable assets." Civil rights had become a matter of foreign policy. Graham, like other centrists, had become by the 1960s much more self-conscious about America's democratic image, and this sensitivity persisted through the end of the cold war.[69]

As the spiritual advisor of all U.S. presidents from Dwight Eisenhower to George W. Bush, he "became the symbol of Protestant Christianity in America," as Boyer notes, "in effect branding evangelicalism as the mainstream American faith." By telling Americans that the fate of their souls, and thus that of the nation as a whole, rested in their own hands, he gave civil religion, and the "Battle Hymn," an evangelical gloss. Only a nation united in faith would allow God to march onward. This theme was especially prominent in one of his last, great sermons, the 9/11 memorial service at Washington National Cathedral. "Now we have a choice," he said, "whether to implode and disintegrate emotionally and spiritually as a people and a nation; or whether we choose to become stronger through all of this struggle—to rebuild on a solid foundation. That foundation," he emphasized, is "trust in God."

Though Graham has been semiretired since the end of the cold war, his Evangelistic Association has moved back toward fundamentalism and the political right; in fact, he declined to serve as an advisor to Barack Obama because of the president's support for abortion rights. Much of this rightward shift can be attributed to his son Franklin Graham, who now presides over Graham's hundred-million dollar organization and is far more conservative, theologically and politically, than his father. Where Billy Graham believes that "God loves even Satan," Franklin is willing to wield the terrible swift sword, placing far less emphasis on the power of forgiveness. While the father acknowledges that "sincere Christians may differ" over such issues as abortion and homosexuality, the son unhesitantly calls the former murder and the latter a "sin in the eyes of God."[70]

This rightward turn in Graham's organization mirrors that of many if not most evangelicals who, with the end of the cold war, exchanged communism for liberalism as the new threat to Christian America. Beginning in the late 1980s, as communism in Europe collapsed, evangelicals had difficulty raising money and organizing. But with the election in 1992 of Bill Clinton, the first president to endorse gay rights, he (and other liberal leaders) became for evangelicals the new "big bad guy," as one leader noted, the new serpent to be crushed.[71]

But Billy Graham has stood apart from other evangelicals during the post–cold war era in his efforts to preserve a vital center. According to Cliff Barrows, Graham has remained true to his conviction of not criticizing people who do not share his theological views, and instead accepting them with love. He has even come close to suggesting that believers of other faiths can become like evangelicals, "saying yes to God." During Clinton's presidency Graham prompted severe criticism from evangelicals by lavishing praise on both him and Hillary. He outraged conservatives by forgiving Clinton within weeks of the Monica Lewinsky scandal. And during his final crusade, in Flushing Meadows, New York, in 2005, Graham invited the Clintons as his special guests, told the crowd of 80,000, "they're a great couple," and added that Clinton should have become an evangelist after leaving the White House, "because he has all the gifts," leaving his wife "to run the country." Franklin Graham was so outraged by his father's comments that he issued a "clarification" under the auspices of the Billy Graham Evangelistic Association, saying that his father had only been "joking" about Clinton becoming an evangelist and emphasizing that his father's comments in no way constituted an endorsement of Senator Hillary Clinton.[72]

During the 2012 presidential campaign, Billy and Franklin Graham hosted the Republican candidate Mitt Romney, and Billy apparently endorsed him by supporting Romney's platform attacking gay rights and affirming anti-abortion policies. "I will turn 94 the day after the upcoming election," Graham said in a prepared statement, "and I believe America is at a crossroads. I hope millions of Americans will join me in praying for our nation and to vote for candidates who will support the biblical definition of marriage, protect the sanctity of life and defend our religious freedoms." Graham then placed full-page advertisements in leading newspapers urging Americans to "vote for biblical values" and to "pray with me that America will remain one nation under God." But given Graham's increasingly frail health, including a severe case of Parkinson's disease, coupled with his son's tendency to issue his own statements under the auspices of the Billy

Graham Evangelistic Association, it is unclear how much of Graham's endorsement of Romney was engineered by Franklin, who has been an outspoken opponent of President Obama. In a sense, Billy Graham and his son exemplify different facets of the "Battle Hymn," the millennial and the apocalyptic. Franklin, the fierce culture warrior, has focused on the cataclysmic battles that Christians must wage against the dark forces imperiling American society. His father has pursued a vision of that society united around the acceptance of Christ as personal Savior; for him, the grand struggle is not between Americans but within them.[73]

At the Billy Graham Evangelistic Association in Minneapolis there is a small multimedia chapel. When you enter, the lights dim and a voice tells of Jesus' death on the Cross and His Resurrection. This is followed by a rousing rendition of the "Battle Hymn of the Republic." At the end of the song the deep voice returns, asking its visitors, "Will you accept or reject Him? This is life's great decision."

VIII

★ ★ ★

THE AFRICAN AMERICAN "BATTLE HYMN"

IN MAY 1932 FIVE busloads of delegates from the annual conference of the National Association for the Advancement of Colored People (NAACP) trekked down from Washington to Storer College in Harpers Ferry. The Storer Normal School for freed men and women had been founded after the Civil War by a contingent of Free-Will Baptists; their choice of the site reflected a commitment to continue John Brown's work in advancing the cause of racial equality—if not through the sword, then through the primer. In 1906 the college had hosted the inaugural meeting on American soil of the Niagara Movement, the NAACP's forerunner. Now NAACP representatives returned once again to place a tablet honoring Brown on the engine house, often called "John Brown's Fort," where Brown and his band had staged their last stand.

The NAACP pilgrimage had been provoked by an effort the previous October to memorialize Brown's raid, when the local chapters of the United Daughters of the Confederacy and the Sons of Confederate Veterans had dedicated on the campus a memorial in honor of Heyward Shepherd, the railroad porter who held the unfortunate distinction of being the first person killed in the raid. The fact that Shepherd was African American granted him a privileged place in the Lost Cause pantheon; his tragedy confirmed the folly of abolitionism and transformed him into a free-born surrogate for the "faithful slave." Shepherd, the stone tablet declared, "exemplif[ied] the character and faithfulness of thousands of Negroes who, under many temptations throughout subsequent years of war, so conducted themselves that no stain was left upon a record which is the peculiar heritage of the American people, and an everlasting tribute to the best of both races."

Despite his initial trepidation that the memorial would stir "unpleasant racial feeling" and despite the fierce opposition from African Americans throughout the country, the white president of Storer, Henry McDonald, authorized the monument and even attended the dedication ceremony. In the official NAACP magazine, its editor and the nation's leading black intellectual, W. E. B. Du Bois, lambasted McDonald's participation as "disgraceful." Another African American journal reported that many of the speeches during the ceremony could not be heard over the derisive laughter of the local blacks in the audience.[1]

The stone tablet offered by the NAACP would answer the Shepherd memorial by depicting John Brown as a crusader for racial justice and his raid as the opening salvo in a righteous war for emancipation in which African Americans enthusiastically enlisted. It would speak not merely to the South but to the North as well, where, as we've seen, Brown was regarded ambivalently at best. Indeed in the decades after his raid, when mainstream American culture dismissed Brown as a bloodthirsty fanatic, black leaders continued to defend his right to employ violence in a noble cause. In 1881 Frederick Douglass had delivered a stirring speech at Storer College honoring Brown's legacy. Brown, he insisted, "began the war that ended American slavery and made this a free Republic. Until this blow was struck, the prospect for freedom was dim, shadowy, and uncertain." Half a century later the NAACP's tablet, with text written by Du Bois, would echo those sentiments.[2]

John Brown
Aimed at Human Slavery
A Blow
That Woke a Guilty Nation.
With Him Fought
Seven Slaves and Sons of Slaves:
Over His Crucified Corpse
Marched 300,000 Black Soldiers
And 4,000,000 Freedmen
Singing—
John Brown's body lies
A-mouldering in the grave
But his soul goes marching on

McDonald had initially authorized the dedication of the NAACP's tablet, but when he received the proposed text he deemed it "ill-advised and historically inaccurate." The phrase "guilty nation" especially perturbed the president, as well as the (all-white) Storer College trustees. In its place he recommended the unadorned phrase "JOHN BROWN 1800–1859 'HIS SOUL GOES MARCHING ON.'" NAACP officials answered that such a "colorless inscription" would not provide an assertive enough counterpoint to the Heyward Shepherd memorial. Still, rather than push the issue they asked if they could still hold their meeting at the college and unveil the tablet, even if it would not be granted a permanent place in John Brown's Fort.[3]

McDonald granted the request, and so the buses, containing several hundred NAACP delegates, rolled into Harpers Ferry for the meeting in May. Many of those who made the trip, however, were not aware of the tablet's fate; they learned the news only when apprised of the standoff by Du Bois from the podium. McDonald, anticipating the unrest that would greet the revelation, made a hasty exit after offering brief welcoming remarks. Sure enough, when Du Bois informed the crowd that they would be bringing the tablet back to the NAACP's New York office "until such a time as public sentiment would make its erection . . . possible," the celebratory mood turned dark. At the ceremony's conclusion, when the presiding officer announced the closing number as directed on the program, the singing of "America," her words were greeted with shouts of protest. "No, let's sing the 'Battle Hymn of the Republic'!" exclaimed one member of the crowd. Assents rang out, and those assembled took up the song. When they concluded, the NAACP representatives hastily boarded their buses, skipping a planned dinner, and returned to Washington.[4]

What did those singers mean by rejecting "America"? They certainly were not rejecting America itself; the spirit of militant separatism that would galvanize a future generation of African American protest did not animate this crowd. By favoring the "Battle Hymn" as an alternative national anthem, they were instead insisting on a radical vision of their nation's millennial promise, one rooted in the emancipatory legacies of the Civil War, while registering their frustrations over the chasm between that promise and the reality of American racism.

They were also vindicating John Brown and his legacy of violence. In fact a debate on Brown's tactics had dominated the thwarted dedication ceremony. The man McDonald had asked to deliver a formal address, Oswald Garrison Villard—the grandson of the famed abolitionist whose middle name he bore and one of the founders of the NAACP—had delivered a carefully calibrated tribute to Brown. Villard instructed the audience on the need to discriminate between "John Brown the man" and his methods. This allowed them "to acknowledge the divine that was in" Brown, while still maintaining the belief that "force gets one nowhere." This hedging did not find many sympathetic ears in the audience. The African American president of the John Brown Memorial Association who followed Villard on the podium put aside his prepared remarks to provide a different perspective. "I am not particular about how John Brown struck his blow at slavery," he announced, describing in vivid detail the hell from which Brown hoped to rescue slaves. "It was in this abattoir, into this lair of the damned that John Brown burst like an avenging knight of God. He came with a sword in his hand and prayer on his lips." At that point, the Storer College trustees and many of the white members of the audience made their exit.

Next came Du Bois. In an address entitled "The Use of Force in Reform" he heaped scorn on both McDonald and the Storer administration for their squeamishness and capitulations to local white prejudice while offering an unembarrassed defense of Brown's ends—and means. Brown "took human lives," Du Bois acknowledged, both in Kansas and on the very ground where the audience had gathered. "He meant to take them. He meant to use force to wipe out an evil he could no longer endure." It was after these remarks that the audience rang out the "Battle Hymn."

The debate that unfolded that day at Storer College—over the legitimacy of violence in the pursuit of racial justice; over the rival claims of integration and nationalism within the tradition of African American protest; over the emancipationist legacy of the Civil War and the memory of John Brown in American life—continued to rage throughout the twentieth century. The "Battle Hymn of the Republic" would continue to shape that debate. For those leading the struggle for racial justice, from Du Bois to Martin Luther King Jr., and for countless less renowned African Americans, the song provided a means of reconciling millennial hope and apocalyptic despair, of turning disappointment into a defiant resolve that would fuel the fight for the battles yet to come.[5]

FROM THE MOMENT OF its composition, African Americans have laid a special claim to the "Battle Hymn." According to one of her granddaughters, Julia Ward Howe had once stated that she had encountered the most impressive, heartfelt rendition of the song in the years after the Civil War, when she was touring the countryside of northern Virginia and visited an African American church outside Washington, D.C. As she entered the church, a soprano was singing an a cappella version of the hymn. That rendition moved her more than any other she had ever heard, she recalled.

In the decades to come, the hymn continued to carry profound meaning for African Americans, as did its kin, "John Brown's Body" and "Solidarity Forever." In fact it was African Americans who sustained the linked vitality of all three songs throughout the twentieth century. Their consanguinity had a certain eloquence. Together they celebrated a tradition of struggle for racial and economic justice that ran from the abolitionism of the nineteenth century to the twentieth-century civil rights movement, a tradition nourished by both the black church (where the "Battle Hymn" was often sung) and the labor movement. The emancipationist legacy of the Civil War and the memory of black soldiers' heroic contributions to the effort animated that tradition; those memories also highlighted the meager recompense African Americans had received for their efforts and therefore underscored the need for the struggle to continue. At a Chicago commemoration of the fiftieth anniversary of the Fifty-fourth Massachusetts' gallant but doomed assault on Fort Wagner, a local chorus performed both the "Battle Hymn" and "John Brown's Body." The songs stoked listeners' pride in African Americans' service to their nation, while also giving voice to their disappointment that though the regiment had made good on the hymn's call to sacrifice—they had died to make men free—their grandchildren had yet to enjoy a full measure of that freedom.

When the members of the Harlem Tenants' League marched in New York's streets against rent-gouging in 1929 and sang "John Brown's Body," they too were incorporating their demonstration into that protest tradition. In the decades that followed, that song continued to hold a special attraction for African American radicals. In Ralph Ellison's 1952 *Invisible Man*, when the novel's unnamed black protagonist speaks at a Communist Party rally, he walks onto the stage while the interracial audience is belting out "John Brown's Body." The song, the narrator recalls in an early draft of the novel, was a favorite of his freethinking grandfather. But the enthusiastic crowd had managed "to make the old song sound new." The Invisible Man's suspicions about the Communists momentarily dissolve, and he joins in the singing.

In the midst of World War II, an African American newspaper from Baltimore invoked the "Battle Hymn" to insist upon the need for the nation to defend the freedom of its own citizens, in order to lend credence to its claim to be fighting to spread freedom abroad. "This gospel war hymn," as the paper called it, can remind Americans, as it did during the Civil War, that even the best-trained armies can fail if those at home cannot "reach up to pull from heaven itself the consciousness that God is on their side." On Lincoln's birthday in 1943, at an interracial prayer pilgrimage at the Lincoln Memorial led by the African American labor organizer A. Philip Randolph, the Howard University Glee Club sang the "Battle Hymn" along with the Negro spiritual "Go Down, Moses." The event drew upon the memory of the Great Emancipator, as well as the spirit of Howe's hymn and of the biblical story of Exodus, to promote racial and economic justice in the current day. And at a social justice dinner held during the 1957 convention of the United Automobile Workers of America, a union whose leadership strongly supported civil rights, the celebrated African American contralto Marian Anderson opened with the first verse of the "Battle Hymn" and then transitioned seamlessly to "Solidarity Forever." In doing so, she established in song the continuities between labor activism and the struggle for racial equality.[6]

Among the three songs, the "Battle Hymn" occupied the most prominent place within the nascent civil rights movement of the 1950s and early 1960s. In the words of Julius Lester, a young musician and photographer active in the movement, in those early years they "sang 'Battle Hymn of the Republic' to death." Of course, they sang much else besides. Indeed no other campaign for social reform in American history has depended so heavily on the music its adherents made for themselves. Civil rights activists sang when they marched; they sang at prayer vigils and at planning meetings; they sang to celebrate victories and to buoy flagging spirits; they sang when they were arrested, when they were jailed, and when they were released. The early prominence of the "Battle Hymn" within the movement (and that of another hymn, "Onward Christian Soldiers") reflected the leadership provided by an established corps of elders from the black church. As it had for nearly a century, the song served as a musical expression of hope and determination and as a storehouse of millennial images and idioms.[7]

When the Supreme Court handed down its decision in *Brown v. Board of Education* in 1954, outlawing segregated education in public high schools, Horace Bond, president of Lincoln University, one of the nation's first historically black universities, prefaced his celebratory remarks with the opening lines of Howe's poem: "Mine eyes have seen the glory of the coming of the Lord." In the first sit-ins to protest segregated accommodations, which began in February 1960 at a Greensboro, North Carolina, Woolworth's lunch counter and spread to cities throughout the South, the song provided vital sustenance. Sit-ins were almost always conducted in silence, at least on the part of those doing the sitting; the students who led them were careful to avoid any hint of unruliness that could be exploited to discredit the movement. Breaking into the "Battle Hymn" once the protest had run its course, on the other hand, was a gesture of supremely *civil* disobedience; the song endowed the protest with respectability while highlighting the determination of the protesters. In March 1960 a crowd of African Americans who had gathered outside a Nashville courthouse to support students who had been arrested for staging a "round-the-clock" protest at the local Greyhound bus station, sang the "Battle Hymn" and "The Star Spangled Banner." That same month, fifty students who had staged a sit-in at a Chattanooga Woolworth's sang the song, as well as "Onward Christian Soldiers," as they were herded into a police van. When more than a thousand black college students convened at the Alabama State Capitol in solidarity for a sit-in strike at the lunchroom of the Montgomery County Court House, they sang the "Battle Hymn" with what a reporter characterized as "an abolitionist fervor."[8]

In these early campaigns against segregation, the "Battle Hymn" was able to amplify one of the most striking characteristics of nonviolent direct action: the combination of subversiveness with an ethic of dignified self-restraint. The hymn did so with a particular resonance in Mississippi's Parchman State Prison during the summer of 1961. Parchman was the last stop for many of the Freedom Riders, the men and women from the North and South who sought to compel the federal government to act against segregated interstate transportation by boarding buses in Washington, D.C. and heading south. Outside Anniston, Alabama, one bus, carrying seven black and six white passengers, was set ablaze. A mob attacked another bus in Birmingham, prompting the riders to call off the campaign. A group of activists from Nashville decided to pick up the journey where it had left off; they made it as far as Jackson, Mississippi, where they were arrested and eventually sent to Parchman, where several spent more than seven weeks in isolated cells.

There was not much to do but sing. Singing helped to banish boredom and to bolster solidarity, and the Riders continued to do so even after guards took away their mattresses for the infraction. (Eventually some of the guards began to hum along.) Among the songs they sang was an improvisation of the "Battle Hymn." "Mine eyes have seen the coming of equality for all," it began, and its chorus proclaimed, "Black and white shall live together / integration is for all."

The borrowed "Battle Hymn" tune reinforced the integrationist message of the revised lyrics, for, by the 1960s, if the song still conjured up abolitionist associations for those continuing the emancipatory struggle, for many others it also expressed the triumph of traditional American values. The Freedom Rides, like many of the campaigns of the early civil rights movement, sought to merge those two meanings. The demand for racial integration called the nation to honor its most fundamental ideals; it insisted that excavating the abolitionist associations of the "Battle Hymn" was a project of restoration. The freedom movement, as its most prominent champion, Martin Luther King Jr., declared, was premised on the belief that "white Americans cherish their democratic traditions over the ugly customs and privileges of generations."[9]

In Parchman a new sort of song had rung out from the cells even more defiantly than did the revised "Battle Hymn." In the campaigns of the previous months, these "freedom songs" had displaced traditional American standards like the "Battle Hymn" and "Onward Christian Soldiers" as the leading anthems of the movement. These songs took the materials of African American Southern culture—gospel tunes, slave chants, spirituals, agricultural union anthems—and repurposed them for contemporary struggles. The old songs' expression of longing for spiritual redemption had always provided a cover for the desire for change in this world. Now that cloak was stripped away and the songs called openly for economic justice, political opportunity, and personal freedom. The old resonances, however, did not disappear. Freedom songs were at once political and spiritual, fueling a quest to have one's God-given humanity recognized by fellow citizens. Sometimes traditional hymns were sung unchanged but granted new meaning; the old gospel song "This Little Light of Mine," for instance, became a statement of both spiritual worth and political agency. And sometimes singers changed a word or a stanza to do new work. While in Mississippi's Hinds County Jail, an Illinois minister who had participated in the Freedom Rides made over an old gospel tune, "Woke Up in the Morning with My Mind Stayed on Jesus," into "Woke Up This Morning with My Mind Stayed on Freedom," which became one of the movement's more popular songs. The song "If You Want to Get to Heaven, Do What Jesus Says" became "If You Want to Get to Heaven, Register and Vote." And in perhaps the most direct translation, "Amen," with its single-word chorus chanted in a rich concatenation of harmonies, saw new life as "Freedom."[10]

These songs were rooted in call-and-response singing, with verses that fed into a simple chorus provided by a song leader or improvised by members of the congregation. The participatory nature of the singing underscored powerful egalitarian strains within a movement increasingly buoyed by the dedication of students. These young activists bristled at any insinuation that they were foot soldiers following the orders of movement elders (which might explain something of the waning appeal of martial hymns like the "Battle Hymn" or "Onward Christian Soldiers," which also lacked the suppleness and adaptability of the freedom songs). At various gatherings of movement leaders, such as the 1960 meeting at Shaw College in Raleigh that gave birth to the Student Non-Violent Coordinating Committee (SNCC), those assembled sought to codify the movement songs. Yet the power of these songs ultimately derived from their responsiveness to local conditions, and most communities had their own favorite variations.[11]

The one song able to transcend these particularities and to speak for the freedom movement as a whole was "We Shall Overcome." As an expression of resolute faith in an ultimate overcoming "someday," the song provided a counterpoint to the triumphant declaration of imminent deliverance announced by the "Battle Hymn." The two songs shared a similar genealogy, with nineteenth-century origins in religious gatherings and a subsequent reincarnation as a labor anthem before assimilation into the repertoire of the civil rights movement. The origins of "We Shall Overcome" extend back at least to the end of the nineteenth century, when an early version, "I'll Be All Right," was a favorite in many black Southern Baptist and Methodist churches. In 1945 the mostly African American workers who had recently formed the Food, Tobacco and Agricultural Workers Union organized a strike against American Tobacco Company in Charleston, South Carolina, and adapted the song for their cause. They collectivized the struggle the song sustained by changing the lyrics to "We Will Overcome," and shifted the focus from personal spiritual transcendence to a campaign for economic justice. It quickly became a standard on the picket line.[12]

In 1947 Zilphia Horton, the musical director of the Highlander Folk School in Monteagle, Tennessee, learned the song from a group of visiting members of the Food, Tobacco and Agricultural Workers Union. She began teaching "We Will Overcome" in all her workshops and passed it on to union organizers throughout the South. She also taught the song to the folk singer Pete Seeger when he visited Highlander that year. Seeger tinkered with it, changing the rhythm slightly and adding a number of lines that honored the burgeoning civil rights movement. He eventually produced the song we now recognize as "We Shall Overcome," which he played at folk gatherings and union meetings throughout the North.

In the 1950s Highlander began to shift its focus from labor to civil rights. Rosa Parks had attended a workshop there shortly before her role in sparking the Montgomery Bus Boycott. In 1957, when Horton died, a California sociologist and folk singer named Gus Carawan assumed her position as Highlander's musical director. Like his predecessor, Carawan sought to teach the African American activists who had begun training there some of the old union classics. Those songs, however, failed to stick. Yet if "Solidarity Forever" did little to inspire, it could at least instruct. As Carawan later explained, he "knew about the old labor-movement tradition of changing an old song into something new, with words for the moment." He cited the way the "Battle Hymn" birthed "Solidarity Forever" as the prime example of the phenomenon. "But the songs that everyone in the South knew, the spirituals and hymns, weren't really being used that way," he added. So he suggested that the black students create their own battle hymns from their community's reserves of spirituals and traditional church songs. At first they resisted, suggesting that it would be almost sacrilegious to employ these "very personal songs about salvation." But Carawan pressed on, insisting that it was the songs' religious resonance that would make them so powerful. Among other songs, Carawan taught them "We Shall Overcome," and it quickly became a favorite. In April 1961 he attended the organizational convention that would lead to the establishment of SNCC and sang the song at the start of a meeting on its opening night.

From then on, "We Shall Overcome" became the leading anthem of SNCC and of the freedom movement more generally. SNCC field secretaries taught the song to communities throughout the South, promoting a standardized Highlander version to take the place of the regional variations and the traditional "I'll Be All Right." They also transformed the singing of the song into a movement ritual, with the singers standing in a circle, linking hands, right over left. In the original publication of the Highlander version, Carawan had included the notation, "With quiet determination," and this is precisely what the song seemed able to express—and to sustain. One SNCC leader who participated in the 1961 Freedom Rides recalled the song's power. When the Riders were being held in Parchman, a guard began beating one of them, who, "with blood streaming down his face . . . began to sing 'We Shall Overcome.' The guard turned red-faced and walked away." "When you get through singing" the song, another SNCC field secretary explained, "you could walk over a bed of hot coals, and you wouldn't feel it."[13]

The history of "We Shall Overcome," braiding together the faiths of Southern black church members, white and black agricultural workers, white folklorists, and black student activists, testified to the interracial potency of the civil rights movement. Freedom songs more generally came to represent the nonviolent and integrationist ideal at the heart of the movement. White audiences and activists quickly embraced the songs, as did the promoters of the folk music revival sweeping the nation. At the 1963 Newport Folk Festival, nearly all the major performers sang their own version of a freedom song. The national media also helped to spread the songs to a broader audience. The *New York Times*'s music critic Robert Shelton described "We Shall Overcome" as the archetypal freedom song, expressing the soul of the movement. In fact many Southern blacks learned it not from traveling SNCC emissaries but from television coverage of protests. Perhaps the most telling sign of the integration of freedom songs into mainstream white society came at the conclusion of a nationally televised speech by President Lyndon Johnson, when he affirmed his commitment to a Voting Rights Bill by emphatically quoting a familiar phrase: "We . . . shall . . . overcome."[14]

Not everyone cheered such a borrowing. For some, it reflected the co-optation of the movement by whites and by a liberal ideology that encouraged submissiveness in the face of brutal repression. Civil rights legal victories of the 1950s and 1960s had triggered an unrelenting and savage counteraction among Southern white reactionaries; by 1966 more than thirty civil rights leaders had been murdered in the previous decade, resulting in only three convictions. A younger generation within the freedom movement, exemplified by Stokely Carmichael, a tall, charismatic Trinidadian who rose to the chairmanship of SNCC, soured on nonviolence as a tactic and integration as an ideal and pushed instead for militant black self-determination. A strong apocalyptic strain pulsed beneath their Black Power rhetoric, most prominently in the preachments of Malcolm X, the Nation of Islam evangelist. With frequent citations of Revelation and prophetic biblical texts, Malcolm X insisted that the nation was living through a time of "prophecy fulfillment" and that God would soon destroy the United States in "a lake of fire" for the sin of slavery. "A day of great separation is at hand," he warned, "the handwriting is on the wall of America."[15]

It was at this moment that the soul of John Brown once again began to stir. The 1959 centennial of his execution had been marked at Harpers Ferry with an uncomfortable combination of reenactments, panel discussions, and a John Brown beard contest. Surveying the commemoration, the *New York Times* remarked, "John Brown's Raid was embarrassing and untimely when it occurred in 1859, and it apparently still is today." But the militant Left that emerged in the following decade refused to be embarrassed by Brown, claiming him as a spiritual forefather as they plotted their own raids on the arsenals of the American establishment. In a tribute to Brown, for example, the Weather Underground, the far-left group responsible for a number of bombings in the late 1960s and 1970s, named their journal *Osawatomie*, the town where Brown and his men, using guerrilla tactics, beat back a much larger proslavery force.

Black radicals wielded Brown's legacy with a particular fierceness, for it served not merely to rouse fellow comrades to action but to chastise white society. Brown became the exception that proved the racialist rule. He was "the only good white the country's ever had," announced Malcolm X. "[He was] the blackest white man anyone had ever known," declared the SNCC militant H. Rap Brown, "the only white man I could respect and he is dead." In these tributes, Brown's dedication to revolutionary violence eclipsed his racial egalitarianism. His memory rebuked white liberals, and their moderate black allies, who spoke of human brotherhood but lacked the will to fight for it. When Malcolm X lampooned attempts by whites to dismiss Brown as a madman, he was not merely making a point about historical memory. "Any white man who is ready and willing to shed blood for your freedom—in sight of other whites, he's nuts," he explained in a speech to the Organization of Afro-American Unity in 1964. "If you are with me," he said the following year, "then you have to be willing to do as old John Brown did."[16]

Unsurprisingly militants and black nationalists showed little love for Howe's "Battle Hymn." Its millennial strains failed to impress them; its abolitionist legacies were mired in the memory of a century of oppression, and they associated the hymn with a complacent American patriotism. As early as 1948 the African American writer James Baldwin, a lifelong admirer of John Brown and the most articulate spokesperson of black rage, dismissed the "Battle Hymn" as quintessentially American . . . banal and brave and cheerful." It did not help the hymn's standing with radicals that it was increasingly appropriated by the opponents of the freedom movement. The crowds who assembled to jeer black students who integrated schools and universities throughout the South often chanted, to the tune of the "Battle Hymn," "Glory, Glory, Segregation / The South shall rise again." Radicals, in turn, promoted their own militant appropriation of the tune. In 1965 Len Chandler, an African American songwriter, attended a commemoration of the Harpers Ferry raid planned by Hunter College students and composed for the occasion an adaptation that invoked Brown. "Mine eyes have seen injustice in each city, town and state," the song began, and went on to reject the standard establishment response: "Wait." Its chorus, soon adopted as a slogan by the Black Panther Party, restored to the song the air of aggressive militancy it had enjoyed as a Union marching tune: "Move on over or we'll move on over you / And the movement's moving on." In fact in the song's second verse, Chandler explicitly recruits Brown to disown the integrationist overtones of the freedom songs—and, in a sense, to repudiate the "Battle Hymn"'s own reconciliationist legacy:

> You conspire to keep us silent in the field and in the slum
> You promise us the vote and sing us, "We Shall Overcome,"
> But John Brown knew what freedom was and died to win us some
> That's why we keep marching on.[17]

Yet many black nationalists had little interest in creating more militant versions of freedom songs. As members of a younger generation that had bypassed the two institutional incubators of black communal singing—the Church and historically black colleges—they rejected the culture of group singing entirely. They demonstrated a particular contempt for freedom songs, which they understood as anthems of accommodation. In a revolution, explained Malcolm X to boisterous laughter in a November 1963 speech, people are too busy *swinging* to do any *singing*.[18]

The most celebrated of the freedom songs naturally attracted the largest share of contempt. When Malcolm X invited the SNCC Freedom Singers to a meeting of the Nation of Islam, he explained, "I just don't believe we're going to overcome, singing. If you're going to get yourself a .45 and start singing 'We Shall Overcome,' I'm with you." In his 1964 speech, "The Ballot or the Bullet," he rejected the passivity that seemed to reside in the song's elevation of a millennial "someday." "We want freedom *now*," he declared, "but we're not going to get it saying 'We Shall Overcome.' We've got to fight until we overcome."[19]

The strains within the freedom movement came to the fore during the last great march of the period, in the summer of 1966. In June, James Meredith, the first African American to gain admission to the University of Mississippi, began a solitary "march against fear" in the state, from the Tennessee border to the state capital of Jackson. On the march's second day, an unemployed Memphis contractor named Aubrey James Norvell ambushed Meredith, shooting him in the back and legs. Leaders of the civil rights movement, including Martin Luther King Jr. and Stokely Carmichael, quickly gathered in the hotel room where Meredith was recovering and promised to continue his march. It was on the way to Jackson that the more militant strains of the movement burst into the open. Carmichael had rebuffed NAACP elders who offered money and media support if the marchers would tone down their militancy and their criticism of the Johnson administration. After the NAACP pulled out, SNCC activists were able to use the march to highlight their opposition to the mainstream civil rights organizations that had previously set the movement's pace and tone. For much of the march, a group of gun-toting black Southerners, the Deacons for Defense, provided an armed escort. There was much angry talk along the way about the failed strategy of nonviolence, about the folly of allowing "white phonies" to participate in the movement. It was at a speech in Greenwood, Mississippi, standing on a truck's tailgate, that Carmichael introduced the Black Power slogan, and it was on the road to Jackson that Len Chandler's "Move on Over or We'll Move on Over You" was first widely sung.

One day, during an afternoon break in the march, King, the movement's leading champion of nonviolence, led the marchers in "We Shall Overcome." As he later recalled, they began it "with all the traditional fervor, the glad thunder and gentle strength that had always characterized the singing" of the song. But when they reached the stanza that speaks of "black and white together," several of the marchers abruptly stopped. When King asked them about it, they responded that in this "new day" they no longer felt comfortable singing those words. In fact they believed that the whole song should be abandoned. "Not 'We Shall Overcome,' but 'We Shall Overrun.'"[20]

That night, in a segregated Memphis motel room, King pleaded with the marchers to "remain true to the time-honored principles" of the movement. He ultimately forged an agreement with the militants that the remainder of the march would be nonviolent and interracial. As he had so often in the past, King found himself in the unenviable role of seeking to bridge the movement's feuding factions. Ideologically he struggled to reconcile "the truth of two opposites—acquiescence and violence—while avoiding the extremes and immoralities of both." He explained his predicament to a reporter: "I have to be militant enough to satisfy the militant, yet I have to keep enough discipline in the movement to satisfy white supporters and moderate Negroes." He was still searching, he explained, for a "synthesis." For all his public acclaim, that synthesis would prove elusive. And in his final years, before his assassination in April 1968, it seemed as if he called off the search by embracing an economic radicalism and an opposition to the Vietnam War that alienated former white allies and black moderates without winning over the champions of Black Power.

Yet that synthesis was not chimerical. The distance between King the nonviolent evangel and the Black Power militants was never as great as the chasm reported by the media. Their relationship was as much complementary as adversarial. Black nationalists like Stokely Carmichael and Malcolm X respected King and continued to work with him, even as they repudiated his tactics and ideology. And King, though he rejected their violent rhetoric and doubted the wisdom of the Black Power slogan (he suggested "Black Equality" in its stead), applauded the "magnificent new militancy" that its advocates had helped to spark. Most significantly, the credible threat of violent black resistance fed the white public's appreciation of nonviolent black resistance. As Malcolm X explained to a group of Islamic students in London in February 1965, "At one time the whites in the United States called [King] a racialist, an extremist, and a Communist. Then the Black Muslims came along and the whites thanked the Lord for Martin Luther King."[21]

In his later years, an increasingly radicalized King would move even closer toward a rapprochement with Black Power. Even before that, however, the millennial and prophetic themes that undergirded much of his oratory pointed to the possibility of that accord. These themes allowed King to affirm the nation's providential identity as well as to rebuke it for its sinfulness. They helped to reconcile militancy and moderation, in part because listeners who preferred either could find favor with his words. And they suggest that the song that can best illuminate the place of Martin Luther King in the civil rights movement is not "We Shall Overcome" but the "Battle Hymn of the Republic." It was this hymn, with its capacity to inspire visions of perfect peace and vengeful retribution, that was able to span King's own ideological transformations. It was this hymn that could celebrate the glory of America's millennial promise while speaking to the frustrations of those who suffered most from the failures to fulfill it.[22]

★

IN JANUARY 1954 Martin Luther King Jr., twenty-five years old, took up a pastorate at Dexter Avenue Baptist Church, in Montgomery, Alabama. He arrived with impressive academic credentials: an undergraduate degree from Morehouse College, a Bachelor of Divinity degree from Crozer Theological

Seminary, and a Ph.D. in systemic theology from Boston University. He also boasted an imposing pedigree: his father and his maternal grandfather were both prominent Baptist ministers in Atlanta. Charismatic and erudite, he possessed a rich, expressive baritone that fed an electric pulpit presence; in divinity school fellow students would crowd the chapel whenever he practiced a sermon. King assumed that he would serve as a pastor for a number of years and then return to academe to become a professor of theology.[23]

In December 1955, nearly two years later, the leaders of Montgomery's African American community selected King to serve as the head of the Montgomery Improvement Association, organized to lead the boycott of the city's segregated buses. The elders were no doubt attracted by King's dynamic presence. They also surely appreciated the fact that, as a recent arrival in the city, he had ensnared himself in few internecine feuds within the African American community and that if the boycott should fail, the youthful King would not have a difficult time extricating himself and moving elsewhere.[24]

Almost overnight King became the public face of the boycott and was catapulted to the forefront of the civil rights movement. The boycott's success, secured by a 1956 Supreme Court ruling desegregating the city's buses, bolstered his stature. To spread the strategy throughout the South, in 1957 King and a number of other ministers founded the Southern Christian Leadership Conference (SCLC); it would "redeem the soul of America" through sustained campaigns of nonviolent direct action to oppose segregation. King moved to Atlanta to take up the presidency of the organization (and to be copastor of his father's Ebenezer Baptist Church). SCLC-led initiatives achieved varying degrees of success—in Birmingham and Selma, Alabama, most prominently—though also suffered a number of frustrating setbacks, such as in Albany, Georgia. Through all these efforts, King came to represent for many Southern blacks and Northern whites a prophetic voice free from bitterness and violence. In 1963 *Time* magazine named him its "Person of the Year." In 1964 he received the Nobel Peace Prize.

During the Montgomery boycott, King had been tutored in the subtleties and rigors of nonviolence by Bayard Rustin and other members of the Fellowship of Reconciliation, an association of devout pacifists. For King, the Montgomery movement confirmed the viability of the strategy. It also sorely tested his own fidelity to it. After his house was firebombed, he talked down the angry mob that had gathered outside and commanded them to love their enemies—"our white brothers," he clarified—no matter the provocation. A trip to India in 1959, a pilgrimage to the land of the guru of nonviolence, Mahatma Gandhi, further deepened his commitment.[25]

Depending on his audience, King could take different approaches to the justification of nonviolent resistance. To those who itched for the sword, he offered tactical arguments. It was ludicrous to imagine that urban guerrillas could do more than pester the strongest military in the world. "We have neither the techniques, the numbers, nor the weapons to win a violent campaign," he admonished militants in 1966. What's more, armed black resistance would sanction the brutal repression some white leaders were all too eager to unleash. He could also call upon his understanding of the appetites of modern media. The evening news would always train its cameras on the few rowdies in a crowd smashing windows, leaving the peaceful protesters marching beyond the lens, and King understood that these images would soon overwhelm any consideration of what had provoked the violence in the first place. Most important, succumbing to violence would strip the movement of its most precious asset, its moral standing, which served as the guarantor of its greatest promise: the formation of an interracial mass coalition. Nonviolent resistance was a means of creating a moral theater that dramatized a clash between the forces of good and the forces of evil, a spectacle that the nation—and the world—could not ignore. It was, King explained, the most effective means of reaching "the conscience of the great decent majority."[26]

For King, these arguments served to nourish the deeper spiritual and moral roots of his own commitment to nonviolent resistance. Nonviolence spoke to his faith in the innate capacities for goodness in all men and women. It was grounded in what he called "an overflowing love" for all men, God's love operating in the human heart, "which seeks nothing in return." As he explained at the opening of the first SNCC meeting, the ultimate aim of nonviolence is "reconciliation," the creation of the "beloved community."[27]

Given his commitment to nonviolence, it is not surprising that King rarely invoked the leading figures within the tradition of militant African American insurrection: Nat Turner, Denmark Vesey, and David Walker. Nor is it surprising that he showed little public regard for John Brown. When King delivered the keynote address at a symposium hosted by the University of Minnesota on the centenary of the Harpers Ferry raid—its theme was "the relevance of John Brown's raid to the Negro problem today"—he spoke about the challenges facing the civil rights movement without once mentioning Brown. In fact a recent scholar has found only one occasion in which King publicly referred to Brown, and this was not to the man but to the song that bore his name. In an 1965 interview with *Playboy*, King linked together "John Brown's Body," the "Battle Hymn" and "We Shall Overcome" as songs that could bear "the *soul* of a movement."[28]

Yet if King demonstrated little respect for the broadsword-wielding Brown, he had stronger affinities with the Brown who ascended the scaffold. As Brown neared his end, he became increasingly confident that his death would help secure the triumph of the antislavery cause. "I am worth inconceivably more to hang than for any other purpose," he famously declared in his prison cell. In the days after the execution, countless Northerners confirmed Brown's self-valuation by equating his death with Christ's crucifixion. The analogy claimed Brown not merely as a martyr but as a figure whose suffering might redeem a guilty nation.[29]

King had an even greater faith in the promise of "unearned suffering." Men have long appreciated that violence could serve as a creative and powerful social force, he explained in a 1961 speech; this belief has fueled the prosecution of countless wars throughout history. But he insisted that unearned "self-suffering" could be just as powerful and creative, and just as redemptive, to both the sufferer and those transfigured by witnessing the act.

Indeed from nearly the moment he was elevated to the leadership of the Montgomery movement, King accepted the possibility that he would be required to make the ultimate sacrifice for the cause of racial justice. After watching television coverage of John F. Kennedy's assassination, King declared to his wife, "This is what is going to happen to me." This was not morbid paranoia. Notwithstanding the persistent sniping from King's critics—white and black—that he excelled at avoiding the risks he urged others to brave, expertly arranging his own release on bail or leaving protests before the police clubs came raining down, King spent much of his time at the forefront of the freedom movement under the constant threat of death. One newspaper counted at least five separate attempts on King's life—before the final, successful one.[30]

To find some meaning in these threats, King increasingly turned to the figure of the suffering Christ. During the 1963 protests in Birmingham, he defied a court injunction prohibiting demonstrations in the city and offered himself up for arrest on Good Friday, keenly aware of the symbolism. "The cross is something that you bear and ultimately that you die on," King told an SCLC gathering in 1967. "And that's the way I have decided to go." "[My work] might get me crucified," he declared during a desegregation campaign in Albany, Georgia. "I may die. But I want it to be said even if I die in the struggle that 'He died to make men free.'"[31]

Others in the freedom movement compared King to Christ. At a mass meeting during the Montgomery movement after King was convicted by a county court of violating an antiboycott law, he was introduced as "the man who today was nailed to the cross for you and me." At another meeting in a Montgomery church, before King rose to speak, the congregation broke out into the hymn "Come Thou Almighty King." Ebenezer churchwomen often referred to him as "Little Lord Jesus." The analogy could also serve as a rebuke. The calls of "De Lawd!" that accompanied his sermons often carried a hint of derision. The analogy became a way for his critics to oppose the public deification of King, to protest the overreliance on his charismatic presence to forward the movement's ends and SCLC's consequent neglect of the cultivation of local leaders and grassroots organizing. King's crown of thorns, they snickered, more resembled a laurel wreath. As Julian Bond complained, King and the institutions that promoted his civil rights ministry had "sold the concept that one man will come to your town and save you."[32]

King's critics saw in his references to crucifixion symptoms of his grandiosity and penchant for self-promotion. Yet as King's own citation of the final lines of the "Battle Hymn" reveal, a more egalitarian intention also emerges from analogies to Christ's redeeming sacrifice. Indeed, for King, bearing the Cross was the essence of Christianity for all believers; his attraction was not to an exceptional but to an exemplary Christ. The nonviolent direct action campaigns that he championed drew sustenance from the plentiful reservoirs of self-sacrifice within the African American community. When King exhorted the activists who had congregated to challenge segregation in Albany, "We will wear them down with our capacity to suffer," he made no special claims to exclusive ownership of that talent. As one historian of the civil rights movement has explained, King's "tactic of massive, peaceful confrontation . . . democratized the attitudes that had until then been held by a special minority." And so King was more than happy to apply the concluding lines of the "Battle Hymn" to the sacrifices made by others. In March 1960 he wrote an encouraging note to a group of Tallahassee students who had been arrested for protesting at a local store. The students had refused to pay the $300 fine and instead had accepted a sixty-day jail sentence. "There is nothing more majestic and sublime than the determined courage of individuals willing to suffer and sacrifice for the cause of freedom," he wrote them. "As Christ died to make men holy, you are suffering to make men free."[33]

King's reference to the "Battle Hymn" was not incidental. Many of his most celebrated public speeches explicitly borrowed from or shared close affinities with Howe's hymn. This is the case with the "I Have a Dream" speech that concluded the 1963 March on Washington for Jobs and Freedom. The march was planned by an interracial group of civil rights organizations for August 28 as a means of pushing Congress to pass the Kennedy administration's civil rights bill. As many as 250,000 people, perhaps a third of them white, gathered at the Washington Monument and made their way down Constitution and Independence Avenues to the Lincoln Memorial. Southern politicians had warned of screaming mobs tearing though the capital's streets and had likened the event to Mussolini's Fascist black shirt march on Rome and Hitler's Nuremberg rallies. But the march's planners had worked diligently to ensure that the day would proceed without unrest of any kind. The only arrest made on Monument grounds that day would be of a Ku Klux Klan sympathizer staging a counterprotest. Reporters compared the march to a well-run revival meeting, a Sunday school picnic, or a fish fry. It was, as King declared, "the greatest demonstration for freedom in the history of our nation."

The interracial crowd was also a testament to his integrationist vision. A button pinned to the lapels of many marchers showed a black hand clasping a white one. The planners had also made sure that the speakers who mounted the stage set up in front of the Lincoln Memorial all held to a resolutely upbeat tone and that the demands they made upon the Kennedy administration and Congress were forceful yet civil. They had even insisted that John Lewis, the young SNCC representative, rewrite a speech they deemed too incendiary. (In it he promised that if segregation was not dismantled, there would be a new Sherman's March through the South that would "burn Jim Crow to the ground—nonviolently.") King was granted the last spot of the day's ten speakers, in part as a tribute to his powerful oratory and in part because other speakers thought they would have a better chance of appearing on the evening news with earlier speaking times.[34]

By the time King ascended to the podium, the crowd had been sweltering in the August sun for hours. The band struck up the "Battle Hymn of the Republic." The song was particularly appropriate since King had spent much of the night before in his room at the Willard Hotel, where a little more than a hundred years earlier Julia Ward Howe had enjoyed a productive night herself. He finished an outline at midnight and then wrote out a draft in longhand, revising it as he went along with his aides and finishing at about four in the morning. Yet for all that work, the draft did not contain the most celebrated sections of the speech. Those he would extemporize on the podium.

King began by recognizing the promise embodied in the Emancipation Proclamation, whose centenary the nation had recently celebrated. Yet, he went on to declare, the promise remained unfulfilled. The nation had given blacks a "bad check," he declared. "One hundred years later, the Negro still is not free." Until the United States made good on the promissory note of its founding principles, black Americans could not rest. "Nineteen sixty-three is not an end, but a beginning," he announced. They needed to continue to struggle for racial equality without succumbing to a spirit of bitterness, and to meet physical force with soul force. As he neared his speech's conclusion, he suddenly paused, put aside his prepared text, and made a decisive turn, dipping instead into one of his favorite rhetorical set pieces. He began to speak of his "dream" of racial harmony. At that moment, his wife later remarked, the words of God seemed to flow through him.[35]

"I have a dream that one day . . . right there in Alabama, little black boys and black girls will be able to join hands with little white boys and white girls as sisters and brothers," he declared. "I have a dream that one day every valley shall be exalted, every hill and mountain shall be made low . . . and the glory of the Lord shall be revealed, and all flesh shall see it together." King had initially offered a private vision: "*I* have a dream." But here he also foretold a collective vision in which the act of witnessing itself would demonstrate the unity of all Americans. In the speech's spirited final lines, he expressed the promise of racial unity through images of geographic and ideological cohesion. He performed a riff on "America," the song that NAACP representatives had once rejected at Storer College, and then complemented it with an image of freedom ringing from mountaintops across the continent.

Taken together, he offered a vision of a unified nationality that rivaled Howe's as the most famous in American letters. And yet, unlike the "Battle Hymn," King did not dwell on the cataclysm that would await those who denied the nation's integrity. There was no discussion of the serpent to be trodden underfoot, little apocalyptic foreboding were the dream not fulfilled. It was, his friend Ralph Abernathy explained, a "prophecy of pure hope."[36]

King's "I Have a Dream" speech both echoed and diverged from the "Battle Hymn." Its words were not quoted, but its spirit was invoked. In other prominent speeches he had borrowed from the hymn more explicitly. In June 1959, for example, speaking before a gathering of young NAACP activists, King extolled the cause of nonviolence, while recognizing that many were frustrated that its fruits took time to ripen. Progress would not come cheap; it would need to be earned through personal sacrifice. Nonetheless the cause of racial justice would ultimately triumph. "The arch of the moral universe is long, but it bends toward justice," he intoned, trying out a variation of a line (possibly borrowed from an article by the Unitarian minister John Haynes Holmes) that he would employ more famously at his speech at the conclusion of the march from Selma to Montgomery. He ended by insisting that he could "see something marvelous unfolding" and illustrated this vision by quoting the first two stanzas of the "Battle Hymn."

Several months later he concluded his valedictory speech as president of the Montgomery Improvement Association by citing the hymn again. "I know you are asking . . . When will our suffering in this righteous struggle come to an end?" King conceded that he could not provide an "exact date," but he could offer his absolute faith in the movement's victory: "[It] grows out of a deep and patient trust in God who leaves us not alone in the struggle for righteousness, and whose matchless power is a fit contrast to the sordid weakness of man. I am certain of the future because: Mine eyes have seen the glory of the coming of the Lord." He then added the first, second, and fourth stanzas of the hymn, and finished with the "Glory, glory hallelujah" chorus.

King omitted two of the hymn's stanzas that most resolutely proclaim violence as an instrument of divine providence. In the third stanza, Howe suggests that God will reward Northerners for the severity with which they "crush the serpent" that is the Confederacy. And the final stanza, its beatific Christ figure notwithstanding, had often been marshaled to sanction killing. King did invoke biblical images of divine retribution, the grapes of wrath and the terrible swift sword. Yet whereas in Howe's poem, those images are tied to Union troops serving as providential agents, King leaves the instrumentality of God's justice unspecified. As early as his 1957 "Prayer Pilgrimage" address, he had warned that the "clock of destiny is ticking out" and had urged the nation to act "before it is too late." A little more than a decade later he proclaimed that, if the nation did not heed his calls to embrace economic justice for all its citizens, "[it was] going straight to Hell." In these pronouncements, as in the unspoken stanzas of the hymn, the possibility of violence hovers over the outskirts of his commitment to nonviolence. The apocalypticism of the "Battle Hymn" enabled King to threaten cataclysm on his oppressors without brandishing the sword himself. Just as Julia Ward Howe could become an advocate for peace in the postbellum years without disavowing the principles of her "Battle Hymn," King could reconcile the violent rhetoric of the song with his dedication to nonviolence by positioning himself as a witness to the imminent arrival of God's justice.[37]

King elaborated on these same themes by invoking the "Battle Hymn" in the peroration of his March 1965 speech in Montgomery, Alabama, at the conclusion of a protest march begun fifty miles away in the town of Selma. The SCLC had led a massive voter registration drive there, an effort steadfastly opposed by local authorities; the town's sheriff wore a gigantic button on his lapel that read, "Never." King planned the march to Montgomery to present a series of grievances to the governor. More than five hundred men and women set off for the capital on March 7, 1965. King was not among them, having returned to Atlanta to minister to his congregation. When they reached the Edmund Pettus Bridge, leading out of town, the marchers were brutally set upon by the sheriff's vigilantes with tear gas, clubs, and cattle prods. The images of the beatings, caught on film, shocked the nation. King immediately called for another march the following week. He led an interracial crowd of three thousand to the Pettus Bridge, but turned back, unwilling to defy a federal injunction. After authorities lifted the injunction, a third march to Montgomery was planned for March 21.

Some eight thousand marchers, Northerners and Southerners, blacks and whites, left Selma. Four days later, their numbers swelling to twenty-five thousand, they reached a Catholic school for blacks on the outskirts of Montgomery. There they heard Peter, Paul and Mary, Joan Baez, Harry Belafonte, Ella Fitzgerald, and a score of others perform. On the morning of the 24th, the crowd began the final leg of the journey into the city. As they marched up Montgomery's main thoroughfare to deliver their petition to Governor George Wallace, they sang the "Battle Hymn" and "Onward Christian Soldiers." On the grounds of the Alabama capitol, a series of dignitaries delivered triumphant speeches to the crowd, while Governor Wallace, who refused to meet with the protesters, watched the day's proceedings through slits in his office blinds. The day's final speaker was King.[38]

He delivered a speech whose central motif was that of the inexorable march. "We are on the move," he declared and urged listeners to continue to march—on segregation, on poverty, on the ballot box. He did warn that the journey would not be an easy one. "I know you are asking today, How long will it take?" It would not be long, King reassured them. And then, initiating a call-and-response exchange, he shouted "How long? Not long, because no lie can live forever. How long?"—and the crowd roared back "Not long!"— "because you shall reap what you sow. . . . How long? Not long! Because the arc of the moral universe is long, but it bends toward justice."

How long? Not long! That refrain, and King's embellishments on it, illuminated the reconciliation of the immediate claims of justice, what King

called "the fierce urgency of now," with a recognition of the disappointments of the moment. To a large extent, the direct action campaigns King
championed sought to effect mass conversions, which, as a student of Billy
Graham's crusades like King appreciated, could be instantaneously transformative. Yet King also came to realize that those transformations might be of
a slower sort. He fought to dispel "the myth of time," the idea that the
justness of their claims and the blindness of their antagonists should lead
African Americans to fall back on a passive faith in long-suffering patience.
Yet he increasingly came to understand that change in racial mores and attitudes *would* take time. So although he considered nonviolent direct action
the strategy "that will bring the Negro into the mainstream of American life
as quickly as possible," and although the SCLC chose "Freedom Now" as
a slogan to counter SNCC's embrace of "Black Power," in his final years
King conceded, "It all doesn't come now. That's a sad fact of life you have
to live with."[39]

In the Montgomery speech's final lines, King reached for the "Battle
Hymn" to cultivate urgency and to combat passivity in the face of the challenges ahead. The hymn's millennial framework helped to put the movement's frustrations into an eschatological context. Questions of secular
duration fell back in the presence of sacred time. The millennium of racial
justice was at hand; God *was* coming. Even disappointments testified to the
imminent arrival of His kingdom.

"How long?" he asked. Not long, because:

Mine eyes have seen the glory of coming of the Lord
He is trampling out the vintage where the grapes of wrath are stored;
He has loosed the fateful lightning of his terrible swift sword;
His Truth is marching on.

He quoted the hymn's second stanza as well, before concluding with four
blasts of the "Glory, glory, hallelujah!" chorus, and then with the hymn's
final refrain: "His truth is marching on."[40]

These last lines held a powerful attraction for King because the act and
symbolism of marching had assumed such a prominent place in the ideology, rhetoric, and tactics of nonviolent resistance. "There is nothing more
powerful than the tramp, tramp of marching feet," he had proclaimed when
he took up Meredith's march against fear. Gandhi's Salt March, the opening
salvo in his campaign of nonviolent civil disobedience against British rule in
India, had been a leading inspiration for the 1963 March on Washington.

There had been countless American precedents as well: the 1957 Prayer Pilgrimage, the 1963 Freedom Walk down Detroit's Woodward Avenue to promote civil rights, and, stretching even further back, the 1894 march of Jacob Coxey's army of unemployed from Ohio to Washington, D.C. And for those in the Montgomery crowd that afternoon, the lines announcing God marching on must have recalled the march they had just completed.[41]

Indeed, by invoking the hymn's final refrain, King aligned the protesters with the force of God's truth, marching on in the hymn. Those witnessing God's truth also helped to bring it to fruition, reflecting King's belief that bearing witness—both to injustices and to the potential for justice to overcome them—was not a passive act but one that demanded courage and conviction. The image of marching also recalled one of King's favorite biblical tropes, the children of Israel's exodus from Egypt. "Walk together, children; don't you get weary, and it will lead us to the Promised Land," he had declared as the marchers prepared to leave Selma. "Alabama will be a new Alabama, and America will be a new America." The Exodus story gave the redemption narrative its pace: it featured prolonged periods of labor, even of wandering, punctuated by moments of millennial rapture and of emancipatory rupture. This had been the template for many spiritual journeys, and King embraced it for the freedom movement as well. Marching suggested determined movement toward a destination; it signaled a faith in the capacity to work toward a collective destiny, even as the biblical resonances of the phrase suggested a higher power leading the way.[42]

Finally, marching conjured up mobilization. Like Gandhi, who spoke of marshaling an army of peace volunteers, and various American religious leaders who claimed to march at the head of an army of believers, King was willing to use martial imagery to describe the discipline and purposefulness of those struggling for the cause of civil rights. "We did not hesitate to call our movement an army," he explained. "But it was a special army . . . that would sing but not slay." He almost always invoked such language to subvert the comparisons to military campaigns. Nonviolent direct action, he declared in 1963, was a "sword that heals," one that "cuts without wounding and ennobles the man who wields it." Yet the language also had a bit of steel in it, especially when reinforced by references to the "Battle Hymn," the marching song of an army that had been willing to sing *and* to slay. Together they reminded listeners how quickly a nonviolent army could turn into a violent one.[43]

For many, the march from Selma represented the high point of the freedom movement, in part because it seemed to foretell the emergence of an interracial "beloved community" and in part because of the disappointments that followed. "The path of Negro-white unity that had been converging crossed at Selma," noted King "and like a giant X began to diverge." Five months after the march, President Johnson signed the Voting Rights Act, prohibiting many of the discriminatory voting practices that had sparked protest in the South. Five days later, the Los Angeles neighborhood of Watts erupted in looting and rioting, leaving thirty-four dead and thousands injured—almost all of them African Americans. It took an army of 14,000 National Guardsmen and 1,600 policemen to restore order.[44]

Watts shocked King, as did his hostile reception when he toured the area in the riot's wake. Many of those he encountered had never heard of him before. Those who had did not seem terribly impressed with his nonviolent program. "'I have a dream' . . . craa-ap," quipped one Watts resident. "We don't want dreams, we want jobs." Those outbursts revealed to King how little the push for legal equality he had promoted in the South had touched African Americans trapped in slums in other parts of the country. He was startled to find Watts residents celebrating the apocalyptic scenes around them and insisting that they had "won" because they had made whites "pay attention." Nonviolent resistance could make little headway against such logic. Although King had been considering for some time a shift of focus to the North and to an engagement with issues of economic and not merely legal equality, Watts sparked a profound realization. As he confided to his advisor Bayard Rustin, "I worked to get these people the right to eat hamburgers, and now I've got to do something . . . to help them get the money to buy [them]." King anticipated that such an effort would prove more difficult than the campaigns against Southern segregation. For it would demand significant sacrifices from white Americans beyond their moral support. He imagined a "Bill of Rights for the Disadvantaged" that would cost $10 billion per year over a decade. And he called for "a radical redistribution of political and economic power," a "reconstruction of the entire society, a revolution of value."[45]

So King initiated what he termed the "second phase" of the freedom movement. It would move beyond civil rights to address broader issues of economic and social justice, challenging not merely racism but the inequities and iniquities of American capitalism and imperialism; it would insist upon a transformed and not merely an integrated nation and would leave King's beloved community badly frayed. He sought to address the poverty of the Northern slums, using the nonviolent tactics he had honed in the South to goad the government to action. Yet those tactics would have to become significantly more aggressive. "Nonviolent protest must now mature to a new level," he declared, "to correspond to heightened black impatience and stiffened white resistance." Such radicalism was the only alternative to an impending apocalypse of black rage, he maintained, and the only rival to the allure of Black Power.

In 1966 he moved his family into a slum tenement in Chicago's west side and planned a massive civil disobedience campaign to draw attention to what he called "the internal colonialism" of the city's slums. But Chicago was not Selma; his organization had little understanding of the urban setting and failed to rally many ghetto residents. He did manage to reach an agreement with Chicago's mayor Richard Daley over housing discrimination and slum conditions, but many black Chicagoans ultimately rejected it as a toothless farce that gained them little.[46]

The disappointing outcome in Chicago did not dampen King's economic radicalism; in fact, in the following months it grew more pronounced and was supplemented by his increasingly vocal opposition to the Vietnam War, which, he came to believe, not only insulted his nonviolent principles but also robbed the government of the funds necessary to address urban poverty. His antiwar stance quickly alienated many of his moderate supporters, white and black, as well as his allies within the Johnson administration, who branded him a traitor. King refused to heed calls to temper his outspoken opposition to the war, though he recognized it would do damage to his standing as a civil rights leader. "I feel so deep in my heart that we are so wrong in this country," he told one colleague, "and the time has come for real prophecy."[47]

He pushed for the inauguration of a broader Poor People's Campaign, despite the reluctance of his SCLC colleagues to make the poverty of all Americans the organization's central focus. The SCLC, King insisted, should recruit three thousand volunteers, an interracial cohort of whites, American Indians, Hispanics, and blacks from cities and rural districts across the nation that would converge on Washington, D.C. in April 1968. There they would erect a tent city and would make daily marches to the Capitol and the White House until their demands, which centered on guaranteed employment, a minimum income, and affordable housing, were met. This campaign of mass civil disobedience, King explained, was an effort to "transmute the inchoate rage of the ghetto into a creative and constructive force," a demonstration that would be "as attention-getting and dramatic as a riot, without destroying life or property." It was his "last, greatest dream."[48]

King threw himself into the Poor People's Campaign with an almost masochistic schedule of meetings, rallies, and speeches. But as the campaign yielded a disappointing crop of recruits and as the attacks on King mounted from his erstwhile liberal allies, he seemed to buckle under the burden, succumbing to fatigue and depression. He seemed a "different person. He was sad and depressed," noted one colleague. He had become "a profoundly weary and wounded spirit," remarked another. The urban riots that erupted in the summer of 1967 deeply distressed King as well. "These have been very difficult days for me," he admitted to a group of psychologists in September. "I'm tired now," he told reporters in August. "I've been in this thing thirteen years now and I'm tired."

Darker strains crept into his speeches and sermons. He began to sound a more ominous prophetic note, as his emphasis on unmerited suffering shifted to a focus on merited retribution. When asked to define the specific demands of his Poor People's Campaign, he responded, "I don't know what Jesus had as his demands other than 'Repent, for the Kingdom of God is at hand.'" "The judgment of God is on America now," he declared when lamenting the failure of Congress to direct funds to antipoverty programs while directing billions to the war in Vietnam; a "curtain of doom" would fall upon the nation soon if it did not change its ways.

King's commitment to nonviolence did not waver, but his faith in his ability to reach the "great decent majority" did. White liberals had badly disappointed him in their failure to support his efforts in the North; he came to understand that though they were willing to rally against the brutality of Southern segregation, their courage faltered when confronted with the possibility of integrating Northern schools and neighborhoods. He began to reconsider the integrity of America's millennial promise, pointing out in numerous speeches that the nation's founding principles, enshrined in the Declaration of Independence, had never been faithfully applied, and hinting that they might never be. "America is a racist country," he announced in early 1968. And so, when he invoked his "dream" of interracial concord, he increasingly did so to express how it had withered. At a Christmas Eve sermon in 1967, he recalled his famous speech at the March on Washington from four years before, when he had "tried to talk to the nation about a dream that [he] had had." He added, "I must confess . . . I started seeing it turn into a nightmare."[49]

IT WAS IN THE midst of this season of disillusionment and infirmity that King arrived in Memphis to support a wildcat strike by the city's garbagemen. Sanitation work was dirty, backbreaking labor, often starting at sunup and finishing past sundown. The city did not provide the men, mostly black, with uniforms or showers, and the workers were at the mercy of white supervisors who routinely devised ways of stripping them of their already meager pay. As one sanitation worker tersely explained, "There is no worse job." Workers had seethed under these conditions for years, but the death of two colleagues who had been crushed in a faulty garbage compressor had provided the final spark for the strike. They demanded that the city recognize their union and agree to payroll deduction of union dues, but they met with fierce opposition from Memphis's mayor Henry Loeb, who quickly mobilized a squad of strikebreakers. During a February march on behalf of the workers, city police maced and beat protesters indiscriminately; the wanton police brutality helped transform the strike from a labor issue into a racial one.

That transformation, as well as a local court's injunction of public union officials from performing any activities that could promote the strike, elevated local black ministers to positions of leadership within the Memphis movement. One of them was James Lawson, who had spent several years in India studying nonviolence, had befriended King as a theology student at Oberlin, and had assumed leadership positions within the SCLC. Lawson invited King to lend his support to the movement by leading a mass rally. King's advisors reminded him of the difficulty of extricating himself from local conflicts once he had parachuted into them; they worried that Memphis would distract from the planning of the Poor People's Campaign. King brushed aside the concerns. He saw the Memphis struggle as a potential springboard for the Campaign, a cause that could unite the poor and the middle class around issues of economic and racial justice.

But King did not appreciate the significant fractures developing underneath the façade of movement unity, divisions that mirrored those within the freedom movement more generally, between older and younger generations, between nonviolent protest and more militant demonstrations of Black Power. The latter perspective was represented in Memphis by the Invaders, a loose network of black militants who sought to organize ghetto youth and who displayed a brazen impatience with the nonviolent tactics of the strike's organizers. Why were black scabs not punished for their racial apostasy, they demanded. Why were the garbage trucks not vandalized? As one Invader explained, "If you expect honkies to get the message, you got to break some windows."[50]

On March 18 King arrived in Memphis and delivered a sermon to the more than twenty thousand men and women who had assembled at the Mason Temple, the national headquarters for the Church of God in Christ, the largest African American Pentecostal denomination in the nation and the largest indoor black facility in the South. With the crowd calling out "Amen" and "Tell it, Doctor," King announced that a victory in Memphis would represent a victory for the poor of the entire nation. He issued a blistering jeremiad, warning of God's coming "indictment on America" for neglecting its least fortunate citizens. And then he suggested a step that had never before been proposed as part of the nonviolent civil rights movement: a general strike. The crowd met the proposal with a roar of support. King fed off their enthusiasm. For a moment he seemed energized, his old hopefulness restored. After sitting down, he quickly returned to the podium to announce that he would return ten days later to lead a protest march to mark a day of work stoppage.[51]

King was walking into a trap. The Invaders had decided that by sabotaging the march, they could win a definitive victory against King's nonviolent ideology. The march on March 28 began several hours late, as planners waited for King to arrive from New York, where he had squeezed in a series of meetings and speeches. The organizers placed a clearly exhausted King at the march's front, along with the striking sanitation workers, while a boisterous crowd of perhaps fifteen thousand surged behind them. Some sang "We Shall Overcome." Others chanted "Down with Loeb." Soon, from the march's rear came the sounds of smashing glass. Young marchers, a few affiliated with the Invaders but many others street folk who saw an opportunity for a quick profit, had begun breaking storefront windows and looting merchandise. From within the crowd rose shouts of "Burn it down, baby!" As the peaceful marchers in front began to realize what was happening and tried to escape, the demonstration descended into chaos. The scene of looting sent the police into a frenzy. They went on a rampage, attacking violent and peaceful protesters alike, dragging diners out of restaurants and killing a teenager. When the nonviolent marchers took refuge in a church, the police lobbed tear gas inside and continued their assault. King's handlers hustled him down a side street, where they flagged down a car and drove him safely back to his hotel. "Now we'll never get anybody to believe in nonviolence," he lamented to Ralph Abernathy as he watched the rioting continue on television. "Maybe we'll have to let violence run its course." The next day he left for Atlanta.[52]

The strike's local opponents used the riot as evidence that the strikers were, as they had always claimed, anarchist troublemakers, and blamed King's presence for inciting them. The national press, which had largely ignored the strike in Memphis until that point, pounced as well, pronouncing

King's image as a nonviolent saint badly tarnished. The *Providence (Rhode Island) Sunday Journal* denounced King as "reckless and irresponsible" and lambasted him for "scurr[ying] to safety" after the violence he had stoked erupted. Never was the precariousness of King's positioning between the civil rights moderates and militants more evident; the elders from the Urban League and NAACP blamed him for failing to control the marchers, while the Invaders pointed to the beatings the demonstrators had endured at the hands of the police as proof of the ineffectiveness of his nonviolent strategy.[53]

The attacks weighed heavily on King. Still, he was convinced of the necessity of leading another march in Memphis, one whose fidelity to nonviolent principles would be guaranteed by the careful preparation that the earlier march had lacked. On Wednesday, April 3, he returned to the city, weighed down by the realization that his leadership and his ideology were undergoing their most profound test yet. "Either the Movement lives or dies in Memphis," he insisted to his aides. As was his custom, he refused police protection once he returned; he believed it violated his status as a nonviolent leader. He settled in at the black-owned Lorraine Motel, despite warnings that, given the mounting threats against his life, its exposed balconies did not provide sufficient protection. (The flak he had received for staying at more expensive, white-owned establishments in previous trips to Memphis left him little choice.)[54]

King had been scheduled to speak that night at another mass meeting at the Mason Temple. Huddled in his motel room with a fever and a sore throat, he dispatched his deputy Ralph Abernathy in his place. It was not merely King's sorry state that led him to send a surrogate; the night had brought a torrential rainstorm, and King worried that the event might draw a poor turnout and that the national press would interpret it as evidence of his waning public support.

When Abernathy walked into the Temple and saw the crowd of some three thousand Memphis citizens who had braved the storm, when he noted the disappointment on their faces as they realized King was not with him, and when he noticed the television cameras prepared to take in the scene, he immediately telephoned King and urged him to come. King jumped into a cab and drove through the storm. When he arrived, the exultant crowd surged toward him.

Many of those at the Mason Temple that night shared the observation of one Memphis minister who noted that King "looked harrowed and tired and worn and rushed." Abernathy delivered a lengthy introduction, praising King extravagantly, in part to give King additional time to gather strength.

When Abernathy sat down, fellow ministers joked that it sounded as if he had just preached King's eulogy. Then King ascended the podium to deliver one of his greatest speeches. It would also be his last.[55]

He began, as was his custom, in measured tones. "Something is happening in Memphis," he declared, "something is happening in our world." From the start, he assigned to the Memphis strike a global import, linking it with anticolonial struggles in Africa and the other uprisings of the dispossessed that were convulsing the world. For King, though, the significance was even grander. And to make this point, he introduced his speech by imagining that God had granted him "a kind of general and panoramic view of the whole of human history" and had asked him to choose an era in which to live. King saw the Exodus from Egypt, the glories of the Greek and Roman Empires, the cultural triumphs of the Renaissance. He saw his namesake nailing his ninety-five theses on the church door at Wittenberg, initiating the Protestant Reformation. He saw Lincoln leading the nation through the Civil War and Franklin D. Roosevelt leading it through the Great Depression. All these moments would hold his interest, but if given the chance to live through any of them, he would decline for the opportunity to live "just a few years in the second half of the twentieth century."[56]

This might seem a strange choice, he conceded, because "the world is all messed up. The nation is sick." And yet it was precisely this sickness that attracted him. For he was promoting the belief that all time had been moving toward a great, final climax, that the tremors and tribulations of the past prefigured the ultimate crises of the current moment, which would culminate in the inauguration of God's perfect Kingdom. And so the conflicts raging throughout the world—and even the disappointments borne by King and his comrades in the freedom movement—became apocalyptic portents. For centuries, King noted, men had spoken of the choice between war and peace. Now the choice had become starker: it was between nonviolence and nonexistence. King was clearly referencing the threat of nuclear holocaust, but he continued to suggest the similarly stark choice posed by the "civil rights revolution" between universal redemption and desolation. "If something isn't done . . . to bring the colored peoples of the world out of their long years of poverty," he warned, "the whole world is doomed." If atomic weapons assumed the role of apocalyptic agents in the first nightmare scenario, in the second King hinted that the pent-up rage of the dispossessed might occupy a similar place in the providential plan. And so though King held true to his nonviolent convictions on the podium of the

Mason Temple, the threat of violence—in Memphis and in troubled nations throughout the world—hung over his words.[57]

The strikers, then, could not quit. He called for another march to be scheduled for the following Monday; he urged a boycott of national and local businesses that failed to hire African American workers (including Coca-Cola, an Atlanta-based company). Performing a gloss on the biblical parable of the Good Samaritan, he exhorted those assembled to assume a "dangerous unselfishness" in support of the less fortunate among them. And then he looked further ahead. His eyes staring off into the distance and pooling with tears, King seemed to foretell his own imminent death. In recent weeks his friends had noted that he had become preoccupied with the subject. A month before, in a sermon at Ebenezer Church, he had delivered a version of his own eulogy, which even his closest aides thought excessively macabre. According to one associate, he had recently developed the habit of scanning the rooms he entered, as if expecting to find hidden assailants within.

On the podium at the Mason Temple, he considered his own end with equanimity. He spoke of the brushes with death he had experienced in the past and revealed that his plane into Memphis had been delayed because the pilot felt the need to search it for a bomb. He thanked God for allowing him to reach this day, and he insisted that he could remain calm in the face of the threats against him because God had vouchsafed to him a final vision more powerful than the creeping premonitions of his own demise.[58] "We've got some difficult days ahead," he intoned. "But it really doesn't matter with me now. Because I've been to the mountain top."

King had used this phrase several times before in his speeches, sometimes to suggest the isolation brought on by privilege and distinction and the need to return to the valley of suffering humanity. Here it conjured up Moses' final ascent to Mount Pisgah, where God granted him a vision of the land of Canaan before he died. Through Moses King expressed his own belief in the imminence of the millennial moment at hand, the assurance that he had gained sight of the Promised Land of racial and economic justice. The allusion combined his faith in the movement's ultimate triumph with his doubts that he would live to enjoy it. In doing so, it linked the first and final lines of the "Battle Hymn," much as his campaign of nonviolence had done more generally, wedding the act of prophetic witness to the act of Christ-like sacrifice.

The audience responded with a gale of shouts and cheers that rivaled the storm raging outside. King barely acknowledged them. "Like anybody, I would like to live a long life—longevity has its place," he continued.

But I'm not concerned about that now. I just want to do God's will. And He's allowed me to go up to the mountain. And I've looked over, and I've seen the Promised Land. I may not get there with you. But I want you to know tonight, that we, as a people, will get to the Promised Land. And so I'm happy tonight; I'm not worried about anything; I'm not fearing any man. Mine eyes have seen the glory of the coming of the Lord![59]

He roared these last lines and seemed about to say more; his wife recalled that she assumed that he planned to finish the hymn's first stanza, as he had often done before. Instead he abruptly turned and walked back to the line of ministers behind him, practically collapsing into the arms of Ralph Abernathy.[60]

When King stopped speaking, the Temple erupted. Men and women shrieked and sobbed openly. The ministers who had joined King on the podium, men who had grown adept at keeping their emotions in check, broke down in tears. King was crying too, a sight that many of his associates had never seen before.

The euphoria eventually subsided. King remained at the Temple a bit longer to greet members of the audience before leaving to attend a strategy session at another nearby church. He did not return to the Lorraine Motel till 4:30 the next morning, where he continued to wage what one aide termed his "war on sleep" by holding several more meetings before finally heading to bed. He seemed energized in those late hours, even lighthearted, engaging in a spirited pillow fight with some of his fellow SCLC workers. The next day he held tough negotiations with Memphis militants, urging them to adopt nonviolent principles and to serve as marshals for the up-coming march. He had dinner plans that night at the home of a local minister. At a little before 6 P.M. a car arrived to drive him there. King stepped out onto the balcony of his room to speak with staff members in the courtyard below.[61]

In midconversation a shot rang out. It came from the roof of a nearby boardinghouse, from a high-powered Remington telescopic rifle, fired by an escaped convict and Klan supporter named James Earl Ray who had been stalking King for weeks. The bullet ripped through King's face, severing his jugular vein and spinal cord. He flew backward as blood poured out from the wound. Within minutes he was dead.

News of King's assassination spread rapidly through the black neighborhoods of Memphis. Some rushed to the motel, but they were blocked by a police cordon; others locked themselves in their homes, sure that violence would soon follow. And in fact the streets quickly filled with young black men, full of hopelessness and rage. "He died for us, and we're going to die for him," one yelled to a reporter, in a grim echo of the concluding lines of the "Battle Hymn." That night Molotov cocktails caused at least seventy-five fires; several stores were firebombed, and dozens of buses were damaged by rocks and bricks. King's SCLC colleagues urged African Americans to respect King's memory by refraining from violence, but unrest spread to cities throughout the nation. In Washington, D.C., within hours of King's death, Stokely Carmichael urged a crowd to go home and get their guns. "When white America killed Dr. King," he declared, "she declared war on us." Soon huge swaths of D.C.'s black neighborhoods were in flames, and looting was rampant in the city's Fourteenth Street corridor, not far from the White House. Fires engulfed large sections of Chicago's west side ghetto, where King had once lived. In Minneapolis a black man vowed to kill the first white person he saw, and then shot his neighbor, pumping six bullets into him while sobbing, "My King is dead." Two days later Black Panthers in Oakland engaged in a ninety-minute shootout with police, leaving two officers wounded and one black militant dead. All told, some 125 cities witnessed rioting or racial unrest, thirty-nine individuals were killed and 3,500 wounded in the wake of the assassination. Some 72,800 army and National Guard troops patrolled the nation's streets, the largest domestic deployment of military forces since the Civil War. Marines mounted machine guns on the Capitol steps. Surveying such scenes, one letter writer to a black newspaper in New York announced, "This country has taken a giant step down the road to Armageddon."[62]

In Memphis on April 7 a stricken James Lawson delivered a fiery speech to a group of nine thousand citizens gathered to promote racial reconciliation. He declared, "[King's death was] God's judgment on you and me and upon our city and our land that it is already too late." Memphis would long be remembered not as the city where blacks and whites united in the cause of economic justice but as "the place where Martin Luther King was crucified." The next day, as many as forty thousand men, women and children joined King's widow in marching, in perfect order, through the city's streets in an effort to keep alive the cause of the striking sanitation workers. The assassination also prompted President Johnson to intervene in the Memphis strike. He sent a labor official to the city to pressure both sides to come to a resolution, which they finally struck on April 16. In it the city finally recognized the sanitation workers' union. King's legacy was honored a month later when thousands of demonstrators descended on Washington and set up camp on a soggy patch of ground near the Reflecting Pool on the National

Mall, which they occupied for six weeks. They called it "Resurrection City."[63]

King had told his friends that when he died, he wanted a simple burial, but the political and media elite who had turned on him in his final years needed something grander, a public ceremony of expiation. On Tuesday, April 9, the vice president, fifty members of the House of Representatives, thirty senators, and a host of national and international dignitaries filed into Ebenezer Baptist Church, where both King and his father had preached, to pay their last respects. When the service concluded, an old farm wagon pulled by two Georgia mules—a symbol selected by his colleagues to represent King's commitment to the poor—carried his casket from the church to Morehouse College for another memorial. A throng of 150,000 mourners marched with him. At first they marched in silence, then they began singing "We Shall Overcome." Some of the other freedom songs followed. As the marchers passed the state capitol, which the segregationist governor, who had refused to call for an official day of mourning, had ringed with state police, they broke into the "Battle Hymn of the Republic."[64]

The song held an ambiguous meaning that day, as Americans strained to see the coming of the Lord in the flames and the rubble and wondered what wonders or terrors his arrival would announce. "Were last week's riots a final paroxysm that might purge angry emotions and clear the way for reconciliation?" asked *Newsweek*. "Or were the pictures of the machine gun on the Capitol steps and Chicago in flames only premonitions of an America without Martin Luther King?"

For all its ambiguity—or perhaps because of it—the hymn had been sung and cited often in the days following King's death, as he was memorialized and his last public utterance recalled. From the pulpit, ministers held up not merely the opening verse of the "Battle Hymn" but its concluding lines as well; as he had foretold, King *had* died to make men free. The "Battle Hymn" was sung at a memorial rally in New Haven, Connecticut, for King the day after his assassination. Its imagery must have resonated especially powerfully that day, for the crowd saved its most enthusiastic applause for the event's most militant speakers. "The age of nonviolence is dead," declared one. "The day and the sunlight belong to white America. But the night belongs to me." Another speaker announced, "We shall not overcome. We shall burn! . . . The white nation must pay for the death of Martin Luther King."

Those charged with putting out the fires also turned to the hymn. In the days after King's assassination, more than 5,700 National Guard troops joined state police and federal troops in patrolling Baltimore's streets. Four days of looting and rioting left six people dead and more than seven hundred injured. But by April 13 the unrest had quieted, the streets were calm, and Maryland's governor ended the state of emergency that he had called a week before. "Domestic tranquility has been returned," he declared, thanking the guardsmen for their service and dismissing them from duty. Before they left the armory where they had been stationed, they attended an Easter service at a nearby train station. On their way to the depot the men sang "Onward Christian Soldiers." On their way back they sang the "Battle Hymn of the Republic."[65]

★ ★ ★

CONCLUSION

The Hymn That Marches On

THE SPRING OF 1961 inaugurated a season of grand centennial celebrations as Americans paused to remember their Civil War. The commission charged by Congress in 1957 with organizing centennial events had dedicated itself to promoting a romantic memory of the conflict, one rooted in the heroic fraternity of the Blue and the Gray. As a member of the commission, a noted Southern historian, declared at its inception, the war's commemoration would be "an American ceremonial, recognizing the sincerity of both contestants and glorying in the greatness that they demonstrated in support of their respective causes." Such a memory would fortify a cold war consensus and inspire Americans in their defense of freedom against the threat of worldwide communism.

Yet given the volatile nature of race relations in the United States in 1961—the first Freedom Rides would begin that May—commission members also recognized the dangers in emphasizing the Civil War as a struggle for freedom. As the commission's deputy chairman explained in 1959, conceding that no commemoration of the Emancipation Proclamation was being planned, "You see there's a bigger theme—the beginning of a new America."[1]

Such efforts, however, did not prevent sectional animosity from spoiling the commission's work. Southern segregationists had little interest in embracing the centennial as a celebration of national unity. Instead they viewed it as an opportunity to reaffirm their opposition to federally mandated integration. "Today the South is facing many of the same problems it faced in 1861," a commentator warned a Montgomery, Alabama, newspaper. "Federal dictatorship is literally being stuffed down our throats. . . . We should stand up and fight as our forefathers did." Exuberant pageants and parades commemorating the establishment of the Confederacy and the inauguration of President Jefferson Davis in Montgomery and the festivities surrounding the commemoration of the Confederate attack on Fort Sumter allowed participants to deploy Civil War memory in a twentieth-century defense of states' rights and white supremacy. When the centennial commission held its national assembly in Charleston, South Carolina, the hotel housing the meeting refused to accommodate a black delegate from New Jersey. Northern state delegations threatened a boycott, and the crisis was averted only with the intervention of the newly elected president John F. Kennedy. (The proceedings were held at a nearby desegregated naval base.)[2]

At the end of August critics of the centennial commission forced the dismissal of its executive director and the resignation of its chairman. President Kennedy placed at the commission's helm Allan Nevins, a prominent Columbia University historian who had recently called for the incorporation of the "darker aspects" of the Civil War into its commemoration. Indeed the change signaled a commitment to a more sober analysis of the conflict that recognized both the significance of the emancipationist memory of the war and the ways that memory resonated with the contemporary struggles for civil rights, and yet still sought, in Nevins's words, to extract a measure of national "unity . . . out of the brothers' war."[3]

It was in this spirit that a group of government officials and cultural luminaries assembled on November 18 at the National Gallery of Art in Washington, D.C., to commemorate the one-hundredth anniversary of the composition of the "Battle Hymn of the Republic." A large portrait of Julia Ward Howe presided over the indoor garden courtyard where the event was held; the marbled interior echoed with the hymn, performed by Ruth Pitts, a prominent contralto, with accompaniment from the U.S. Marine Band Orchestra and the U.S. Army Chorus. Bruce Catton, the noted Civil War historian (who had borrowed from the hymn the title of the second work, *Terrible Swift Sword*, in his popular trilogy), provided a commemorative address. He praised the "Battle Hymn" as an expression of "the dedicated spirit" that could inspire the nation at a time of fading faith. It was, he announced, "the great affirmation of our belief—our belief in ourselves, in the significance of what we do and mean, in the eternal value that lies beyond life." In speaking of a *singular*, cohesive public united around the core values trumpeted in the "Battle Hymn," Catton recruited the song in service of cold war consensual patriotism.[4]

And yet the uses Americans actually made of the "Battle Hymn" in the years during the Civil War centennial made clear the fragility of that consensus. On the anniversary of Howe's vision at the Willard Hotel, as President Kennedy gave an address at the Hollywood Palladium, three thousand protesters congregated outside, holding signs declaring "CommUNism Is Our Enemy" and "Unmuzzle the Military," while joining together to sing the "Battle Hymn." A few months earlier, in Montgomery, Alabama, an angry mob of five hundred whites had surrounded the Negro First Baptist Church, where 1,500 men, women, and children had come to attend a pro-integration meeting and welcome a troop of Freedom Riders. At one point a driver in a passing car lobbed a tear-gas canister into a basement window of the church. Led by Martin Luther King Jr., the besieged sang the "Battle Hymn" to lift their spirits till National Guardsmen drove the mob away.[5]

That those outside the Hollywood Palladium and those inside Montgomery's Negro First Baptist Church could both call on the same song for inspiration demonstrates the ability of the "Battle Hymn" to span the gulf between millennial hope and apocalyptic anxiety. The beliefs the hymn affirmed held out the promise of a redeemed and unified republic while serving as the battleground for fratricidal conflict. In these years freedom, enshrined in the hymn's final stanza as Americans' highest and holiest ideal, proved a particularly contentious field of combat, a conceptual Antietam. The journalist Theodore White was struck by the ferocity of those battles. Covering the 1964 presidential race, he recorded the eerie overlap in the rhetoric of supporters of the conservative candidate Barry Goldwater and of progressive civil rights protesters. "The dominant word of these two groups, which loathe each other, is 'freedom,'" White noted. "Both demand Freedom Now or Freedom for All." But the word held so much "emotive power," that when White tried to extract a definition of the term from each camp, he was "instantly denounced." Now more than ever, White concluded, the nation needed "a commonly agreed-on concept of freedom."

In the final decades of the twentieth century, and in the opening decade of the twenty-first, even as the "Battle Hymn" continued to express the fears and feuds that divided Americans, the power of its vision of a providentially blessed millennial nation, serving the world in the cause of freedom, held out the promise of a citizenry united in glorious, triumphant concord. Despite the clashes over values and ideals that continued to roil the body politic—and perhaps even because of them—Americans still witnessed in the righteous campaigns of their fellow citizens the glory of the coming of the Lord.[6]

★

AS IT HAD EARLIER in the century, the "Battle Hymn" inspired and consoled Americans during World War II. Although the more secular-minded Franklin D. Roosevelt was less likely to employ millennial idioms than had President Wilson, he also spoke of the war against Nazism and fascism as a crusade the American people would take on "in their righteous might" against the forces of ultimate evil. FDR too used the "Battle Hymn" as a central text in the liturgy of America's civil religion. At a 1942 Thanksgiving service, broadcast from the White House to the nation, he led the Supreme Court justices, cabinet members, and other governmental leaders assembled in singing "Onward Christian Soldiers" and the "Battle Hymn."

The song also remained a favorite within the military, as Fred Waring, the leader of one of the nation's most popular singing groups, the Pennsylvanians, learned during a wartime concert for troops at a New York theater. Rehearsing the song shortly before the curtain was to rise, Waring grew frustrated that he could not get the proper sound from his performers' microphones. Stopping them mid-song to consult with the engineer, he quickly realized the problem when the singing continued: the audience had heard them and had carried the song forward. "We raised the curtain and let them join in the rehearsal with us," he recalled "These soldiers, sailors, and marines sang as I've never heard any group sing before."

The hymn held its power closer to the scene of battle. When, on Independence Day 1941, a memorial tablet was unveiled in London's St. Paul's Cathedral to honor one of the first American casualties in the war, the pilot Billy Fiske, members of his squadron gathered around the plaque to sing the song. In the early morning of June 6, 1944, aboard the attack transport USS *Bayfield*, Brigadier General Theodore Roosevelt Jr., deputy commander of the Fourth Infantry Division and eldest son of Teddy Roosevelt, turned to the hymn to rally his troops as they approached the Normandy coast on the first wave of the D-Day assault. As Roosevelt walked among his men, offering words of reassurance to those who had assembled on deck, he began singing the "Battle Hymn" and urged those around him to join in. One officer on board recalled, "This was a very sobering time to sing the words, 'As God died to make men holy, let us die to make men free.'" The beachhead on which the *Bayfield* would soon deposit its cargo would become sacred ground in the American civil religion, and the "Battle Hymn" was called upon to commemorate its exalted status: the war memorial honoring the American dead at Omaha Beach, a twenty-two-foot bronze statue representing "The Spirit of American Youth Rising from the Waves," rests on a granite stone on which is carved, "Mine eyes have seen the glory of the coming of the Lord."[7]

At midcentury, as the United States emerged from the war brimming with confidence in its own economic, military, and moral might, the "Battle Hymn" served as a favored means of projecting that triumphalism abroad. In June 1942 the first broadcast of the Voice of America, the government-sponsored radio station tasked with disseminating American war policies overseas, opened with the hymn. Five years later, when the U.S. State Department began its broadcasts into the Soviet Union in a sonic infiltration of the "iron curtain," the musical program included the "Battle Hymn," along with a medley of cowboy songs and a Cole Porter selection.

Yet victory in the war had also inaugurated the nuclear age, and the scenes of the devastation of Hiroshima and Nagasaki, as well as the atomic anxieties released with the knowledge that the Soviets possessed a countervailing arsenal of annihilation, bolstered a premillennial strain in American religious thought, one that envisioned the United States hurtling to the precipice of a providentially mandated catastrophe. Unlike other imagined ends, which had encompassed varieties of naturalistic disasters or supernatural interventions, this one was of Americans' own devising. And so if the "Battle Hymn" captured postwar American confidence, it also fed darker visions of the nation's future.[8]

In the postwar decades, no version of the song captured Americans' patriotic zeal—and perhaps their insecurity—more ably than that of the Mormon Tabernacle Choir. The Choir had been created in the mid-nineteenth century to sing devotional works at official Tabernacle services, but by the end of the century it had begun to perform outside the church and had incorporated secular songs into its repertoire. The Church's leaders appreciated the Choir's missionary value; its harmonies were an effective means of countering anti-Mormon bias and dispelling the taint of polygamy. In 1929 the Choir began a weekly 4 P.M. broadcast directly from the Tabernacle on an NBC affiliate station in Salt Lake City, and on the night of President Franklin Roosevelt's death, April 12, 1945, performed an on-air memorial service that was broadcast to 143 stations nationwide. Four years later the Choir signed a record deal with Columbia Records.

In 1959 the Choir recorded an album, *The Lord's Prayer*, and released a single drawn from it of the "Battle Hymn," arranged by Peter Wilhousky and accompanied by Eugene Ormandy and the Philadelphia Symphony Orchestra. It was, the director of Columbia Records wrote to the Choir's president, "a genuine 24 karat hit," selling some 300,000 copies in its first few months. The song became the first "classical" single to appear on the popular music charts, peaking at number 13 on Billboard's Hot 100 (between Santo & Johnny's "Sleep Walk" and Johnny and the Hurricanes' "Red River Rock"). When, in September, Nikita Khrushchev made a visit to the United States, one Dayton, Ohio, disk jockey played the song continuously so that the Soviet leader might hear "the sound of freedom." In November the National Academy of Recording Arts and Sciences awarded the Choir a Grammy for best performance by a chorus. The awards ceremony, the first ever televised, ended with the nearly three-hundred-member Choir bursting through the doors to the NBC Television Studio stage singing the "Battle Hymn."[9]

There was a logic, and perhaps even a certain irony, in the song serving as an instrument of Mormon integration into mainstream American culture. By midcentury the Choir was frequently touring Europe, where they were often greeted more as cold war ambassadors than as religious proselytizers. Mormon conversion rates began to soar. No longer regarding them as religious outcasts, many came to see them as paragons of squeaky-clean respectability. But since the earliest prophecies of Joseph Smith, foretelling the return of Christ to Jackson County, Missouri, the Church had harbored visions of the end times that strained against the bounds of mainstream conventionality. It is not surprising that the Choir representing a church that foretold a Second Coming on American soil developed a special claim to the "Battle Hymn," the quintessential expression of American millennialism. Yet in the decades after World War II, the Church's religious leaders de-emphasized a literal interpretation of its apocalyptic preachments. "We don't spend a lot of time talking about or dreaming about the millennium to come," the Church's president, Gordon Hinkley, told an interviewer for a 1999 book. Those strains never disappeared entirely, however. "If the president were to blink an eye toward Jackson County, Missouri, people would flow there," insisted Richard Bushman, a leading scholar on Mormon history, when appraised of Hinkley's comments. "The belief is still potent, but it's latent."

At midcentury the same could be said of the apocalyptic strains that coursed through the "Battle Hymn." They had been muted by the associations with traditionalism and respectability that the song had accumulated over the years. But in times of crisis, real or imagined, they could erupt to the surface and threaten the visions of national unity that the song extolled. And so the hymn did not merely give voice to an American consensus. It also hinted at its fragility.[10]

Indeed by the 1960s that consensus had seemingly fractured beyond repair, imploded by battles over civil rights and the war in Vietnam. The popularity of the "Battle Hymn" during these years stemmed from its ability to communicate anger and fear at the fracturing as well as a hopefulness that something better might emerge from the shards.

When John Steinbeck visited Lyndon Johnson at the White House in June 1964, shortly after the president had unveiled his Great Society legislative program, he brought as a gift an 1862 copy of the *Atlantic*, containing Howe's original version of the hymn. Steinbeck told Johnson and his wife about finding the title of his most famous novel within the poem. (Decades before, Johnson, who grew up in rural poverty in south central Texas, had seen the movie version of *Grapes of Wrath* with Lady Bird and had wept quietly for nearly the entire two hours.) With his gift, Steinbeck suggested that Johnson's ambitious agenda of bolstering the nation's social safety net had answered the calls for a revolutionary renewal of brotherhood that he had issued with his account of Dust Bowl impoverishment. When the Mormon Tabernacle Choir performed the "Battle Hymn" at Johnson's inauguration in January 1965, the song reinforced the president's own calls in his inaugural address for the nation to unite in fulfilling the "covenant" their forefathers had made to bring justice and liberty to the land (though some Southern politicians did grumble about the sectional nature of the hymn).

As the nation sank deeper into the quagmire of the Vietnam War, Johnson's appreciation of the "Battle Hymn" took on a darker cast. Hawks had begun to stake a claim to the song in order to affirm America's conduct and mission in the conflict, frequently appropriating the tune for pro-war anthems. Johnson too seemed increasingly drawn to the song, especially as performed by Anita Bryant. On March 14, 1968, just two weeks before he announced that he would not seek another term in office, Johnson requested that Bryant perform the "Battle Hymn" at a White House event honoring the Somali prime minister. "Sir, I do know the words of other songs," she pleaded. We can only surmise how differently the hymn sounded in Johnson's ears that night than it had in the more hopeful days of his presidency.[11]

For many Americans, the "Battle Hymn" was able to capture both the patriotic imperative to support the nation at war and a growing uneasiness with the conflict, which seemed to produce little more than body bags and cascading revelations of American misconduct. Most damning of these were reports that on March 16, 1968, the troops of Charlie Company, First Battalion, Twentieth Infantry, on a search-and-destroy mission against Vietcong fighters, systematically murdered more than five hundred civilians, mostly women, children, and elderly, at the South Vietnamese village of My Lai. After an initial cover-up, the army charged twenty-six-year-old Second Lieutenant William L. Calley with masterminding the My Lai massacre. On March 29, 1971, a court-martial convicted Calley of the premeditated murder of twenty-two Vietnamese; a few days later he was sentenced to life imprisonment. Almost immediately a wave of public sympathy, cresting especially dramatically in the South, swelled for Calley, who was regarded as a scapegoat sacrificed to propitiate antiwar sentiment.

The reaction prompted radio stations across the South to begin playing a recent adaptation of the "Battle Hymn" tune, written after Calley's court martial by a pair of Alabamans and performed by a disc jockey named Terry Nelson and an impromptu band calling themselves "C Company." For a few months the "Battle Hymn of Lt. Calley" achieved a nearly unprecedented degree of popularity and controversy; it sold 200,000 copies in the three days after Calley's conviction and hit the one million mark in the next few weeks. Others were disgusted with the song and its valorization of Calley. Played continuously on Armed Forces Radio, broadcasting out of Saigon, the military ultimately banned it from the air. Some radio stations on the home front also refused to play it, and in bars throughout the country fistfights erupted when the hymn was requested on the juke box.

Whereas Howe's "Battle Hymn" had abstracted the individual soldier as an instrument of divine providence, Calley's hymn took up his personal, aggrieved perspective—punctuated at the end of each stanza by the claim that he and his men had simply been doing their duty and "marching on," and then at the song's end, by an angelic rendition of the "Glory, glory, Hallelujah" chorus. Calley's persecution becomes a stand-in for the shameful and contemptuous treatment of American troops more generally. A spoken-word introduction informs listeners that Calley had wished to serve his country from the time he paraded around with a saucepan on his head, a wooden sword in one hand and an American flag in the other. But he and his dutiful, uncomplaining fellow soldiers had been betrayed by a sinister confluence of conspirators. The Vietcong guerrillas refused to fight fairly and attacked American troops from within civilian populations, thereby courting the slaughter of innocents. (The song explains the My Lai massacre, echoing Calley's own attempts at exoneration, by claiming the men had been following orders to take the village and had returned enemy fire.) An incompetent military command gave territory back to the enemy after it had been purchased with the blood of brave American GIs. And while soldiers were "dying in the rice fields," antiwar protesters in American streets were "helping our defeat" and "sounding a retreat," an ironic recasting of Howe's description of God's trumpet that "shall never call retreat."

Calley's hymn stands in an ambiguous relationship with its predecessor. It did not seek to expose hypocrisy by using the song to protest the betrayal of Americans' mission to die to make men free, as Mark Twain had done with his appropriation of the song. If there was more than a hint of the common soldier's defiance of authority that had characterized "John Brown's Body," it was tempered by the insistence that the soldier had merely been doing his duty, an imperative that the song prizes among all other virtues. And the violence that the soldier directs to the shifty enemy seems detached from any higher cause. In his ballad, Calley makes no mention at all of his reasons for fighting; it is the fact that he is willing to fight that is stressed. Calley's song personalizes Howe's vision of providence inexorably "marching on" through the uncomplaining and unquestioning obedience of the soldier. And so Calley's hope for redemption lies not in this world but in the next, when he will enter that "final campground" and the "great commander" will ask, "Did you fight or did you run?" In the ballad's final stanza, Calley finds self-assurance in knowing that he will be able to respond, "Count me only as a soldier who never left his gun."[12]

Yet in those regions where the "Battle Hymn of Lt. Calley" was most popular—the Bible Belt, most prominently—listeners likely extracted a considerable portion of ideological sustenance from the song's use of the "Battle Hymn" tune. For in the 1960s the hymn was also embraced by a nascent political conservatism. The various grievances and anxieties that intertwined and fueled the movement's growth, linked together by a fear that traditional American values and institutions were under attack by a conspiracy of malignant forces—liberalism and communism, chiefly—each could draw from the hymn's association with a righteous patriotism committed to the preservation of an idealized Union. Despite the hymn's abolitionist legacy, Southern opponents of desegregation could stake their own claim to the song; at one counterdemonstration after civil rights proponents had marched through the town of Bogalusa, Louisiana, in July 1965, a group calling itself Christian Mothers confused onlookers by waving Confederate flags while singing the "Battle Hymn."

The hymn held a special appeal to anti-Communist zealots. In December 1958, at the inaugural meeting of the John Birch Society, the right-wing organization that rallied Americans against "a vast conspiracy to enslave mankind," extending from the Kremlin all the way into the White House, the Supreme Court, and the highest levels of the military command, its founder, Robert Welsh, concluded his speech outlining the society's mission by invoking the "Battle Hymn." The struggle against communism, Welch insisted, was "a world-wide battle, the first in history, between light and darkness; between freedom and slavery; between the spirit of Christianity and the spirit of anti-Christ for the souls and bodies of men." If need be, those assembled must be willing to give their very lives to the cause. And if that need arose, Welch suggested, they should take as inspiration "the end of a great and stirring hymn, written to inspire men to fight against a far less extensive slavery of their fellow men." He concluded by quoting that hymn's final stanza.[13]

The status of the "Battle Hymn" as a conservative anthem was given confirmation during the 1964 presidential campaign of Senator Barry Goldwater of Arizona. Its ability to meld the traditional and the insurgent perfectly fit Goldwater's efforts to defy the power of the Republican Party's "East Coast elite" and to overthrow the liberal establishment in order to recover the values of the "real" God-fearing America. As early as 1962, at a massive rally at Madison Square Garden, the band played the "Battle Hymn" when Goldwater took the stage, and a giant banner proclaimed, "For the Future of Freedom: Goldwater in '64." The crowd erupted and sang the "Glory, Hallelujah" chorus for nearly ten minutes.

During the campaign itself, as the hymn became known as Goldwater's "favorite song," bands frequently played it when he made his appearance. A half-hour pro-Goldwater film, which the campaign planned to broadcast on NBC in October 1964, a month before the election, also made use of the song. The film opened with a frenzied jazz tune blaring in the background and scenes of criminals resisting arrest, African Americans clamoring violently at civil right protests, and debauched revelers (including a shot of a topless female dancer, which ultimately led the network to ban the film). Then the "Battle Hymn" took over, accompanied by images of the Statue of Liberty, the Declaration of Independence, and rolling hills and valleys, while an announcer intoned, "Now there are two Americas. One is words like 'allegiance' and 'Republic.' . . . The other America—the other America is no longer a dream but a nightmare."[14]

The hymn blared as Goldwater strode onto the podium during the Republican convention in San Francisco to make his nomination speech.

Much as it had a half-century before, during the Progressive convention, the *New York Times* took this musical selection, and the fervor of Goldwater's faithful delegates, as a prompt to compare the gathering to a "revival." "Our people have followed false prophets," Goldwater declared. "We must and we shall return to proven ways . . . [and become] freedom's missionaries in a doubting world." The crowd erupted with nearly every sentence, gaining enthusiasm as Goldwater neared his peroration. "I would remind you that extremism in the defense of liberty is no vice," he intoned. "And let me remind you also—that moderation in the pursuit of justice is no virtue." The galleries roared their approval. A lengthy standing ovation ensued, with a number of overzealous delegates shaking the planks holding up the ABC broadcast booth, toppling the newsmen inside.

Predictably representatives of the moderate wing of the Republican Party were less impressed. Upon hearing the remarks, Senator Kenneth Keating of New York bolted out of the convention hall, marching (symbolically) down the center aisle. A few days later Governor Nelson Rockefeller of New York denounced the statement, explaining that "terrorists" always justified their lawlessness through "the defense of liberty." His remarks were soon seconded, and amplified, on the op-ed pages of the nation's major newspapers. A few weeks later Goldwater clarified his remarks in a response to a letter from former vice-president Richard Nixon, who had asked for an explanation. He had not been promoting lawlessness but merely "whole-hearted devotion to liberty," he insisted. And his defense of extremism should be understood in the context of his speech's embrace of the broader values of ordered freedom and equal justice under the law.

Yet if those had been Goldwater's intended meanings, the echoes of the "Battle Hymn of the Republic" still reverberating through the convention hall helped to betray them. For the song linked a resurgent conservatism to the tradition of American millennialism, one that could release energies that, as the frenzied delegates on the convention floor demonstrated, would not soon yield to calls to order.[15]

BY THE END OF the decade, however, Goldwater was not the political figure most closely associated with the "Battle Hymn." That distinction belonged to Robert Kennedy, who, during the 1968 presidential campaign, championed a progressive vision that could also find sustenance in the song. Kennedy's campaign, competing for the antiwar vote with the campaign of Senator

Eugene McCarthy of Minnesota, floundered in its opening months. Not until the assassination of Martin Luther King, and the riots that followed, did Kennedy's candidacy surge. He began to present himself as the candidate of national reconciliation, as the one figure who could bring together the white working class and African Americans into a powerful, progressive coalition. Had this campaign been allowed to run its course, the "Battle Hymn of the Republic" might have served as a rallying cry to the disenfranchised and the dispossessed. There is some evidence that the song had been a favorite of Kennedy's for some time. During a South American tour in 1965, he once found himself mobbed by admirers in Linares, Chile. As men and women rushed in to touch Kennedy, he took refuge on top of a police car and quieted the crowd by singing the "Battle Hymn."

Yet Kennedy's association with the song was firmly established only after the promise that he represented was extinguished. During a party celebrating the candidate's victory in the California primary, Kennedy was assassinated by a Jordanian national infuriated by his support of Israel. In the ceremonies of mourning held over the following week—some carefully scripted, others unfolding spontaneously—the "Battle Hymn" assumed a central place. Some found its prominence, and the apocalyptic themes it introduced, uncomfortable since, as the *Boston Globe* pointed out, the assassination had "come at a time of national introspection about violence as a way of life in America." Yet the song clearly helped to assuage many of those anxieties. In planning the requiem high mass held at St. Patrick's Cathedral in New York, Ethel Kennedy insisted on deviating from the traditional liturgy and concluding the service with the hymn in order to lend the service a more triumphant and less despondent air. As soon as Andy Williams, the television crooner and Kennedy's friend, began the first verse, those in the pews joined in. As one reporter remarked, the singing "served as an ablution for despair," producing a catharsis "wincingly painful and spiritually reinforcing." From that moment on, the "Battle Hymn," another writer declared, "spontaneously became the anthem of the day."[16]

The funeral cortege left the cathedral and made its way to Penn Station, where a twenty-one-car train waited, the last of which, hung with black bunting, held Kennedy's flag-draped coffin. More than 1,100 passengers made the journey to Washington, D.C., where Kennedy would be buried at Arlington National Cemetery, not far from his brother. All along the 225-mile route, mourners crowded the edge of the tracks, standing at attention on factory roofs, removing their hats on highway overpasses, waiting for the train to speed by. (Some got too close; in New Jersey a man and a woman were killed when they stood in the path of an express train traveling in the opposite direction.) Some knelt in prayer as the cortege passed; others waved flags and handkerchiefs or saluted. In northeast Philadelphia on-lookers scattered roses on the tracks. At select depots, the train would slow to a solemn crawl so those on board could acknowledge the mourners on the platform. No slow-down had been scheduled for New Brunswick, New Jersey, where a large crowd had gathered. A high school brass band began to play the "Battle Hymn" and those assembled sang along. The tribute so moved Kennedy's family that they instructed the conductor to reduce the train's speed in a sort of return salute.

In fact spectators from New York to Washington took up the hymn. In Baltimore, in the gathering dusk, a crowd of more than ten thousand assembled at the station; minutes before the train was scheduled to arrive, they began singing the hymn. When they finished, they began "We Shall Overcome." But when they heard the grumble of the approaching cars, they took up the "Battle Hymn" again. "As that noble old hymn floated across the tracks," recorded one journalist traveling on the train, "the awful dignity of all those grave faces on the edge of night seemed to embrace the entire train with awe and pity." The scene, another reporter recalled, offered a corrective to the tragedy. "If the assassination resulted in the unfair excoriation of America at its worst, this tribute in song was sure a moment of America at its best."[17]

The train, four hours behind schedule, reached Union Station in the late afternoon. All along the route from the station to Arlington Cemetery, mourners had gathered, and as it grew dark, many held candles to light the way. Before reaching the Memorial Bridge, the funeral procession stopped for several minutes in front of the Lincoln Memorial. As the cortege approached, a Marine Corps choir began performing the "Battle Hymn," and the large crowd that had assembled there joined in. The pause allowed one slain presidential aspirant to rest for a moment in the presence of the nation's most revered martyr. But it was also a deliberate tribute to those encamped nearby at Resurrection City, some of whom took up the hymn as well. Other protesters remained silent, simply raising their fists in the Black Power salute.[18]

Kennedy's memory breathed life into the hymn as an expression of national unity in the face of tragedy. Mere weeks later it arose again as an anthem of protest and polarization. The 1968 Democratic convention, held in August in Chicago, exposed the deep fractures within the Democratic Party and within the nation as a whole. In the city's streets, some twelve thousand police and five thousand National Guardsmen, mobilized by Mayor Richard Daley, battled with thousands of leftist protesters, savagely beating a group who had sought to march to the International Amphitheater, where the delegates had gathered. Groups of police stormed the headquarters of the antiwar candidate Eugene McCarthy in the Hilton Hotel, clubbing his campaign workers. Inside the Amphitheater, surrounded by a seven-foot barbed-wire fence, the Democrats' establishment and insurgent factions, deeply divided over the war in Vietnam, race relations, and the politics of law and order, also battled, if a bit less savagely.

During the convention's second day, occupied mostly with parliamentary procedures, Anita Bryant sparked a rare burst of enthusiasm with her rendition of the "Battle Hymn" (she had also performed the song at the Republican convention in Miami). The next day the hymn made another appearance at one of the most fateful moments of the convention, following the adoption of a plank supporting President Johnson's policy in Vietnam. When the dovish New York delegation realized that the antiwar plank, which demanded an immediate de-escalation of hostilities, had been defeated, they broke into a mournful version of the hymn, accompanied by the chorus of "We Shall Overcome." The official convention orchestra played military marches and show tunes in an effort to drown them out.

The following day the convention achieved a brief moment of unity when Edward Kennedy mounted the podium to introduce a half-hour video tribute to his brother. All the delegates watched in respectful silence. "It was the first occasion this week that had found the Democrats unanimous about anything," noted the *New York Times*. But that unanimity proved fleeting, and the "Battle Hymn," rather than sustain consensus, expressed its unraveling. When the video ended, delegates, led by those from New York and California—the core of the progressive factions—began to clap and cheer. The chairman of the convention sought to bring them to order, but they refused, and in a show of defiance began singing the "Battle Hymn." Soon almost all the delegates in the hall were singing along, stamping their feet, and drowning out the chairman's gaveling—except for the Texas and Illinois delegations, leaders of the old guard, who remained seated and stony-faced. Wave upon wave of the "Glory, glory, Hallelujah" chorus rose and fell within the Amphitheater, drowning out the chairman's calls for silence. The demonstration lasted for nearly half an hour, ending only when supporters of Mayor Daley, whom he had packed into the galleries, successfully shouted down the insurgent Kennedy tribute.[19]

So powerful was the association between the hymn and the fallen senator that the man who finally captured the presidency in the 1968 election, Richard Nixon, initially shunned the song in many of his subsequent public appearances; when an aide suggested citing the "Battle Hymn" in a speech, Nixon rebuffed him. "That's a Kennedy song," he snapped. (For all his antipathy toward the hymn, Nixon did select as his campaign headquarters the Willard Hotel, which had closed earlier in the year.) By Nixon's second term, the noxious liberal associations had apparently dissipated, for he requested members of the Mormon Tabernacle Choir to perform the "Battle Hymn" at a service marking his first full day in office.[20]

As conservatives gained power and confidence in the decades after Goldwater's defeat, each of the three political tributaries whose convergence fueled the movement—anticommunism, antitaxation, and the Religious Right—could claim the "Battle Hymn" as a call to arms. The song resonated with the Manichaean proclivities of cold warriors, who regarded America's confrontation with the Soviet Union as an ultimate battle, waged in the shadows of nuclear brinksmanship. Even as it addressed contemporary anxieties, the song also conjured up an idyllic American past, one in which traditional values thrived, untroubled by an intrusive federal bureaucracy. Finally, the hymn spoke to the growing electoral clout of evangelical Christians, who had shed the political alienation encouraged by fundamentalism and begun to stride unabashedly into the political arena; it became, for instance, a staple at anti-abortion rallies and was frequently played at protests against the government's banning of prayer in public schools.

A premillennial perspective animated this newly charged political activism. Many of the denominations whose members made up the Religious Right foretold Christ's imminent return and rejected the postmillennial vision of the world's progressive salvation through man's benevolent striving. Once, this attitude had led to political quiescence, but in the final decades of the century it led to a sense of heightened urgency. The martial images in the "Battle Hymn" helped to reinforce the premonition that the forces of the adversary were closing in.[21]

In fact despite its heterodox theological foundations, the "Battle Hymn" became a rallying cry for the religious orthodox protesting the inroads of secularism, atheism, and religious liberalism in American culture. Liberals and conservatives within denominations had clashed before over the liturgical meaning of the "Battle Hymn," yet the terms of the debate had now changed. In the early 1960s, for instance, when the United Methodist Church initiated a revision of its hymnal, opposition to the inclusion of the

"Battle Hymn" came from Southerners, who still resented the Unionist associations of the song. When the denomination began a revision two decades later, in May 1986, Northern liberals led the opposition. Fired by the campaign for nuclear disarmament in the wake of the Chernobyl power plant disaster, they sought to remove "Onward Christian Soldiers" and all but the chorus of the "Battle Hymn" from hymnals because of their "unrelenting use of military images." They hoped to counterbalance what they considered to be an overly masculine and aggressive divinity with feminine metaphors for God and to correct sexist and racially insensitive language with more inclusive terms.

The proposed changes infuriated the more conservative within the denomination, who charged the revision committee with being anti-American, "soft-headed," Communists, and "liberal ignoramuses." In July the hymnal commission received over eleven thousand letters, only forty-four of which supported the proposed revisions. So many protest phone calls flooded the denomination's headquarters in Nashville that for nearly two weeks the staff had to make outgoing calls from a public payphone in the lobby. Overwhelmed by the response, the committee ultimately decided to restore the two controversial hymns (though they added an extra stanza to "Onward Christian Soldiers" clarifying that the enemy to be combated was Satan). Their decision met with wide acclaim; even the *New York Times* called the committee's initial revision "the liturgical equivalent of changing the formula for Coke" and applauded them for reversing the move.[22]

It is no coincidence that the man who synthesized the various strands of conservatism most expertly was also the national leader most closely identified with the "Battle Hymn" since Theodore Roosevelt. On multiple occasions Ronald Reagan declared the hymn his "favorite song," and it threaded its way through his ascent to the presidency. Early in his career, when he served as a "traveling ambassador" for General Electric, giving patriotic (and pro-corporate) speeches at the company's plants throughout the nation, Reagan often spoke to the musical accompaniment of the hymn's tune. A high school band played the "Battle Hymn" at Reagan's inauguration as California's governor; the Mormon Tabernacle Choir, massed in front of the Lincoln Memorial, sang the hymn during his presidential inauguration; and the U.S. Army Chorus performed the song at his funeral.[23]

Reagan's critics associated his fondness for the hymn with his ties to political and religious fundamentalism. It was, to them, an anthem of immoderacy. An ally of Gerald Ford, who battled Reagan for the Republican presidential nomination in 1976, urged Ford to give up courting the right wing of the party. "We're never, never going to get those crazies back with us," he told the *New York Times*. "They're going to march down the street with Reagan singing 'Battle Hymn of the Republic.'"

Reagan's relation to the hymn was more complex, however. The tension between those millennial hopes and apocalyptic fears reflected his own bifurcated personality, as genial eschatologist and cheerful cold warrior. The song clearly fed his predilection for moral absolutes, his commitment to ultimate victory over an "Evil Empire," and his fascination with end times. His apocalyptic views and their connection to his nuclear policy in fact became a point of controversy during his presidency, especially after his secretary of defense, Caspar Weinberger, insisted that his reading of the Book of Revelation convinced him that "time is running out" and his nominee for secretary of the interior responded to questions about preserving the environment for future generations by insisting that he did not know "how many future generations we can count on before the Lord returns." Reagan had previously suggested a similar intuition of the end's imminence and had once explicitly linked Armageddon to nuclear catastrophe, a common association in fundamentalist prophecy writing of the period. As he told a lobbyist for Israel in 1983, he often wondered whether this generation would not become the one that would witness Armageddon. The prophecies in Revelation "certainly describe the times we're going through," he remarked. Critics grew concerned: in the nuclear age, might such a fascination with end times represent a self-fulfilling prophecy?

Reagan deflected the uproar generated by such comments by insisting during one 1984 presidential debate that he held a merely "philosophical" interest in the Apocalypse and had no idea when it might actually arrive. (That it *would* arrive, he did not seem to doubt.) Improved relations with the Soviet Union helped to quell the controversy. So too did the fact that Reagan's own overpowering optimism frequently eclipsed his doomsday streak; his faith in America's promise mitigated whatever terrors might attend the coming of the Lord. In fact he seemed to appreciate the "Battle Hymn" primarily as an expression of patriotism and traditional conservative values, not as an expression of prophecy. "Nothing thrilled me more," he recounted in his autobiography, "than looking up at a wind-blown American flag while listening to a choir sing 'The Battle Hymn of the Republic,'" hardly a vision from Revelation.[24]

Conservatives secured their appropriation of the "Battle Hymn" as the movement's partisans increasingly clothed their various policy preferences in the language of freedom, making the hymn's final stanza a catch-all anthem for their religious and ideological enthusiasms. This emphasis on freedom as the cardinal value pointed to the possibility of some common ground with progressives. However, as progressives increasingly ceded the rhetoric of freedom to the Right, favoring instead a political discourse centered on rights, emancipatory exhortations were more often wielded as instruments of partisanship. The same might be said for the "Battle Hymn" itself. Unsurprisingly the hymn played a leading role in one of the ceremonies of the Right's ascendancy, the installation of Newt Gingrich as speaker of the House in January 1995. That morning Gingrich had joined his congressional colleagues at a Capitol Hill church. The service had featured readings of biblical texts calling for reconciliation and peace and concluded with a black choir performing a stirring rendition of the hymn. Later that afternoon, after his swearing in, Gingrich referred to the song in the peroration of a lengthy address in which the partisan incendiary proclaimed his commitment to bipartisanship. Speaking within sight of the Lincoln Memorial, Gingrich remarked, it was hard not to appreciate "how painful and how difficult that Battle Hymn is." It called on Americans to accept a sacred charge, expressed in its last lines, "As he died to make men holy, let us live to make men free." Gingrich gave that final word an expansive meaning that he hoped might appeal to both Republicans and Democrats: "If you can't afford to leave the public housing project, you're not free. If you don't know how to find a job and you don't know how to create a job, you're not free." He called on his fellow congressmen to find an inspiration in those verses for nonpartisan public service.[25]

Of course, those verses could yield other, less pacific interpretations as well, hinted at by the fact that, before the day was done, the new speaker had found an opportunity to denounce Democrats as "cheap, nasty and destructive." For much of the next decade, Democrats were more often treated as antagonists than as allies in the struggle to make men free. In July 2001, for instance, during a congressional debate over an amendment that would prohibit the "physical desecration of the flag of the United States," John Duncan Jr., a Republican representative from Tennessee, invoked the "Battle Hymn" and quoted its final stanza. In doing so, however, he transformed an abolitionist hymn into a libertarian call to arms, one in which Democratic supporters of an enlarged federal government were paired with foreign totalitarian despots. "[The hymn's final lines are] what so much of what we do today is all about," he declared. "The battle or the struggle for freedom is ongoing. It is never ending. There are always tyrants and dictators from abroad who would take our freedom away if they had the slightest chance to do so, and there are always liberal elitists and bureaucrats from within who want to live our lives for us and spend our money for us and take away our freedom, slowly but surely."[26]

Just a few months later the sight of the crumbling Twin Towers and the smoldering Pentagon muted much of that divisiveness. The response to the 9/11 attacks, including the service at Washington National Cathedral, brought to the fore those strains of the "Battle Hymn" that promoted national unity in a time of crisis. The song affirmed a core of values and a tradition of sacrifice that inspired and consoled Americans of all backgrounds and stations. Yet, as we have seen, the consensus that the song fostered was always tenuous, and the hymn continued to unleash forces that threatened to sow divisiveness even as it celebrated unity.

Such tensions were on display in April 2008, when Pope Benedict XVI became only the second pontiff to visit the White House. The White House organized the largest welcoming ceremony in its history, with over 13,500 guests on hand, who spontaneously serenaded the pope (who turned eighty-one that day) with a version of "Happy Birthday." In his remarks President George W. Bush linked the nation's struggle against Islamic terrorism abroad with the campaign to abolish abortion at home and with broader struggles against moral relativism flaring up throughout the West (and in doing so, seemed to lump Democratic defenders of reproductive rights with terrorist militants). The ceremony concluded with a rousing four-part arrangement of the "Battle Hymn" performed by the U.S. Army Chorus, whose members shouted out the final lines with a startling staccato vigor.[27]

Many conservatives applauded the event, interpreting it as a worthy gesture in support of ecumenical orthodoxy and as a savvy effort to cement the growing political alliance between evangelical Protestants and Catholics. Special attention was focused on the "Battle Hymn." "[It is] a patriotic, yet spiritual song, uniquely American, that we know the Holy Father will enjoy," one White House aide explained. Conservative talk-show host Rush Limbaugh was so impressed with the selection—"God's music," he called it—that he played the song on his radio program for weeks afterward. It represented, he informed his listeners, a vigorous effort to reinstall God in the public sphere and an unembarrassed articulation of American exceptionalism. When President Bush called his show a few days after the White House ceremony, Limbaugh gushed that the performance of the hymn had "stirred" his soul: "It was so uplifting. It was so timely."[28]

But some Catholic observers expressed discomfort with the choice, which they interpreted quite differently. The Vatican had, after all, honored its traditional commitment to pacifism by opposing the Iraq War, with then-Cardinal Ratzinger (soon to be Pope Benedict) expressing his skepticism of America's justifications for the invasion. Some had hoped that the pope would use his visit to the United States as an opportunity to reaffirm publicly the vocation of peacemaking, yet except for a brief call for "the patient efforts of international diplomacy to resolve conflicts" and a passing paean to the United Nations, he was pointedly restrained on the subject. Indeed while some interpreted the selection of the song as a militaristic affront to His Holiness, the request for the "Battle Hymn" had come from the Vatican itself. When the White House asked if there were any songs the pope would like played at the ceremony, his American representative mentioned the one with the "Glory, glory Hallelujah!" chorus. By the final verse, the pope could be seen faintly mouthing the "Hallelujah" refrain with the army singers. In this context the prominence accorded to the "Battle Hymn" seemed like a vindication of the Bush administration's military engagements and of America's millennial mission more generally, much to the disappointment of those who opposed the president's foreign policy or the conflation of worldly triumphs and spiritual redemption.[29]

The election of Barack Obama in 2008 intensified the power of the "Battle Hymn" to polarize. The results galvanized the political Right, amplifying their fears that the traditional order was being dismantled before their eyes by a host of liberal enemies. Unsurprisingly the song quickly became a favorite at Tea Party rallies. Yet at the same time, Obama's election also vindicated the millennial tradition of the black church, and the "Battle Hymn" was called upon to express the hope of many Americans that a sort of political millennium had in fact arrived. Progressives, many of whom had long felt marginalized from mainstream political culture, now felt the weight of their alienation removed. They were suddenly free to embrace American civil religion. In an article on the resurgence of "progressive patriotism" following Obama's election, one historian recalled being overwhelmed with the impulse to hear the "Battle Hymn" in church.[30]

The rival political interpretations of the hymn were on display in a controversy surrounding a group of New Jersey elementary school students who performed a song, to the tune of the "Battle Hymn," celebrating Obama's election at a Black History Month assembly. ("Hello, Mr. President we honor you today! / For all your great accomplishments, we all do say hooray!") A video of the assembly leaked to the press, and conservatives pounced on the performance as an example of "political indoctrination." Activists picketed the school, singing the original "Battle Hymn" while they marched. On his popular show, the right-wing television host Glenn Beck used the controversy to issue a contemporary jeremiad. After showing a video of a sixteen-year-old boy beaten to death when he was caught in a melee between two Chicago gangs, Beck asked his viewers, "What has happened to us? How have we come to a place where the value on human life is so incredibly low?" The answer, he insisted, was because "God is no longer trusted in America." He then called attention to the New Jersey adaptation of the "Battle Hymn" as an illustration of this failing, suggesting that political messianism had supplanted traditional religious belief. That act of grade school revisionism illustrated for Beck the moral declension at the heart of all jeremiads; there was something especially damning in the tampering with Howe's lyrics, which Beck explained were his "favorite collection of words in any song." He quoted the final verse with tears in his eyes.[31]

Around the same time, a law student, aggravated by "the whole of this latest election process," composed a "divorce settlement" between the Left and the Right that spread quickly among conservatives on the Internet. Conservatives would keep guns, capitalism, Wal-Mart, Wall Street, Bibles, and Judeo-Christian values, he suggested. Liberals would keep the ACLU, abortion clinics, Oprah, and illegal aliens. The Left would get "Kumbaya," while the Right would retain the "Battle Hymn of the Republic."

There was a certain irony in the student's claiming the "Battle Hymn," a song originally composed to celebrate the efforts of those who fought to keep the Union whole against those who would split it apart, on behalf of a national divorce along partisan lines. On the other hand, the proposed settlement laid bare tensions that have long coursed through the hymn. For in heralding America's millennial promise and fostering national reconciliation, the "Battle Hymn of the Republic" has also celebrated the final, cataclysmic sifting of the righteous from the unrighteous. It contains visions both of perfect peace and of violent discord and underscores the kinship between the two. When we reach for one, we have often taken in the other. The "Battle Hymn" reminds us that our most powerful visions of the coming of the Lord are pierced by the gleaming of the terrible swift sword. It reminds us as well that beyond the wrath and the trampling and the sword, the glory endures.

APPENDIX

Lyrical Lineage of the "Battle Hymn of the Republic"

- "Grace Reviving in the Soul" (from Stith Mead, *A General Selection of the Newest and Most Admired Hymns and Spiritual Songs*, 1807)

I feel the work reviving, I feel the work reviving,
I feel the work reviving, reviving in my soul.
I'm on my way to Zion, I'm on my way to Zion,
I'm on my way to Zion, the new Jerusalem.

CHORUS

We'll shout and give him glory, we'll shout and give him glory,
We'll shout and give him glory, for glory is his own.

O Christians will you meet me, O Christians will you meet me,
O Christian will you meet me, on Canaan's happy shore.
    There we'll shout and give him glory, &c.

Question. O brothers will you meet me, O brother[s] will you meet me,
O brothers will you meet me, on Canaan's happy shore?
Answer. By the grace of God I'll meet you, by the grace of God I'll meet you,
By the grace of God I'll meet you, on Canaan's happy shore.
    There we'll shout and give him glory, &c.

Question. O sisters will you meet me, &c.

Answer. By the grace of God I'll meet you, &c.

There we'll shout and give him glory, &c.

Question. O mourners will you meet me, &c.

Answer. By the grace of God I'll meet you, &c.

There we'll shout and give him glory, &c.

Question. O Sinners will you meet me, &c.

O will you try to meet me on Canaan's happy shore.

I am sorry for to leave you, &c.

I am sorry for to leave you, to leave you in your sins.

Fare you well my dearest Brethren, &c.

Fare you well my dearest Brethren, until we meet again.

I am sorry for to leave you, &c.

I am sorry for to leave you, to leave you all behind.

But we'll shout and give him glory, &c.

- John Brown's Body (Songsheet, arranged by C.B. Marsh, published by C. S. Hall, Boston, 1861)

John Brown's Body lies a mouldering in the grave,

John Brown's Body lies a mouldering in the grave,

John Brown's Body lies a mouldering in the grave,

His soul's marching on!

CHORUS

Glory, Hally, Hallelujah! Glory, Hally, Hallelujah! Glory, Hally, Hallelujah!

His soul's marching on!

He's gone to be a soldier in the army of the Lord,

He's gone, &c.

He's gone, &c.

His soul's marching on!

CHORUS

Glory, Hally, Hallelujah! &c.

His soul's marching on!

John Brown's knapsack is strapped upon his back—

John Brown's, &c.

John Brown's, &c.

His soul's marching on!

CHORUS

Glory, Hally, Hallelujah! &c.

His soul's marching on!

His pet lambs will meet him on the way—
His pet lambs, &c.
His pet lambs, &c.
> They go marching on!

CHORUS

Glory, Hally, Hallelujah! &c.
> His soul's marching on!

They will hang Jeff Davis to a tree!
They will hang, &c.
They will hang, &c.
> As they march along!

CHORUS

Glory, Hally, Hallelujah! &c.
> His soul's marching on!

Now, three rousing cheers for the Union!
Now, &c.
Now, &c.
> As we are marching on!

CHORUS

Glory, Hally, Hallelujah! Glory, Hally, Hallelujah! Glory, Hally, Hallelujah!
> Hip, Hip, Hip, Hip, Hurrah!

• The New John Brown Song (Rev. W. W. Patton, *Chicago Tribune*, December 16, 1861)

Old John Brown's body lies a-mouldering in the grave,
While weep the sons of bondage, whom he ventured all to save;
But though he lost his life in struggling for the slave,
> His soul is marching on. Glory, Hallelujah!

John Brown was a hero, undaunted, true, and brave,
And Kansas knew his valor, when he fought her rights to save;
And now, though the grass grows green above his grave,
> His soul is marching on. Glory, etc.

He captured Harper's Ferry with his nineteen men so few,
And he frightened "Old Virginny" till she trembled through and through;
They hung him for a traitor, themselves a traitorous crew.
> But his soul is marching on. Glory, etc.

John Brown was John the Baptist, of the Christ we are to see—
Christ, who of the bondman shall the Liberator be;
And soon throughout the sunny South, the slaves shall all be free,
> For his soul is marching on. Glory, etc.

The conflict that he heralded, he looks from Heaven to view,
On the army of the Union, with its flag red, white, and blue;
And Heaven shall ring with anthems o'er the deed they mean to do,
    For his soul is marching on. Glory, etc.

Ye soldiers of Freedom, then strike while strike ye may,
The death-blow of oppression, in a better time and way;
For the dawn of old John Brown has brightened into day.
    And his soul is marching on. Glory, etc.

- "Words That Can be Sung to the 'Hallelujah Chorus'" (Henry H. Brownell, in *Songs of the Soldiers*, ed. Frank Moore, 1864)

Old John Brown lies a-mouldering in the grave,
Old John Brown lies slumbering in his grave—
But John Brown's soul is marching with the brave,
        His soul is marching on.
    Glory, glory, hallelujah!
    Glory, glory, hallelujah!
    Glory, glory, hallelujah!
        His soul is marching on.

He has gone to be a soldier in the army of the Lord,
He is sworn as a private in the ranks of the Lord—
He shall stand at Armageddon with his brave old sword—
        When Heaven is marching on.
    Glory, glory, hallelujah, &c.
        For heaven is marching on.

He shall file in front where the lines of battle form,
He shall face to front when the squares of battle form—
Time with the column, and charge in the storm,
        Where men are marching on.
    Glory, glory, hallelujah, &c.
        True men are marching on.

Ah! foul tyrants! do ye hear him where he comes?
Ah! black traitors! do ye know him as he comes?
In thunder of the cannon and roll of the drums,
        As we go marching on.
    Glory, glory, hallelujah, &c.
        We all are marching on.

Men may die, and moulder in the dust,
Men may die, and arise again from dust,
Shoulder to shoulder, in the ranks of the just,

When Heaven is marching on.
Glory, glory, hallelujah, &c.
The Lord is marching on.

- "Song of the First of Arkansas" (Supervisory Committee for Recruiting Colored Regiments, c. 1864)

Oh! we're de bully soldiers of de "First of Arkansas,"
We are fightin' for de Union, we are fightin' for de law,
We can hit a Rebel furder dan a white man eber saw,
As we go marching on.
Glory, glory, hallelujah, &c.

See dar! above de centre, where de flag is wavin' bright;
We are goin' out of slavery; we are bound for freedom's light;
We mean to show Jeff. Davis how the Africans can fight,
As we go marching on.

We hab done wid hoein' cotton, we hab done with hoein' corn,
We are colored Yankee soldiers now, as sure as you are born;
When de Massas hear us yellin', dey'll tink it's Gabriel's horn,
As we go marching on.

Dey will hab to pay us wages, de wages ob their sin,
Dey will hab to bow their foreheads to their colored kith and kin,
Dey will hab to gib us house-room, or de roof shall tumble in,
As we go marching on.

We heard de proclamation, massa hush it as he will;
De bird he sing it to us, hoppin on de cotton hill,
And de possum up de gum tree, he couldn't keep it still,
As he went climbing on.

Dey said, "Now colored bredren, you shall be forever free,
From the first of January, eighteen hundred and sixty-three."
We heard it in de riber goin' rushin' to de sea,
As it went soundin' on.

Father Abraham has spoken and de message has been sent,
De prison doors he opened, and out de pris'ners went,
To join de sable army of de "African descent,"
As we go marching on.

Den fall in, colored bredren, you'd better do it soon,
Don't you hear de drum a-beatin' de Yankee Doodle tune?
We are wid you now dis mornin', we'll be far away at noon,
As we go marching on.

- "Battle Hymn of the Republic" (facsimile of the first draft, November 1861, in Julia Ward Howe, *Reminiscences*, 1899, inset)

Mine eyes have seen the glory of the coming of the Lord.
He is trampling out the wine press where the grapes of wrath are stored,
He hath loosed [bared] the fateful lightnings of his terrible swift sword,
    His truth is marching on.

I have seen him in the watchfires of an hundred circling camps
They have builded him an altar in the evening dews and damps,
I can read his righteous sentence by the dim and flaring lamps
    His day is marching on.

I have read a burning Gospel writ in fiery rows of steel,
As ye deal with my contemners, so with you my grace shall deal
Let the hero born of women crush the serpent with his heel,
    Our God is marching on.

He has sounded out the trumpet that shall never call retreat,
He has waked the earth's dull bosom with a high ecstatic beat,
Oh! be swift my soul to answer him, be jubilant my feet.
    Our God is marching on.

In the ~~glory~~ whiteness of the lilies he was born across the sea
With a glory in his bosom that shines out on you and me,
As he died to make men holy, let us die to make men free
    Our God is marching on.

He is coming like the glory of the morning on the wave
He is wisdom to the mighty, he is ~~glory~~ honour to the brave
So the world shall be his footstool, and the soul of Time his slave
    Our God is marching on.[1]

- "Battle Hymn of the Republic" (Julia Ward Howe, *Atlantic*, February 1862)

Mine eyes have seen the glory of the coming of the Lord:
He is trampling out the vintage where the grapes of wrath are stored;
He hath loosed the fateful lightning of His terrible swift sword:
His truth is marching on.

I have seen Him in the watch-fires of a hundred circling camps,
They have builded Him an altar in the evening dews and damps;
I can read His righteous sentence by the dim and flaring lamps:
His day is marching on.

I have read a fiery gospel writ in burnished rows of steel:
"As ye deal with my contemners, so with you my grace shall deal;

Let the Hero, born of woman, crush the serpent with his heel,
Since God is marching on."

He has sounded forth the trumpet that shall never call retreat;
He is sifting out the hearts of men before His judgment-seat:
Oh, be swift, my soul, to answer Him! be jubilant, my feet!
Our God is marching on.

In the beauty of the lilies Christ was born across the sea,
With a glory in His bosom that transfigures you and me:
As He died to make men holy, let us die to make men free,
While God is marching on.

- "Battle Hymn of the Republic (Brought Down to Date)" 1901, Mark Twain, *Collected Tales,
  Sketches, Speeches, & Essays, 1891–1910* (New York: Library of America, 1992), 474–75

Mine eyes have seen the orgy of the launching of the Sword;
He is searching out the hoardings where the stranger's wealth is stored;
He has loosed his fateful lightning, & with woe & death has scored;
His lust is marching on.

I have seen him in the watch-fires of a hundred circling camps;
They have builded him an altar in the Eastern dews & damps;
I have read his doomful mission by the dim & flaring lamps—
His might is marching on.

I have read this bandit gospel in burnished rows of steel,
As ye deal with my pretensions, so with you my wrath shall deal,
Let the faithless sons of freedom, crush the patriot with his heel
Lo, Greed is marching on.

We have legalized the Strumpet & are guarding her retreat;
Greed is seeking out commercial souls before his judgment seat;
Oh be swift, ye clods, to answer him! Be jubilant my feet!
Our God is marching on!

In a sordid slime harmonious, Greed was born in yonder ditch;
With a longing in his bosom—for other's goods an itch;
Christ died to make men holy, let men die to make us rich;
Our God is marching on.[2]

- "Solidarity Forever!" (From *I.W.W. Songs,* 1923)

When the Union's inspiration through the worker's blood shall run,
There can be no power greater anywhere beneath the sun.
Yet what force on earth is weaker than the feeble strength of one?
    But the Union makes us strong.

CHORUS

Solidarity forever!
Solidarity forever!
Solidarity forever!
But the Union makes us strong.

Is there aught we hold in common with the greedy parasite
Who would lash us into serfdom and would crush us with his might?
Is there anything left for us but to organize and fight?
For the Union makes us strong.

It is we who plowed the prairies; built the cities where they trade.
Dug the mines and built the workshops; endless miles of railroad laid.
Now we stand, outcast and starving, 'mid the wonders we have made;
But the Union makes us strong.

All the world that's owned by idle drones, is ours and ours alone.
We have laid the wide foundations; built it skywards, stone by stone.
It is ours, not to slave in, but to master and to own,
While the Union makes us strong.

They have taken untold millions that they never toiled to earn.
But without our brain and muscle not a single wheel can turn.
We can break their haughty power; gain our freedom when we learn
That the Union makes us strong.

In our hands is placed a power greater than their hoarded gold;
Greater than the might of armies, magnified a thousand fold.
We can bring to birth the new world from the ashes of the old,
For the Union makes us strong.

- "Battle Hymn of Lt. Calley" (From C Company featuring Terry Nelson with Julian Wilson, James M. Smith, Plantation Records, 1971; from *Next Stop is Vietnam: The War on Record: 1961–2008*, Bear Family Records, 2010, disk 14, #29)

Once upon a time there was a little boy who wanted to grow up and be a soldier and serve his country in whatever way he could. He would parade around the house with a sauce pan on his head for a helmet, a wooden sword in one hand and the American flag in the other. As he grew up, he put away the things of a child but he never let go of the flag.

My name is William Calley, I'm a soldier of this land
I've tried to do my duty and to gain the upper hand
But they've made me out a villain they have stamped me with a brand
As we go marching on

I'm just another soldier from the shores of U.S.A.
Forgotten on a battle field ten thousand miles away

While life goes on as usual from New York to Santa Fe
As we go marching on

I've seen my buddies ambushed on the left and on the right
And their youthful bodies riddled by the bullets of the night
Where all the rules are broken and the only law is might
As we go marching on

While we're fighting in the jungles they were marching in the street
While we're dying in the rice fields they were helping our defeat
While we're facing V.C. bullets they were sounding a retreat
As we go marching on

With our sweat we took the bunker, with our tears we took the plain
With our blood we took the mountain and they gave it back again
Still all of us are soldiers, we're too busy to complain
As we go marching on

When I reach my final campground in that land beyond the sun
And the great commander asks me, "Did you fight or did you run?"
I'll stand both straight and tall stripped of medals, rank and gun
And this is what I'll say:

Sir, I followed all my orders and I did the best I could
It's hard to judge the enemy and hard to tell the good
Yet there's not a man among us would not have understood

We took the jungle village exactly like they said
We responded to their rifle fire with everything we had
And when the smoke had cleared away a hundred souls lay dead

Sir, the soldier that's alive is the only one can fight
There's no other way to wage a war when the only one in sight
That you're sure is not a VC is your buddy on your right

When all the wars are over and the battle's finally won
Count me only as a soldier who never left his gun
With the right to serve my country as the only prize I've won

Glory, glory hallelujah
Glory, glory hallelujah
Glory, glory hallelujah
As we go marching on
As we go marching on

NOTES

INTRODUCTION

1. Timothy S. Goeglein, *The Man in the Middle* (Nashville: B&H, 2011), 74–75; Karl Rove, *Courage and Consequence: My Life as a Conservative in the Fight* (New York: Threshold Editions, 2010), 268–69; Karen Hughes, *Ten Minutes to Normal* (New York: Viking Penguin, 2004), 251; phone interview with Margaret Shannon, March 11, 2011; phone interview with Timothy Goeglein, May 21, 2012.

2. Bill Sammon, *Fighting Back: The War on Terrorism—from Inside the Bush White House* (Washington, D.C.: Regnery, 2002), 153–68; *Washington Post*, January 30, 2002.

3. "No Higher Honor: A Conversation with Condoleezza Rice," *Baylor Magazine*, Winter 2011, http://www.baylor.edu/alumni/magazine/1002/news.php?action=story&story=105966; Mary Beth Brown, *Condi: The Life of a Steel Magnolia* (Nashville: Thomas Nelson, 2007), 26; *Washington Times*, October 9, 2002.

4. Goeglein, *Man in the Middle*, 74–75; Hughes, *Ten Minutes to Normal*, 251; phone interview with Timothy Goeglein, May 21, 2012.

5. *Washington Post*, September 24, 2001; (London) *Daily Mail*, September 15, 2001.

6. Richard T. Hughes, "Christianity Was Never Designed as a Tool for War," *Vital Speeches of the Day* 73, no. 12 (2007): 537; Jim Wallis, *God's Politics: Why the Right Gets It Wrong and the Left Doesn't Get it* (New York: HarperCollins, 2005), 143–44; George F. Will, "Battle Hymn," *Washington Post*, September 23, 2001; Gregg Easterbrook, "What Would Jesus Sing?" Beliefnet, http://www.beliefnet.com/News/2001/09/What-Would-Jesus-Sing.aspx.

7. Phone interview with Doug Major, July 14, 2011; *Washington Post*, September 22, 2001; *Washington Post*, January 26, 1991; phone interview with Margaret Shannon; materials on the Lincoln Bay Bosses in National Cathedral Archives, Record Group 165, Box 2, Folder 20.

8. Richard M. Gamble, *The War for Righteousness: Progressive Christianity, the Great War, and the Rise of the Messianic Nation* (Wilmington, Del.: ISI Books, 2003); Ernest Lee Tuveson, *Redeemer Nation: The Idea of America's Millennial Role* (Chicago: University of Chicago Press, 1968).

9. James H. Moorhead, *American Apocalypse: Yankee Protestants and the Civil War, 1860–1869* (New Haven: Yale University Press, 1978), 53; Margaret Prescott Montague, "Good Friday, 1917," *Atlantic Monthly* 119, no. 6 (1917): 753; William Crowell Edgar, *England During the Last Four Months of the War* (Minneapolis: Powers Mercantile Co., 1919), 34; *Los Angeles Times*, January 31, 1965.

10. *Columbus* (Ga.) *Ledger*, December 1, 1913; for details of the United Daughters of the Confederacy contest, see Annie Forney Daugette to Boyd Stutler, August 16, 1937, Stutler to Louis Crenshaw Ray, April 3, 1939, Brown/Boyd B. Stutler Database, West Virginia Memory Project at http://www.wvculture.org/history.

11. Tuveson, *Redeemer Nation*, 120; Moorhead, *American Apocalypse*, 14–15, 28 (quote).

12. Samuel T. Pickard, *Life and Letters of John Greenleaf Whittier* (Boston: Houghton, Mifflin, 1894), 2:611; Fanny Bixby Spencer, *The Repudiation of War* (Costa Mesa, Calif.: H. F. Schick, n.d.), 13–14.

13. Beverly Gage, "Terrorism and the American Experience: A State of the Field," *Journal of American History* 98, no. 1 (2011): 83; David S. Reynolds, *John Brown: Abolitionist* (New York: Vintage Books, 2005), 498–502; Sarah Vowell, "John Brown's Body," in Sean Wilentz and Greil Marcus, eds., *The Rose and the Briar: Death, Love and Liberty in the American Ballad* (New York: Norton, 2005), 83; Dave Marsh, "Where the Grapes of Wrath Are Stored," *Counterpunch*, October 4, 2001, http://www.counterpunch.org/2001/10/04/where-the-grapes-of-wrath-are-stored.

14. For a collection of these schoolyard variations, see Josepha Sherman and T. K. F. Weisskopf, *Greasy Grimy Gopher Guts: The Subversive Folklore of Children* (Little Rock, Ark.: August House, 1995), 103–8. Tuveson, *Redeemer Nation*, 214.

15. John Updike, *Self-Consciousness* (New York: Knopf, 1989), 103.

CHAPTER 1

1. Stith Mead, *A General Selection of the Newest and Most Admired Hymns & Spiritual Songs, Now in Use* (Richmond, Va.: Seaton Grantland, 1807), title page; Stith Mead, "Camp Meeting," *William and Mary Quarterly*, second series, 4, no. 3 (1924): 210; Dickson D. Bruce, *And They All Sang Hallelujah: Plain-Folk Camp Meeting Religion, 1800–1845* (Knoxville: University of Tennessee Press, 1974), 53. On camp meetings, see also Christine Leigh Heyrman, *Southern Cross: The Beginnings of the Bible Belt* (New York: Knopf, 1997); Ellen Jane Lorenz, *Glory, Hallelujah! The Story of the Campmeeting Spiritual* (Nashville, Tenn.: Abingdon, 1980); John B. Boles, *The Great Revival, 1787–1805: The Origins of the Southern Evangelical Mind* (Lexington: University Press of Kentucky, 1972); Ellen Eslinger, *Citizens of Zion: The Social Origins of Camp Meeting Revivalism* (Knoxville: University of Tennessee Press, 1999); Leigh Eric Schmidt, *Holy Fairs: Scottish Communions and American Revivals in the Early Modern Period* (New York: Cambridge University Press, 1989); Charles A. Johnson, "The Frontier Camp Meeting: Contemporary and Historical Appraisals, 1805–1840," *Mississippi Valley Historical Review* 37, no. 1 (1950):

91–110; Charles A. Johnson, "Camp Meeting Hymnody," *American Quarterly* 4, no. 2 (1952): 110–26.

2. Mead, "Camp Meeting," 210.

3. Heyrman, *Southern Cross*, 117–25, quotation 119, 121; Stith Mead, *A Short Account of the Experiences and Labors of the Reverend Stith Mead: Preacher of the Gospel, and an Elder in the Methodist Episcopal Church: To Which are Added Extracts of Letters From Himself and Others in a Religious Correspondence* (Lynchburg, Va.: published for and sold by the author, 1829).

4. Mead, *General Selection of the Newest and Most Admired Hymns*, 2.

5. Mead, *General Selection of the Newest and Most Admired Hymns*, 2–3, 80–81.

6. George Pullen Jackson, *White and Negro Spirituals: Their Life Span and Kinship* (Locust Valley, N.Y.: J. J. Augustin, 1943), 38–39, 42 43, 54–59, 62–76, quotation 66; John Powell, preface to *Spiritual Folk-Songs of Early America*, collected and edited by George Cullen Jackson (New York: J. J. Augustin, n.d.), vii–x; Bruce, *And They All Sang Hallelujah*, 90–95; David Warren Steel with Richard H. Hulan, *The Makers of the Sacred Harp* (Urbana: University of Illinois Press, 2010), 57–69. We are immensely grateful for Richard Hulan's advice via email during our research on the origins of "Say Brothers."

7. Jackson, *Spiritual Folk-Songs of Early America*, 7–11; Jackson, *White and Negro Spirituals*, 79–87.

8. Heyrman, *Southern Cross*, 3–27; Jackson, *White and Negro Spirituals*, 79–81; Eslinger, *Citizens of Zion*, 187–212; Johnson, "Frontier Camp Meeting," 91–110; Bruce, *And They All Sang Hallelujah*, 3–12, 51, 70–75, 80–86; Mead, "Camp Meeting," 210; Heyrman, *Southern Cross*, 231–32; John F. Garst, "Mutual Reinforcement and the Origins of Spirituals," *American Music* 4, no. 4 (1986): 390–406.

9. Bruce, *And They All Sang Hallelujah*, 5–9, 36–46.

10. Bruce, *And They All Sang Hallelujah*, 53–54, quotation 53; Heyrman, *Southern Cross*, 79–80, quotation 80.

11. James B. Finley, *Autobiography of Rev. James B. Finley, or, Pioneer Life in the West*, ed. W. P. Strickland (Cincinnati: E. P. Thompson, 1856), 166–67; Heyrman, *Southern Cross*, 212.

12. Finley, *Autobiography*, 167–68; Heyrman, *Southern Cross*, 212.

13. Finley, *Autobiography*, 166; Jackson, *White and Negro Spirituals*, 80–81, quotation 80; Sydney E. Ahlstrom, *A Religious History of the American People* (New Haven: Yale University Press, 1972), 432–35.

14. Heyrman, *Southern Cross*, 4–5. As Heyrman notes, the sites in which these conversions occurred often became sacred, with converts returning year after year. The camp meeting at Indian Fields, South Carolina, remains a sacred site. Bishop Francis Ashbury preached there in 1801 and 1803, and it has held annual revivals for over two hundred years. See the article on Indian Fields in the Charleston, S.C., *News and Courier*, September 25, 1949; Charleston *News and Courier*, August 26, 1973.

15. On the popularity of "Say Brothers," see Jackson, *Spiritual Folk-Songs*, 206–7; Jackson, *White and Negro Spirituals*, 178–79.

16. Jackson, *Spiritual Folk-Songs*, 7; Jackson, *White and Negro Spirituals*, 38–43; Bruce, *And They All Sang Hallelujah*, 90–95; Johnson, "Camp Meeting Hymnody," 116–17.

17. Mead, *General Selection of the Newest and Most Admired Hymns*, 1; Jackson, *White and Negro Spirituals*, 39–43, 84–85, 178; Johnson, "Camp Meeting Hymnody," 114–15.

18. David B. Mintz, ed., *Collection of Hymns, and Spiritual Songs, Mostly New* (New Bern, N.C.: John M'Williams and Christopher D. Neale, 1806), 18–20, quotation of "Say Brothers" stanza 19–20; Jackson, *White and Negro Spirituals*, 66, 84–85, 119–22; Bruce, *And They All Sang Hallelujah*, 90–95; Johnson, "Camp Meeting Hymnody," 120.

19. Samuel Holyoke, ed., *The Christian Harmonist: Containing a Set of Tunes Adapted to all the Metres in Mr. Rippon's Selection of Hymns, in the Collection of Hymns by Mr. Joshua Smith, and in Dr. Watt's Psalms and Hymns* (Salem, Mass.: Joshua Cushing, 1804), 142, Hymn No. 211; Jackson, *White and Negro Spirituals*, 85. Jackson refers to the publication of "Say Brothers" in Mintz's 1808 North Carolina hymnbook and notes that "despite the absence of *tunes* from the Mintz booklet, there can be little doubt of this song's being an early form of the old spiritual which inspired Julia Ward Howe, nearly half a century later, in the writing of her 'Battle Hymn of the Republic'" (85, emphasis added).

The website Hymnary.org has been invaluable for analyzing "Say Brothers" and "Almighty Love Inspire." It includes sixty-five hymnals featuring "Almighty Love Inspire" from 1799 to 1869, and it includes eighty-nine hymnals featuring "Say Brothers" from 1858 to 1951. For examples of "Say Brothers," see http://www.hymnary.org/text/say_brothers_will_you_meet_us. For examples of "Almighty Love Inspire," see http://www.hymnary.org/text/almighty_love_inspire_my_heart_with_sacr.

Deborah Cunningham, an accomplished violinist, kindly played "Almighty Love Inspire" from the 1804 hymnal, which clarified that its melody is distinct from "Say Brothers."

20. Jackson, *White and Negro Spirituals*, 84–85; Bruce, *And They All Sang Hallelujah*, 93. On Caleb Jarvis Taylor, see "The Early Camp-Meeting Song Writers," *Methodist Quarterly Review* 11 (July 1859): 401. Bruce notes that "spiritual choruses, like the camp meeting, were the creations of the frontier church-folk and were group religious statements which were sung by those who had been converted." Bruce, *And They All Sang Hallelujah*, 93. The editor of an 1878 hymnbook calls "Say Brothers" a "refrain song." See Jackson, *Spiritual Folk-Songs*, 181; William Hauser, ed., *The Olive Leaf: A Collection of Beautiful Tunes, New and Old* (Wadley, Ga.: William Hauser and Benjamin Turner, 1878).

21. Mead, *General Selection of the Newest and Most Admired Hymns*, 79–81, quotation 80–81, emphasis added.

22. For an example of the inclusion of "Say Brothers" in an African American hymnal, see *Jubilee Songs: Complete. As Sung by the Jubilee Singers*, compiled by Theodore F. Seward and George L. White (New York: Biglow & Main, 1872), 14, 140. Jackson, *White and Negro Spirituals*, 83–85, 178–79, 230, 262, quotation 230; Albert J. Raboteau, *Slave Religion: The "Invisible Institution" in the Antebellum South* (New York: Oxford University Press, 1978), 68–70; Sterling Stuckey, *Slave Culture: Nationalist Theory and the Foundations of Black America* (New York: Oxford University Press, 1987), 16, 30, 84–85, 87, 89–91.

23. Heyrman, *Southern Cross*, 51, 119, quotation 119; Raboteau, *Slave Religion*, 59–61, 67, 74; William Tallmadge, "The Black in Jackson's White Spirituals," *Black Perspective in Music* 9, no. 2 (1981): 139–60; Lawrence Levine, *Black Culture and Black Consciousness* (New York: Oxford University Press, 1977), 23, 30; Dena J. Epstein, "A White Origin for the Black Spiritual? An Invalid Theory and How It Grew," *American Music* 1, no. 2 (1983): 53–59; Steve Vaughn, "Making Jesus Black: The Historiographical Debate on the Roots of African-American Christianity," *Journal of Negro History* 82, no. 1 (1997): 37–38; James H. Cone,

The Spirituals and the Blues: An Interpretation (1972; reprint, New York: Orbis Books, 2004), 1–96; Mechal Sobel, *Trabelin' On: The Slave Journey to an Afro-Baptist Faith* (Princeton: Princeton University Press, 1988), 79–88; Stuckey, *Slave Religion*, 89–91; Samuel A. Floyd Jr., "On Black Music Research," *Black Music Research Journal* 3 (1983): 47–48; Eileen Southern, *The Music of Black Americans: A History*, 3rd ed. (New York: Norton, 1997), 82–88; John Wesley Work, ed., *American Negro Songs and Spirituals* (New York: Crown, 1940); James Weldon Johnson and J. Rosamund Johnson, *The Book of American Negro Spirituals* (New York: Da Capo Press, 1942); John Lovell, *Black Song: The Forge and the Flame* (New York: Macmillan, 1972); Darius Thieme, "Afro-American Folksong Scholarship," *Black Music Research Journal* 10, no. 1 (1990): 10; John E. Taylor, "Somethin' on My Mind: A Cultural and Historical Interpretation of Spiritual Texts," *Ethnomusicology* 19, no. 3 (1975): 387–99; LeRoy Moore Jr., "The Spiritual: Soul of Black Religion," *American Quarterly* 23, no. 5 (1971): 658–76.

24. "Contrabands and Christmas," *Daily Cleveland Herald*, January 31, 1862; Raboteau, *Slave Religion*, 69–70, quotation 70; Stuckey, *Slave Culture*, 16, 30, 57.

25. James Hosmer, *The Thinking Bayonet* (Boston: Walker, Fuller, 1865), v–vi, 259–61, quotation 260.

26. John Watson, *Methodist Error; or, Friendly, Christian Advice, to those Methodists, Who Indulge in Extravagant Emotions and Bodily Exercises* (Trenton, N.J.: D. & E. Fenton, 1819), 62–64; Raboteau, *Slave Religion*, 67. See also Levine, *Black Culture and Black Consciousness*, 30–54; Sobel, *Trabelin' On*, 79–98.

27. Raboteau, *Slave Religion*, 67–72, quotations 67, 69, 72.

28. A. D. Betts, *Experience of a Confederate Chaplain, 1861–1864*, ed. W. A. Betts (Greenville, S.C.: privately printed, 1901), 92, http://docsouth.unc.edu/fpn/betts/betts.html; *The Southern Zion's Songster; Hymns Designed for Sabbath Schools, Prayer, and Social Meetings, and the Camps* (Raleigh: N.C. Christian Advocate, 1864), 117, Hymn 114; *Hymns for the Camp*, 2nd ed. (Raleigh: General Tract Agency, Strother & Marcom, 1862), 126, Hymn 148; *A Collection of Sabbath School Hymns. Compiled by a Sabbath School Teacher, for the Benefit of the Children in the Confederate States* (Raleigh, N.C.: Raleigh Register Steam-Power Press, 1863), 61, Hymn 68.

29. Eugene A. Nolte, "Downeasters in Arkansas: Letters of Roscoe G. Jennings to His Brother" *Arkansas Historical Quarterly* 18 no. 2 (1959), 3; Kate Cumming, *Kate: The Journal of a Confederate Nurse*, ed. Richard Barksdale Harwell (Baton Rouge: Louisiana State University Press, 1987), 254; Heyrman, *Southern Cross*, 4, 127–29, quotation 4. See also Drew Gilpin Faust, *Confederate Nationalism: Ideology and Identity in the Civil War South* (Baton Rouge: Louisiana State University Press, 1988), 22–32, 60, 58–81.

30. Frederick Douglass, *My Bondage and My Freedom*, ed. John Stauffer (New York: Modern Library, 2003), 159–60.

31. Harriet Beecher Stowe, *Uncle Tom's Cabin: A Norton Critical Edition*, ed. Elizabeth Ammons (New York: Norton, 2010), 2, 236–39, quotations 2, 238, 239. Lawrence Levine notes that black spirituals were more rooted in the temporal than the eschatological world. See Levine, *Black Culture and Black Consciousness*, 30; Vaughn, "Making Jesus Black," 38.

32. Johnson, "Camp Meeting Hymnody," 114; *The Boston Collection of Sacred and Devotional Hymns: Intended to Accommodate Christians on Special and Stated Occasions* (Boston: Manning and Loring, 1808), 2, 155 (Hymn 159), quotation 2. Kay Norton notes that most scholars have described the migration of folk hymns from the North to the South, and she deftly refutes the

argument by focusing on a specific hymnal, Jesse Mercer's *Cluster of Spiritual Songs*, published in Georgia in 1810. See Kay Norton, "Who Lost the South?," *American Music* 21, no. 4 (2003): 391–411.

33. On New Jerusalem as a common symbol in New England, Sacvan Bercovitch provides many examples of Puritans and their descendants characterizing New England as "a type and emblem of New Jerusalem." Cotton Mather characterized New England as "our American Jerusalem," and in his biography of John Winthrop he substituted "New England" for "Jerusalem." See Sacvan Bercovitch, *The Puritan Origins of the American Self* (New Haven: Yale University Press, 1975), 1, 26, 39–70, 78, 90–102, 107, 114, 120–35, 148–60, 170, 191, quotations 39, 40, 51.

34. Jackson, *White and Negro Spirituals*, 119–23; Bruce, *And They All Sang Hallelujah*, 56–57; Johnson, "The Frontier Camp Meeting," 98–99.

35. Milton Meltzer and Patricia G. Holland, eds., *Lydia Maria Child: Selected Letters, 1817–1880* (Amherst: University of Massachusetts Press, 1982), 394; Timothy L. Smith, *Revivalism and Social Reform: American Protestantism on the Eve of the Civil War* (New York: Harper & Row, 1957), 7–9, 15–21; David Hempton, *Methodism: Empire of the Spirit* (New Haven: Yale University Press, 2005), 1–10, 68–85, 202–9; Christian McWhirter, *Battle Hymns: The Power and Popularity of Music in the Civil War* (Chapel Hill: University of North Carolina Press, 2012), 42, 223n21. On Mormons using the John Brown tune as their own, see Samuel Morris Brown, *In Heaven As It Is on Earth: Joseph Smith and the Early Mormon Conquest of Death* (New York: Oxford University Press, 2012), 29.

On Millerites using the John Brown tune, see Colonel Nicholas Smith, *Stories of Great National Songs* (Milwaukee, Wis.: Young Churchman, 1899), 85, 103. As Smith notes, in 1843 Millerites coupled the "Say Brothers" melody to the following lyrics:

We'll see the angels coming through the old church yards, [x2]
Shouting through the air.
Glory, glory Hallelujah. (85)

On the American Sunday School Union using the song, see A. Taylor, ed., *Union Prayer Meeting Hymns* (Philadelphia: American Sunday School Union, 1858), Hymn 192; *Union Prayer Meeting Hymns* (Boston: American Sunday School Union, 1859), Hymn 192.

The Sons of Temperance wrote a variant of "Say Brothers" called "The Temperance Compact" to the "Say Brothers" tune: "Say, brothers, will you join us? / The drunkard's child to save?" See, for example, Horace Waters, ed., *The Sabbath School Bell: A New Collection of Choice Hymns and Tunes, Original and Standard* . . . (Philadelphia: Presbyterian Board of Publication, 1859), 120. Four other versions of "The Temperance Compact" are listed on http://www.hymnary.org/text/say_brother_will_you_join_us.

36. William Lichtenwanger, quoted in William Charles Eugene Claghorn, "*Battle Hymn* (The Story behind *The Battle Hymn of the Republic*)," *Papers of the Hymn Society of America* 29 (1974): 7; Jackson, *Spiritual Folk-Songs of Early America*, 7. On Lichtenwanger, see Carol June Bradley, "William Lichtenwanger, Reference Librarian," *Notes*, second series, 62, no. 2 (2005): 299–321.

37. *Songs & Ballads As Sung by R. Bishop and G. Swain Buckley of Buckley's Minstrels* (Boston: Henry Tolman, 1855), 4, The Lester S. Levy Collection of Sheet Music, Special Collections at the

Sheridan Libraries of the Johns Hopkins University. We are grateful to Masato Sakurai for pointing out this sheet music to us.

The "Say Brothers" melody also fit comfortably within music's highest cultural form. It shared "a remarkable similarity of theme" with aspects of Johannes Brahms's *Second Piano Concerto*, as musicologists have noted. There is no evidence that Brahms, a German who completed his *Concerto* in 1881 in Budapest, knew anything about "Say Brothers," "John Brown's Body," or the "Battle Hymn." But he was deeply interested in European folksong. After finishing the *Concerto* he wrote "Hungarian Dances," his most popular work, which is heavily based on folksong. And he dedicated the *Concerto* to his music teacher, Eduard Marxsen, himself a student of folksong. Brahms helped Marxsen publish "Hundred Variations on a Folk-Song," and some of Marxsen's folksongs, such as "Der Post," closely resemble the "Battle Hymn" melody. "Say Brothers" was thus "in the air" in America *and* Europe. The coupling of folksongs with concertos, or secular melodies with sacred texts, was part of the formula for creating popular music in multiple genres. See S. J. Sackett, "Johannes Brahms's Body," *Journal of American Folklore* 79, no. 314 (1966): 609–11. We are grateful for Charles Parker for pointing out to us the similarities between the "Battle Hymn" and Brahms's Second Piano Concerto.

38. David S. Reynolds, *John Brown, Abolitionist* (New York: Knopf, 2005), 4; Moncure Conway, quoted in *The Martyrdom of John Brown: The Proceedings of a Public Meeting, Held in London on the 2nd December 1863, to Commemorate the 4th Anniversary of John Brown's Death* (London: Emancipation Society, 1864), 4. "Blow Ye the Trumpet Blow" was among the most popular hymns in America from 1830 to 1860, appearing in 30 to 40 percent of published hymnals. See http://www.hymnary.org/text/blow_ye_the_trumpet_blow.

39. *Richmond Whig*, November 22, 1859; *Richmond Enquirer*, October 25, 1859. Allan Nevins similarly concludes that secessionist voices became dominant after Harpers Ferry. See *The Ordeal of the Union, Vol. 2: Prologue to Civil War, 1857–1861* (1950; reprint, New York: Collier Books, 1992), 114–15. See also David M. Potter, *The Impending Crisis, 1848–1861* (New York: Harper & Row, 1976), 382–84; John Stauffer and Zoe Trodd, eds., *The Tribunal: Responses to John Brown and the Harpers Ferry Raid* (Cambridge, Mass.: Harvard University Press, 2012), xix–lix.

40. "The Day of Execution," *The Independent*, November 24, 1859; Frederick Douglass and Hermann von Holst, quoted in Stauffer and Trodd, *The Tribunal*, 499, 421.

41. Zoe Trodd and John Stauffer, eds., *Meteor of War: The John Brown Story* (Maplecrest, N.Y.: Brandywine Press, 2004), ii; Brown, "To Mr. Henry L. Stearns," July 15, 1857, in Stauffer and Trodd, *Tribunal*, 19–25. See also Tony Horwitz, *Midnight Rising: John Brown and the Raid That Sparked the Civil War* (New York: Henry Holt, 2011), 9, 11; and John Stauffer, *The Black Hearts of Men: Radical Abolitionists and the Transformation of Race* (Cambridge, Mass.: Harvard University Press, 2002), 88–92.

42. Brown, "To Mr. Henry L. Stearns," July 15, 1857, in Stauffer and Trodd, *Tribunal*, 22; Stauffer, *Black Hearts*, 89–90

43. Reynolds, *John Brown*, 48–49.

44. Stephen B. Oates, *To Purge This Land With Blood: A Biography of John Brown* (1970; reprint, Amherst, Mass.: University of Massachusetts Press, 1984), 22–50, quotation 37; Stauffer, *Black Hearts*, 119.

45. Stauffer, *Black Hearts*, 120; Oates, *To Purge This Land*, 44. Several historians, notably Louis DeCaro, argue that Brown was a Calvinist in the tradition of Jonathan Edwards. But a central

tenet of such Edwardsian Calvinism is God's inscrutability. For a Calvinist, presuming to know God's will, as Brown thought he did, was hubris. Edwards repudiated free will and antinomianism, which contradicts Brown's faith. However, as many scholars have noted, Edwards's emphases on a future millennium and the "spiritual affections" of the heart opened the way for prophecy and an impending new age either by dismantling Edwards's Calvinist determinism or by embracing antinomianism. See Ahlstrom, *Religious History of the American People*, 301–13, quotations 303; Joseph A Conforti, *Jonathan Edwards, Religious Tradition, and American Culture* (Chapel Hill: University of North Carolina Press, 1995), 36–61; Nicholas Parrillo, "Lincoln's Calvinist Transformation: Emancipation and War," *Civil War History* 46, no. 3 (2000): 227–53; Phillip S. Paludan, *A People's Contest: The Union and Civil War, 1861–1865* (New York: Harper & Row, 1988), 372.

46. J. Newton Brown, "The Beginning of John Brown's Career," *Nation*, February 12, 1914, 157; Justus Newton Brown, "Lovejoy's Influence on John Brown," *Magazine of History, with Notes and Queries* 23 (July–December 1916): 101; Oates, *To Purge This Land*, 41–42; Reynolds, *John Brown*, 64–65; Stauffer, *Black Hearts*, 118–19.

47. Oates, *To Purge This Land*, 54–55; Franklin B. Sanborn, ed., *The Life and Letters of John Brown* (Boston: Roberts Brothers, 1885), 35, 43; Reynolds, *John Brown*, 66–85; Louis Ruchames, ed., *John Brown: The Making of a Revolutionary* (New York: Grosset, 1969), 26–27.

48. John Brown, letter of November 8, 1846, in Ruchames, *John Brown*, 64. See also Oates, *To Purge This Land*, 55–56.

49. Frederick Douglass, "Editorial Correspondence," *North Star*, February 11, 1848; John Brown, "Sambo's Mistakes," 1848, in Stauffer and Trodd, *Tribunal*, 5; Stauffer, *Black Hearts*, 168–69.

50. Gerrit Smith, quoted in *Fifth Annual Report of the Executive Committee of the American Anti-Slavery Society* (New York: William S. Dorr, 1838), 35; Gerrit Smith, letter to the editor, *Oneida Morning Herald*, October 13, 1848; Stauffer, Black Hearts, 134–44.

51. Brown, quoted in Sanborn, *Life and Letters*, 97; Brown, quoted in Ralph Volney Harlow, *Gerrit Smith: Philanthropist and Reformer* (New York: Henry Holt, 1939), 246. See also Ruchames, *John Brown*, 75; Oswald Garrison Villard, *John Brown, 1800–1859: A Biography Fifty Years After* (1910; reprint New York: Alfred A. Knopf, 1943), 71–77. Of the three thousand recipients of Smith's gift, only about a hundred people moved to Timbucto. The main reason for this low turnout was start-up costs. Before moving, would-be pioneers needed wagons, mules or oxen, tools, and enough supplies to survive until the first harvest. All this amounted to about $100, roughly one-third of the annual earnings of the working poor. Many recipients did not have that much, and Smith didn't have an extra $300,000 in cash to enable settlers to make the move. Additionally, the land was of poor quality and the climate harsh, and settlers had to generate surplus in order to generate yearly taxes. Some settlers could not pay their taxes and faced foreclosure by the New York State Treasury. Finally, some whites living in the region tried to cheat grantees out of their deeds. See Stauffer, *Black Hearts*, 157.

52. Richard Henry Dana Jr., "How We Met John Brown," *Atlantic Monthly*, July 1871, 1–9, quotation 6.

53. Frederick Douglass, *The Life and Times* (Boston: De Wolfe & Fiske, 1892), 340, 341; Frederick Douglass, "Slavery, The Slumbering Volcano," speech of April 23, 1849, in *The Frederick Douglass Papers, Series One: Speeches: Debates and Interviews*, vol. 2, ed. John W. Blassingame et al. (New Haven: Yale University Press, 1982), 148–58, quotation 151. See also Matthew Clavin,

"A Second Haitian Revolution: John Brown, Toussaint Louverture, and the Making of the American Civil War," *Civil War History* 54, no. 2 (2008): 138, 142–45.

54. *Proceedings of the Convention of Radical Political Abolitionists . . .* (New York: Central Abolition Board, 1855), 17, 52. See also Stauffer, *Black Hearts*, 22–27.

55. John Brown Jr., letter quoted in Villard, *John Brown*, 83. See also *Proceedings of the Convention*, 62–63; Richard O. Boyer, *The Legend of John Brown: A Biography and a History* (New York: Knopf, 1973), 524–27.

56. William Phillips, *The Conquest of Kansas, by Missouri and Her Allies* (Boston: Phillips, Sampson, 1856), 297; Reynolds, *John Brown*, 149, 156–57; Robert E. McGlone, *John Brown's War Against Slavery* (New York: Cambridge University Press, 2009), 74, 355n11.

57. *New York Herald*, June 8, 1856. See also Reynolds, *John Brown*, 154–57, 171–73. News from Washington would not reach Kansas for at least one week, which means that Brown had not yet learned of Sumner's caning when he attacked the settlers at Pottawatomie Creek. See McGlone, *John Brown's War*, 74, 355n11.

58. Frederick Douglass, "The Danger of the Republican Movement," speech of May 28, 1856, in *The Life and Writings of Frederick Douglass*, vol. 5, ed. Philip S. Foner (New York: International Publishers, 1975), 385–90, quotation 389.

59. Sandra Harbert Petrulionis, *To Set This World Right: The Antislavery Movement in Thoreau's Concord* (Ithaca, N.Y.: Cornell University Press), 117–21; Reynolds, *John Brown*, 206–38; Horwitz, *Midnight Rising*, 74–79; Len Gougeon, *Virtue's Hero: Emerson, Antislavery, and Reform* (Athens: University of Georgia Press, 1990), 218–49.

60. Randolph Paul Runyon, *Delia Webster and the Underground Railroad* (Lexington: University Press of Kentucky, 1996), 207; Petrulionis, *To Set This World Right*, 121; Gougeon, *Virtue's Hero*, 229; Reynolds, *John Brown*, 222–24.

61. Emerson, quoted in Reynolds, *John Brown*, 222–23.

62. James Freeman Clarke, "Charles Sumner," in *Memorial and Biographical Sketches* (Boston: Houghton, Osgood, 1878), 102; Beverly Wilson Palmer, ed., *The Selected Letters of Charles Sumner, vol. 2: 1859–1874* (Boston: Northeastern University Press, 1990), 11.

63. Runyon, *Delia Webster*, 207; Reynolds, *John Brown*, 259–62; Stauffer, *Black Hearts*, 255–56.

64. "Old Brown's Parallels," *New York Tribune*, January 22, 1859; "Brown's Rescued Negroes Landed in Canada," *New York Daily Tribune*, March 17, 1859; Horwitz, *Midnight Rising*, 88–89, quotation 88; McGlone, *Brown's War*, 210–12.

65. Stauffer, *Black Hearts*, 173–74; Paul Schneider, *The Adirondacks: A History of America's First Wilderness* (New York: Henry Holt, 1997), 110.

66. Osborne P. Anderson, *A Voice from Harpers Ferry* (Boston: self-published, 1861), 31. See also Horwitz, *Midnight Rising*, 128–29.

67. Testimony of Daniel Whelan, *Report of Select Committee on the Harpers Ferry Invasion*, U.S. Congress, June 15, 1860, 22.

68. Reynolds, *John Brown*, 305; Horwitz, *Midnight Rising*, 131; McGlone, *Brown's War*, 258, 413n71. Horwitz says blacks made up less than 10 percent of the population of Harpers Ferry, but Reynolds and McGlone argue that they constituted about 50 percent. We are convinced by Horwitz's research.

69. "General Orders No. 1," *Calendar of Virginia State Papers and Other Manuscripts* (Richmond: R. F. Walker, 1893), 11:274–75.

70. "Testimony of Lewis W. Washington," *Report of Select Committee*, 34. Brown could have attempted a preemptive strike on the few hundred white men in Harpers Ferry, much as he had done against proslavery men at Pottawatomie Creek in Kansas Territory in 1856. But doing so would have been at least as risky as staying where he was in the armory, and it would not have endeared him to antislavery Northerners. However, instead of waiting at the armory, he could have fled to the mountains with guns and hostages. Arguably it would have been easier to elude capture, use hostages as ransom, and give blacks days and weeks rather than a few hours to decide whether or not to join his army.

71. "The Inhabitants," *New York Herald*, November 1, 1859; Douglass, *Life and Times*, 389. On the "suicidal" nature of slave rebellions, see David Brion Davis, *Inhuman Bondage: The Rise and Fall of Slavery in the New World* (New York: Oxford University Press, 2006), 206.

72. Testimony of Lewis W. Washington, in Robert M. Fogelson and Richard E. Rubenstein, eds., *Mass Violence in America: Invasion at Harper's Ferry* (New York: Arno Press and The New York Times, 1969), 31, 34, 40, quotation 34.

73. Stauffer, *Black Hearts*, 256; Horwitz, *Midnight Rising*, 123.

74. Testimony of Conductor Phelps, in Robert De Witt, *The Life, Trial and Execution of Captain John Brown* (New York: Robert M. De Witt, 1859), 69. See also "Statement of W. E. Throckmorten," *New York Herald*, October 24, 1859; Horwitz, *Midnight Rising*, 137–40; McGlone, *Brown's War*, 262–64; Reynolds, *John Brown*, 309, 318–19, 322. We agree with Horwitz, who uses "Heyward Shepherd." McGlone says "Hayward Shepherd" and Reynolds uses "Shepherd Hayward."

75. "A. J. Phelps to W. P. Smith," October 17, 1859, in *The Senate of Maryland, Correspondence Relating to the Insurrection at Harpers Ferry, 17th October, 1859* (Annapolis: B. H. Richardson, 1860), 5.

76. Horwitz, *Midnight Rising*, provides the clearest narrative of the raid and a concise summary in his tables on 291–92.

77. Horwitz, *Midnight Rising*, 291–92.

78. Anderson, *Voice from Harpers Ferry*, 29. During and after each of the three largest slave revolts in North America—the Stono Rebellion of 1739, the Louisiana Slave Revolt of 1811, and Nat Turner's Rebellion of 1831—over a hundred blacks were killed. See Peter Charles Hoffer, *Cry Liberty: The Great Stono River Slave Rebellion of 1739* (New York: Oxford University Press, 2010); Daniel Rasmussen, *American Uprising: The Untold Story of America's Largest Slave Revolt* (New York: HarperCollins, 2011); Kenneth S. Greenberg, ed., *Nat Turner: A Slave Rebellion in History and Memory* (New York: Oxford University Press, 2003).

79. Sanborn, *Life and Letters of Brown*, 131; Reynolds, *John Brown*, 309, 334–35.

80. John Brown, "Interview with Senator Mason and Others," October 18, 1859 in Stauffer and Trodd, *Tribunal*, 48; Brown, "Last Speech to the Court," November 2, 1859, in James Redpath, *The Public Life of Capt. John Brown* (Boston: Thayer and Eldridge, 1860), 341–42. Emerson would later call Brown's speech and Lincoln's Gettysburg Address the two greatest speeches in American history. See Reynolds, *John Brown*, 355.

81. Brown to Sanborn, quoted in Oates, *To Purge This Land*, 289; Villard, *John Brown*, 334; Judges 16:28–30.

82. Brown, quoted in Sanborn, *Life and Letters of Brown*, 573, 579; Brown, quoted in Richard Warch and Jonathan Fanton, eds., *John Brown* (Englewood Cliffs, N.J.: Prentice-Hall, 1973), 91, 94, 96, 99.

83. Villard, *John Brown*, 554–55; Ruchames, *John Brown*, 167; Oates, *To Purge This Land*, 349–52; *The Life, Trial and Execution of Captain John Brown, Known as "Old Brown of Ossawatomie,"* *Compiled from Official and Authentic Sources* (1859; reprint, New York: Da Capo, 1969), 100–101.

CHAPTER II

1. Robert E. Lee to Mrs. M. C. Lee, December 1, 1859, in Robert Edward Lee, ed., *Recollections and Letters of General Robert E. Lee* (New York: Doubleday, Page, 1904), 22; David S. Reynolds, *John Brown: Abolitionist* (New York: Vintage Books, 2005), 340 (*New York Tribune* quote), 392–93; Elizabeth Brown Pryor, *Reading the Man: A Portrait of Robert E. Lee through His Private Letters* (New York: Viking, 2007), 279–83; Peter Wallenstein, "Incendiaries All: Southern Politics and the Harpers Ferry Raid," in Paul Finkelman, ed., *His Soul Goes Marching On: Responses to John Brown and the Harpers Ferry Raid* (Charlottesville: University Press of Virginia, 1995), 151.

2. Reynolds, *John Brown*, 337–39, 392–93; Chester G. Hearn, *Six Years of Hell: Harpers Ferry During the Civil War* (Baton Rouge: Louisiana State University Press, 1996), 40; Lewis Sayre quoted in Franny Nudelman, *John Brown's Body: Slavery, Violence and the Culture of War* (Chapel Hill: University of North Carolina Press, 2004), 4, 7, 178n7.

3. Reynolds, *John Brown*, 398–400, quotation 406–7; Gary Alan Fine, "John Brown's Body: Elites, Heroic Embodiment, and the Legitimation of Political Violence," *Social Problems* 46, no. 2 (1999): 225–49.

4. *Mt. Carroll Weekly Mirror*, August 6, 1862, quoted in Reynolds, *John Brown*, 468; Holmes quoted in Christian McWhirter, *Battle Hymns: The Power and Popularity of Music in the Civil War* (Chapel Hill: University of North Carolina Press, 2012), 46–47, 63–64.

5. *The Nation*, August 6, 1874, 89; Brander Matthews, "The Songs of the Civil War," *Century Illustrated* 34, no. 4 (1887): 622; *Morning Oregonian*, July 31, 1887; Nicholas Smith, *Stories of Great National Songs* (Milwaukee: The Young Churchman, 1899), 77; Edward Whipple, "America's Literature," *Harper's New Monthly Magazine*, March 1876, 517.

6. Christian McWhirter, "'Liberty's Great Auxiliary': Music and the American Civil War," Ph.D. diss., University of Alabama, 2009, 46–53 (*Liberator* quote on 53); Cecil D. Eby Jr., "The National Hymn Contest and 'Orpheus C. Kerr,'" *Massachusetts Review* 1, no. 2 (1960): 400–409. For an account of the contest from one of the committee members, see Richard Grant White, *National Hymns: How They Are Written and How They Are Not Written* (New York: Rudd & Carleton, 1861).

7. Boyd Stutler, an amateur historian who became one of the leading collectors of and authorities on Brown memorabilia, spent decades testing the stories of these various claimants and ultimately concluded that they were all spurious. Boyd Stutler, *Glory, Glory, Hallelujah! The Story of "John Brown's Body" and "Battle Hymn of the Republic"* (Cincinnati: C. J. Krehbiel, 1960), 13. For the articles that precipitated the investigation of the song's origins, see Abram E. Cutter, *The John Brown Song Scrapbook*, Boston Public Library. "John Brown's Body," *Independent*, June 30, 1887; "John Brown's Body," *Lance*, May 9, 1885, clipping in John Brown/Boyd B. Stutler Database, West Virginia Memory Project at http://www.wvculture.org/history (hereafter Stutler Database); John J. MacIntyre, *The Composer of the Battle Hymn of the Republic*

(New York: William H. Conklin, 1916); Katherine Little Bakeless, *Glory, Hallelujah! The Story of the Battle Hymn of the Republic* (Philadelphia: J. B. Lippincott, 1944), 29–32, 43; "Hymn from Maine," *Time*, July 1, 1935, 37.

8. In a 1974 article, Charles Claghorn, a prominent musicologist, claimed to have identified and interviewed William Steffe's grandson, who informed him that Steffe was the organist and choirmaster at a South Carolina Methodist camp meeting festival. Given the possibility that the "Say Brothers" hymn originated in Carolina revival meetings, Steffe might have heard the tune there. We have not, however, been able to verify the grandson's claims. Charles Eugene Claghorn, "Battle Hymn: The Story behind *The Battle Hymn of the Republic*," *Papers of the Hymn Society of America* 39 (1974): 5. "The term "bummer" did not acquire its association with vagrancy until after the Civil War. Before then, it referred generally to a loafer or idler, but could also refer to an individual who left off his assigned task for another, such as a soldier who went on the prowl for food. It is perhaps this latter association that Steffe had in mind in reference to the traveling fire company, though his intended meaning still remains a mystery. Kenneth L. Kusmer, *Down & Out, On the Road: The Homeless in American History* (New York: Oxford University Press, 2002), 37; "bummer," *Oxford English Dictionary*, 2nd ed. 1989, 650. Stutler to Bernice Larrabee, September 2, 1950, Stutler Database; William Steffe to Richard Hinton, December 11, 1885; Steffe to Hinton, January 15, 1887; Steffe to Hinton, March 4, 1887, Stutler Database. Steffe was first publicly identified with the song in an 1883 article by Major O. S. Bosbyshell, a Civil War veteran, amateur historian, and future superintendent of the U.S. Mint, in an obscure Philadelphia journal. The claim was then circulated in an influential 1887 *Century* article on Civil War music. See O. C. Bosbyshell, "Origin of 'John Brown's Body,'" *Grand Army Scout and Soldier's Mail*, typescript copy in Stutler Database; Matthews, "The Songs of the Civil War."

9. Stutler, *Glory, Glory, Hallelujah!*, 15; James Howard Jenkins, "Author of the John Brown Song," *New York Evening Post*, November 27, 1909, clipping in Stutler Database; Frederick Morse Cutler, *The Old First Massachusetts Artillery in War and Peace* (Boston: Pilgrim Press, 1917), 12; George Kimball, "My Army Life," in *Stories of Our Soldiers* (Boston: Journal Newspaper Company, 1893), 82; George Kimball, "Origin of the John Brown Song," *New England Magazine* 1, no. 4 (1889): 371.

10. Jenkins, "Author of the John Brown Song"; Kimball, "Origins of the John Brown Song," 372; Stutler, *Glory, Glory, Hallelujah!*, 16.

11. In their reminiscences, several members of the Tigers mentioned the *Melodeon* as a source for the tune; however, the "Say Brothers" hymn does not appear in the 1860 edition. However, intriguingly, one hymn that does not seem to share the "Say Brothers" tune, "Sweet Rest in Heaven," does contain the line, "These bodies soon will moulder in the dark and dreary tomb." J. W. Dadmun, *The Melodeon* (Boston: J. P. Magee, 1860), 164. Kimball, "Origins of the John Brown Song," 371; Kimball, "My Army Life," 81; Stutler to James J. Fuld, March 17, 1957, Stutler Database; "Story of 'John Brown's Body,'" *Daily Inter Ocean*, January 19, 1889; "'John Brown's Body': Some Light on the Authorship of the Famous War Song," *Morning Oregonian*, August 9, 1887; John D. Hall, "John Brown's Body," *Morning Oregonian*, August 13, 1887.

12. J. E. G. [James E. Greenleaf], "Author of 'John Brown's Body,'" undated clipping in Stutler Database; John S. Wise, *The End of an Era* (Boston: Houghton, Mifflin, 1901), 136; Tracy

Melton, *Hanging Henry Gambrill: The Violent Career of Baltimore's Pug Uglies, 1854–1860* (Baltimore: Maryland Historical Society, 2005), 110–11; *Nation*, August 20, 1874, 123; *Nation*, August 6, 1874, 89; "The John Brown Song," *Lowell Daily Citizen and News*, July 6, 1875; "Rest in Heaven," in *The Day Spring; or, Union Collection of Songs for the Sanctuary*, compiled by Sylvester Main (New York: F. J. Huntington, 1859), 260; "Rest in Heaven" in *Sacred Music for Social Worship* (1859), http://www.hymnary.org/text/how_often_am_i_weary; Mary Louise Bringle, "Truth Is Marching On: Nineteenth Century U.S. Women Singing for Change," manuscript in authors' possession. We are grateful to Mary Bringle for calling to our attention the "Rest in Heaven" hymn.

13. Another verse that was incorporated into "John Brown's Body"—"The Stars of heaven are looking kindly down / on Old John Brown"—was borrowed from a song sung by the Fourth Massachusetts, stationed in nearby Fort Monroe. Stutler, *Glory, Glory, Hallelujah!*, 21. James Howard Jenkins, "Origins of the Famous War Song of John Brown," in *War Papers Read before the Commandery of the State of Wisconsin, Military Order of the Loyal Legion of the United States* (Milwaukee: Burdick and Allen, 1914), 4: 212–13; Stutler, *Glory, Glory, Hallelujah!*, 20; Boyd Stutler to Kirke Mechem, March 23, 1938, Stutler Database. Jenkins, a member of the choral group, claimed that only this verse about Brown's knapsack referred to the Scottish Brown and that all the rest were composed with the abolitionist in mind. "It was merely a coincidence that sergeant Brown should be a member of the first quartette to use the song," he noted.

14. Kimball, "Origins of the John Brown Song," 374; Boyd Stutler, "John Brown's Body," *Civil War History* 4, no. 3 (1958): 254; Jenkins, "Origins of the Famous War Song of John Brown," 210; "The President's Pet Lambs," *New York Times*, May 21, 1861. The verse "His pet lambs will meet him on the way" became disassociated from the commemoration of Ellsworth and was incorporated into versions of the song that referred only to John Brown. One member of the battalion explained the persistence of the verse by suggesting that the "pet lambs" actually referred to the members of the Twelfth Regiment, sometimes referred to as "Webster's Cattle." James Beale, "John Brown's Body: Something about the Origins of the Famous War Song," *Oregonian*, November 18, 1894. For an example of a song sheet featuring Fort Warren verses with only Ellsworth's name, see "Ellsworth's Body Lies Mouldering in the Grave" (Philadelphia: A. W. Auner, n.d.), in America Singing: Nineteenth-Century Song Sheets database, Library of Congress, digital ID cw101640. For a version that brackets both Ellsworth's and Brown's names, see "Glory, Hallelujah" (Boston: Oliver Ditson, 1861) and "Glory Hallelujah" (New York: Firth, Pond, 1862).

15. Jenkins, "Author of the John Brown Song"; Stutler, *Glory, Glory, Hallelujah!*, 42.

16. Members of the Second Battalion offered different accounts of the first public performance of "John Brown's Body," some claiming that Gilmore's Band played it after the flag-raising ceremony, others recalling that the Brockton Band played it during the ceremony itself, as the flag was raised. Kimball, "My Army Life," 84; Jenkins, "Origins of the Famous War Song," 210–11; "Story of 'John Brown's Body,'" *Daily Inter Ocean*, January 19, 1889; Stutler to James J. Fuld, March 17, 1957, Stutler Database; Beale, "John Brown's Body"; Greenleaf, "Author of 'John Brown's Body'"; Stutler, *Glory, Glory, Hallelujah!*, 24. Stutler obtained an 1895 copy of the original musical transcription of the John Brown song that Greenleaf had made for Gilmore. See "John Brown Song" (July 2, 1895), Stutler Database.

17. "John Brown in Song," *Chicago Tribune*, August 9, 1861; "The Twelfth Massachusetts Regiment," *New York Times*, July 25, 1861.

18. *Dwight's*, July 27, 1861, quoted in James J. Fuld, *The Book of World-Famous Music: Classical, Popular and Folk*, 5th ed. (New York: Dover, 2000), 133; Stutler, *Glory, Glory, Hallelujah!*, 27–28; Stutler to James J. Fuld, March 21, 1957, Stutler Database; undated clipping in Cutter, *John Brown Song Scrapbook*, 45.

19. Stutler, *Glory, Glory, Hallelujah!*, 31–32; "List of versions of the John Brown song," Stutler Database; Stutler to Glynn Harvey, September 8, 1951, Stutler Database.

20. Caroline Moseley, "Irrepressible Conflict: Differences between Northern and Southern Songs of the Civil War," *Journal of Popular Culture* 25, no. 2 (1991): 48; McWhirter, *Battle Hymns*, 12–17, quotation 16.

21. Benjamin F. Cook, *History of the Twelfth Massachusetts Volunteers* (1882; Salem, Mass.: Higginson, 1998), 17–22; Kimball, "Origin of the John Brown Song," 376; "The Twelfth Massachusetts Regiment," *New York Times*, July 25, 1861; *New York Herald*, July 25, 1861; "John Brown, Dead Yet Speaketh," *Independent* 13, no. 665 (1861): 1; "John Brown's Body," *Morning Oregonian*, August 9, 1887; *New York Tribune*, July 28, 1861; Jenkins, "Author of John Brown Song."

22. "Glory, Hallelujah" (Boston: Oliver Ditson, 1861); McWhirter, *Battle Hymns*, 41; James C. Cannon, *Record of Service of Company K, 150th O.V.I. 1864* (N.p., 1903), 8.

23. Steven Woodworth, *While God Is Marching On: The Religious World of Civil War Soldiers* (Lawrence: University Press of Kansas, 2001), 180; Charles Nelson Kent, *History of the Seventeenth Regiment, New Hampshire Volunteers Infantry, 1862–1863* (Concord: Seventeenth New Hampshire Veterans Association, 1898), 211; Morgan Ebenezer Wescott to Mother, March 11, 1865, in *Civil War Letters, 1861 to 1865: Written by a Boy in Blue to His Mother* (Mora, Minn.: 1909), 29.

24. The only song that rivaled "John Brown's Body" in its ability to rally troops was "The Battle Cry of Freedom." See, for instance, the account of the song's effect on troops during the Battle of the Wilderness in "Songs of the Soldiers," *St. Louis Globe-Democrat*, May 12, 1883. Orville J. Victor, *History of American Conspiracies* (New York: James D. Torrey, 1863), 523; McWhirter, *Battle Hymns*, 127; Habberton quoted in Fred Winslow Adams, "Our National Songs: 'Battle Hymn of the Republic,'" *Zion's Herald*, July 27, 1898, 938; "In Front of Yorktown: A Reminiscence," quoted in McWhirter, *Battle Hymns*, 43–44.

25. Cook, *History of the Twelfth Massachusetts Volunteers*, 53, 140; Kimball, "My Army Life," 82; Beale, "John Brown's Body"; Smith, *Stories of Great National Songs*, 88.

26. Reynolds, *John Brown*, 112; George T. Stevens, *Three Years in the Sixth Corps* (Albany: S. R. Gray, 1866), 390; Smith, *Stories of Great National Songs*, 82; *History of the First Regiment Minnesota Volunteer Infantry, 1861–1864* (Stillwater, Minn.: Easton and Masterman, 1916), 86; McWhirter, *Battle Hymns*, 45, 144.

27. Moseley, "Irrepressible Conflict," 53; "John Brown in Song," *Chicago Tribune*, August 9, 1861.

28. Reynolds, *John Brown*, 474; *Liberator*, May 16, 1862; McWhirter, *Battle Hymns*, 45; Benjamin Quarles, *Allies for Freedom: Blacks and John Brown* (New York: Oxford University Press, 1974), 162; John W. Ames to his mother, November 12, 1861, quoted in James McPherson, *For Cause and Comrades: Why Men Fought in the Civil War* (New York: Oxford University Press, 1997), 19.

29. S. M. Fox, *The Seventh Kansas Cavalry: Its Service in the Civil War. An Address before the State Historical Society, December 2, 1902* (Topeka: State Printing Office, 1908), 20, 22, 29–30; Mark

A. Lause, *Race and Radicalism in the Union Army* (Urbana: University of Illinois Press, 2009), 50; *Chicago Tribune*, October 22, 1861.

30. For another account of an African American singer's merging the secular and sacred by combining the words of "Say Brothers" with "John Brown's Body," see "Jeff Davis on Canaan's Happy Shore," *Youth's Companion*, February 6, 1868, 22; *New York Times*, September 15, 1862; [Justus Clement French and Edward Cary], *The Trip of the Steamer Oceanus to Fort Sumter and Charleston, S.C.* (Brooklyn: "The Union" Steam Printing House, 1865), 90–91.

31. *Boston Daily Advertiser*, February 20, 1863; "Slaves Singing the John Brown Chorus," *Providence Journal*, October 30, 1862, quoted in Louis A. DaCaro Jr., "Black People's Ally, White People's Bogeyman: A John Brown Story," in Andrew Taylor and Eldrid Herrington, eds., *The Afterlife of John Brown* (New York: Palgrave Macmillan, 2005), 13.

32. McWhirter, *Battle Hymns*, 156–58; Quarles, *Allies for Freedom*, 161, 162 (quote from *Journal of Charlotte Forten*), 164; Willie Lee Rose, *Rehearsal for Reconstruction: The Port Royal Experiment* (1964; Athens: University of Georgia Press, 1999), 196–97; *Liberator*, February 10, 1865.

33. Thomas Wentworth Higginson, December 3, 1862 and T. W. Higginson to Mother, August 4, 1861, in Thomas Wentworth Higginson, *The Complete Civil War Journal and Selected Letters of Thomas Wentworth Higginson*, ed. Christopher Looby (Chicago: University of Chicago Press, 2000), 59, 224. For one of the members of Higginson's regiment, who also served for a time as his manservant, the song held a particularly personal meaning. This elderly black soldier, whom the men called "Uncle York," had a son named John Brown, who was killed leading a pursuit of Confederate guerrillas hiding out on St. Simon's Island, off the Georgia coast. Higginson reported that Brown's death—the "first armed encounter," he suspected, "between the rebels and their former slaves"—provided "John Brown's Body" with an additional resonance for the young man's father. "He fully believed, to his dying day, that the 'John Brown Song' related to his son, and to him only." Thomas Wentworth Higginson, *Army Life in a Black Regiment* (1870; East Lansing: Michigan State University Press, 1960), 212–13.

34. *Douglass Monthly* 5, no. 6 (1863): 818, 828; David W. Blight, *Frederick Douglass' Civil War: Keeping Faith in Jubilee* (Baton Rouge: Louisiana State University Press, 1989), 158–59; Luis Emilio, *History of the Fifty-Fourth Regiment of Massachusetts Volunteer Infantry, 1863–1865* (Boston: Boston Book, 1894), 32; Don H. Doyle, *New Men, New Cities, New South: Atlanta, Nashville, Charleston, Mobile, 1860–1910* (Chapel Hill: University of North Carolina Press, 1990), 59. In his reminiscences, Saint-Gaudens recalls a moment thirty years before, when the same song had moved him nearly as much as it had during the monument's unveiling. While apprenticing for a cameo cutter with an office on Broadway, he had watched "New England volunteers" marching by, singing "John Brown's Body." Augustus Saint-Gaudens, *Reminiscences of Augustus Saint-Gaudens* (New York: Century, 1913), 1:41, 2:83.

35. David Walls, "Marching Song of the First Arkansas Colored Regiment: A Contested Attribution," *Arkansas Historical Quarterly* 66, no. 4 (2007): 403, 404–5; *The War of the Rebellion: A Compilation of the Official Records of the Union and Confederate Armies* (Washington, D.C.: Government Printing Office, 1889), 1:24, 517; John Y. Foster, *New Jersey and the Rebellion* (Newark: Martin R. Dennis, 1868), 764; Edwin Charles Hill, *The Historical Register: A Record of People, Places and Events in American History* (New York: Edwin C. Hill, 1920), 127; Frank Preston Stearns, *The Life and Public Services of George Luther Stearns* (Philadelphia: J. B. Lippincott, 1907), 297.

36. Lindley Miller to Mary Louisa Miller, January 20, 1864, quoted in Walls, "Marching Song," 415; Walls, "Marching Song," 410; *National Anti-Slavery Standard*, February 27, 1864.

37. Walls, "Marching Song," 407, 415, 408, 417; "Song of the First of Arkansas" (N.p., n.d.), in America Singing: Nineteenth-Century Song Sheets database, Library of Congress, digital ID, cw105500.

38. *National Anti-Slavery Standard*, February 27, 1864; "Song of the First of Arkansas"; Foster, *New Jersey and the Rebellion*, 764.

39. Walls, "Marching Song," 413, 402.

40. McPherson, *For Cause and Comrades*, 117, 121; *New York Herald*, July 25, 1861; "Glory Hallelujah: The Popular Army Hymn" (New York: Wm. Hall & Son, 1862).

41. Chandra Manning, *What This Cruel War Was Over: Soldiers, Slavery, and the Civil War* (New York: Vintage Books, 2007), 45; McWhirter, "'Liberty's Great Auxiliary,'" 134; David Nichol to father, January 4, 1863, in McPherson, *For Cause and Comrades*, 122.

42. Manning, *What This Cruel War Was Over*, 77, 200; McPherson, *For Cause and Comrades*, 119, 124.

43. James Freeman Clarke, *Autobiography, Diary, and Correspondence*, ed. Edward Everett Hale (1891; Boston: Houghton, Mifflin, 1899), 279; Reynolds, *John Brown*, 474.

44. Nudelman, *John Brown's Body*, 14–16; Reynolds, *John Brown*, 433, 463; Drew Gilpin Faust, *This Republic of Suffering: Death and the American Civil War* (New York: Vintage Books, 2008), xi.

45. McWhirter, *Battle Hymns*, 44; Gail Hamilton [Mary Abigail Dodge], *Skirmishes and Sketches* (Boston: Ticknor and Fields, 1865), 17.

46. Reynolds, *John Brown*, 163 (Albert D. Richardson quote), 164 (Phillips quote).

47. Cox quoted in Reynolds, *John Brown*, 482; Susan Bradford Eppes, diary entry for April 23, 1865, in *Through Some Eventful Years* (Macon, Ga.: J. W. Burke, 1926), 279–80. An actual copy of Eppes's diary has not been located, and it is possible that she recorded these events years later. David Coles, "Eppes, Susan Branch Bradford," in *Women in the American Civil War*, vol. 1, ed. Lisa Tendrich Frank (Santa Barbara, Calif.: ABC-CLIO, 2008), 243.

48. McWhirter, *Battle Hymns*, 46; Matthews, "The Songs of the Civil War," 623; "Glory Hallujah" (Philadelphia: n.p., n.d.), in America Singing: Nineteenth-Century Song Sheets database, Library of Congress, digital ID cw102070.

49. McWhirter, *Battle Hymns*, 129, 130.

50. Whipple, "America's Literature," 517; Robert H. Kellogg, *Life and Death in Rebel Prisons* (Hartford, Conn.: L. Stebbins, 1865), 36; Sheldon Thorpe, *The History of the Fifteenth Connecticut Volunteers in the War for the Defense of the Union 1861–1865* (New Haven: Price, Lee and Adkins, 1893), 39.

51. Perhaps the song's association with Union triumphs explains the claim of one Milwaukee newspaper that the popularity of "John Brown's Body" seemed to wane in the middle years of the war but then waxed again in the war's final months. *Milwaukee Daily Sentinel*, May 24, 1865. Adin B. Underwood, *The Three Years' Service of the Thirty-Third Mass. Infantry Regiment, 1862–1865*, quoted in McWhirter, *Battle Hymns*, 46; Reynolds, *John Brown*, 475–76; *Memoirs of General W. T. Sherman* (New York: Library of America, 1990), 655–56; *New York Daily Tribune*, April 4, 1865; Quarles, *Allies for Freedom*, 163.

52. Perhaps the most subversive appropriation of the "John Brown's Body" tune was the one that pledged to hang the abolitionist Wendell Phillips to a sour apple tree and, in another verse, to

hang Gerrit Smith, one of Brown's most avid supporters, to a "hickory pine-post." "Union Emotions" (New York: H. De Marsan, n.d.), in America Singing: Nineteenth-Century Song Sheets database, Library of Congress, digital ID sb40539b. Quarles, *Allies for Freedom*, 169; McWhirter, *Battle Hymns*, 101; Boyd Stutler to Glynn Harvey, September 8, 1951, Stutler Database; (San Francisco) *Daily Evening Bulletin*, September 22, 1862.

53. Hamilton, *Skirmishes and Sketches*, 10; *Lowell Daily Citizen and News*, December 21, 1865; Oliver Wendell Holmes, "Poetry of the War," quoted in Alice Fahs, *The Imagined Civil War: Popular Literature of the North and South, 1861–1865* (Chapel Hill: University of North Carolina Press, 2001), 77; Richard Grant White, *Poetry, Lyrical, Narrative and Satirical, of the Civil War* (New York: American News, 1866), 66.

54. For a discussion of soldiers' motivations, see McPherson, *For Cause and Comrades*.

55. John Richards Boyle, *Soldiers True: The Story of the One Hundred and Eleventh Regiment Pennsylvania Veteran Volunteers* (New York: Eaton and Mains, 1903), 298; James Harrison Wilson and William. P. Stedman, "Pursuit and Capture of Jefferson Davis," *Century Illustrated Monthly Magazine* 39, no. 4 (1890): 596; Varina Davis to Colonel John J. Craven, October 10, 1865, quoted in John J. Craven, *Prison Life of Jefferson Davis* (New York: Carleton, 1866), 341.

56. McWhirter, *Battle Hymns*, 167; *North American and United States Gazette*, May 24, 1865; *Liberator*, April 7, 1865.

57. Garrison quoted in French and Cary, *Trip of the Steamer Oceanus*, 119; Rose, *Rehearsal for Reconstruction*, 342; David Blight, *Race and Reunion: The Civil War in American Memory* (Cambridge, Mass.: Belknap Press, 2001), 67–68.

58. Roe quoted in Stutler, *Glory, Glory, Hallelujah!* 11.

CHAPTER III

1. Plebs [W. W. Patton], "War Songs for the Army and the People," *Chicago Daily Tribune*, December 16, 1861; "His Soul Is Marching On," *Chicago Daily Tribune*, September 11, 1887; William W. Patton, "More about the John Brown Song," *American Missionary* 41, no. 12 (1887): 339.

2. Brownell's version portrays Brown as a decidedly apocalyptical figure, "stand[ing] at Armageddon with his brave old sword," echoing the themes of the "Battle Hymn." Henry Howard Brownell, "Words That Can Be Sung to the 'Hallelujah Chorus,'" in Frank Moore, ed., *Songs of the Soldiers*, quoted in Terrie Dopp Aamodt, *Righteous Armies, Holy Cause: Apocalyptic Imagery and the Civil War* (Macon, Ga.: Mercer University Press, 2002), 47. See Aamodt, *Righteous Armies*, 207–8 for the full lyrics of Brownell's song.

3. Laura E. Richards and Maud Howe Eliot, *Julia Ward Howe, 1819–1910* (Boston: Houghton Mifflin, 1916), 1:21; Julia Ward Howe, *Reminiscences, 1819–1899* (Boston: Houghton, Mifflin, 1899), 11; Mary H. Grant, *Private Woman, Public Person: An Account of the Life of Julia Ward Howe from 1819 to 1868* (Brooklyn: Carlson, 1994), 19.

4. Howe, *Reminiscences*, 12, 15, 18, 47; Deborah Pickman Clifford, *Mine Eyes Have Seen the Glory: A Biography of Julia Ward Howe* (Boston: Little, Brown, 1978), 16, 31; Richards and Eliot, *Julia Ward Howe*, 1:31–32.

5. Grant, *Private Woman*, 35; Richards and Eliot, *Julia Ward Howe*, 1:45–46; Howe, *Reminiscences*, 57, 60.

6. Richards and Eliot, *Julia Ward Howe*, 1:58, 59, 66, 325, 2:315.

7. Howe, *Reminiscences*, 81–82; Richards and Eliot, *Julia Ward Howe*, 1:74–78; Clifford, *Mine Eyes Have Seen the Glory*, 54–56.

8. Howe, "The Darkest Moment" (1844), quoted in Grant, *Private Woman*, 62; "La Veille des Noees" (1843), quoted in Valerie Ziegler, *Diva Julia: The Public Romance and Private Agony of Julia Ward Howe* (Harrisburg, Pa.: Trinity Press International, 2003), 32; JWH to her sister Annie [Ward], 1846, quoted in Richards and Eliot, *Julia Ward Howe*, 1:118; JWH to Louisa Ward Crawford, n.d., quoted in Ziegler, *Diva Julia*, 41.

9. Clifford, *Mine Eyes Have Seen the Glory*, 66, 84; Samuel Gridley Howe to Charles Sumner, March 16, 1844, quoted in Clifford, *Mine Eyes Have Seen the Glory*, 80; JWH to Louisa Ward Crawford, November 1845, quoted in Ziegler, *Diva Julia*, 41; Richards and Eliot, *Julia Ward Howe*, 1:102–3.

10. Clifford, *Mine Eyes Have Seen the Glory*, 120–22; Ziegler, *Diva Julia*, 73; JWH to her sister Annie [Ward Mailliard], January 19, 1855, quoted in Richards and Eliot, *Julia Ward Howe*, 1:166; Grant, *Private Woman*, 108; JWH to Louisa Ward Crawford, January 31, 1847, quoted in Ziegler, *Diva Julia*, 8; JWH to Louisa Ward Crawford, ca. February 16, 1846, quoted in Ziegler, *Diva Julia*, 42.

11. Ziegler, *Diva Julia*, 102, 80 (selection from *Passion-Flowers*); Grant, *Private Woman*, 118, 170.

12. Ziegler, *Diva Julia*, 177n16; Grant, *Private Woman*, 134; JWH diary, May 31, 1865, quoted in Richards and Eliot, *Julia Ward Howe*, 1:224–25; David S. Reynolds, *John Brown: Abolitionist* (New York: Vintage Books, 2005), 358, 482.

13. Howe, *Reminiscences*, 254.

14. Howe's dissembling infuriated another member of the Secret Six. "Is there no such thing as honor among confederates?" demanded Thomas Wentworth Higginson. Reynolds, *John Brown*, 343. Howe, *Reminiscences*, 254, 256; Grant, *Private Woman*, 134; *New York Tribune*, November 16, 1859 quoted in Reynolds, *John Brown*, 342–43; JWH to Annie [Ward Mailliard], November 6, 1859, quoted in Richards and Eliot, *Julia Ward Howe*, 1:177.

15. Scholars have dated the emergence of Julia Ward Howe's abolitionism differently, some suggesting she held strong antislavery beliefs in the mid-1850s and others arguing that it was the arrest and execution of Brown that solidified her abolitionism. Ziegler, *Diva Julia*, 191n4. Grant, *Private Woman*, 130; Julia Ward Howe, *A Trip to Cuba* (1860), quoted in Grant, *Private Woman*, 132; *Liberator*, May 6, 1859; Howe, *Reminiscences*, 236.

16. JWH to Anne Ward Mailliard, May 24, 1861, quoted in Clifford, *Mine Eyes Have Seen the Glory*, 141; Howe, *Reminiscences*, 273–74.

17. Julia Ward Howe, "Note on the 'Battle Hymn of the Republic,'" *Century Illustrated Magazine* 34, no. 4 (1887): 629; Howe, *Reminiscences*, 270–72; Howe-Lincoln reminiscence, Series 2 Item 55, Julia Ward Howe Papers, Schlesinger Library, Cambridge, Mass., MC272/M133; Margaret Leech, *Reveille in Washington, 1860–1865* (1941; New York: New York Review of Books, 2011), 10; Florence Howe Hall, *The Story of the Battle Hymn of the Republic* (New York: Harper and Brothers, 1916), 44.

18. In his memoirs, Rufus Dawes, then in command of the Sixth Wisconsin Volunteer Infantry, claimed it was his regiment that had marched around Howe's carriage and started singing "John Brown's Body." Rufus R. Dawes, *Service with the Sixth Wisconsin Volunteers* (Marietta, Ohio: E. R. Alderman & Sons, 1890), 29.

19. She continued this routine even after the babies had grown and left her bed. Early one morning in February 1909, when Howe was eighty-nine, she awoke with some lines in her head for a poem commemorating Lincoln's birthday, and jotted them down. Richards and Eliot, *Julia Ward Howe*, 2:287, 387; Howe, *Reminiscences*, 275; Hall, *Story of the Battle Hymn*, 47.

20. Howe was quite happy to have her original composition, and especially the final excised stanza, lost to oblivion and only reluctantly acceded to the request of the publishers of her *Reminiscences* to reproduce the original draft of the poem. She was right to be concerned. An October 1915 letter on the hymn in the London *Times* included the expurgated sixth stanza in its version of the song; several years later a Church of England hymnal printed the "Battle Hymn" with the additional stanza, provoking fierce objections from Howe's children. The sixth stanza also appeared in the United States in the 1964 Methodist hymnal. Richards and Eliot, *Julia Ward Howe*, 2:267; "Papers concerning the 'Battle Hymn of the Republic,'" MS AM 2195, Folder 3, Julia Ward Howe Papers; (London) *Times* October 6, 1915; Samuel J. Rogal, "Textual Change in Popular Occasional Hymns Found in American Evangelical Hymnals," in Mark Noll and Edith L. Blumhofer, eds., *Sing Them Over Again to Me: Hymns and Hymnbooks in America* (Tuscaloosa: University of Alabama Press, 2006), 109. Howe, *Reminiscences*, 274–75; Richards and Eliot, *Julia Ward Howe*, 1:188.

21. We borrow the phrase *origin myth* from Anne J. Randall, "A Censorship of Forgetting: Origins and Origin Myths of 'Battle Hymn of the Republic,'" in Anne J. Randall, ed., *Music, Power and Politics* (New York: Routledge, 2005). Louise Hall Tharp, "The Song That Wrote Itself," *American Heritage* 8, no. 1 (1956): 10–11; *Macon Telegram*, May 26, 1907; Florence Howe Hall, "The Building of a Nation's War Hymn," *Independent* 50, no. 2 (1898): 832.

22. James Randall, a New Orleans literature professor, awoke one night, unable to shake thoughts of a recent attack by Baltimore citizens on Union troops that had entered the city. Possessed by "some powerful spirit," he "rose, lit a candle, and went to [his] desk," where he "rapidly" composed "Maryland, My Maryland," which became one of the Confederacy's most popular songs. Randall quoted in Alice Fahs, *The Imagined Civil War: Popular Literature of the North and South, 1861–1865* (Chapel Hill: University of North Carolina Press, 2001), 80. Brander Matthews, "The Songs of the Civil War," *Century Illustrated* 34, no. 4 (1887): 619.

23. Melinda Lawson, *Patriot Fires: Forging a New American Nationalism in the Civil War North* (Lawrence: University Press of Kansas, 2002), 19; Franny Nudelman, *John Brown's Body: Slavery, Violence and the Culture of War* (Chapel Hill: University of North Carolina Press, 2004), 166.

24. Similar arguments could further more progressive attitudes toward gender. In 1870 Massachusetts suffragists, for example, invoked Howe's composition of the "Battle Hymn" as evidence of the service women had granted the state that should have merited the vote. *Boston Daily Advertiser*, April 20, 1870; *Philadelphia Inquirer*, June 3, 1898.

25. Harriet Beecher Stowe, "Introduction to the New Edition," *Uncle Tom's Cabin* (Boston: Houghton, Osgood, 1879), xi; Michael Anesko, "What Was an Author?," *American Literary History* 3, no. 3 (1991): 588.

26. Ernest Lee Tuveson, *Redeemer Nation: The Idea of America's Millennial Role* (Chicago: University of Chicago Press, 1968), 187; Steven E. Woodworth, *While God Is Marching On: The Religious World of Civil War Soldiers* (Lawrence: University Press of Kansas, 2001), 94; Phillip Shaw Paludan, *"A People's Contest": The Union and Civil War, 1861–1865* (New York: Harper & Row,

1988), 348; Fahs, *Imagined Civil War*, 79; Lawson, *Patriot Fires*, 5; George C. Rable, *God's Almost Chosen Peoples: A Religious History of the American Civil War* (Chapel Hill: University of North Carolina Press, 2010), 51–68.

27. Kenneth A. Bernard, *Lincoln and the Music of the Civil War* (Caldwell, Idaho: Caxton Printers, 1966), 51; Hall, *Story of the Battle Hymn*, 114; Julia Ward Howe, "Our Country," in *Later Lyrics* (Boston: J. E. Tilton, 1866), 9; Lawson, *Patriot Fires*, 6; Grant, *Private Woman*, 139.

28. Edward D. Snyder, "The Biblical Background of the 'Battle Hymn of the Republic,'" *New England Quarterly* 24, no. 2 (1951): 231–38; Aamodt, *Righteous Armies*, 20, 81–85; Tuveson, *Redeemer Nation*, 197–201; James. H. Moorhead, *World without End: Mainstream American Protestant Visions of the Last Things, 1880–1925* (Bloomington: Indiana University Press, 1999); Keith D. Miller, *Martin Luther King's Biblical Epic: His Final, Great Speech* (Jackson: University Press of Mississippi, 2012), 139–44.

29. The "Glory, Hallelujah" chorus inherited from "John Brown's Body" and "Say Brothers" also recalls the angelic chorus after the fall of Babylon (Revelation 19:1). As Ernest Tuveson has pointed out, in the original version Howe composed in Willard's Hotel, the borrowing from the biblical text was even more explicit, since she initially used the term *winepress*, which is how the phrase from Revelation appeared in the King James version she would have read. The image of the winepress is used in Joel (3:13) as well as in (Third) Isaiah (63:3). Tuveson, *Redeemer Nation*, 200; Miller, *Martin Luther King's Biblical Epic*, 140.

30. The line merges several biblical references to serpents, most prominently Genesis 3:14–15, when God tells the serpent that a descendent of Eve's will crush the beast's head with his heel, and the dragon of Revelation 12. Gary Wills, *Under God: Religion and American Politics* (New York: Simon and Schuster, 1990), 210; Snyder, "Biblical Background of the 'Battle Hymn,'" 234.

31. Aamodt, *Righteous Armies*, 83; Tuveson, *Redeemer Nation*, 202.

32. Mark A. Noll, *The Civil War as a Theological Crisis* (Chapel Hill: University of North Carolina Press, 2006), 81; Aamodt, *Righteous Armies*, 30, 42.

33. James H. Moorhead, *American Apocalypse: Yankee Protestants and the Civil War, 1860–1869* (New Haven: Yale University Press, 1978), 25–28, 33, 38, 56; Tuveson, *Redeemer Nation*, 193; Paludan, *"A People's Contest,"* 347.

34. Moorhead, *American Apocalypse*, 39, 157; Aamodt, *Righteous Armies*, 77.

35. Woodworth, *While God Is Marching On*, 138; Aamodt, *Righteous Armies*, 53–54; Wise quoted in Jackson Lears, *Rebirth of a Nation: The Making of Modern America, 1877–1920* (New York: HarperCollins, 2009), 17.

36. Hollis Read, *The Coming Crisis of the World*, quoted in Moorhead, *American Apocalypse*, 61; Moorhead, *American Apocalypse*, 99, 109–11.

37. Woodworth, *While God Is Marching On*, 102; Moorhead, *American Apocalypse*, 45–46; Tuveson, *Redeemer Nation*, 195–96; "A Hymn for Northern People," quoted in Aamodt, *Righteous Armies*, 121.

38. Moorhead, *American Apocalypse*, 80–81, 148; Aamodt, *Righteous Armies*, 83; Frothingham quoted in George M. Frederickson, *The Inner Civil War: Northern Intellectuals and the Crisis of the Union* (1965; Urbana: University of Illinois Press, 1993), 83.

39. In the short term, however, Howe's initial anonymity encouraged various misattributions of the poem to other prominent literary figures—the abolitionist poet John Greenleaf Whittier

and the novelist Harriet Beecher Stowe, among others. Richards and Eliot, *Julia Ward Howe*, 2:273; "The Battle Hymn of the Republic," *Lowell Daily Citizen and News*, November 25, 1868. The *New York Daily Tribune* published the poem in its January 14, 1862, issue, from an advance proof of the February *Atlantic*. Frank Luther Mott, *A History of American Magazines 1850–1865* (Cambridge: Harvard University Press, 1938), 2:505n47; Clifford, *Mine Eyes Have Seen the Glory*, 128; "Battle Hymn of the Republic," *Atlantic Monthly*, 9 no. 52 (1861): 145; J.W.H. to Fields, December 2, 1861, quoted in James C. Austin, *Fields of the* Atlantic Monthly (San Marino, Calif.: Huntington Library, 1953), 104.

40. Howe, *Reminiscences*, 275–76; "Battle Hymn of the Republic, adapted to the favorite melody, Glory, Hallelujah" (Boston: Oliver Ditson, 1862); Reynolds, *John Brown*, 6. According to Howe, the first public singing of the "Battle Hymn" occurred during a celebration of Washington's birthday at the Congregational Church at the Centre, in Framingham, Massachusetts (later Plymouth Church). Julia Ward Howe to C. C. Esty, October 9, 1899, in Stephen W. Herring, *Framingham: An American Town* (Framingham, Mass.: Framingham Historical Society, Framingham Tercentennial Commission, 2000), 178–80.

41. Frank Milton Bristol, *The Life of Chaplain McCabe: Bishop of the Methodist Episcopal Church* (New York: Fleming H. Revell, 1908), 194, 195, 125, 90, 129, 132.

42. Bristol, *Life of Chaplain McCabe*, 95, 188, 197, 135; Hall, *Story of the Battle Hymn*, 66–68; Edward P. Smith, *Incidents of the United States Christian Commission* (Philadelphia: J. B. Lippincott, 1869), 397; William E. Ross, "The Singing Chaplain: Bishop Charles Cardwell McCabe and the Popularization of the 'Battle Hymn of the Republic,'" *Methodist History* 28, no. 1 (1989): 22–32.

43. Bristol, *Life of Chaplain McCabe*, 119, 192.

44. In other accounts, McCabe recalled that Lincoln made his request for him to sing the song again by passing him a note. Since McCabe recorded the scene of Lincoln's making a vocal request just a few days after the meeting, and others in attendance recalled the scene similarly, it seems most likely that Lincoln called for McCabe to sing the "Battle Hymn" again both vocally and in writing. Bristol, *Life of Chaplain McCabe*, 202. McCabe to his wife, February 3, 1864, in Bristol, *Life of Chaplain McCabe*, 198–200; B. R. Frick, "Battle Hymn of the Republic," *Christian Advocate* 64, no. 32 (1889): 4; "Once Again—'The Battle Hymn of the Republic,'" *Christian Advocate* 64 no. 36 (1889): 572; Bristol, *Life of Chaplain McCabe*, 203. See also George Stuart to Abraham Lincoln, June 18, 1864, in Abraham Lincoln Papers, Library of Congress, http://memory.loc.gov/ammem/index.html.

45. Hall, *Story of the Battle Hymn*, 71, 72.

46. Christian McWhirter, *Battle Hymns: The Power and Popularity of Music in the Civil War* (Chapel Hill: University of North Carolina Press, 2012), 50; H. S. Hale, letter to the editor, *New York Times*, September 19, 1908.

47. Randall, "A Censorship of Forgetting," 9.

48. Hall, "Building of a Nation's War Hymn," 832; *Biloxi Daily Herald*, March 25, 1909; Reynolds, *John Brown*, 6.

49. Emerson had actually borrowed the line from a similar pronouncement made by the Kentucky-born abolitionist Mattie Griffith. Reynolds, *John Brown*, 366 (Emerson quote); Carol Brink, *Harps in the Wind: The Story of the Singing Hutchinsons* (New York: Macmillan, 1947), 203.

50. Letter of Rebecca Harding Davis, April 20, 1865, quoted in Nina Silber, *The Romance of Reunion: Northerners and the South, 1865–1900* (Chapel Hill: University of North Carolina Press, 1993), 16; Moorhead, *American Apocalypse*, 173–76; Leon F. Litwack, *Been in the Storm So Long: The Aftermath of Slavery* (New York: Vintage Books, 1979), 527; Bristol, *Life of Chaplain McCabe*, 211.

51. Mark A. Noll, *America's God: From Jonathan Edwards to Abraham Lincoln* (New York: Oxford University Press, 2002), 425–26.

52. Ronald C. White Jr., *Lincoln's Greatest Speech: The Second Inaugural* (New York: Simon & Schuster, 2002), 17–19, 29, 31, 32, 39, 42.

53. As Ernest Tuveson has pointed out, in invoking the biblical verse that ends his penultimate paragraph, "The judgments of the Lord are true and righteous altogether," Lincoln suggests he has taken it from an Old Testament source, "said three thousand years ago," likely Psalm 119:137. But the citation more closely resembles a similar declaration in Revelation 16:7. Tuveson, *Redeemer Nation*, 206–7.

54. Noll, *America's God*, 428, 430–31; Abraham Lincoln to Thurlow Weed, March 15, 1865, quoted in White, *Lincoln's Greatest Speech*, 198; Abraham Lincoln, "Second Inaugural Address," in *The Portable Abraham Lincoln* (New York: Penguin Books, 1992), 320.

55. "Monopoets," *New York Times*, January 12, 1874; Julia Ward Howe diary, May 18, 1864, bMS Am 2119 (814), Houghton Library, Harvard University, Cambridge, Mass.; *Salt Lake Telegram*, May 6, 1904; Richards and Eliot, *Julia Ward Howe*, 1:190; Hall, *Story of the Battle Hymn*, 89.

56. *Atchison (Kansas) Champion*, June 14, 1890; *Oregonian*, July 31, 1887.

57. Clifford, *Mine Eyes Have Seen the Glory*, 168; Grant, *Private Woman*, 141, 163; JWH. to Fields, December 2, 1861, quoted in Austin, *Fields of the Atlantic Monthly*, 113; Howe, *Reminiscences*, 305.

58. Richards and Eliot, *Julia Ward Howe*, 1:195, 197; Clifford, *Mine Eyes Have Seen the Glory*, 159; JWH diary, April 23, 1865, quoted in Clifford, *Mine Eyes Have Seen the Glory*, 164; JWH diary, March 23, 1865, quoted in Grant, *Private Woman*, 162.

59. Richards and Eliot, *Julia Ward Howe*, 1:356; Clifford, *Mine Eyes Have Seen the Glory*, 205; Ziegler, *Diva Julia*, 114, 122, 148–49; Richards and Eliot, *Julia Ward Howe*, 2:186–213; Howe, *Reminiscences*, 400; Richards and Eliot, *Julia Ward Howe*, 1:292.

60. Ziegler, *Diva Julia*, 154; *New York Times* quoted in Clifford, *Mine Eyes Have Seen the Glory*, 257; Richards and Eliot, *Julia Ward Howe*, 1:257, 2:283; *Daily Oklahoman*, June 26, 1898; Ziegler, *Diva Julia*, 145.

61. Howe, "Moral Trigonometry," quoted in Grant, *Private Woman*, 154–55.

62. Tom Appleton quoted in Richards and Eliot, *Julia Ward Howe*, 1:360; Clifford, *Mine Eyes Have Seen the Glory*, 162, 175, 178–79; Grant, *Private Woman*, 168, 179; Ziegler, *Diva Julia*, 6, 153; Howe, *Reminiscences*, 217.

63. *Daily Inter Ocean*, March 30, 1888; *Galveston Daily News*, April 30, 1893; *Grand Forks Herald*, November 15, 1895; *Philadelphia Inquirer*, December 3 1900; *Boston Journal*, February 25, 1891; *Dallas Morning News*, March 7, 1898; Hall, *Story of the Battle Hymn*, 81.

64. Moorhead, *World without End*; Jean B. Quandt, "Religion and Social Thought: The Secularization of Postmillennialism," *American Quarterly* 25, no. 4 (1973): 390–409.

65. Aamodt, *Righteous Armies*, 120.

CHAPTER IV

1. William L. Richter, *Overreached on All Sides: The Freedmen's Bureau Administrators in Texas, 1865–1868* (College Station: Texas A&M University Press, 1991), 127–32; William L. Richter, "The Brenham Fire of 1866: A Texas Reconstruction Atrocity," *Louisiana Studies*, 14 no. 3 (1975): 287–314; (New Orleans) *Daily Picayune*, September 6, 1866.

2. *New York Herald*, June 18, July 9, September 23, 1863; *Journal of the Board of Education of the City of New York, 1863* (New York: C. S. Westcott, 1863), 172; Austin Abbott and Benjamin Abbott, *Reports of Practice Cases, Determined in the Courts of the State of New York* (New York: John S. Voorhier, 1865), 18:166; *New York Tribune*, June 18, 1863.

3. David M. Barnes, *The Draft Riots in New York* (New York: Baker and Goodwin, 1863), 104; Iver Bernstein, *The New York City Draft Riots: Their Significance for American Society and Politics in the Age of the Civil War* (New York: Oxford University Press, 1990), 3. For the list of Ninth Ward trustees and the membership of the Board of Education, see *Twenty-Second Annual Report of the Board of Education of the City and County of New York for the year ending December 31, 1863* (New York: C. S. Westcott, 1864), 41, 48. For biographical information on Trustee Augustus F. Dow, see *New York Times*, October 13, 1858, November 1, 1860, November 30, 1861, September 10, 1865. For Trustee Henry P. See, see *Seventeenth Annual Report of the New York Association for Improving the Condition of the Poor* (New York: John F. Trow, 1860), 3. For Trustee William H. Gedney, see *New York Times*, July 12, 1862, December 1, 1864, November 1, 1876. For Trustee William W. Cornell, see "William W. Cornell," *Ladies' Repository* 30 (July 1870): 49–53.

4. Diane Ravitch, *The Great School Wars: A History of the New York City Public Schools* (Baltimore: Johns Hopkins University Press, 2000), 83; Willis Rudy, *The College of the City of New York: a History, 1847–1947* (New York: City College Press, 1949), 44–45; Trustee Augustus F. Dow quoted in *Journal of the Board of Education*, 180; *New York Herald*, February 14, 1870.

5. *Omaha World Herald*, July 24, 1898; James Rankin Young and J. H. Moore, *Reminiscences and Thrilling Stories of the War by Returned Heroes* (Philadelphia: Shepp, 1899), 22.

6. Edward J. Blum, *Reforging the White Republic: Race, Religion, and American Nationalism, 1865–1898* (Baton Rouge: Louisiana State University Press, 2005), 22; (Baltimore) *Sun*, March 18, 1868; Eric Foner, *Reconstruction: America's Unfinished Revolution 1863–1877* (New York: HarperCollins, 1988), 317; *Encyclopedia of North Carolina*, ed. William S. Powell (Chapel Hill: University of North Carolina Press, 2006), "Convention of 1868," 289–90; U.S. Congress, *Report of the Select Committee on the New Orleans Riots* (Washington, D.C.: Government Printing Office, 1867), 392, 393.

7. Blum, *Reforging the White Republic*, 88 (Beecher quote), 93; Debby Applegate, *The Most Famous Man in America: The Biography of Henry Ward Beecher* (New York: Doubleday, 2006), 362; *New York Times*, September 12, 1866.

8. *Daily Arkansas Gazette*, September 26, 1866; *New York Times*, August 2, 1867; (Harrisburg) *Weekly Patriot and Union*, November 9, 1865.

9. David W. Blight, *Race and Reunion: The Civil War in American Memory* (Cambridge: Harvard University Press, 2001), 100, 103; *Flakes Bulletin* (Galveston, Texas), September 8, 1868; *Pittsfield (Massachusetts) Sun*, March 11, 1869.

10. Blum, *Reforging the White Republic*, 113–16; (Baltimore) *Sun*, June 7, 1872; *Cleveland Morning Daily Herald*, August 12, 1872.

11. *Boston Daily Advertiser*, January 2, 1867; Daniel E. Sutherland, *The Confederate Carpetbaggers* (Baton Rouge: Louisiana State University Press, 1988), 236; Blight, *Race and Reunion*, 68–70.

12. Eric Foner, *Freedom's Lawmakers: A Directory of Black Officeholders During Reconstruction* (New York: Oxford University Press, 1993), xi; Blum, *Reforging the White Republic*, 88, 108, 126; Nina Silber, *The Romance of Reunion: Northerners and the South, 1865–1900* (Chapel Hill: University of North Carolina Press, 1993), 95.

13. Silber, *Romance of Reunion*, 39–65; Bushnell quoted in Mark A. Noll, *The Civil War as a Theological Crisis* (Chapel Hill: University of North Carolina Press, 2006), 77.

14. James H. Moorhead, *American Apocalypse: Yankee Protestants and the Civil War, 1860–1869* (New Haven: Yale University Press, 1978), 203; George M. Fredrickson, *The Inner Civil War: Northern Intellectuals and the Crisis of the Union* (Urbana: University of Illinois Press, 199), 183–98; Tilden G. Edelstein, *Strange Enthusiasm: A Life of Thomas Wentworth Higginson* (New Haven: Yale University Press, 1968), 300–301, 322, quotation 329–34. See also, T. W. Higginson, "Some War Scenes Revisited," *Atlantic Monthly*, July 1878, 1–9.

15. Blight, *Race and Reunion*, 149 (Lee quote), 157; (Providence, Rhode Island) *Daily Journal*, May 26, 1876, and (Worcester, Massachusetts) *Daily Spy*, May 28, 1877, quoted in Silber, *Romance of Reunion*, 61; Jackson Lears, *Rebirth of a Nation: The Making of Modern America, 1877–1920* (New York: HarperCollins, 2009); (Trenton, New Jersey) *State Gazette* quoted in Silber, *Romance of Reunion*, 96.

16. Blight, *Race and Reunion*, 22, 84, 88, 171; *New York Herald*, May 29, 1877, quoted in Blight, *Race and Reunion*, 87.

17. Christian McWhirter, "'Liberty's Great Auxiliary': Music and the American Civil War," Ph.D. diss., University of Alabama, 2009, 262; Drew Gilpin Faust, *This Republic of Suffering: Death and the American Civil War* (New York: Vintage Books, 2008). For examples of the "Battle Hymn" being sung at Memorial Day celebrations, see *New York Herald-Tribune*, May 31, 1886; *Morning Oregonian*, May 31, 1888. For examples of the "Battle Hymn" being sung at GAR events, see *San Francisco Chronicle*, August 5, 1886; (Chicago) *Daily Inter Ocean*, September 16, 1895. For examples of the "Battle Hymn" being sung at Republican rallies, see (San Francisco) *Daily Evening Bulletin*, September 20, 1876; *St. Louis Post-Dispatch*, June 16, 1888; *Chicago Daily Tribune*, September 12, 1896.

18. This symmetry was granted even more significance by the popular attribution of the "Battle Hymn" tune to William Steffe and the identification of Steffe as a Southerner, as well as by claims that the tune had originated at Methodist camp meetings in the South. When coupled with the fact that Daniel Emmett, the composer of "Dixie," was from Ohio and that the song had first achieved its popularity at Northern minstrel shows, the Southern roots of the "Battle Hymn" suggested the tangled cultural chords that lent the nation a degree of cohesiveness even in the midst of a brutal internecine conflict. Coleman Hutchinson, "Whistling 'Dixie' for the Union (Nation, Anthem, Revision)," *American Literary History* 19, no. 3 (2007): 603–28; *Columbus* (Georgia) *Daily Enquirer*, June 17, 1900. Norman S. Stevens, review of *Banners in the Air: The Eighth Ohio and the Spanish American War*, by Curtis Hard and Robert Ferrell, *Journal of Military History* 54, no. 4 (1990): 507.

19. To make matters even more confusing for turn-of-the-century Georgia students, "Glory, Glory to Old Georgia" was also a favorite of the captain of the university's baseball team, whose name happened to be John Brown. For lynching statistics, see http://memory.loc.

gov/ammem/aap/timelin2.html. *Red and Black* (University of Georgia student newspaper), June 2, 1906, http://redandblack.libs.uga.edu; *Worcester (Massachusetts) Daily Spy*, May 30, 1895; F. N. Boney, *A Pictorial History of the University of Georgia* (Athens: University of Georgia Press, 1984), 112; John F. Stegeman, *The Ghosts of Herty Field: Early Days on a Southern Gridiron* (Athens: University of Georgia Press, 1966); *Atlanta Journal*, November 10, November 11, 1906; *Macon (Georgia) Telegraph*, January 20, 1905. The school has since developed an elaborate ritual showcasing what is now called "The Battle Hymn of the Bulldog Nation" before football games. A lone trumpeter stands in the upper decks of the south side of the stadium and begins playing the "Battle Hymn" tune. During the solo, Georgia fans remove their hats and point them at the trumpeter in reverential silence.

20. Julia Ward Howe, "Robert E. Lee," in *At Sunset* (Boston: Houghton Mifflin, 1910), 62; Florence Howe Hall, *The Story of the Battle Hymn of the Republic* (New York: Harper and Brothers, 1916), 93; Julia Ward Howe, "Note on the 'Battle Hymn of the Republic,'" *Century* 34 (August 1887): 629–30; *Oregonian*, October 30, 1910.

21. Hall, *Story of the Battle Hymn*, 97; Silber, *Romance of Reunion*, 161, 172.

22. Ernest Lee Tuveson, *Redeemer Nation: The Idea of America's Millennial Role* (Chicago: University of Chicago Press, 1968), 207.

23. James McPherson, *For Cause and Comrades: Why Men Fought in the Civil War* (New York: Oxford University Press, 1997), 170; Eric Foner, *The Story of American Freedom* (New York: Norton, 1998), 95.

24. Foner, *Story of American Freedom*, 120; Moorhead, *American Apocalypse*, quotation 112–19.

25. *New York Times*, February 8, 1903.

26. *Daily Rocky Mountain News* (Denver, Colorado), October 3, 1878; *Boston Daily Advertiser*, November 9, 1887; *St. Louis Globe-Democrat*, October 27, 1876; (Chicago) *Daily Inter Ocean*, September 18, 1880; Blight, *Race and Reunion*, 259–60, 264; *New York Times*, April 29, 1886; *Chicago Daily Tribune*, April 28, 1886; (Baltimore) *Sun*, April 30, 1886; *New York Herald*, April 30, 1886.

27. *Philadelphia Record*, quoted in *Macon (Georgia) Telegraph*, June 26, 1883; *Georgia Weekly Telegraph*, October 29, 1878; *Boston Evening Journal*, September 20, 1878; (Baltimore) *Sun*, August 1, 1888.

28. Blight, *Race and Reunion*, 92–93, 306; (Chicago) *Inter Ocean*, October 9, 1876; (Chicago) *Daily Inter Ocean*, November 8, 1888; *Independent*, June 29, 1911, 1438.

29. *Atlanta Daily Constitution*, August 23, 1879; John Clark Ridpath, *The Life and Trial of Guiteau the Assassin* (Cincinnati: Jones Brothers, 1882), 105; Charles E. Rosenberg, *The Trial of the Assassin Guiteau: Psychiatry and Law in the Gilded Age* (Chicago: University of Chicago Press, 1968), 201, 212–14.

30. *Manchester (U.K.) Courier*, January 14, 1875, quoted in Sandra Jean Graham, "The Fisk Jubilee Singers and the Concert Spiritual: The Beginnings of an American Tradition," Ph.D. diss., New York University, 2001, 217–18, 442–444; Darius E. Jones, "Patriotic Songs," *Advance* 2, no. 69 (1868): 2; David W. Stone, "'An Inestimable Blessing': The American Gospel Invasion of 1873," *ATQ* 16, no. 3 (2002): 192; Toni Anderson, *"Tell Them We Are Singing for Jesus": The Original Fisk Jubilee Singers and Christian Reconstruction, 1871–1878* (Macon, Ga.: Mercer University Press, 2010), 122, 125.

31. Paul Gilroy, *The Black Atlantic: Modernity and Double Consciousness* (Cambridge: Harvard University Press, 1993), 90; Anderson, *"Tell Them We Are Singing for Jesus,"* 125; Gustavus D. Pike, *The Singing Campaign for Ten Thousand Pounds; or, The Jubilee Singers in Great Britain* (New York: American Missionary Association, 1875), 53–54, 76; Stone, "'An Inestimable Blessing,'" 192, 196.

32. *Milwaukee Journal*, January 24, 1895.

33. "Not Historical Truth," *Oregonian*, September 10, 1899; F. H. Hodder, "Propaganda as a Source of American History," *Mississippi Valley Historical Review* 9, no. 1 (1922): 13; *Philadelphia Inquirer*, December 21, 1909.

34. Not surprisingly, the most successful effort to rehabilitate the memory of John Brown within mainstream American culture was achieved by incorporating him into a culture of reunion. In 1928 Stephen Vincent Benét published *John Brown's Body*, a fifteen-thousand-line epic poem telling the story of the Civil War that used Brown's life as a central motif. The book was an immense success, selling 100,000 copies in the first few months and winning the Pulitzer Prize the year after. Benét, who had grown up in both the North and the South and whose grandfathers had fought on opposites sides of the Civil War, had sought to write an "impartial" account of the conflict, chronicling a war that produced "on both sides, men and deeds of the heroic kind." In this account, Brown is a noble but misguided warrior, kin to the proud, misguided heroes of the Confederacy. In the poem's concluding pages, Benét intersperses lines from "John Brown's Body" with calls to transcend the memory of both Brown and the Lost Cause so that the nation can embrace its grand destiny. "Bury the South together with this man," he writes. "Out of John Brown's strong sinews the tall skyscrapers grow, / Out of his heart the chanting buildings rise, / Rivet and girder, motor and dynamo." R. Blakeslee Gilpin, *John Brown Still Lives! America's Long Reckoning with Violence, Equality, and Change* (Chapel Hill: University of North Carolina Press, 2011), 106–19; Merrill D. Peterson, *John Brown: The Legend Revisited* (Charlottesville: University of Virginia Press, 2002), 108–10; Bruce A. Ronda, *Reading the Old Man: John Brown in American Culture* (Knoxville: University of Tennessee Press, 2008), 97–108; Stephen Vincent Benét, *John Brown's Body* (Garden City, N.Y.: Country Life Press, 1928), 373, 374, 376.

35. Henry George, *Social Problems* (Chicago: Belford, Clarke, 1883), 127; Eugene V. Debs, "John Brown: History's Greatest Hero," *Appeal to Reason*, no. 25 (November 23, 1907), 1; Zoe Trodd, "Writ in Blood: John Brown's Charter of Humanity, the Tribunal of History, and the Thick Link of American Political Protest," *Journal for the Study of Radicalism* 1, no. 1 (2006): 19; Merle Curti, *The Roots of American Loyalty* (New York: Atheneum, 1968), 191; Foner, *Story of American Freedom*, 134; *Harper's Weekly*, April 23, 1904.

36. Stuart Miller, *"Benevolent Assimilation": The American Conquest of the Philippines* (New Haven: Yale University Press, 1982), 6–11; David Traxel, *1898: The Tumultuous Year of Victory, Invention, Internal Strife, and Industrial Expansion That Saw the Birth of the American Century* (New York: Knopf, 1998), 107–26.

37. *Washington Post*, March 2, 1898; *New York Times*, March 25, 1898; *Chicago Daily Tribune*, March 25, March 26, 1898.

38. Traxel, *1898*, 115, 120; Miller, *"Benevolent Assimilation,"* 9; *Boston Daily Advertiser*, April 19, 1898.

39. Miller, *"Benevolent Assimilation,"* 17–18; Traxel, *1898*, 140; Blum, *Reforging the White Republic*, 213; General James Rusling, "Interview with President William McKinley," *Christian Advocate*,

January 22, 1903, in Daniel B. Schirmer and Stephen Rosskamm Shalom, eds., *The Philippines Reader: A History of Colonialism, Neocolonialism, Dictatorship, and Resistance* (Boston: South End Press, 1987), 22.

40. Miller, *"Benevolent Assimilation,"* 38, 88, 220, 248.

41. Moorhead, *American Apocalypse*, 74, 53; Blum, *Reforging the White Republic*, 214, 219–20; James Mills Thoburn, *The Christless Nations* (New York: Hunt and Eaton, 1895), 30; Beveridge quoted in Miller, *"Benevolent Assimilation,"* 131.

42. Blight, *Race and Reunion*, 345–54; Miller, *"Benevolent Assimilation,"* 58; Gaines Foster, *Ghosts of the Confederacy: Defeat, the Lost Cause, and the Emergence of the New South, 1865 to 1913* (New York: Oxford University Press, 1987), 145–46; Blum, *Reforging the White Republic*, 226–27, 231, 232 (McKinley quote), 234.

43. Some black troops did in fact express reservations about fighting men of their "own hue and color" and remarked that they received better treatment from Filipino citizens than they did from their countrymen back home. Miller, *"Benevolent Assimilation,"* 193. Blight, *Race and Reunion*, 348, 352; Miller, *"Benevolent Assimilation,"* 179, 80.

44. Miller, *"Benevolent Assimilation,"* 124, 134, 263.

45. Blight, *Race and Reunion*, 353; Foster, *Ghosts of the Confederacy*, 147.

46. Blum, *Reforging the White Republic*, 232; Traxel, *1898*, 181; JWH to Maud Howe Elliot, December 25, 1898, quoted in Deborah Pickman Clifford, *Mine Eyes Have Seen the Glory: A Biography of Julia Ward Howe* (Boston: Little, Brown, 1978), 267; Miller, *"Benevolent Assimilation,"* 117; *Boston Daily Globe*, September 12, 1898; Julia Ward Howe, "The Uses of Victory," *Christian Register* 77, no. 38 (1898): 1069–71.

47. Hall, *Story of the Battle Hymn*, 77–78; Blight, *Race and Reunion*, 353.

48. *Hawaiian Gazette*, July 5, 1898; E. L. Powell, "Battle Hymn of the Republic: An Interpretation," in *Savonarola; or The Reformation of a City. With Other Address on Civic Righteousness* (Louisville, Ky.: Sheltman, 1903), 99, 100; O. O. Howard, "Religious Work among the Soldiers," *Independent*, May 26, 1898, 16.

49. William E, Mason, "Universal Liberty," in *Republic or Empire: The Philippine Question* (Chicago: Independence Company, 1899), 486–87; (Raleigh, North Carolina) *News and Observer*, March 23, 1899; *Irish World and American Industrial Liberator*, May 20, 1899; *Boston Transcript*, quoted in the *Springfield (Massachusetts) Republican*, May 23, 1899.

50. "Battle Hymn of the Empire," *Public*, November 3, 1900, 479; S. P. Butler, "Battle Hymn of the Republic: Revised to Date," *(Baltimore) Sun*, May 25, 1899.

51. Philip S. Foner, *Mark Twain: Social Critic* (New York: International Publishers, 1959), 278.

52. R. Kent Rasmussen, *Critical Companion to Mark Twain: A Literary Reference* (New York: Facts on File, 2007), 34; *New York Times*, February 12, 1901; Foner, *Mark Twain*, 239, 256, 267.

53. "The Stupendous Procession," another unpublished piece composed by Twain at around the same time as his parody, also invokes the memory of the "Battle Hymn" to underscore America's moral failings. Foner, *Mark Twain*, 256, 285–88; Joe B. Fulton, *The Reconstruction of Mark Twain: How a Confederate Bushwhacker Became the Lincoln of Our Literature* (Baton Rouge: Louisiana State University Press, 2010), 157–77.

54. Blight, *Race and Reunion*, 255–99; (New Orleans) *Times-Picayune*, August 8, 1904; *San Francisco Chronicle*, December 14, 1904; McWhirter, "'Liberty's Great Auxiliary,'" 260; *Chicago Tribune*, April 13, 1904; *Southern Historical Society Papers* (Richmond, Va.: Southern Historical Society,

1903), 31:364; James M. McPherson, "Long-Legged Yankee Lies: The Southern Textbook Crusade," in Alice Fahs and Joan Waugh, eds., *The Memory of the Civil War in American Culture* (Chapel Hill: University of North Carolina Press, 2004), 64–78.

55. A similar confusion over the interpretation of the "Glory, Hallelujah" tune reigned at the 1924 Democratic convention in New York City, when the band struck up the song. *New York Times*, June 25, 1924; *Washington Post*, June 28, 1924; *Columbus (Ga.) Enquirer-Sun*, August 24, 1905; *Montgomery Advertiser*, August 23, 1905; *Indianapolis Freeman*, September 30, 1905; Beth Taylor Muskat, "The Last March: The Demise of the Black Militia in Alabama," *Alabama Review* 43, no. 1 (1990): 18–34, Guards quotation 31.

56. *Washington Post*, June 28, 1920; Virginius Dabney, *The Last Review: The Confederate Reunion, Richmond, 1932* (Chapel Hill: Algonquin Books, 1984), 24.

CHAPTER V

1. Lewis L. Gould, *Four Hats in the Ring: The 1912 Election and the Birth of Modern American Politics* (Lawrence: University Press of Kansas, 2008), 69–70; Edmund Morris, *Colonel Roosevelt* (New York: Random House, 2010), 195–96.

2. Gould, *Four Hats in the Ring*, 75; Morris, *Colonel Roosevelt*, 32, 82–87.

3. Morris, *Colonel Roosevelt*, 170; *Washington Post*, June 18, 1912; Gould, *Four Hats in the Ring*, 125.

4. Pennsylvania delegates also sang a version of "John Brown's Body," featuring the reactionary Pennsylvania senator Boise Penrose, one of Taft's leading supporters, on the sour apple tree. William Menkel, "The Progressives at Chicago," *American Review of Reviews* 46, no. 3 (1912): 310–17; *New York Times*, August 6–8, 1912; *Atlanta Constitution*, August 6, 1912; Donald Richberg, "We Thought It Was Armageddon," *Survey* 61, no. 11 (1929): 723; "A Speech at St. Johnsbury, Vermont, August 30, 1912," in Lewis L. Gould, ed., *Bull Mouse on the Stump: The 1912 Campaign Speeches of Theodore Roosevelt* (Lawrence: University Press of Kansas, 2008), 49.

5. During the Progressive convention, Straus led the New York delegation marching into the Chicago hall singing "Onward, Christian Soldiers." Morris, *Colonel Roosevelt*, 221. *New York Times*, October 1, 1912; *Boston Journal*, September 7, 1912; *Philadelphia Inquirer*, October 6, 1906, October 19, 1910; *Salt Lake (Utah) Telegram*, April 13, 1911.

6. Copyright descriptive material for *The Battle Hymn of the Republic*, LP10059, 1917, Motion Picture and Television Reading Room, Library of Congress, Washington, D.C.; "The Battle Hymn of the Republic—Vitagraph," *Moving Picture World* 8, no. 26 (1911): 1497; Michael Devine, "'Mine Eyes Have Seen the Glory': The Cinematic Adaptation of American Poetry," *Adaptation* 5, no. 1 (2012): 2; Vachel Lindsay, *The Art of the Moving Picture* (New York: Macmillan, 1915), 73–77; William Uricchio and Roberta E. Pearson, *Reframing Culture: The Case of the Vitagraph Quality Films* (Princeton: Princeton University Press, 1993), 195; *Fort Worth Star-Telegram*, June 30, 1911; *Morning Oregonian*, July 3, 1911; *Jonesboro (Ark.) Daily Tribune*, August 19, 1911; *Savannah Tribune*, August 26, 1911; *Trenton (New Jersey) Evening Times*, August 28, 1911.

7. John Milton Cooper Jr., *The Warrior and the Priest: Woodrow Wilson and Theodore Roosevelt* (Cambridge: Harvard University Press, 1983), 38–40.

8. Note from Theodore Roosevelt, ca. 1900, in John Brown/Boyd B. Stutler Database, West Virginia Memory Project, http://www.wvculture.org/history; H. E. Armstrong, "Theodore Roosevelt as a Volunteer Soldier," *Independent*, September 26, 1901, 2281; email correspondence, Danny Smith to Benjamin Soskis, October 22, 2011; Edward Wagenknecht, *The Seven Worlds of Theodore Roosevelt* (New York: Longmans, Green, 1958), 59; Laura E. Richards and Maud Howe Eliot, *Julia Ward Howe, 1819–1910* (Boston: Houghton Mifflin, 1916), 2:305; Theodore Roosevelt, *Fear God and Take Your Own Part* (1916; New York: Cosimo, 2005), v, vii.

9. Archie Butt to "My Dear Mother," June 15, 1908, in Lawrence F. Abbott, ed., *The Letters of Archie Butt, Personal Aide to President Roosevelt* (Garden City, N.Y.: Doubleday, Page, 1924), 30–36; "President Roosevelt Presents a Suggestion to You," *Uncle Remus's The Home Magazine* 23, no. 6 (1908): 5–6; David W. Blight, *Race and Reunion: The Civil War in American Memory* (Cambridge: Harvard University Press, 2001), 225–31.

10. Julia Ward Howe to Capt. Archibald W. Butt, August 8, 1908, quoted in *Los Angeles Times*, February 1, 1924; "Not Our National Anthem," *New York Times*, July 28, 1908; *New York Times*, August 8, August 15, 1908; Harriet Stevens, "Don't Like the Suggestion," *Atlanta Constitution*, August 3, 1908; *Biloxi Daily Herald*, August 10, 1908.

11. *New York Times*, August 8, 1912.

12. Morris, *Colonel Roosevelt*, 36, 711; Wagenknecht, *Seven Worlds*, 182, 184; "Theodore Roosevelt's Religion," *Current Opinion* 72, no. 1 (1922): 82–83; Christian F. Reisner, "Roosevelt and Religion," *New York Times*, October 30, 1921.

13. Robert S. La Forte, "Theodore Roosevelt's Osawatomie Speech," *Kansas Historical Quarterly* 32, no. 2 (1966): 187–200; Morris, *Colonel Roosevelt*, 108–14.

14. The *Outlook* article reflected Roosevelt's view more accurately than his Osawatomie speech, which he had farmed out to a number of advisors, especially Gifford Pinchot and William Allen White. *Springfield (Massachusetts) Republican*, September 1, 1910; La Forte, "Theodore Roosevelt's Osawatomie Speech," 192; William Allen White to Colonel Theodore Roosevelt, August 4, 1910; Roosevelt to White, August 9, 1910, William Allen White Papers, Manuscript Division, Library of Congress, Washington, D.C.; Theodore Roosevelt, "The Progressives, Past and Present," *Outlook* 96, no. 1 (1910): 19–20, 20–21.

15. For more on the general tendency of Progressives to avoid abolitionists as models, see John T. Cumbler, *From Abolition to Rights for All: The Making of a Reform Community in the Nineteenth Century* (Philadelphia: University of Pennsylvania Press, 2008), 3. Cooper, *Warrior and the Priest*, 35 (Roosevelt quote); Gould, *Four Hats in the Ring*, 144; Merrill D. Peterson, *John Brown: The Legend Revisited* (Charlottesville: University of Virginia Press, 2002), 103–4; *Atlanta Constitution*, August 7, 1912.

16. Gould, *Four Hats in the Ring*, 158, quotation 170.

17. Morris, *Colonel Roosevelt*, 217; Gould, *Four Hats in the Ring*, 142; Oscar King Davis, *Released for Publication: Some Inside Political History of Theodore Roosevelt and His Times 1898–1918* (Boston: Houghton Mifflin, 1925), 332–34.

18. *Financial World* 19, no. 10 (1912): 27; "A Defective Crusader," *Nation*, August 8, 1912, 116.

19. Nick Salvatore, *Eugene V. Debs: Citizen and Socialist* (Urbana: University of Illinois Press, 1982), 101 (Debs quote), 186–93, 229.

20. Clarence Darrow, the famed attorney who defended the McNamaras, also invoked the legacy of John Brown. Like Brown, Darrow argued, the McNamara brother ultimately

charged with the dynamiting was both a criminal and a martyr, who "risked his life because he believed in a cause." *Chicago Daily Tribune*, May 19, 1915. Salvatore, *Eugene V. Debs*, 199, 253–58 (quotations 254), 275, 294; Gould, *Four Hats in the Ring*, 116; Eugene Debs, "Arouse, Ye Slaves!," in *Debs: His Life, Writing, and Speeches* (Chicago: Charles H. Kerr, 1908), 310; Rebecca N. Hill, *Men, Mob, and Law: Anti-Lynching and Labor Defense in U.S. Radical History* (Durham, N.C.: Duke University Press, 2008), 135–39; Eugene V. Debs, "The McNamara Case and the Labor Movement," *International Socialist Review* 12 (January 1912): 397–401; Gould, *Four Hats in the Ring*, 108–10; Eugene Debs, speech delivered June 16, 1918, Canton, Ohio, E. V. Debs Internet Archive, http://www.marxists.org/archive/debs/works/1918/canton.htm.

21. Morris, *Colonel Roosevelt*, 227–28; Gould, *Four Hats in the Ring*, 134.

22. Gould, *Four Hats in the Ring*, 134–35, 145; *Crisis* 5, no. 1 (1912): 19. See also "Battle Hymn of the Black Delegates," *Los Angeles Times*, August 18, 1912.

23. Morris, *Colonel Roosevelt*, 101, 164, 174 (Root quote), 198; A. Lincoln, "Theodore Roosevelt, Hiram Johnson, and the Vice-Presidential Nomination of 1912," *Pacific Historical Review* 28, no. 3 (1959): 272; Gould, *Four Hats in the Ring*, 51, 53; *Los Angeles Times*, June 23, 1912.

24. Morris, *Colonel Roosevelt*, 245–48; Gould, *Four Hats in the Ring*, 171; Reisner, "Roosevelt and Religion."

25. James H. Moorhead, *World without End: Mainstream American Protestant Visions of the Last Things, 1880–1925* (Bloomington: Indiana University Press, 1999), xii, xv, xvi, 42–46; Richard M. Gamble, *The War for Righteousness: Progressive Christianity, the Great War, and the Rise of the Messianic Nation* (Wilmington, Del.: ISI Books, 2003), 29–40.

26. Moorhead, *World without End*, 42, 45–46; James Henry Snowden, *The Coming of the Lord: Will It Be Premillennial?* (New York: Macmillan, 1919), 124, 128; Gamble, *War for Righteousness*, 58, 64–65, 132, quoting Sidney Gulick, *The Fight for Peace* (1915); Gifford Pinchot, *The Fight for Conservation* (New York: Doubleday, Page, 1910), 92.

27. Although Machen became a spokesman for fundamentalism, unlike most fundamentalists he did not hold premillennial views. He believed instead that fundamentalists had focused too much attention on the exact "order of future events" at the end of history, about which Christians could never achieve certitude. J. Gresham Machen, *Christianity and Liberalism* (New York: Macmillan, 1923), 126, 179–80; Daryl G. Hart, *Defending the Faith: J. Gresham Machen and the Crisis of Conservative Protestantism in Modern America* (Baltimore: Johns Hopkins University Press, 1994), 64, 69–71, 75.

28. The "Battle Hymn" was frequently sung at national and state meetings of the Women's Christian Temperance Union, one of the nation's most powerful reform groups. *New York Times*, November 15, 1891; *Colorado Springs Gazette Telegraph*, April 22, 1899. Strangely enough, the program for the World's Peace Jubilee referred to the "Battle Hymn" as the "John Brown Song." The Fisk Jubilee Singers won plaudits for performing the song in the difficult key of E flat. Toni Anderson, *"Tell Them We Are Singing for Jesus": The Original Fisk Jubilee Singers and Christian Reconstruction, 1871–1878* (Macon, Ga.: Mercer University Press, 2010), 68; Sandra Jean Graham, "The Fisk Jubilee Singers and the Concert Spiritual: The Beginnings of an American Tradition," Ph.D. diss., New York University, 2001, 392–94; *Chicago Daily Tribune*, October 10, 1893; *Hartford (Connecticut) Courant*, October 21, 1919; *Chicago Daily Tribune*, March 6, 1931; *New York Tribune*, October 14, 1904.

29. For the anguished letter that Howe wrote to Sammy after his death, see Richards and Elliot, *Julia Ward Howe*, 1:179–83. For more on the ways Willie's death shaped Lincoln's moral and theological views, see Phillip Shaw Paludan, *"A People's Contest": The Union and Civil War, 1861–1865* (New York: Harper & Row, 1988), 369–72. Julia Ward Howe, *Reminiscences, 1819–1899* (Boston: Houghton, Mifflin, 1899), 327–28; *Oregonian*, May 15, 1913; Deborah Pickman Clifford, *Mine Eyes Have Seen the Glory: A Biography of Julia Ward Howe* (Boston: Little, Brown, 1978), 185–87, 156; Franny Nudelman, *John Brown's Body: Slavery, Violence and the Culture of War* (Chapel Hill: University of North Carolina Press, 2004), 168–70; Richards and Elliot, *Julia Ward Howe*, 1:302.

30. John T. Trowbridge quoted in Edwin D. Mead, *Woman and War: Julia Ward Howe's Peace Crusade* (Boston: World Peace Foundation, 1914), 9.

31. Richards and Elliot, *Julia Ward Howe*, 2:377–78; Clifford, *Mine Eyes Have Seen*, 270.

32. Clifford, *Mine Eyes Have Seen*, 267–68; Richards and Elliot, *Julia Ward Howe*, 2:264.

33. Morris, *Colonel Roosevelt*, 130; Roosevelt quoted in Gamble, *War for Righteousness*, 119.

34. Theodore Roosevelt, "The Peace of Righteousness," *Outlook*, September 9, 1911, 67; Morris, *Colonel Roosevelt*, 132, 146 (Taft quote), 476, 481, 487; Cooper, *Warrior and the Priest*, 35–36, 284 (Taft quote).

35. Morris, *Colonel Roosevelt*, 283, 348, quotation 395; Theodore Roosevelt, *America and the World War* (New York: Charles Scribner's Sons, 1915), 93.

36. Morris, *Colonel Roosevelt*, 294 (Roosevelt quote), 400, 446; Oscar Cesare, "The Real Armageddon," *New York Sun*, June 1, 1916; Cooper, *Warrior and the Priest*, 250; John Milton Cooper Jr., *Woodrow Wilson: A Biography* (New York: Knopf, 2009), 338.

37. Cooper, *Woodrow Wilson*, 6, 451; Gamble, *War for Righteousness*, 73, 115 (Lyman Abbott quote), 95 (Count von Bernstorff quote), 156; [Lyman Abbott], "The Duty of Christ's Church To-Day," *Outlook*, May 2, 1917, 15.

38. "Christianity and War," *Outlook*, January 13, 1915, 61–63; "An Open Letter," *Outlook*, April 25, 1917, 730. See also "Unforeseen Forces in the War," *Outlook*, June 6, 1917, 216.

39. Gamble, *War for Righteousness*, 147 (Kitchin quote), 142–43; Moorhead, *World without End*, 150.

40. Cooper, *Woodrow Wilson*, 342; J. W. Schulte Nordholt, *Woodrow Wilson: A Life for World Peace*, trans. Herbert P. Rowen (Berkeley: University of California Press, 1991), 223.

41. Wilson was waging his own battle for self-control while he was entreating citizens to "put a curb upon our sentiments" in order to sustain the nation's neutrality. Ellen Wilson, his wife of nearly thirty years, died from complications due to Bright's disease in August 1914, a week after the war began. "Dead in heart and body," he confided to a friend, "I never understood before what a broken heart meant. . . . It just means that he lives by the compulsion of duty only." That compulsion served him admirably as he managed his grief in order to attend to his presidential duties. Cooper, *Woodrow Wilson*, 240, 244, 263, 268, 278, 287, 375, 382.

42. Cooper, *Woodrow Wilson*, 286, 352.

43. Cooper, *Woodrow Wilson*, 373, 385, 387; *New York Times*, April 3, 1917; *St. Louis Post-Dispatch*, April 3, 1912.

44. *Boston Transcript* quoted in the *Trenton (New Jersey) Evening Times*, April 4, 1917; *Salt Lake (Utah) Telegram*, May 24, 1917.

45. Gamble, *War for Righteousness*, 100, 148, 153; *New York Times*, April 6, August 16, 1917; Robert Jewett and John Shelton Lawrence, *Captain America and the Crusade Against Evil: The Dilemma*

of *Zealous Nationalism* (Grand Rapids, Mich.: W. B. Eerdmans, 2003), 73; Moorhead, *World without End*, 152.

46. Cooper, *Woodrow Wilson*, 431, 464; Gould, *Four Hats in the Ring*, 77; Gamble, *War for Righteousness*, 157.

47. Cooper, *Woodrow Wilson*, 509, 527; Moorhead, *World without End*, 152; Ernest Lee Tuveson, *Redeemer Nation: The Idea of America's Millennial Role* (Chicago: University of Chicago Press, 1968), 210–11.

48. *Chicago Daily Tribune*, May 19, 1918.

49. *New York Times*, April 3, April 5, 1917; *Atlanta Constitution*, April 1, 1918; "One Community Gives Its Best," *Outlook*, June 26, 1918, 334; *Chicago Daily Tribune*, February 24, 1918; *Oregonian*, March 4, 1917; Gamble, *War for Righteousness*, 174.

50. *Trenton (New Jersey) Evening Times*, April 20, 1917; *Independent*, April 28, 1917, 195; "America Day: Service at St. Paul's Cathedral," *Musical Times*, May 1, 1917, 207; *San Francisco Chronicle*, December 30, 1918.

51. Florence Howe Hall suggested that her mother had absorbed an internationalist perspective, which inspired the "Battle Hymn," from Samuel Gridley Howe's engagements in multiple foreign causes. *Duluth (Minnesota) News-Tribune*, August 26, 1917. Lyman Abbott, "An International Battle Hymn," *Outlook*, June 27, 1917, 321; Gamble, *War for Righteousness*, 171. For more on the universality of the "Battle Hymn," see Robert J. Burdette, "The Battle Hymn of the Republic," *Los Angeles Times*, October 19, 1910.

52. "The Real End of the War," *Independent*, June 8, 1918, 395; *Macon (Georgia) Telegraph*, quoted in "After the Years," *Confederate Veteran* 26, no. 6 (1918): 238.

53. Gamble, *War for Righteousness*, 175; George Creel, *How We Advertised America* (New York: Harper & Brothers, 1920), 204–6.

54. Gavin James Campbell, "'A Higher Mission Than Merely to Please the Ear': Music and Social Reform in America, 1900–1925," *Musical Quarterly* 84, no. 2 (2000): 265, 272–73; *New York Times*, May 12, 1918; Donald Wilhelm, "Shoot Straight and Live Straight," *Independent*, December 15, 1917, 516.

55. Eric Foner, *The Story of American Freedom* (New York: Norton, 1998), 177; Gamble, *War for Righteousness*, 175–76; Cooper, *Woodrow Wilson*, 432; Salvatore, *Eugene V. Debs*, 291–94.

56. Cooper, *Woodrow Wilson*, 509.

57. Cooper, *Woodrow Wilson*, 462; Joseph P. Tumulty, *Woodrow Wilson as I Know Him* (Garden City, N.Y.: Doubleday, Page, 1921), 125–26, 336–37; Tuveson, *Redeemer Nation*, 131; James H. Moorhead, *American Apocalypse: Yankee Protestants and the Civil War, 1860–1869* (New Haven: Yale University Press, 1978), 243; Gamble, *War for Righteousness*, 236–44; Ernest Hemingway, *A Farewell to Arms* (1929; Norwalk, Conn.: Easton Press, 1957), 177.

58. *Columbus* (Georgia) *Ledger*, June 9, 1920; *Lexington (Kentucky) Herald*, June 10, 1920; Michael Jacobs, "Co-opting Christian Chorales: Songs of the Ku Klux Klan," *American Music* 28, no. 3 (2010): 368–75; Danny O. Crew, *Ku Klux Klan Sheet Music: An Illustrated Catalogue of Published Music, 1867–2002* (Jefferson, N.C.: McFarland, 2003), 112, 133–34, 156–57, 158, 176–77, 237. The Klan also manufactured its own adaptations of the "Battle Hymn," creating versions like "The Battle Hymn of the Klansmen" ("I have seen them in the evenings by the bright and fiery cross, / They stand for all that's righteous but are sifting out the dross") and "Battle

Hymn of the Klan" ("Mine eyes have seen the parades of the Nation's Ku Klux Klan; / They are stamping out rebellion to our glorious country's plan").

59. Robert DeMott has suggested that Carol Steinbeck might have been inspired in her selection of the title from hearing Pare Lorenz's radio drama, *Ecce Homo!*, which ended with a stirring version of Howe's hymn. Robert DeMott, introduction to John Steinbeck, *Working Days: The Journals of the Grapes of Wrath 1938–1941* (New York: Viking, 1989), xxvi. Diary entry 63, September 3 [1938], John Steinbeck, *Working Days*, 65; Steinbeck to Elizabeth [Otis], [1938], in *Steinbeck: A Life in Letters* (New York: Viking Press, 1975), 173; Steinbeck to Elizabeth [Otis], September 10, 1938, in *Steinbeck: A Life in Letters*, 171.

60. In condemning the California farmers' practice of destroying badly needed fruit in order to keep prices high, Steinbeck made use of the image in his title. "There is a sorrow here that weeping cannot symbolize," he wrote. "In the souls of the people the grapes of wrath are filling and growing heavy, growing heavy for the vintage." DeMott, introduction, xxii. Steinbeck to Elizabeth [Otis], September 10, 1938; Jackson J. Benson, *The True Adventures of John Steinbeck, Writer* (New York: Viking Press, 1984), 385–87.

61. Steinbeck to Pat [Covici], January 1, 1939, in *Steinbeck: A Life in Letters*, 174; Steinbeck to Elizabeth [Otis], [1938], in *Steinbeck: A Life in Letters*, 173; Steinbeck to Covici, December 22, 1938, quoted in Peter Lisca, *The Wide World of John Steinbeck* (New Brunswick, N.J.: Rutgers University Press, 1958), 148.

62. John Steinbeck, *The Grapes of Wrath* (New York: Viking Press, 1939); Steinbeck to Pat [Covici], [received March 31, 1939], in *Steinbeck: A Life in Letters*, 182.

CHAPTER VI

1. "Women Help Slug Police: Bullets Fly," *Chicago Daily Tribune*, January 18, 1915; Ralph Chaplin, *Wobbly: The Rough-and-Tumble Story of an American Radical* (Chicago: University of Chicago Press, 1948), 168. Jane Addams was away at a peace meeting.

2. William M. Adler, *The Man Who Never Died: The Life, Times, and Legacy of Joe Hill, American Labor Icon* (New York: Bloomsbury, 2011), 7–8; William Preston Jr., *Aliens and Dissenters: Federal Suppression of Radicals, 1903–1933* (1963; reprint, Urbana: University of Illinois Press, 1994), 36–37; U.S. Commission on Industrial Relations, *Final Report and Testimony* (Washington, D.C.: Government Printing Office, 1916), 5:8–16, 23–76; Chaplin, *Wobbly*, 166.

3. Adler, *Man Who Never Died*, 7; Michael McGerr, *A Fierce Discontent: The Rise and Fall of the Progressive Movement in America, 1870–1920* (New York: Free Press, 2003), 64–65; Cary Nelson, *Repression and Recovery: Modern American Poetry and the Politics of Cultural Memory, 1910–1945* (Madison: University of Wisconsin Press, 1989), 58–61.

4. We have been unable to find any historical treatment of the 1917 Chicago hunger demonstration. Our account has been reconstructed from contemporaneous newspaper accounts and Chaplin's autobiography, *Wobbly*. Chaplin, *Wobbly*, 168–69; Joyce L. Kornbluh, ed., *Rebel Voices: An IWW Anthology* (Chicago: Charles H. Kerr, 1988), 174–75.

5. "Women Help Slug Police: Bullets Fly," *Chicago Daily Tribune*, January 18, 1915; "Gemmill Rules Police Can't Bar Jobless Parade," *Chicago Daily Tribune*, January 29, 1915; Chaplin, *Wobbly*, 168.

6. "Women Help Slug Police: Bullets Fly," *Chicago Daily Tribune*, January 18, 1915.

7. "Women Help Slug Police: Bullets Fly," *Chicago Daily Tribune*, January 18, 1915; "Riot Views of Different Sides," *Chicago Daily Tribune*, January 18, 1915.

8. "Women Help Slug Police: Bullets Fly," *Chicago Daily Tribune*, January 18, 1915; Illinois vs. August Spies et al. trial transcript no. 1: Testimony of Herman Schuettler, July 28, 1886, http://www.chicagohistory.org/hadc/transcript/volumek/501–550/K515–529.htm; Timothy Messer-Kruse, *The Trial of the Haymarket Anarchists: Terrorism and Justice in the Gilded Age* (New York: Palgrave Macmillan, 2011); Robert A. Ferguson, *The Trial in American Life* (Chicago: University of Chicago Press, 2007), ch. 6; "I.W.W. Faction Row Involved in Street Riot," *Chicago Daily Tribune*, January 19, 1915.

9. Several years earlier, the U.S. Supreme Court had declared unconstitutional a Chicago ordinance authorizing the police to require permits for parades. Such authority was "oppressive, tyrannical, and unconstitutional," the Court had stated. Chicago municipal judge William Gemmill echoed the Court's ruling in the wake of the hunger march: "The unemployed have a legal right to parade the streets of Chicago. No permits from the police are necessary. The police have no right to interfere with parades if they are orderly." See "Gemmill Rules Police Can't Bar Jobless Parade," *Chicago Daily Tribune*, January 29, 1915. "Women Help Slug Police: Bullets Fly," *Chicago Daily Tribune*, January 18, 1915; Chaplin, *Wobbly*, 169.

10. "Women Help Slug Police: Bullets Fly," *Chicago Daily Tribune*, January 18, 1915; "1,500 Idle Riot around Hull House," *Chicago Daily Tribune*, January 18, 1915; "Gemmill Rules Police Can't Bar Jobless Parade," *Chicago Daily Tribune*, January 29, 1915; "I.W.W. Faction Row Involved in Street Riot," *Chicago Daily Tribune*, January 19, 1915; Chaplin, *Wobbly*, 169–70.

11. Chaplin, *Wobbly*, 167–68, 170. It is unclear from Chaplin's autobiography whether he scribbled these stanzas before or after the hunger march. Chaplin says he wrote them "lying on the rug in the living-room" while a colleague had "dinner." At the time, "dinner" usually implied a midday meal. Neither Chaplin nor the Chicago newspapers mention what time the march and "riot" occurred. In his narrative Chaplin describes writing the song before the hunger march, but his narrative often does not follow chronology.

12. Chaplin, *Wobbly*, 167, 169, 122–23; Elliott J. Gorn, *Mother Jones: The Most Dangerous Woman in America* (New York: Hill and Wang, 2001), ch. 7, esp. 185–94. The train's name, Bull Moose Special, stemmed from some Progressives who had financed it. See "The Bull Moose Special," West Virginia Encyclopedia, http://www.wvencyclopedia.org/articles/707.
Chaplin organized the miners with Mother Jones, the famous labor radical and orator. When he was attacked, he was en route to speak in place of Mother Jones, who had been arrested and thrown in a bull pen.

13. Chaplin, *Wobbly*, 119, 121, 125; Gorn, *Mother Jones*, 356n56; Ralph Chaplin, "The Two John Browns," Ralph Chaplin Papers, Washington State Historical Society (hereafter WSHS), Ms. 71, Box 3. The Socialist John Brown was locked up with Mother Jones. Chaplin's awareness that a few abolitionists had planned to rescue Brown during his imprisonment at Harpers Ferry reveals a considerable depth of knowledge about Brown and his raid.

14. Chaplin, *Wobbly*, 123; Ralph Chaplin, "Why I Wrote 'Solidarity Forever,' with an Introduction by Bruce Le Roy," *American West* 5, no. 1 (1968): 25, 27; Stewart Bird, Dan Georgakas, and Deborah Shaffer, eds., *Solidarity Forever: An Oral History of the IWW* (Chicago: Lake View Press, 1985), 146; Nelson, *Repression and Recovery*, 58–63. In the IWW's "Little Red

Songbook," "Solidarity Forever" appears under the parenthetical "(Tune: John Brown's Body)." See, for example, *I.W.W. Songs: To Fan the Flames of Discontent* (Chicago: Industrial Workers of the World, 1923), 25.

Chaplin specifically refers to the labor battles in Kanawha County as "civil war" (*Wobbly*, 123).

15. "Solidarity Forever" has been widely published. One of the best contextualized sources is Joyce L. Kornbluh, ed., *Rebel Voices: An IWW Anthology* (Chicago: Charles H. Kerr, 1988), 26–27.

16. Chaplin, "Why I Wrote 'Solidarity Forever,'" 19–27, 73; Nelson, *Repression and Recovery*, 62; John Greenway, *American Folksongs of Protest* (New York: Octagon Books, 1971), 181.

17. No one knows why "Wobbly" became a pseudonym for the IWW. The most colorful explanation credits a Chinese cook in a West Coast railroad camp, who mispronounced "I-W-W" as "Eye-Wobble-U, Wobble-U." Another derivation is the "wobble saw," a circular saw mounted unevenly in order to cut a wide groove. Max Hayes, an American Socialist, first used "Wobbly" to mean unstable. See Upton Sinclair, *Singing Jailbirds: A Drama in Four Acts* (Long Beach, Calif.: self-published, 1924), 39; Patrick Renshaw, *The Wobblies: The Story of the IWW and Syndicalism in the United States* (1967; reprint, Chicago: Ivan R. Dee, 1999), 1–2; Adler, *Man Who Never Died*, 2; Chaplin, "Why I Wrote 'Solidarity Forever,'" 23, 24.

18. In his autobiographical writings, Chaplin sometimes criticizes his younger self for being an atheist, but he clearly uses atheism to mean his repudiation of mainline religious *institutions*. He describes his younger self as an atheist in order to dramatize his conversion to Catholicism (discussed later in this chapter). For examples of Chaplin's describing his younger self as an atheist, see Chaplin, *Wobbly*, 98–99, 275; Ralph Chaplin with William J. Barker, "Confessions of a Radical," part 1, *Empire: The Magazine of the Denver Post*, February 17, 1957, 12; Ralph Chaplin with William J. Barker, "Confessions of a Radical," part 2, *Empire: The Magazine of the Denver Post*, February 24, 1957, 10; Chaplin, quoted in "Only Crusaders Sing, Says Veteran Crusader," *Work Magazine*, September 1958, 7.

19. Chaplin, "Why I Wrote 'Solidarity Forever,'" 73.

20. Surprisingly scholars and biographers have all but ignored Chaplin. The best assessment of his career, aside from his own fair-minded autobiography, is John R. Salter Jr., "Reflections on Ralph Chaplin, the Wobblies, and Organizing in the Save the World Business—Then and Now," *Pacific Historian* 30, no. 1 (1986): 5–19.

21. Melvyn Dubofsky notes that Wobblies liked to compare themselves to the antebellum abolitionists. He quotes an organizer as saying, "We are the modern abolitionists fighting against the wage system." See Dubofsky, *We Shall Be All: A History of the Industrial Workers of the World*, abridged edition, ed. Joseph A. McCartin (Urbana: University of Chicago Press, 2000), 91. Unless stated otherwise, we cite this abridged edition of Dubofsky's *We Shall Be All* rather than the original 1969 edition.

On the abolitionists' "sacred vocation," see Donald M. Scott, "Abolition as a Sacred Vocation," in Lewis Perry and Michael Fellman, eds., *Antislavery Reconsidered: New Perspectives on the Abolitionists* (Baton Rouge: Louisiana State University Press, 1979), 51–74.

22. Chaplin, *Wobbly*, 3–14, quotation 3.

23. Chaplin, *Wobbly*, 4–14, quotation 6. Chaplin kept a manuscript of his father's eyewitness account of the Pullman Strike. See E. L. Chaplin, "Eye Witness Account of 'Deb's Rebellion,'" holograph (11 handwritten pages), Ralph Chaplin Papers, Ms. 71, Box 5, Folder 22, WSHS.

24. Chaplin, *Wobbly*, 15–24, 28, quotation 23.

25. Chaplin, *Wobbly*, 34–36, quotations 35.

26. Chaplin, *Wobbly*, 40–47.

27. Chaplin, *Wobbly*, 48–49.

28. Chaplin, *Wobbly*, 48–55, quotations 48, 55.

29. Chaplin, *Wobbly*, 98–99; Michael Robertson, *Worshipping Walt: The Whitman Disciples* (Princeton: Princeton University Press, 2008), 1–13, 232–76. Robertson brilliantly notes that "one of the keys to Debs's success was that he enabled Americans disenchanted with traditional religion to transfer their millennial aspirations from individual salvation to the transformation of society." In *Leaves of Grass*, Whitman satisfied the thirst among American radicals for "alternative models of spirituality, politics, sexuality, and gender identity." Debs's rhetoric was "perfectly congruent" with Whitman's poetry (251, 254, 255). On Whitman's *Leaves of Grass* as a stimulus for American spirituality, see also Leigh Eric Schmidt, *Restless Souls: The Making of American Spirituality* (San Francisco: HarperSanFrancisco, 2005), 13, 101–6, 232–35, 288–90.

   The Kerr Publishing Company, a Socialist publisher, had recently issued a volume of *Leaves of Grass*, which is the edition Chaplin read. Chaplin became a director. Chaplin, *Wobbly*, 98, 165.

30. Chaplin, "Why I Wrote 'Solidarity Forever,'" 27. "Walt Whitman's Caution" first appeared as one of the "Messenger Leaves" in the 1860 edition of *Leaves of Grass*. The poem was later titled "To the States" and appeared as one of the "Songs of Insurrection" in the 1871 and 1876 editions of *Leaves of Grass*. See Walt Whitman, *Leaves of Grass: A Norton Critical Edition*, ed. Sculley Bradley and Harold W. Blodgett (New York: Norton, 1973), 9. Whitman wrote his warning in response to Southerners' aggressiveness at nationalizing slavery, which also inspired him to publish his 1855, 1856, and 1860 editions of *Leaves of Grass*. See Betsy Erkkila, *Whitman: The Political Poet* (New York: Oxford University Press, 1989), 185.

31. Chaplin, "Why I Wrote 'Solidarity Forever,'" 24, 27.

32. Chaplin, *Wobbly*, 94–118, quotations 114. Chaplin's autobiography is not entirely clear about when he joined the IWW. John Salter says Chaplin joined in 1913, but Chaplin says he "rejoined the IWW" in 1913, after returning to the Midwest from Kanawha County, West Virginia, where he worked as an artist and organized the miners. He doesn't specifically say whether or not he joined the IWW in 1910, simply that its "direct action tactics" answered the needs of the downtrodden. See Chaplin, *Wobbly*, 114, 133; Salter, "Reflections on Ralph Chaplin," 9.

33. Dubofsky, *We Shall Be All*, 84–97, esp. 94–95. See also Renshaw, *Wobblies*, 21–74. On black Wobblies, see Peter Cole, *Ben Fletcher: The Life and Times of a Black Wobbly* (Chicago: Charles H. Kerr, 2007); Paul Garon and Gene Tomko, eds., *Black Hoboes and Their Songs* (Chicago: Charles H. Kerr, 2006), 199–205.

34. Haywood, quoted in Dubofsky, *We Shall Be All*, 95; Adler, *Man Who Never Died*, 8.

35. Dubofsky, *We Shall Be All*, 34–47, 80, 89, quotations 89; Nick Salvatore, *Eugene V. Debs: Citizen and Socialist* (Urbana: University of Illinois Press, 1982), 206–8, quotations 208; Renshaw, *Wobblies*, 48–73.

36. Dubofsky, *We Shall Be All*, 89–93, quotations 90, 92, 93; Chaplin, *Wobbly*, 207; Adler, *Man Who Never Died*, 9.

37. Dubofsky, *We Shall Be All*, 96; Renshaw, *Wobblies*, 52–62; Paul Frederick Brissenden, *The I.W.W.: A Study in American Syndicalism* (New York: Columbia University Press, 1919); IWW Preamble, quoted in Chaplin, *Wobbly*, 148; Chaplin, "Why I Wrote 'Solidarity Forever,'" 20.

38. Adler, *Man Who Never Died*, 5. As Morgan Miller notes, "while Haywood may never have read *Capital*," most labor radicals had read Marx's lectures to workers on economic laws, *Value, Price and Profit*, which inspired the Preamble of the IWW. See Morgan Miller to authors, September 13, 2012; Karl Marx, *Wage-Labour and Capital & Value, Price and Profit* (New York: International Publishers, 1976).

39. *I.W.W. Songs: To Fan the Flames of Discontent*; Chaplin, *Wobbly*, 200; Nelson, *Repression and Recovery*, 58–66; Joe Hill, quoted in *Solidarity*, December 29, 1914; Adler, *Man Who Never Died*, 12; Bird et al., *Solidarity Forever*, 217; Greenway, *American Folksongs of Protest*, 174–89; R. Serge Denisoff, *Great Day Coming: Folk Music and the American Left* (Urbana: University of Illinois Press, 1971), 9. Denisoff suggests that the IWW used the Salvation Army as a model to create its "Little Red Songbook," but the evidence for this connection is unpersuasive.

40. Chaplin, *Wobbly*, 146; Wallace Stegner, *Joe Hill: A Biographical Novel* (1950; reprint, New York: Penguin Books, 1990), 11; Walter B. Rideout, *The Radical Novel in the United States, 1900–1954: Some Interrelations of Literature and Society* (1956; reprint, New York: Columbia University Press, 1992), 93; James Jones, *From Here to Eternity* (1951; reprint, New York: Avon Books, 1975), 612. See also Donald E. Winters Jr., *The Soul of the Wobblies: The I.W.W., Religion, and American Culture in the Progressive Era, 1905–1917* (Westport, Conn.: Greenwood Press, 1985).

41. Adler, *Man Who Never Died*, 12; Kornbluh, *Rebel Voices*, 29–30, 132–33; Greenway, *American Folksongs of Protest*, 173–76; John Pietaro, "Solidarity Forever: The IWW and the Protest Song," online on Pietaro's blog, "The Cultural Worker," http://theculturalworker.blogspot.com/2010/12/solidarity-forever-iww-and-protest-song.html.

42. Hester L. Furey, "IWW Songs as Modernist Poetry," *Journal of the Midwest Modern Language Association* 34, no. 2 (2001): 51 (quotation from Bruce ("Utah") Phillips); Kornbluh, *Rebel Voices*, vii, 442; Chaplin, *Wobbly*, 148, 199.

43. Furey, "IWW Songs as Modernist Poetry," 53.

44. Dubofsky, *We Shall Be All*, 200; Adler, *Man Who Never Died*, 3; Chaplin, *Wobbly*, 203; Chaplin, "Why I Wrote 'Solidarity Forever,'" 24; Bird et al., *Solidarity Forever*, 21–28, 108–13, quotation 21; Renshaw, *Wobblies*, ch. 8.

45. Chaplin, *Wobbly*, 89; 184, 186; Kornbluh, *Rebel Voices*, 133–34, 143, 145–49; Adler, *Man Who Never Died*, 18–22.

46. Tony Bubka, "Time to Organize! The IWW Stickerettes," *American West* 5, no. 1 (1968): 21–22, 25–26; Chaplin, *Wobbly*, 194–96, 205–6.

47. Bernard Bailyn et. al., *The Great Republic: A History of the American People* (Boston: Little, Brown, 1977), 1017–27; Michael Kazin, *A Godly Hero: The Life of William Jennings Bryan* (New York: Anchor Books, 2006), 232–39; Dubofsky, *We Shall Be All*, 200, 204–6.

48. Adler, *Man Who Never Died*, 3, 8, quotation 3; Dubofsky, *We Shall Be All*, 98–113, 215–27, quotation 215; Renshaw, *Wobblies*, 93–95; James W. Silver, "Mississippi: The Closed Society," *Journal of Southern History* 30, no. 1 (1964): 3–34; Scott Nearing, introduction to *Bars and Shadows: The Prison Poems of Ralph Chaplin* (New York: Leonard Press, 1922), 9; Clement Eaton, *The Freedom-of-Thought Struggle in the Old South* (New York: Harper & Row, 1964); Michael Cohen, "'The Ku Klux Government': Vigilantism, Lynching, and the Repression of the IWW," *Journal for the Study of Radicalism* 1, no. 1 (2006): 31–56.

49. Renshaw, *Wobblies*, 160–64; Dubofsky, *We Shall Be All*, 223–24.

50. Chaplin, *Wobbly*, 196, 206–10; Renshaw, *Wobblies*, 161–63; Dubofsky, *We Shall Be All*, 223–24; Adler, *Man Who Never Died*, 1–24, quotation 4. Adler's brilliant book all but erases lingering questions over Hill's innocence or guilt. Deeply researched and beautifully written, it uncovers new evidence, including a letter found in an attic in Michigan that exonerates Hill and points to the guilt of another man in the murder of the grocer.

51. Adler, *Man Who Never Died*, 1–24, quotation 17, 19; Chaplin, *Wobbly*, 150.

52. Bubka, "Time to Organize," 25; Chaplin, *Wobbly*, 209; Dubofsky, *We Shall Be All*, 204, 219, 226, 231–33. The "Young Man" stickerette, written by Wallace D. Wattles, has often been attributed to Jack London. See Ora Ellen Cox, "The Socialist Party in Indiana Since 1896," *Indiana Magazine of History* 12, no. 2 (1916): 127.

53. Chaplin, *Wobbly*, 220–24; Dubofsky, *We Shall Be All*, 233.

54. Chaplin, *Wobbly*, 227–28.

55. Chaplin, *Wobbly*, 226, 247; Salter, "Reflections on Ralph Chaplin," 4; Nelson, *Repression and Recovery*, 59; Dubofsky, *We Shall Be All*, 247–48.

56. Dubofsky, *We Shall Be All*, 204, 246–50; Chaplin, *Wobbly*, 220; Harrison George, ed., *Mass Violence in America: The I.W.W. Trial* (New York: Arno Press, 1969), 71; *United States v. Haywood, et al.*, IWW Collection, box 109, Archives of Labor and Urban Affairs, Wayne State University; Mark W. Van Wienen, *Partisans and Poets: The Political Work of American Poetry in the Great War* (New York: Cambridge University Press, 1997), 190–200.

57. Chaplin was briefly released on appeal, but the Supreme Court refused to review the IWW cases. See Chaplin, *Wobbly*, 250–83, 306, 309–10, 318–19, 418, quotations 257, 309, 318, 418; Salter, "Reflections on Ralph Chaplin," 11; Chaplin, "Confessions of a Radical," part 2, 10, which includes an image of his Christ portrait, done in a traditional and respectful style: Jesus holds a candle, a halo of light surrounds his head, and he looks up to heaven; Morgan Miller email to authors, September 13, 27, 2012. We are grateful to Morgan Miller for pointing out the influence of the Mennonites on Chaplin.

58. Chaplin, *Bars and Shadows*, 25; Chaplin, *Wobbly*, 250, 311, 321–24; Aaron Abell, "Revolutionist Turned Reformer," *The Review of Politics* 11, no. 2 (1949): 260; Edith Chaplin to First Lady Florence Harding, undated letter [1923], Ralph Chaplin Papers, Box 2, Folder 7, WSHS; Laura Harlan to Edith Chaplin, February 27, 1923, Box 2, Folder 7, WSHS; President Harding's Letter of Commutation, June 19, 1923, Ralph Chaplin Papers, Box 5, Folder 28, WSHS.

59. Chaplin, "Confessions of a Radical," part 2, 10; Abell, "Revolutionist Turned Reformer," 260; Fred W. Thompson and Jon Bekken, *The Industrial Workers of the World: Its First 100 Years* (Cincinnati: Industrial Workers of the World, 2006), 142–43; John S. Gambs, *The Decline of the I.W.W.* (New York: Columbia University Press, 1932), 243–51; "The Communist Party of America (1919–1946) Membership Figures," http://www.marxisthistory.org/subject/usa/eam/cpamembership.html; Dubofsky, *We Shall Be All*, 264–66. As Morgan Miller notes, in the 1920s Wobblies no longer enjoyed hegemony among radical labor organizations. Miller, email to authors, September 27, 2012. We are immensely grateful to Miller for sharing his deep knowledge of the Wobblies with us.

60. As a Communist song, "Solidarity Forever" was probably more popular in eastern cities than it had been as an IWW song, but less popular in the western United States. This was because of the Communist Party USA's greater influence in eastern cities.

61. "Five Injured in Riot as Police Drive Reds from City Hall Park," *New York Times*, February 28, 1930; "Millions March against 'Imperialism,'" *Pittsburgh Courier*, May 10, 1930; "15,000 Anti-War Folk Parade in New York," *Daily Boston Globe*, August 5, 1934; "20,000 Hear Thomas Point Way to Reds," *New York Times*, November 28, 1935.

62. Ronald D. Cohen and Dave Samuelson, *Songs for Political Action: Folk Music, Topical Songs, and the American Left* (Hambergen, Germany: Bear Family Records, 1996), 59, 65; Greenway, *American Folksongs*, 181–82. According to Cohen and Samuelson, the Manhattan Chorus was also Communist. The first stanza of Chaplin's "Solidarity Forever" becomes the third stanza of the Almanac Singers' version of the song.

63. Wilbur Patterson Thirkfield, "An Untrained Minister and a Declining Church," *Baltimore Afro-American*, July 22, 1933, 7. The demonstration in which the black Communist was killed is covered in "Harlem 'Reds' Protest Race Comrade's Murder," *Pittsburgh Courier*, July 12, 1930.

64. Chaplin, *Wobbly*, 361; Chaplin, "Confessions of a Radical," part 2, 11.

65. Chaplin, *Wobbly*, 360; Robertson, *Worshipping Walt*, 50, 246–51, 270; Frederic Babcock, "Beginning of a Friendship," *Journal of the Illinois State Historical Society* 45, no. 4 (1952): 326.

66. Chaplin, "Resignation Letter," April 20, 1936, included in General Organization Bulletins (the IWW's Internal newsletter) for 1936, collection of Morgan Miller; Morgan Miller, email to authors, September 13, 28, 2012; Chaplin, *Wobbly*, 364–65. We are deeply grateful to Morgan Miller for sending us the IWW's General Organization Bulletins for 1936.

67. Chaplin, *Wobbly*, 338, 352–419, quotations 356, 357, 404. See also John Stauffer, "Fighting the Devil with His Own Fire," in Andrew Delbanco, *The Abolitionist Imagination* (Cambridge: Harvard University Press, 2012), 57–80.

68. Chaplin, *Wobbly*, 410, 412, 416, 417.

69. Ralph Chaplin, "Gimmicks, Gimme and the Grace of God," *Partners: The Magazine of Labor and Management* 4, no. 7 (1950): 7–11, copy in the Ralph Chaplin Papers, WSHS; Peter F. Drucker, "The New Society, I: Revolution by Mass Production," *Harper's Magazine*, September 1949, in the Ralph Chaplin Papers, WSHS; Peter F. Drucker, "Is Management Legitimate? The New Society, Part II," *Harper's Magazine*, October 1949; Peter F. Drucker, "The Insecurity of Labor Unions: The New Society, Part III," *Harper's Magazine*, November 1949, all three essays in the Ralph Chaplin Papers, WSHS; Chaplin, *Wobbly*, 408–27; John Kenneth Galbraith, *American Capitalism: The Concept of Countervailing Power* (1952; reprint, New Brunswick, N.J.: Transaction, 2008); Chaplin, "Why I Wrote 'Solidarity Forever,'" 27, 73.

70. Chaplin, *Wobbly*, 417; Chaplin, "Why I Wrote 'Solidarity Forever,'" 27.

71. Chaplin, "Why I Wrote 'Solidarity Forever,'" 26–27.

72. Chaplin, "Why I Wrote 'Solidarity Forever,'" 26–27; Timothy P. Lynch, "'Sit Down! Sit Down!' Songs of the General Motors Strike, 1936–1937," *Michigan Historical Review* 22, no. 2 (1996): 1–47; Robert Dallek, "Modernizing the Republic, 1920 to the Present," in *The Great Republic: A History of the American People*, 4th ed. (Lexington, Mass.: D. C. Heath, 1992), 402; W. E. B. Du Bois, "As the Crow Flies: Now—Anything Can Happen!," *New York Amsterdam News*, November 20, 1943, 12.

73. "UAW Local 6888," http://www.uawlocal6888.org/.

74. Jim Pope, "Worker Lawmaking, Sit-Down Strikes, and the Shaping of American Industrial Relations, 1935–1958," *Law and History Review* 24, no. 1 (2006): 49–55, 75, 84, 99, quotation 50.

75. Edith Fowke and Joe Glazer, eds., *Songs of Work and Freedom* (Chicago: Labor Division of Roosevelt University, 1960), 5, 206. Its precursor was *The AFL-CIO Songbook* (Washington: AFL-CIO Dept. of Education, 1958). The AFL and CIO merged in 1955.

76. Fowke and Glazer, *Songs of Work and Freedom*, 13; Chaplin, "Why I Wrote 'Solidarity Forever,'" 27; Ralph Chaplin, "Time to Sing Out for a Cause, Says 'Solidarity Forever' Author," *Work*, May 1960, 10, copy in the Ralph Chaplin Papers, WSHS.

77. Chaplin, "Time to Sing Out," 10; Ed Marciniak, "Unionists Don't Sing Any More: Too Much 'Business Unionism,'" *Work*, September 1958, 7, copy in the Ralph Chaplin Papers, WSHS.

78. Chaplin, "Time to Sing Out," 10; "Humphrey Woos Labor with Song," *New York Times*, March 13, 1960, copy in the Ralph Chaplin Papers, WSHS; Chaplin, "Why I Wrote 'Solidarity Forever,'" 27.

79. Chaplin, "Time to Sing Out," 10.

80. Chaplin, "Confessions of a Radical," part 2, 11; Chaplin, *Wobbly*, 318–19, 426–27. During World War II Chaplin worked for the Red Cross, the USO, and the Selective Service as a reemployment officer, helping veterans find jobs. He received a merit award from President Truman for his service with the Red Cross. See "The American National Red Cross to Ralph Chaplin" and "Selective Service System, Certificate of Service," Ralph Chaplin Papers, Box 1, Folder 27, WSHS.

81. Chaplin, *Wobbly*, 420; Ralph Chaplin, "Held in Trust for You," *Tower* 2, no. 7 (1944), Ralph Chaplin Papers, Box 1, Folder 13, WSHS.

82. Paul J. Murphy to Ralph Chaplin, December 3, 1948, Ralph Chaplin Papers, WSHS. On Murphy, see the obituary, "Rev. Paul J. Murphy, Pornography Opponent, 82," *New York Times*, August 29, 1990. For sixteen years Murphy served as director of St. Joseph's Retreat League. He was president of Morality in Media, an antipornography organization, from 1985 to 1988.

83. Paul J. Murphy to Chaplin, January 6, 1949; Murphy to Chaplin, April 4, 1949, in Ralph Chaplin Papers, WSHS; Joseph McSorley to Ralph Chaplin, January 18, 1949, Ralph Chaplin Papers, WSHS; Jim Forest, *All Is Grace: A Biography of Dorothy Day* (Maryknoll, N.Y.: Orbis Books, 2011), 28–29, 59–60, 110, 141, quotation 60; Salter, "Reflections on Ralph Chaplin," 15.

84. "Baptism" of Ralph Chaplin, December 23, 1949, St. Patrick Catholic Church, 1122 North Jay St., Tacoma, Washington; "Holy Sacrament of Confirmation" of Ralph Chaplin, December 21, 1952, Church of Christ the King, Evergreen, Colorado, in Ralph Chaplin Papers, Box 2, Folder 27, WSHS; Roger Baldwin to Bruce Le Roy, October 10, 1967, Ralph Chaplin Papers, WSHS; Calendar for October 1950, Ralph Chaplin Papers, Box 1, Folder 40, WSHS; McSorley to Chaplin, October 9, 1950; Murphy to Chaplin, December 16, 1950, Ralph Chaplin Papers, WSHS; Salter, "Reflections on Ralph Chaplin," 15–17.

85. John Sheerin, editor, *Catholic World*, to Ralph Chaplin, January 7, 1950; McSorley to Chaplin, September 9, 1950; Murphy to Chaplin, September 29, 1950, all in Ralph Chaplin Papers, WSHS; Ralph Chaplin, "Religion and the Workingman," *Catholic World*, September 1950, 406–12, quotations 408, 409, 412; Salter, "Reflections on Ralph Chaplin," 17.

86. Ralph Chaplin, letter to the editor, *National Review*, December 28, 1955, 31; William F. Buckley Jr. to Ralph Chaplin, January 6, 1956, Ralph Chaplin Papers, Box 2, Folder 5, WSHS.

87. Senator Harry P. Cain to Ralph Chaplin, March 15, 1947, Ralph Chaplin Papers, Box 2, Folder 3, WSHS; Salter, "Reflections on Ralph Chaplin," 6. The scholars who have largely dismissed Chaplin for his alleged right turn include Dubofsky, *We Shall Be All*, 532; Joseph Conlin, *Big*

Bill Haywood and the Radical Union Movement (Syracuse, N.Y.: Syracuse University Press, 1969), 217; Philip Foner, *The Industrial Workers of the World, 1905–1917* (New York: International Publishers, 1965), 155; Len De Caux, *The Living Spirit of the Wobblies* (New York: International Publishers, 1965), 155. Salter's essay is an invaluable corrective to these dismissive treatments of Chaplin.

88. Examples of essays in *National Review* emphasizing Buckley's hatred of bureaucracy and regimentation and his preference for anarchy over statism during Chaplin's life are E. V. Kuehnelt-Leddihn, "Letter from the Continent: The Blight of Bureaucracy," *National Review*, April 13, 1957, 354; Murray N. Rothbard, "In a Glorious—and Radical—Tradition," *National Review*, June 21, 1958, 14–15; Frank S. Meyer, "The Roots of Libertarian Conservatism," *National Review*, April 6, 1957, 331–32, 339. On Buckley, see Carl T. Bogus, *William F. Buckley Jr. and the Rise of American Conservatism* (New York: Bloomsbury, 2001).

89. Chaplin, *Wobbly*, 254–57, 261–69, 270–83, 307–24, 400–19; Salter, "Reflections on Ralph Chaplin," 15–18. Chief Leschi was exonerated in the slaying of a militia officer. See Rebecca Cook, "Nisqually Indian Chief Cleared in Slaying," http://groups.yahoo.com/group/NatNews/message/36848?var=1.

90. Stegner, *Joe Hill*, 11; Rideout, *Radical Novel*, 93; Nelson, *Repression and Recovery*, 62.

91. Anthony Arthur, *Radical Innocent: Upton Sinclair* (New York: Random House, 2006); Kevin Mattson, *Upton Sinclair and the Other American Century* (New York: John Wiley & Sons, 2006); Upton Sinclair, *The Jungle: A Norton Critical Edition*, ed. Clare Virginia Eby (New York: Norton, 2003); Sinclair, *Singing Jailbirds*. In writing *The Jungle*, Sinclair said he tried to do for Chicago's meatpacking workers what Stowe had done for antebellum slaves. "In many respects I had 'Uncle Tom's Cabin' in mind as a model of what I wished to do," he wrote after *The Jungle* prompted the passage of the Food and Drug Act. He called meatpacking workers "modern wage slaves" and said he had hoped to effect a Socialist revolution that would abolish wage slavery. But his novel was read as a consumerist critique against the *quality* of meat rather than an exposé of the dehumanization of workers. "I wished to frighten the country by a picture of what its industrial masters were doing to their victims; entirely by chance I had stumbled on another discovery—what they were doing to the meat-supply of the civilized world. In other words, I aimed at the public's heart, and by accident I hit it in the stomach." See Upton Sinclair, "What Life Means to Me," *Cosmopolitan* 44 (October 1906): 593–94, reprinted in *The Jungle*, 299 (emphasis added), 350, 351.

92. Sinclair, *Singing Jailbirds*, 87–95; Arthur, *Radical Innocent*, 189.

93. Sinclair, *Singing Jailbirds*, 20–24.

94. Sinclair, *Singing Jailbirds*, 77–78.

95. Sinclair, *Singing Jailbirds*, 83–86.

96. Upton Sinclair, "Editorial," *New York Times*, December 23, 1928; Max Beerbohm, "Punch, Wifebeater and Street Rowdy," *New York Times*, October 5, 1924. Scholars have almost entirely ignored *Singing Jailbirds*.

97. Upton Sinclair, "Editorial," *New York Times*, December 23, 1928; *Boston Daily Globe*, May 24, 1925; *New York Times*, January 15, 1927; C. Hooper Trask, "Upton Sinclair Abroad," *New York Times*, May 20, 1928 (quoted); *Wall Street Journal*, December 6, 1928; John Steele, "British Cabinet Aids London's New Socialist Theater," *Chicago Daily Tribune*, November 15, 1929; *New York Times*, February 10, 1930; *New York Times*, November 23, 1934.

98. Michael Denning, *The Cultural Front: The Laboring of American Culture in the Twentieth Century* (London: Verso Books, 1997), 163–70, quotation 163; Virginia Spencer Carr, *Dos Passos: A Life* (Garden City, N.Y.: Doubleday, 1984), 536; Townsend Ludington, *John Dos Passos: A Twentieth Century Odyssey* (New York: E. P. Dutton, 1980), 352–55.

99. Denning, *Cultural Front*, 163–70; Carr, *Dos Passos*, 348–51, 380–85, 536, quotation 536; Ludington, *John Dos Passos*, 353–59; Jean-Paul Sartre, "John Dos Passos and 1919," in *Literary Philosophical Essays* (New York: Collier, 1962), 103.

100. Denning, *Cultural Front*, 169. On Dos Passos's use of history, see Barbara Foley, "From *U.S.A.* to *Ragtime*: Notes on the Forms of Historical Consciousness in Modern Fiction," *American Literature* 50 (March 1978): 85–105; Barbara Foley, "History, Fiction, and Satirical Form: The Example of Dos Passos' 1919," *Genre* 12 (Fall 1979): 357–78; Barbara Foley, "The Treatment of Time in *The Big Money*: An Examination of Ideology and Literary Form," *Modern Fiction Studies* 26 (Autumn 1980): 447–67.

101. John Dos Passos, *The 42nd Parallel, First in the Trilogy U.S.A.* (New York: Signet 1969), 312, 354.

102. Dos Passos to Chaplin, undated letter, Ralph Chaplin Papers, Box 2, Folder 26, WSHS; Dos Passos to Chaplin, 1933, Box 1, Ralph Chaplin Papers, University of Michigan, Special Collections Library; Chaplin, *Wobbly*, 336–37; Thomas Larson, "The Good Shoemaker and the Poor Fish Peddler," *San Diego Reader*, August 18, 2005, http://www.sandiegoreader.com/news/2005/aug/18/good-shoemaker-and-poor-fish-peddler/. Dos Passos was deeply sympathetic to the Wobblies; see Carr, *Dos Passos*, 173. In 1933 Chaplin invited Dos Passos to contribute to the Wobbly organ, *Industrial Worker*, but Dos Passos declined owing to sickness and "stacked up work." But he expressed great admiration for *Industrial Worker* and said Chaplin's editorials "hit nearer the truth than those in most labor publications" (Dos Passos to Chaplin, 1933).

103. Dos Passos, *The 42nd Parallel*, 50–52, 101–2, 112–14, 121, 144, quotation 121; John Dos Passos, *Nineteen Nineteen: Second in the Trilogy U.S.A.* (New York: Signet 1969), 281–82; John Trombold, "Popular Songs as Revolutionary Culture in John Dos Passos' 'U.S.A.' and Other Early Works," *Journal of Modern Literature* 19, no. 2 (1995): 289–316, esp. 309–10; Arnold Goldman, "Dos Passos and His U.S.A.," *New Literary History* 1, no. 3 (1970): 471–83.

104. Dos Passos, *The 42nd Parallel*, 121, 138, 144.

105. John Dos Passos, *The Big Money: Third in the Trilogy U.S.A.* (New York: Signet 1969), 468–69; Carr, *Dos Passos*, 262, 550–51; Denning, *Cultural Front*, p. 504n7.

Dos Passos tacitly recognized the need for Wobblies to rewrite "John Brown's Body" and the "Battle Hymn" in order to reclaim national ideals of freedom. He was fascinated by both "John Brown's Body" and "Solidarity Forever." His first critically acclaimed novel, *Three Soldiers* (1921), ends with the protagonist identifying with John Brown and planning a new version of the John Brown song.

John Andrews, a World War I soldier, has deserted and now lives in Paris. Andrews changes his name on his passport to John Brown, and after doing so he hears "John Brown's Body" so vividly "that he thought for an instant someone must be standing beside him singing it." Hearing the song inspires him to expand it into a symphony, "The Body and Soul of John Brown."

After finishing the first movement, Andrews realizes that his identification with Brown stemmed from his own sense of enslavement. As a soldier he had felt himself a slave "on a treadmill. . . . Half by accident he had managed to free himself from the treadmill. Couldn't he have helped others?" He realizes that "he had not lived up to the name of John Brown." The novel ends with an M.P. arresting him for desertion, a capital crime.

In shifting his musical focus from "John Brown's Body" in *Three Soldiers* to "Solidarity Forever" in *U.S.A.*, Dos Passos implies the need for new language to restore the ideals of freedom. Andrews, like Brown, hopes to draw attention to the dehumanization of individuals. In *U.S.A.* capitalists replace the military as the source of dehumanization, and the Wobblies and "Solidarity Forever" replace Andrews and "John Brown's Body" as the noble but failed efforts to fight such dehumanizing forces. Dos Passos was himself a World War I veteran, and, according to Ludington, John Andrews was "the most nearly autobiographical character" in the novel. See Dos Passos, *Three Soldiers* (1921; reprinted, New York: Carroll & Graf, 1988), 410–33, quotations 414, 415, 420, 431; Ludington, *John Dos Passos*, 179; Carr, *Dos Passos*, 171.

106. On Dos Passos's ideological shift, see Carr, *Dos Passos*, 171–72, 357–77, 518–33, quotation 518; Denning, *Cultural Front*, 167, 504n7; Ludington, *John Dos Passos*, xvii–xviii, 377, 389–90, 404–5, 500–504; John P. Diggins, "Dos Passos and Veblen's Villains," *Antioch Review* 23, no. 4 (1963–64): 485–500; Daniel Aaron, "The Riddle of John Dos Passos," *Harper's*, March 1962, 55–60.

107. Diggins, "Dos Passos and Veblen's Villains," 485; John Dos Passos, introduction to William F. Buckley Jr., *Up from Liberalism* (New York: McDowell, Obolensky, 1959), xi–xvi; Ludington, *John Dos Passos*, 500.

108. Carr, *Dos Passos*, 534; Diggins, "Dos Passos and Veblen's Villains," 485–86; Dos Passos, *The 42nd Parallel*, 354.

109. Mattathias Schwartz, "Pre-Occupied: The Origins and Future of Occupy Wall Street," *New Yorker*, November 28, 2011, 30, 32, 33, quotations 32, 33; "Occupy Wall Street," http://occupywallst.org/about/; "NYC Metro Raging Grannies and Their Daughters: Songs to Sing at Occupy Wall Street," http://nycmetro.raginggrannies.org/OccupyWallStreet.htm.

110. Schwartz, "Pre-Occupied," 34.

CHAPTER VII

1. William G. McLoughlin Jr., *Billy Sunday Was His Real Name* (Chicago: University of Chicago Press, 1955), xvii–xxix, quotations xvii; Roger A. Bruns, *Preacher: Billy Sunday and Big-Time American Evangelism* (New York: Norton, 1992), 202–24; Lyle W. Dorsett, *Billy Sunday and the Redemption of Urban America* (1990; reprint, Macon, Ga.: Mercer University Press, 2004), 105–8; Robert F. Martin, *Hero of the Heartland: Billy Sunday and the Transformation of American Society, 1862–1935* (Bloomington: Indiana University Press, 2002), 118–22; W. A. Firstenberger, *In Rare Form: A Pictorial History of Baseball Evangelist Billy Sunday* (Iowa City: University of Iowa Press, 2005), 60–63; William A. "Billy" Sunday, *The Sawdust Trail: Billy Sunday in His Own Words* (Iowa City: University of Iowa Press, 2005), 77–81; Karen Gullen, ed., *Billy Sunday Speaks* (New York: Chelsea House, 1970); Francis Hackett, "Billy Sunday, Salesman," *New Republic*, April 28, 1917, 370–72; "Billy's Rubicon," *Literary Digest*, April 21, 1917, 1168; Joseph Collins, "Revivals, Past and Present," *Harper's Monthly* 135 (November 1917): 856–65. See especially Robert Shuster, ed., *The*

Papers of William and Helen Sunday, Microform, 29 reels, Andover-Harvard Theological Library (hereafter Sunday Papers). McLoughlin's biography remains the most thorough and analytically sophisticated.

2. Bruns, *Preacher*, 202–5, quotations 204; McLoughlin, *Billy Sunday*, xviii–xxii, quotation xviii.

3. McLoughlin, *Billy Sunday*, xix–xxi, 5, quotation xix; Bruns, *Preacher*, 204–7.

4. McLoughlin, *Billy Sunday*, xix–xx, quotation 19; Bruns, *Preacher*, 207–9.

5. McLoughlin, *Billy Sunday*, xix–xxi, quotations xx; Bruns, *Preacher*, 208–9.

6. McLoughlin, *Billy Sunday*, xix–xxi, xvi, quotations xx; Bruns, *Preacher*, 207–10, quotation 209. Sunday had declined an offer of $1 million to star in a Hollywood film, and another offer to preach at a circus for $2,000 a day, he said.

7. McLoughlin, *Billy Sunday*, xxi–xxii, quotations xxi–xxii; Bruns, *Preacher*, 205–10, quotation 210; undated clipping, Sunday Papers, Reel 25 (quoted); Billy Sunday, "Sermons, New York Campaign," holograph, Sunday Papers, Reel 9. Sunday likened Germany to hell: "If you turn hell upside down, you will find 'Made in Germany' stamped on the bottom." Sunday was himself part German, his great-grandfather Heinrich Sundag having immigrated in the early nineteenth century and changed his name to Sunday. In his sermon he distinguished the nation from the people. See Firstenberger, *In Rare Form*, 61.

8. Bruns, *Preacher*, 210; McLoughlin, *Billy Sunday*, xxi–xxii. Sunday got so excited promoting the war effort that soon after his New York campaign, he announced his intention to go to France to inspire the troops and shoot Germans. "I'll bet that I know half the boys over there now," he declared in February 1918. "If General Pershing will only stake me to a rifle so that I can get a crack at that dirty German bunch, I'll be satisfied." But soon after his announcement, President Wilson summoned him to the White House and asked him to stay home, where his services were more urgently needed. "We have speakers and singers and entertainers enough overseas," Wilson told him. "Not everyone here at home is doing his part like the soldiers are and you have the ears of the people and can go from city to city." Sunday agreed, shaking Wilson's hand: "Mr. President, your wish is law with me." See David T. Morgan, "The Revivalist as Patriot: Billy Sunday and World War I," *Journal of Presbyterian History*, Summer 1973, 213; *Washington Post*, February 18, 1918; Bruns, *Preacher*, 257–58.

9. McLoughlin, *Billy Sunday*, xxiv–xxix; Bruns, *Preacher*, 217–18, 222–24, quotations 217. Sunday did not seek converts on the opening night of his "campaigns," as his revivals were called. And he kept audiences, and his staff, in the dark about when the first call for accepting Jesus would come, partly to add to the excitement of his campaigns. In New York he requested the first call for faith on April 19, the twelfth day of the campaign.

10. McLoughlin, *Billy Sunday*, 84; "'Going Fine,' Sunday Says at the End of Week," *Boston Daily Globe*, April 11, 1915; "Billy Sunday and Boston," *Pacific*, November 23, 1916, 5. For a few among many examples of Sunday's treating the "Battle Hymn" as his anthem, see "Sunday Opens War on the Unitarians," *New York Times*, April 11, 1915; "I.W.W. Flanks Sunday as He Baffles Devil," *New-York Tribune*, April 11, 1915; "'Young America,' Asleep, Dreams of Billy Sunday," *New York Times*, May 6, 1917; "Billy Sunday in Sizzling Sermon Jolts Aurora Sin," *Chicago Daily Tribune*, April 11, 1927.

11. Paul Boyer, *When Time Shall Be No More: Prophecy Belief in Modern American Culture* (Cambridge: Harvard University Press, 1992), 100–105, quotation 101; Firstenberger, *In Rare Form*, 62.

12. *Boston Herald*, December 14, 1916; McLoughlin, *Billy Sunday*, 127–28.

13. H. L. Mencken, *Prejudices*, fourth series (1924; reprint, New York: Octagon Books, 1977), 78–79; George M. Marsden, *Fundamentalism and American Culture: The Shaping of Twentieth-Century Evangelicalism, 1870–1925* (New York: Oxford University Press, 1980), 1.

14. Sunday, *The Sawdust Trail*, 1–4; Martin, *Hero of the Heartland*, 1–6; Dorsett, *Billy Sunday*, 6–8.

15. Sunday, *The Sawdust Trail*, 3–15; Martin, *Hero of the Heartland*, 2–11; Dorsett, *Billy Sunday*, 7–9.

16. Sunday, *Sawdust Trail*, 21–29, 4–7, 18–19, quotation 26; Martin, *Hero of the Heartland*, 4–7; Dorsett, *Billy Sunday*, 9–13.

17. Sunday, *Sawdust Trail*, 27–36, quotation 36; Martin, *Hero of the Heartland*, 4–23; Dorsett, *Billy Sunday*, 12–16; Bruns, *Preacher*, 28–32.

18. Sunday, *Sawdust Trail*, 36–44, quotation 41; Martin, *Hero of the Heartland*, 7–23, 25–30; Dorsett, *Billy Sunday*, 15–22.

19. Dorsett, *Billy Sunday*, 20–26, quotation 22; Gullen, *Billy Sunday Speaks*, 5; Martin, *Hero of the Heartland*, 25–30; Sunday, *Sawdust Trail*, 43–36; Bruns, *Preacher*, 33–45.

20. Sunday, *Sawdust Trail*, 47–52, quotations 49–50; McLaughlin, *Billy Sunday*, 1–7, quotation 6; Martin, *Hero of the Heartland*, 32–40; Dorsett, *Billy Sunday*, 23–29.

21. Sunday, *Sawdust Trail*, 48–51 quotations 48, 50, 51; Dorsett, *Billy Sunday*, 23–31; Martin, *Hero of the Heartland*, 32–37.

22. Sunday, *Sawdust Trail*, 50–51; Dorsett, *Billy Sunday*, 23–31; Martin, *Hero of the Heartland*, 32–37; McLoughlin, *Billy Sunday*, 6–8.

23. Sunday, *Sawdust Trail*, 52–54, quotation 53; McLoughlin, *Billy Sunday*, 5.

24. Dorsett, *Billy Sunday*, 34–38.

25. Sunday, *Sawdust Trail*, 63, 64 (quoted); Dorsett, *Billy Sunday*, 32–36.

26. Sunday, *Sawdust Trail*, 69–71; Dorsett, *Billy Sunday*, 35–42; Martin, *Hero of the Heartland*, 35–44.

27. Sunday, *Sawdust Trail*, 69–71, quotation 70; Dorsett, *Billy Sunday*, 35–42; Martin, *Hero of the Heartland*, 35–44.

28. Walter Rauschenbusch, *Christianity and the Social Crisis* (New York: Macmillan, 1907), 60–61 (quoted); Dorsett, *Billy Sunday*, 43–52; McLoughlin, *Billy Sunday*, 7–10; Sunday, *Sawdust Trail*, 82–86.

29. Sunday, *Sawdust Trail*, 82–86, quotation 84; Dorsett, *Billy Sunday*, 43–52.

30. Dorsett, *Billy Sunday*, 43–52; Marsden, *Fundamentalism and American Culture*, 3–48. The growing divide between modernists and evangelicals stemmed in part from the influence of modern scholarship. Darwinism, which contradicted Genesis, and other scientific theories led modernists to interpret the Bible as one would a work of literature and *discover* the nature of God within it. By contrast, evangelicals believed that God was *revealed*, not discovered, in the Bible. The Bible was the inspired Word of God.

31. Rauschenbusch, *Christianity and the Social Crisis*, 45, 65, 72; Dorsett, *Billy Sunday*, 45–47.

32. Dorsett, *Billy Sunday*, 45–47.

33. McLoughlin, *Billy Sunday*, 8–9; Dorsett, *Billy Sunday*, 44–52.

34. Dorsett, *Billy Sunday*, 54, 55 (quoted); McLoughlin, *Billy Sunday*, 8–10.

35. Dorsett, *Billy Sunday*, 56–68; McLoughlin, *Billy Sunday*, 8–23.

36. Dorsett, *Billy Sunday*, 61–72; McLoughlin, *Billy Sunday*, 9–25.

37. Dorsett, *Billy Sunday*, 68–76, quotation 71; Gullen, *Billy Sunday Speaks*, 103.

38. Dorsett, *Billy Sunday*, 70–76.

39. Dorsett, *Billy Sunday*, 76–77 (quoted).

40. McLoughlin, *Billy Sunday*, 23; Dorsett, *Billy Sunday*, 22 (quoted).

41. McLoughlin, *Billy Sunday*, 26–29, quotations 27.

42. Richard Hofstadter, *Anti-Intellectualism in American Life* (New York: Vintage Books, 1962), 114–22, quotations 114, 115; Clifford Putney, *Muscular Christianity: Manhood and Sports in Protestant America, 1880–1920* (Cambridge: Harvard University Press, 2001), 59–60; Constance Rourke, *American Humor: A Study of the National Character* (1931; reprint, Tallahassee: Florida State University Press, 1959); Nicole Etcheson, "Manliness and the Political Culture of the Old Northwest, 1790–1860," *Journal of the Early Republic* 15, no. 1 (1995): 59–77.

43. Lindsay Denison, "The Rev. Billy Sunday and His War on the Devil," *American Magazine* 64, no. 5 (1907): 451–68, quotation 452; McLoughlin, *Billy Sunday*, 28–29.

44. Firstenberger, *In Rare Form*, 120–23; McLoughlin, *Billy Sunday*, 49, 114–17. Sunday's lifetime total converts have been estimated at 1.25 million.

45. McLoughlin, *Billy Sunday*, 35–37, 121, 146–49, 224–25 suggests a few of these connections.

46. Francis Hackett, "Billy Sunday, Salesman," *New Republic*, April 28, 1917, 370–72, quotation 371; Margaret Bendroth, "Why Women Loved Billy Sunday: Urban Revivalism and Popular Entertainment in Early Twentieth-Century America," *Religion and American Culture* 14, no. 2 (2004): 251–71; Putney, *Muscular Christianity*, 1–44, 58–61, quotation from 25; June Hadden Hobbs, *I Sing for I Cannot Be Silent: The Feminization of American Hymnody, 1870–1920* (Pittsburgh: University of Pittsburgh Press, 1997), 144.

47. McLoughlin, *Billy Sunday*, 36–37.

48. Bruns, *Preacher*, 204; McLoughlin, *Billy Sunday*, 35–36; Michael McGerr, *A Fierce Discontent: The Rise and Fall of the Progressive Movement in America, 1870–1920* (New York: Free Press, 2003), 77–117; Reinhold Niebuhr, "Billy Sunday: His Preachments and His Methods," *Detroit Saturday Night*, October 14, 1916 (quoted); McLoughlin, *Billy Sunday*, 36–37, 121, 146–49, 224–25; Martin, *Hero of the Heartland*, 111–14.

49. Bendroth, "Why Women Loved Billy Sunday," 251–71, quotations 251, 255; Gullen, *Billy Sunday Speaks*, 112.

50. Bruns, *Preacher*, 225–47; Martin, *Hero of the Heartland*, 116–19, quotation 117; Dorsett, *Billy Sunday*, 152–57; McLoughlin, *Billy Sunday*, 258–61.

51. Dorsett, *Billy Sunday*, 85–123, quotation 86.

52. McLoughlin, *Billy Sunday*, 75, 81, 83, 84, quotation 83; Jack Reed, "Back of Billy Sunday," *Metropolitan Magazine*, May 1915, reprinted in Daniel W. Lehman, *John Reed and the Writing of Revolution* (Athens: Ohio University Press, 2002), 254 (quoted); Bert H. Wilhoit, *Rody: Memories of Homer Rodeheaver* (Greenville, S.C.: Bob Jones University Press, 2000), xvi; Dorsett, *Billy Sunday*, 101–2; Homer Rodeheaver, *Twenty Years with Billy Sunday* (New York: Cokesbury Press, 1936).

53. Dorsett, *Billy Sunday*, 72.

54. "Adds to Sunday's 'Hell List,'" *New York Times*, May 7, 1917; Bruns, *Preacher*, 266; McLoughlin, *Billy Sunday*, 276–83.

55. Martin, *Hero of the Heartland*, 124 (quoted); Dorsett, *Billy Sunday*, 124–42; McLoughlin, *Billy Sunday*, 288. At one point during Billy Graham's early career as a revivalist, he found out that Nell Sunday was in town and invited her out for the evening. She urged him,

with tears streaming down her cheeks, "[Do not] neglect your family. I did. I traveled with Pa all over the country, and I sacrificed my children." See Martin, *Hero of the Heartland*, 124.

56. Virginia Waring, *Fred Waring and the Pennsylvanians* (Urbana: University of Illinois Press, 1997), 182–83, quotation 182; Kevin Parks, *Music and Copyright in America: Toward the Celestial Jukebox* (Chicago: American Bar Association, 2012), 109–11; McLoughlin, *Billy Sunday*, 260.

57. McLoughlin, *Billy Sunday*, 260–78, quotation 260.

58. McLoughlin, *Billy Sunday*, 288–89; Martin, *Hero of the Heartland*, 140 (quoted).

59. William Martin, *A Prophet with Honor: The Billy Graham Story* (New York: William Morrow, 1991), 52, 63–64. On Graham, see also William Martin, *With God on Our Side: The Rise of the Religious Right in America* (New York: Broadway Books, 1996); John Pollock, *Billy Graham: Evangelist to the World* (New York: Harper & Row, 1979); John Pollock, *Billy Graham: The Authorized Biography* (New York: McGraw-Hill, 1966); Steven P. Miller, *Billy Graham and the Rise of the Republican South* (Philadelphia: University of Pennsylvania Press, 2010); William G. McLoughlin, *Billy Graham: Revivalist in a Secular Age* (New York: Ronald Press, 1960).

60. Martin, *Billy Graham*, 55–62.

61. Martin, *Billy Graham*, 93; *Youth for Christ Magazine*, January 1954, Billy Graham Center Archives, Wheaton College (hereafter BGCA); Edward B. Fiske, "The Closest Thing to a White House Chaplain," *New York Times Magazine*, June 8, 1969; Peter J. Boyer, "The Big Tent: Billy Graham, Franklin Graham, and the Transformation of American Evangelicalism," *The New Yorker*, August 22, 2005, 47

62. Cliff Barrows interview with authors (quoted); BGCA, Box 2, Folder 1.

63. Billy Graham, *Hour of Decision*, BGCA.

64. Graham, *Hour of Decision*, BGCA; Jason Stevens, "Interventions: Should We Forget Reinhold Niebuhr?," *boundary 2*, Summer 2007, 137; Boyer, "Big Tent," 44. It was during the 1950s that Graham began to define himself as "a theological conservative but a social liberal," as he later put it. See Boyer, "Big Tent," 51.

65. Barrows interview; Stevens, "Interventions," 137.

66. Barrows interview; Billy Graham, *Just As I Am: The Autobiography of Billy Graham* (New York: HarperOne, 1997), 554.

67. Graham, "Morality in the United States," Speech to the Commonwealth Club of California, September 8, 1972, BGCA, and http://www.commonwealthclub.org/archive/20thcentury/72; Graham, *Hour of Decision*, BGCA.

68. Miller, *Billy Graham and the Rise of the Republican South*, 2–3, 4, 13, 18; Boyer, "Big Tent," 42, 44, 51.

69. George M. Fredrickson, *Racism: A Short History* (Princeton: Princeton University Press, 2002), 132; Dean Rusk, "Fulfilling Our Basic Commitments as a Nation," *Department of State Bulletin*, July 29, 1963; Philip A. Klinkner, with Rogers M. Smith, *The Unsteady March: The Rise and Decline of Racial Equality in America* (Chicago: University of Chicago Press, 1999), 269.

70. Boyer, "Big Tent," 42, 44, 52; Graham, *Just As I Am*, 754; http://www.cc.org/news/billy_graham_will_not_be_advisor_obama_because_his_abortion_position.

71. Martin, *With God on Our Side*, 329; Boyer, "Big Tent," 42, 44, 51–55.

72. Boyer, "Big Tent," 42, 44, 50, 51.

73. Matthew Schmitz, "Billy Graham Endorses Mitt Romney," http://www.firstthings.com/blogs/firstthoughts/2012/10/11/billy-graham-endorses-mitt-romney/; Eric Marrapodi, "Billy Graham Buys Election Ads After Romney Meeting," http://religion.blogs.cnn.com/2012/10/18/billy-graham-buys-election-ads-after-romney-meeting/

CHAPTER VIII

1. Mary Johnson, "An 'Ever Present Bone of Contention': The Heyward Shepherd Memorial," *West Virginia History* 56 (1997): 1–26; Teresa S. Moyer and Paul A. Shackel, *The Making of Harpers Ferry National Historical Park: A Devil, Two Rivers, and a Dream* (Lanham, Md.: Altamira Press, 2008), 155–56; Caroline E. Janney, "Written in Stone: Gender, Race, and the Heyward Shepherd Memorial," *Civil War History* 52, no. 2 (2006): 117–41.

2. Merrill Peterson, *John Brown: The Legend Revisited* (Charlottesville: University of Virginia Press, 2002), 49; Benjamin Quarles, *Allies for Freedom: Blacks and John Brown* (New York: Oxford University Press, 1974).

3. In the 1980s protests over the Heyward Shepherd memorial led the National Park Service to remove it from public view. Protests from the United Daughters of the Confederacy and the Sons of Confederate Veterans resulted in the removal of the covering in 1995, but it is now accompanied by a wayside that includes information about its controversial history under the heading "Another Perspective," including W. E. B. DuBois's text honoring John Brown. In July 2006, as part of the NAACP's centennial celebration, members of the organization once again made the trip down from Washington to Harpers Ferry carrying a replica of the "Great Tablet" (the original was lost in the 1950s), which they installed at the spot where Brown's Fort stood in 1932. *Times Dispatch* (Richmond, Virginia), July 15, 2006; Moyer and Shackel, *The Making of Harpers Ferry*, 157.

4. The subversive exchange of the "Battle Hymn" for "America" recalled a widely remarked-upon incident from four decades before, when a group of one thousand African Americans convened in 1892 at a Chicago church for an "indignation meeting" to protest a surge of lynching in the South; they refused to sing "America" and sang "John Brown's Body" instead. Lynn Abbott and Doug Seroff, *Out of Sight: The Rise of African American Pop Music: 1889–1895* (Jackson: University Press of Mississippi, 2002), 213; *Washington Bee*, April 23, 1892. Moyer and Shackel, *Making of Harpers Ferry*, 157, 166–67. *Afro-American* (Baltimore), May 28, 1932; *Philadelphia Tribune*, May 26, 1932; *Atlanta Daily World*, May 25, 1932. The *Daily World* reports that the NAACP representatives sang "John Brown's Body" to conclude the proceedings, not the "Battle Hymn."

5. Du Bois believed that Brown's use of violence was justified by the monstrous nature of the system of American slavery. But he was reluctant to endorse similar tactics to address the condition of African Americans and the poor in the twentieth century. Speaking to comrades who wholeheartedly embraced communism and looked toward the Russian Revolution as a millennial movement, Du Bois cautioned in an 1921 *Crisis* editorial that though there might have been rare circumstances in the past when "organized murder" proved the only means to enact radical change, now activists must rely on "reason, human sympathy and the education

Notes to Pages 233–238

of children, and not . . . murder." David Levering Lewis, *W. E. B. Du Bois: The Fight for Equality and the American Century, 1919–1963* (New York: Henry Holt, 2000), 195. R. Blakeslee Gilpin, *John Brown Still Lives! America's Long Reckoning with Violence, Equality, and Change* (Chapel Hill: University of North Carolina Press, 2011), 103–5; *Afro-American* (Baltimore), May 28, 1932.

6. Email, Danny Smith to Benjamin Soskis, October 22, 2011; *Chicago Defender*, July 19, 1913, January 17, 1970; *Afro-American* (Baltimore), January 2, 1943; Ralph Ellison, *Invisible Man* (New York: Random House, 1952), 256; Barbara Foley, "Race, Class, and Communism: The Young Ralph Ellison and the 'Whole Left,'" in Laura Gray-Rosendale and Steven Rosendale, eds., *Radical Relevance: Toward a Scholarship of the Whole Left* (Albany: State University of New York Press, 2005), 44–45; Scott Sandage, "A Marble House Divided: The Lincoln Memorial, the Civil Rights Movement, and the Politics of Memory, 1939–1963," *Journal of American History* 80, no. 1 (1993): 153; *Proceedings, Sixteenth Constitutional Convention, United Automobile, Aircraft and Agricultural Implement Workers of America*, April 7–12, 1957, Atlantic City (n.p.: The Union, 1957) 241.

7. Josh Dunson, *Freedom in the Air: Song Movements of the Sixties* (New York: International Publishers, 1965), 35; Bernice Johnson Reagon, "Songs of the Civil Rights Movement 1955–1965: A Study in Culture History," Ph.D. diss., Howard University, 1975, 15; William G. Roy, *Reds, Whites, and Blues: Social Movements, Folk Music, and Race in the United States* (Princeton: Princeton University Press, 2010), 181; Jon Michael Spencer, *Protest and Praise: Sacred Music of Black Religion* (Minneapolis: Fortress Press, 1990), 92.

8. *Chicago Defender*, May 22, 1954; Reagon, "Songs of the Civil Rights Movement," 101; *Chicago Daily Defender*, March 1, 1960; *Afro-American* (Baltimore), March 12, 1960; *Washington Post*, March 2, 1960; Bobby L. Lovett, *The Civil Rights Movement in Tennessee: A Narrative History* (Knoxville: University of Tennessee Press, 2005), 150.

9. The singing in Parchman was not always solemn. Another variation of the "Battle Hymn" sung by Freedom Riders began "Mine eyes have seen the disintegration of my underwear" and featured a chorus of "Grab the sheets, the men are coming [x3], / It's the Parchman fashion flair." Guy Carawan and Candie Carawan, *We Shall Overcome: Songs of the Southern Freedom Movement* (New York: Oak Publications, 1963), 53; Roy, *Reds, Whites, and Blues*, 201; James H. Cone, *Martin and Malcolm and America: A Dream or a Nightmare* (Maryknoll, N.Y.: Orbis Books, 1991), 217.

10. Spencer, *Protest and Praise*, 83; Reagon, "Songs of the Civil Rights Movement," 102, 121–22.

11. Reagon, "Songs of the Civil Rights Movement," 25–27, 114, 85; Spencer, *Protest and Praise*, 86.

12. Reagon, "Songs of the Civil Rights Movement," 64–89.

13. Reagon, "Songs of the Civil Rights Movement," 76 (Miles Horton quote), 132, 83 (Cordell Hull Reagon quote); Carawan quoted in Pete Seeger and Bob Reiser, *Everybody Says Freedom: A History of the Civil Rights Movement in Songs and Pictures* (New York: Norton, 1989), 38–39; Carawan and Carawan, *We Shall Overcome*, 11.

14. Reagon, "Songs of the Civil Rights Movement," 140–41, 173–74; Eric J. Sundquist, *King's Dream* (New Haven: Yale University Press, 2009), 124–25; Roy, *Reds, Whites, and Blues*, 200–202.

15. *New York Times*, July 3, 1966; Peniel E. Joseph, *Waiting 'Til the Midnight Hour: A Narrative History of Black Power in America* (New York: Henry Holt, 2006), 149; Cone, *Martin and Malcolm*, 109, 159–60, 171, 182.

16. Peterson, *John Brown*, 143, 153; Gilpin, *John Brown Still Lives!*, 184–86; Zoe Trodd, "Writ in Blood: John Brown's Charter of Humanity, the Tribunal of History, and the Thick Link of American Political Protest," *Journal for the Study of Radicalism* 1, no. 1 (2006): 22, 24; Quarles, *Allies for Freedom*, 196.

17. In the early 1970s the feminist movement also embraced Chandler's song. Denise Sullivan, *Keep On Pushing: Black Power Music from Blues to Hip-Hop* (Chicago: Lawrence Hill Books, 2011), 146. Baldwin quoted in David W. Blight, *American Oracle: The Civil War in the Civil Rights Era* (Cambridge: Harvard University Press, 2011), 209; Russell Banks, "John Brown's Body: James Baldwin and Frank Shatz in Conversation," *Transition* 9, no. 1 (2000): 250–66; *Los Angeles Sentinel*, December 11, 1969; *New York Times*, November 15, 1960; *Baltimore Sun*, October 9, 1962; *St. Petersburg Times*, November 17, 1960; Seeger and Reiser, *Everybody Says Freedom*, 216.

18. Reagon, "Songs of the Civil Rights Movement," 175; Roy, *Reds, Whites, and Blues*, 190; Joseph, *Waiting 'Til the Midnight Hour*, 90 (Malcolm X quote).

19. Malcolm X quoted in Roy, *Reds, Whites, and Blues*, 217, and Spencer, *Protest and Praise*, 98; Spencer, *Protest and Praise*, 217 (Lester quote).

20. As Jon Spencer suggests, King might have been thinking of remarks by Alvin F. Poussaint of the Medical Committee for Human Rights, during a Meredith March rally in which he endorsed exchanging "We Shall Overcome" with "We Shall Overthrow." Spencer, *Protest and Praise*, 96. *New York Times*, July 3, 1966; Joseph, *Waiting 'Til the Midnight Hour*, 133–46; Guy Carawan and Candie Carawan, eds., *Sing for Freedom: The Story of the Civil Rights Movement through Its Songs* (Montgomery, Ala.: New South Books, 2007), 103; Martin Luther King Jr., *Where Do We Go From Here: Chaos or Community?* (New York: Harper & Row, 1967), 25–26.

21. Or as James Baldwin declared, "This country is only concerned about non-violence if it seems as if I'm going to get violent." Cone, *Martin and Malcolm*, 263. Sundquist, *King's Dream*, 121; *New York Times*, July 17, 1966; Cone, *Martin and Malcolm*, 2, 100, 131, 209 (Malcolm X quote), 215, 227, 263–64, 268; Joseph, *Waiting 'Til the Midnight Hour*, 131, 137; David L. Lewis, *King: A Biography* (2nd ed.; Urbana: University of Illinois Press, 1978), 196.

22. Lewis, *King*, 395.

23. Lewis, *King*, 46; Drew D. Hansen, *The Dream: Martin Luther King, Jr., and the Speech That Inspired a Nation* (New York: Ecco, 2003), 99; Cone, *Martin and Malcolm*, 33.

24. Lewis, *King*, 56.

25. Lewis, *King*, 70, 72, 99, 105; Sundquist, *King's Dream*, 118.

26. King quoted in Lewis, *King*, 85, 332; Sundquist, *King's Dream*, 120–22.

27. Lewis, *King*, 86, 116; Martin Luther King Jr., "Love, Law, and Civil Disobedience," in James Melvin Washington, ed., *A Testament of Hope: The Essential Writings of Martin Luther King, Jr.* (San Francisco: Harper & Row, 1986), 46.

28. At a 1963 address in Atlanta, King referenced Walker, Turner, Vesey, Gabriel Turner, and "other unsung heroes [who] plotted and planned and fought and died to make the American dream a reality for their people." Cone, *Martin and Malcolm*, 73–74. Peterson, *John Brown*, 155; Gilpin, *John Brown Still Lives*, 184, 242n14.

29. Franny Nudelman, "John Brown, Martin Luther King, and the Art of 'Creative Suffering,'" paper presented at the eleventh annual Gilder Lerhman Center International Conference,

Yale University, October 29–21, 2009; David S. Reynolds, *John Brown: Abolitionist* (New York: Vintage Books, 2005), 370 (Brown quote).

30. Lewis, *King*, 83, 300, 70; Michael K. Honey, *Going Down Jericho Road: The Memphis Strike, Martin Luther King's Last Campaign* (New York: Norton, 2007), 452; *Boston Globe*, April 5, 1968.

31. Cone, *Martin and Malcolm*, 127; Keith D. Miller, *Voice of Deliverance: The Language of Martin Luther King, Jr. and Its Sources* (New York: Free Press, 1992), 173–75; Sundquist, *King's Dream*, 113; *Boston Globe*, April 5, 1968.

32. Richard Lischer, *The Preacher King: Martin Luther King Jr. and the Word That Moved America* (New York: Oxford University Press, 1995), 187; Scott Hoffman, "Holy Martin: The Overlooked Canonization of Dr. Martin Luther King, Jr.," *Religion and American Culture* 10, no. 2 (2000): 123–48; Bond quoted in Lewis, *King*, 231.

33. Cone, *Martin and Malcolm*, 128; Lewis, *King*, 148, 208; King to Rev. C. K. Steele, March 19, 1960, in Clayborne Carson, ed., *The Papers of Martin Luther King, Jr.* (Berkeley: University of California Press, 2005), 5:391.

34. Hansen, *Dream*, 24, 29–30, 38, 41, 52 (King quote), 142 (Lewis quote); Sundquist, *King's Dream*, 50–53; Cone, *Martin and Malcolm*, 83.

35. King remarked to his dissertation advisor, Harold DeWolf, that the dream existed first in the mind of God and that he merely outlined it to the nation. Hansen, *Dream*, 153. Lewis, *King*, 227; Hansen, *Dream*, 58, 65, 69, 95, 111; Sundquist, *King's Dream*, 14, 18.

36. Sundquist, *King's Dream*, 10 (Abernathy quote), 103.

37. "Address at the Fiftieth Annual NAACP Convention," July 17, 1959, in Carson, *Papers of Martin Luther King*, 5:249–50; "Address at the Fourth Annual Institute on Nonviolence and Social Change at Bethel Baptist Church," December 3, 1959, in Carson, *Papers of Martin Luther King*, 5:343; Cone, *Malcolm and Martin*, 68 (King quote); Hansen, *Dream*, 205. See also King's invocation of the opening lines of the "Battle Hymn" at his speech before an interracial crowd of fifty thousand at Wrigley Field in Los Angeles in May 1963. Diane McWhorter, *Carry Me Home: Birmingham, Alabama, the Climactic Battle of the Civil Rights Revolution* (New York: Simon & Schuster), 452.

38. *Chicago Tribune*, March 25, 1965; Lewis, *King*, 272; *New York Times*, March 26, 1965.

39. Graham and King admired each other. Graham invited King to deliver a prayer during his 1957 New York crusade, and the two even discussed the possibility of organizing joint crusades in the same city, though nothing came of the idea. Tyler Branch, *Parting the Waters: America in the King Years, 1954–1963* (New York: Simon & Schuster, 1988), 227. Martin Luther King Jr., "Address at the Conclusion of the Selma to Montgomery March," in Clayborne *Call to Conscience: The Landmark Speeches of Dr. Martin Luther King, Jr.*, 122, 126, 130–31; King, "Love, Law, and Civil Disobedience," 51; Lewis, *King*, 331, 350.

40. Cone, *Martin and Malcolm*, 218; King, "Address at the Conclusion of the Selma to Montgomery March," 130–32.

41. Honey, *Going Down Jericho Way*, 84; Lewis, *King*, 91; Joseph, *Waiting 'Til the Midnight Hour*, 81–84.

42. Lewis, *King*, 287 (King quote); Miller, *Martin Luther King's Biblical Epic*, 45, 49.

43. It was perhaps in recognition of such resonances that King, while delivering his "I Have a Dream" speech, decided to leave out the reference to the mobilization of a "biracial army" that had appeared in his prepared text. Hansen, *Dream*, 87. Spencer, *Protest and*

Praise, 93–94 (King quote on 94); Lewis, *King*, 101; Sundquist, *King's Dream*, 47, 121 (King quote).

44. Cone, *Martin and Malcolm*, 218, 219, 221; Sundquist, *King's Dream*, 59 (King quote).

45. Lewis, *King*, 306, 354 (King quote); Cone, *Martin and Malcolm*, 222 (King quote); Hansen, *Dream*, 184–85 (Watts quote), 191.

46. Honey, *Going Down Jericho Road*, 93–96, 176; Lewis, *King*, 370 (King quote); Joseph, *Waiting 'Til the Midnight Hour*, 161; Hansen, *Dream*, 186.

47. Lewis, *King*, 364; Honey, *Going Down Jericho Road*, 180; Cone, *Martin and Malcolm*, 242 (King quote).

48. Honey, *Going Down Jericho Road*, 289, 290; Lewis, *King*, 373; Hansen, *Dream*, 197, 198, 199 (King quote).

49. Honey, *Going Down Jericho Road*, 174, 189 (quote); Hansen, *Dream*, 190, 192, 194, 200–202; Cone, *Martin and Malcolm*, 232, 240 (King quote); Lischer, *Preacher King*, 158–59; Sundquist, *King's Dream*, 20.

50. Honey, *Going Down Jericho Road*, 53–82 (quote on 55), 292, 381 (Invaders quote); Miller, *Martin Luther King's Biblical Epic*, 10.

51. Honey, *Going Down Jericho Road*, 292, 297–304.

52. Honey, *Going Down Jericho Road*, 335–61 (quote on 345); Hansen, *Dream*, 205 (King quote).

53. Lewis, *King*, 382–83; Honey, *Going Down Jericho Road*, 367–70 (*Journal* quote on 368); Miller, *Martin Luther King's Biblical Epic*, 11.

54. Honey, *Going Down Jericho Road*, 318 (King quote), 403, 365.

55. Honey, *Going Down Jericho Road*, 416 (Harold Middlebrook quote).

56. Martin Luther King Jr., "I've Been to the Mountaintop," speech delivered April 3, 1968, Memphis, Tennessee, in Carson and Shepard, *A Call to Conscience*, 207–9.

57. King, "I've Been to the Mountaintop," 210.

58. Lewis, *King*, 377, 386.

59. Honey, *Going Down Jericho Road*, 189; King, "I've Been to the Mountaintop," 222–23.

60. Miller, *Martin Luther King's Biblical Epic*, 138; Honey, *Going Down Jericho Road*, 424.

61. Honey, *Going Down Jericho Road*, 174; Lewis, *King*, 388.

62. Honey, *Going Down Jericho Road*, 443, 444 (Carmichael quote); *Newsweek*, April 15, 1968, 31; Joseph, *Waiting 'Til the Midnight Hour*, 227–28; *New York Amsterdam News*, April 13, 1968.

63. Honey, *Going Down Jericho Road*, 468, 473–74 (Abernathy quote).

64. Lewis, *King*, 390–91; *Newsweek*, April 22, 1969, 31; *Baltimore Sun*, April 10, 1968.

65. *Newsweek*, April 15, 1968, 34; *Hartford (Connecticut) Courant*, April 6, April 10, 1968; *Baltimore Sun*, April 15, 1968.

CONCLUSION

1. The Commission was nearly torn apart along sectional lines when Northerners insisted on planning a commemoration of the Emancipation Proclamation at the Lincoln Memorial. President Kennedy threaded the needle by declining to attend himself, but sent his brother Attorney General Robert Kennedy in his place. By all accounts, the high point of the event was its stirring climax, when the gospel singer Mahalia Jackson, herself the granddaughter of

slaves, led the audience in an impromptu version of the "Battle Hymn." *New York Times*, September 23, 1962. Robert J. Cook, *Troubled Commemoration: The American Civil War Centennial, 1961–1965* (Baton Rouge: Louisiana State University Press, 2007), 34, 40–41 (Bell Wiley quote), 42 (K. S. Betts quote).

2. David W. Blight, *American Oracle: The Civil War in the Civil Rights Era* (Cambridge: Harvard University Press, 2011), 12–16.

3. Cook, *Troubled Commemoration*, 141, 146, 147; Blight, *American Oracle*, 16.

4. *Gettysburg Times*, November 10, 1961; *Washington Post*, November 19, 1961; "Commemoration Ceremony Honoring Julia Ward Howe and the One Hundredth Anniversary of the Battle Hymn of the Republic," November 18, 1961, District of Columbia Civil War Centennial pamphlet collection, Special Collections, Gelman Library, George Washington University, Washington, D.C.

5. *New York Times*, November 19, 1961, January 28, 1962; *Baltimore Sun*, May 23, 1961.

6. White quoted in Eric Foner, *The Story of American Freedom* (New York: Norton, 1998), 307.

7. Robert Jewett and John Shelton Lawrence, *Captain America and the Crusade against Evil: The Dilemma of Zealous Nationalism* (Grand Rapids, Mich.: William B. Eerdmans, 2003), 75–78; *New York Times*, November 27, 1942; *Chicago Daily Tribune*, July 25, 1943; Alexander Woollcott, "She Sounded Forth the Trumpet," *Reader's Digest* 40, no. 241 (1942): 49; Steven Ambrose, *D-Day June 6, 1944: The Climactic Battle of World War II* (New York: Simon & Schuster, 1994), 258; *New York Times*, August 6, 1953. Although the version of the "Battle Hymn" performed by Waring's Pennsylvanians no doubt expressed the patriotic pride of many of his listeners, by midcentury the conductor had introduced a subversive strain into the song. According to his widow, Waring had insisted on changing the final words of the hymn to "let us *live* to make men free" in protest over American involvement in the Korean War. Waring had used and published Roy Ringwald's arrangement of the song. Ringwald's arrangement became one of the most popular versions of the hymn among choral groups, who also inherited the revised last line. Those who used the other most popular arrangement, by Peter Wilhousky, more often learned the song with its last verse in its original version (although the Mormon Tabernacle Choir's 1959 version of the song, using Wilhousky's arrangement, included the revised final line as well). Politics clearly determined many people's preferences as well. One letter writer to the *Los Angeles Times* denounced Waring's revision as embodying "the Communist-sponsored propaganda of 'peaceful coexistence.'" The Union soldiers who sang the song, like those languishing behind the Iron Curtain, the writer declared, had no illusions about the price necessary to win freedom. *Los Angeles Times*, December 17, 1959. *Washington Post*, February 4, 1995, September 22, 2001.

8. Walter L. Hixson, *Parting the Curtain: Propaganda, Culture, and the Cold War, 1945–1961* (New York: St. Martin's Griffin, 1997), 2; Angela M. Lahr, *Millennial Dreams and Apocalyptic Nightmares: The Cold War Origins of Political Evangelicalism* (New York: Oxford University Press, 2007), 93–94; Paul Boyer, *When Time Shall Be No More: Prophecy Belief in Modern American Culture* (Cambridge: Harvard University Press, 1992), 115; *New York Times*, February 18, 1947.

9. Mark David Porcaro, "The Secularization of the Repertoire of the Mormon Tabernacle Choir, 1949–1992," Ph.D. diss., University of North Carolina, 2006, 21, 25, 65, 82, 83, 88; Michael Hicks, *Mormonism and Music* (Urbana: University of Illinois Press, 2003), 153; Charles Jefferson Calman, *The Mormon Tabernacle Choir* (New York: Harper & Row, 1979), 99; *Billboard*, September 14, 1959, October 26, 1959.

10. There was perhaps no more eloquent statement of the Mormon Church's confidence that its integration into the American mainstream was secure than the Mormon Tabernacle Choir director's admission, during a 1972 interview, that he had actually grown "sick" of the "Battle Hymn," since he had "heard it too many times to enjoy it anymore." *Reading (Pa.) Eagle*, September 27, 1972. Hicks, *Mormonism and Music*, 162–63; Richard N. Ostling and Joan K. Ostling, *Mormon America: The Power and the Promise* (New York: HarperOne, 2007), 93 (Hinkley quote), 94 (Bushman quote). On millennialism in early Mormon thought, see Ernest Lee Tuveson, *Redeemer Nation: The Idea of America's Millennial Role* (Chicago: University of Chicago Press, 1968), 175–86.

11. Johnson also asked that Bryant sing the "Battle Hymn" at his funeral. Bryant, a prominent figure in the Christian Right, frequently sang the hymn at performances and titled her 1970 memoir *Mine Eyes Have Seen the Glory*. Anita Bryant, *Mine Eyes Have Seen the Glory* (Old Tappan, N.J.: Revell, 1970). *Washington Post*, January 24, 1973; Lady Bird Johnson, *A White House Diary* (Austin: University of Texas Press, 2007), 156–57; *New York Times*, January 8, 1965; James. E. Perone, *Songs of the Vietnam Conflict* (Westport, Conn.: Greenwood Press, 2001), 71; *Washington Post*, March 15, 1968.

12. Terry Nelson and C Company, *The Battle Hymn of Lt. Calley*, Plantation Record PL-73, 45 RPM; Perone, *Songs of the Vietnam Conflict*, 10, 101–2; Michael Bilton and Kevin Sim, *Four Hours in My Lai* (New York: Viking, 1992), 340; *Los Angeles Times*, April 3, 1971; *Chicago Tribune*, April 3, 1971; *Billboard*, April 17, 1971, April 24, 1971; *Washington Post*, April 20, 1971; *New York Times*, May 1, 1971.

13. The *New York Times* gestured toward the regional basis of the song's popularity, noting that radio stations in the New York area showed little interest in "The Battle Hymn of Lt. Calley." *New York Times*, May 1, 1971. *Los Angeles Times*, July 18, 1965; Robert Welch, *The Blue Book*, quoted in William McPherson, *Ideology and Change: Radicalism and Fundamentalism in America* (Palo Alto, Calif.: National Press Books, 1973), 274.

14. *New York Times*, March 8, 1962; *Chicago Tribune*, July 19, 1964; *Washington Post*, September 19, 1964; Rick Perlstein, *Before the Storm: Barry Goldwater and the Unmaking of the American Consensus* (New York: Hill and Wang, 2001), 494–95.

15. San Francisco church and labor groups held a Freedom March to protest Goldwater's candidacy, at which the "Battle Hymn" was continuously blared from loudspeakers. *New York Amsterdam News*, July 18, 1964. *New York Times*, July 19, 1964; Perlstein, *Before the Storm*, 391–92; *Chicago Tribune*, August 10, 1964.

16. Allen J. Matusow, *The Unraveling of America: A History of Liberalism in the 1960s* (New York: Harper & Row, 1984), 406; *New York Times*, November 18, 1965; *Boston Globe*, June 9, 1968, June 16, 1968; *Baltimore Sun*, June 9, 1968.

17. *Boston Globe*, June 9, June 16, 1968; *New York Times*, June 9, June 11, 1968; *Baltimore Sun*, June 9, 1968.

18. *New York Times*, June 9, 1968; *Baltimore Sun*, June 9, 1968.

19. Matusow, *Unraveling of America*, 411–22; *Chicago Tribune*, August 28, 1968; *New York Times*, August 29, August 30, 1968; *Boston Globe*, August 30, 1968.

20. Robert Schlesinger, *White House Ghosts: Presidents and Their Speechwriters* (New York: Simon & Schuster, 2008), 192; *New York Times*, July 16, 1968; *Wall Street Journal*, August 29, 1968; *New York Times*, January 22, 1973.

21. For examples of the "Battle Hymn" being sung at pro-life rallies, see *New York Times*, January 23, 1981, April 29, 1990; *St. Petersburg Times*, July 23, 1989. For examples of the hymn used in the protests over school prayer, see *Washington Post*, July 23, 1979, April 30, 1980; *Seattle Post-Intelligencer*, August 2, 2000.

22. Carlton R. Young, *Companion to the United Methodist Hymnal* (Nashville, Tenn.: Abingdon Press, 1993), 135–36, 622; *Los Angeles Times*, July 6, 1986; *New York Times*, May 24, July 7, 1986.

23. Ronald Reagan with Richard G. Hubler, *Where's the Rest of Me?* (New York: Duell, Sloan and Pearce, 1965), 265; *Christian Science Monitor*, January 7, 1967; *Washington Post*, January 9, 1981; *New York Times*, June 12, 2004.

24. A striking illustration of the place of the "Battle Hymn of the Republic" in late twentieth-century premillennial apocalypticism occurs in Charles Colson's 1987 *Kingdoms and Conflict*. Colson, a former Nixon associate who became a born-again Christian while serving a prison sentence for his Watergate crimes, offers a fictive and cautionary scenario in which an evangelical president with premillennial views allows Israel to destroy the Dome of the Rock in Jerusalem, one of the holiest sites in Islam, bringing the region to the brink of nuclear war. As the president watches the scene unfold on the Christian Broadcasting Network, the network begins playing a recording of a choir singing the "Battle Hymn." Boyer, *When Time Shall Be No More*, 142–47; Stephen D. O'Leary, *Arguing the Apocalypse: A Theory of Millennial Rhetoric* (New York: Oxford University Press, 1994), 180–85; *New York Times*, May 6, 1976; Ronald Reagan, *An American Life: The Autobiography* (New York: Simon & Schuster, 1990), 387.

25. In 2012 Gingrich mined the hymn's final stanza yet again to provide the title for a book he cowrote on the history of the Civil War "Battle of the Crater," which he titled *To Make Men Free*. Foner, *Story of American Freedom*, 304; *Washington Post*, January 5, 1995.

26. 107th Congress, 1st sess., *Congressional Record* 147 (July 17, 2001), H 4102.

27. *Washington Post*, April 17, 2008; *Wall Street Journal*, April 23, 2008. A video of the ceremony is available at http://uspapalvisit.org/index.htm.

28. Anita McBride, chief of staff to Laura Bush, on *CNN Newsroom*, April 15, 2008, transcript available at http://transcripts.cnn.com/TRANSCRIPTS/0804/15/cnr.06.html; *The Rush Limbaugh Show*, April 16, April 18, 2008, transcripts available at http://www.rushlimbaugh.com/daily/2008/04/16/white_house_ceremony_for_pope_praises_god_and_american_exceptionalism3 and http://www.rushlimbaugh.com/daily/2008/04/18/rush_and_president_bush_discuss_welcoming_ceremony_for_the_pope3.

29. Laura Bush, *Spoken from the Heart* (New York: Scribner, 2010), 409; *Wall Street Journal*, April 23, 2008; *Washington Post*, April 17, 2008. For an example of a dismayed interpretation of the selection of the "Battle Hymn," see Scott P. Richert, "His God Is Marching On," *Chronicles*, May 2, 2008, http://www.chroniclesmagazine.org/2008/05/02/mine-eyes-have-seen-the-horror-of-the-coming-of-the-bush/.

30. Jill Lepore, "Tea and Sympathy: Who Owns the American Revolution," *New Yorker* 86, no. 11 (2010): 32; *Arkansas Democrat-Gazette*, April 18, 2010; *Hickory (North Carolina) Daily Record*, April 16, 2009; Warren Goldstein, "Progressive Patriotism," *Chronicle of Higher Education* 55, no. 14 (2008): 20.

31. *Philadelphia Inquirer*, September 26, October 13, 2009; *Beck*, September 29, 2009, transcript available at http://www.livedash.com/transcript/glenn_beck/5202/FNC/Tuesday_September_29_2009/90145/.

APPENDIX

1. Readers have deciphered Howe's scrawled sixth stanza in various ways; because Howe excised the stanza before publishing the poem, and disavowed it afterward, there is no official version.
2. In his letter to a friend in which he quotes the poem, Twain first cites what would be the third stanza, corresponding to Howe's hymn, and then cites the rest of the poem in order.

INDEX

Early, Jubal, 92
Ebenezer Baptist Church, 253, 267, 270
economic justice, 260
education, 107–9, 110–11, 137–38
Edwardsian Calvinism, 309–10n45
Eisenhower, Dwight, 232
Eisenhower Executive Office Building, 3
Elizabeth II, Queen of Great Britain, 6
Elliot, Maud Howe, 169, 226
Ellison, Ralph, 239
Ellsworth, Elmer E., 49–50
emancipation
    and Civil War objectives, 55, 63–72, 73
    Emancipation Day celebrations, 96,
        354–55n1
    Emancipation Proclamation, 64,
        113–14, 120, 138, 255, 272
    and "John Brown's Body," 55, 59,
        70–72
    Preliminary Emancipation
        Proclamation, 89–90
    and southern blacks, 57
    and the Spanish-American War, 13
    and Twain, 137
Emerson, Ralph Waldo, 35, 43, 96, 323n49
Emmett, Daniel, 326n18
England, 124–26
English Civil War, 53
Episcopalians, 7
eschatology, 10, 96, 156
Espionage Act, 191, 226
European audiences, 125
evangelical Christians, 25, 148, 212–27,
    286, 347n30
Everest, Wesley, 205
Everett, Edward, 52
Exodus, 240, 259, 266
Ezekiel, book of, 86, 230

A Farewell to Arms (Hemingway), 173
fascism, 175
Fear God and Take Your Own Part
    (Roosevelt), 146
Federalists, 12

Fellowship of Reconciliation, 250
"Fellow-Worker Jesus," 192
feminism, 104
Fields, James T., 91–92, 101
Fifteenth Amendment, 114
Fifty-fourth Massachusetts, 59–60, 239
financial panics, 30–31
Finley, James, 20–21
First Amendment, 177
First Arkansas Volunteer Infantry
    (African Descent), 60–62
First Congregational Church of Tacoma,
    Washington, 199
First Connecticut Voluntary Infantry,
    118
First Massachusetts Heavy Artillery, 82
First Regiment, Kansas Colored
    Volunteers, 59
First Volunteer Corps, 118
Fischer, Fred, 225
Fisk Jubilee Singers, 125, 158, 332n28
Fiske, Billy, 275
Fitzgerald, Ella, 257
Flag Day, 127
Florida Bible Institute, 228
Floyd, John, 39
Food, Tobacco and Agricultural Workers
    Union, 243
Food and Drug Act, 343n91
Ford, Gerald, 287–88
Ford, Patrick, 135
foreign missionary movement, 131, 134
foreign policy, 7, 137, 161, 260
Fort Sumter, 71, 86, 88, 273
Fort Wagner, 239
Fort Warren, 47, 48, 50–53, 64, 68, 158
The 42nd Parallel (Dos Passos), 204
Fosdick, Harry Emerson, 164
Fourteenth Amendment, 114
Fourth Battalion, Massachusetts
    Thirteenth Regiment, 53, 315n13
Fourth Michigan Cavalry, 70
Franco-Prussian War, 158, 159
Fredericksburg, battle of, 67

May Day, 193
McCabe, Charles, 92–93, 97, 323n44
McCarthy, Eugene, 283, 285
McCarthy, Joseph, 200
McClellan, George, 67, 69
McClintock, Harry ("Haywire Mack"),
    187
McCormack, John, 171
McDonald, Henry, 236, 237–38
McGean, Catherine, 107–9
McKinley, William, 128–29, 131–33, 146
McLoughlin, William, 227
McNamara brothers, 153, 331–32n20
McSorley, Joseph, 199, 200
McVeigh, Timothy, 14
Mead, Stith, 17–18, 19, 21–24
Mead, Walter Russell, 6
Medin, Edith, 184
Melodeon, 48, 314n11
Memorial Day celebrations, 113–14,
    116–17, 118, 133, 159
Memphis, Tennessee, 264–67
Mencken, H. L., 212
Menonites, 192
Meredith, James, 247–48, 258
Meriam, Francis, 36
messianism, 167. *See also* Christ figures
    and imagery
Methodists, 19–20, 21, 24–25, 27, 90,
    182–83, 243
Mexico, 161–62, 165
migratory workers, 185
militarism, 15, 162, 210, 211, 278
military training, 171
millennialism
    and American isolationism, 172
    and Brown, 31, 44, 58, 74
    and Calvinism, 309–10n45
    and civil rights, 237, 238, 246, 247, 259,
        267
    and the Civil War, 90, 117, 131, 170
    and conservatism, 286–88
    and cultural impact of the Battle
        Hymn, 12–16

and elections, 69
and emancipation, 89
and evangelical Christians, 229–30,
    234
and evolution of "John Brown's Body,"
    72
and Howe, 85–86, 86–91, 102, 104–5
and labor struggles, 181, 186, 193, 196,
    202, 203, 205–6
and Lincoln's Second Inaugural,
    93–94, 166–67
and lyrics of the Battle Hymn, 10
and Mormonism, 277
and origin of the Battle Hymn, 86–88,
    96–97
and Progressivism, 142–43, 144, 146,
    150, 152–54, 154–62, 164, 165–68,
    170, 172–74
and Reconstruction, 117
and revivalism, 211–12, 228
and Roosevelt, 173
and social conservatism, 291–92
and the Spanish-American War, 131
and Twain, 136
and World War I, 165–68, 168–69, 170,
    172–74
Miller, Lindley, 60–62
Millerites, 27
Mills, Ruth, 29–30
miners' strikes, 179–80
minstrelsy, 62
Mintz, David, 21–22
missionaries, 56, 131, 134
Mississippi, 241, 248
Missouri, 36
modernism, 217–18, 223, 227, 347n30
Montgomery Bus Boycott, 244, 250, 253,
    258
Montgomery Improvement Association,
    250, 256
Moody, Dwight, 218
Moorehouse, J. Ward, 205
Morehouse College, 270
Morgan, J. P., 151

Pottawatomie Creek massacre, 34–35,
312n70
Powell, E. L., 134
Prayer Pilgrimage, 256, 259
"The Preacher and the Slave," 187, 189
Preliminary Emancipation Proclamation,
89–90
premillennialism, 156, 286, 332n27,
357n24
Prentiss, Benjamin, 121
Presbyterians, 19–20, 88, 156–57, 168,
215, 218–20
primitive Christians, 40
Princeton Theological Seminary, 157
Progressive Party, 142, 143, 150, 153–54,
219, 282–83
Progressivism
  and American messianism, 173–74
  and Brown's legacy, 150, 154, 158
  and Episcopalian theology, 7
  and Kennedy (Robert), 282–83
  and millennial themes, 142–43, 144,
    146, 150, 152–54, 154–62, 164,
    165–68, 170, 172–74
  and music education, 171
  and Obama, 291–92
  progressive Christianity, 15, 223
  and Roosevelt (Theodore), 142–44,
    145–54, 154–65
Prohibition, 223, 225
proslavery apologists, 66
protest culture, 109, 121, 123
Protestantism
  and anti-Catholic sentiment, 224–25
  and Howe's background, 75–76
  and Northern race relations, 108–9
  and postmillennialism, 87
  and Progressivism, 156
  and Republican conservatism, 290
  and the Spanish-American War, 130, 131
Providence (Rhode Island) Sunday Journal,
265
Pullman strike, 182–83
Pure Food and Drug Act, 201

racism and race relations, 19, 81, 106,
118, 132, 154. *See also* civil rights
movement
Radical Abolition Party, 33–34, 34–35
Radical Reconstruction, 72, 110–11, 122
Radical Republicans, 110
radio, 226
Ram's Horn, 32
Randall, Anne J., 95
Randolph, A. Philip, 240
Rauschenbusch, Robert, 216–17
Ray, James Earl, 268
Reagan, Ronald, 287–88
"Rebel Girl," 189
Reconstruction, 72, 100, 132–33
Red Cross, 169, 210, 342n80
Red Scare, 226. *See also* anticommunism
"Religion and the Workingman," 200
Religious Right, 286, 289
Reminiscences (Howe), 76, 92, 101, 159,
321n20
Republican National Committee, 141,
145
Republican Party
  and American messianism, 173–74
  and draft riots, 108
  and Gingrich, 289
  and Goldwater, 281–82
  and Greeley, 113
  and Lincoln's reelection, 69
  and Northern race relations, 108–9
  and Reagan era conservatism, 287–88
  and Reconstruction, 112
  and Roosevelt (Theodore), 141,
    145–46, 150
  and sectional conflict, 148
  use of "John Brown's Body," 121
"Rest in Heaven" ("Rest in Home"), 48
Resurrection City, 270, 284
retributive justice, 61, 65–66
Revelation, book of
  and apocalyptic imagery, 9–10
  and the "Glory, Hallelujah" chorus,
    322n29

and "grapes of wrath" imagery, 174
and Howe's poetry, 86–87
and Lincoln's Second Inaugural, 98
and Manichaeism, 89
and Reagan era conservatism, 288
and Sunday, 211–12
in *Uncle Tom's Cabin*, 26
revivalism
    and American exceptionalism, 85–86
    and camp meetings, 17–18, 19–28
    and the "Glory, Hallelujah" chorus,
        210
    and Goldwater, 282
    and Graham, 227–34
    and Howe, 75
    and "John Brown's Body," 18, 46
    and labor unionism, 197–98
    and origins of the Battle Hymn, 9,
        17–18, 19–28
    and Progressivism, 142
    and "Say Brothers," 84
    and Sunday, 208–12, 212–27
Revolutionary War, 10, 36–37, 161
Rice, Condoleeza, 5
Richmond, Virginia, 71
Richmond Enquirer, 29
Richmond Whig, 29
ring shouts, 24–25
Ringwald, Roy, 355n7
RMS *Lusitania*, 166
robber barons, 204
Robertson, Michael, 338n29
Rockefeller, John D., Jr., 208
Rockefeller, Nelson, 282
Rodeheaver, Homer, 225, 228, 229
Roe, Alfred S., 71
Romney, Mitt, 233–34
Roosevelt, Franklin D., 275, 276
Roosevelt, Quentin, 162–63
Roosevelt, Theodore
    and apocalyptic imagery, 162–63
    assassination attempts on, 155–56
    and conservatism, 287
    and millennial themes, 173

path to presidency, 145–46
and Progressivism, 142–44, 145–54,
    154–65
and the Spanish-American War,
    129–30, 145–46
and Sunday, 208
and World War I, 168
Roosevelt, Theodore, Jr., 275–76
Root, Elihu, 132, 155
Rough Riders, 129–30, 145–46, 208
Rove, Karl, 3
Rusk, Dean, 232
Russian Army Chorus, 231
Russian Revolution, 10–11, 350n5
Rustin, Bayard, 250, 260

Sacco, Nicola, 204, 205
Saint-Gaudens, Augustus, 60, 317n34
Salt March, 258
Salter, John, 338n32
Salvation Army, 187–88
Samson (biblical), 40
Sanborn, Franklin, 35
Sandburg, Carl, 194
Saratoga, battle of, 182
Sartre, Jean-Paul, 204
Savage, Richard Ellsworth, 205
"Say, Bummers, Will You Meet Us?", 46
"Say Brothers Will You Meet Us"
    and adaptability of music, 18–19
    and black churches, 58
    and changing meaning of the Battle
        Hymn, 138
    and the "Glory, Hallelujah" chorus, 24,
        28, 49, 322n29
    introduction to Northerners, 27
    Mead's version, 22–23
    and national hymn campaign, 46–49
    and northern hymnals, 26–27
    origins of, 314n8
    and origins of the Battle Hymn, 9,
        21–28, 84
Schrank, John, 155
Schuettler, Herman, 177

Index

375